"For years, Roman Catholics have been important providers of competent and compassionate care to people living with HIV infection around the globe. In this important new book, Catholic ethicists engage their tradition and provide nuanced analyses of public health initiatives (such as condom distribution and needle exchange). It discusses the critical social, economic, and gender issues which play a dominant role in the spread of the epidemic, especially among marginalized populations. This volume is a welcome addition to global efforts to stem the spread of HIV/AIDS. It serves as an invitation to other faith communities to similarly commit their resources to prevention as well as care."

Peter Piot, M.D.
Executive Director
UNAIDS

"There are few more pressing moral and social challenges today than HIV prevention, and few in which the Church has responded so inadequately. This comprehensive, moving, diverse, and powerful collection of essays is a beginning in that effort. It is intellectually serious, theologically rigorous, and pastorally engaged. We need this discussion desperately—in America and, increasingly, around the world."

Andrew Sullivan
columnist, *New York Times Magazine*
senior editor, *The New Republic*
author of *Virtually Normal* and *Love Undetectableable.*

"This book is a landmark contribution to worldwide efforts to respond to HIV/AIDS. It finally brings to bear on this issue, in a unified (though still importantly diverse) way, the resources of the Roman Catholic tradition of moral theology. In doing so, it contributes not only to the pastoral and medical responses needed for HIV/AIDS prevention, but also to the coherence required of ethicists and moral theologians from every strand of Christianity and from other world religions. It will be an extraordinary practical and theoretical catalyst, one that is necessary if churches and nations are to be more responsible and just."

Margaret A. Farley
Gilbert L. Stark Professor of Christian Ethics
Yale University Divinity School

"The gift of fire to mankind by the Titan Prometheus was considered by many of the early Greeks as the singular event that changed the course of human history. James F. Keenan's brilliantly conceived and edited *Catholic Ethicists on HIV/AIDS Prevention* is a parallel gift with potential to significantly affect the course of the global HIV pandemic. The pristine clarity of logic that underscores the papers in the section on 'Fundamental Moral Issues for HIV Prevention' provides the key to effectively mediate the conflict perceived by some between the moral teachings of the Roman Catholic church and the moral responsibility to use effective HIV-prevention resources. I have ordered four dozen copies to send to Catholic bishops in Latin America."

Gordon Nary
Founding Director
International Association of Physicians in AIDS Care

"I am frequently asked whether my work on AIDS prevention and control in Latin America and the Caribbean is particularly difficult due to 'religious constraints.' These questions stem from the widespread assumption that Catholic communities tend to be reactionary, bigoted, and reluctant to change. As any other generalization, this is a prejudiced stereotype that does not accurately represent the variety of positions, approaches, and perspectives within Catholicism. The Catholic Church does not oppose actions against AIDS. In fact, it is already involved in the joint social effort against the pandemic. Moreover, almost always one recognizes an authentic interest among the religious sector in finding approaches that are evidence-based and contribute to prevention and control of HIV infection in a rational, albeit principled manner.

"This book explores the voyage of a living church seeking evolving solutions in these changing times. It has not been conceived to provide prescriptions or dogmatic responses but to stimulate analysis, discussion, reflection, and a revision of attitudes."

Rafael Mazin, M.D.
Regional Advisor on HIV/AIDS and STD
Pan American Health Organization

CATHOLIC ETHICISTS ON HIV/AIDS PREVENTION

Edited by
James F. Keenan, S.J.

Assisted by
John D. Fuller, S.J., M.D.
Lisa Sowle Cahill
Kevin Kelly

continuum

NEW YORK • LONDON

2005

The Continuum International Publishing Group Inc
15 East 26 Street, New York, NY 10010

The Continuum International Publishing Group Ltd
The Tower Building, 11 York Road, London SE1 7NX

www.continuumbooks.com

Printed in the United States of America

Library of Congress Cataloging-in-Publication Data
Catholic ethicists on HIV/AIDS prevention / edited by James F. Keenan;
assisted by Lisa Sowle Cahill, Jon Fuller, Kevin Kelly.
     p. cm.
  ISBN 0-8264-1230-0 (paperback : alk. paper)
  1. AIDS (Disease)—Prevention—Moral and ethical aspects. 2. AIDS
    (Disease)—Prevention—Religious aspects—Catholic Church. I.
    Keenan, James F. II. Cahill, Lisa Sowle. III. Fuller, Jon. IV. Kelly,
    Kevin T., 1933–

    RA644.A25 C376 2000
    261.8'321969792—dc21

                         99-057307

To

Jonathan Mann

1947—1998

CONTENTS

About this Book

JAMES F. KEENAN, S.J.

IN EARLY JANUARY of 1999, Dr. Jon Fuller, S.J., assistant director of the Clinical AIDS Program at Boston Medical Center and founding president of the National Catholic AIDS Network (USA), and I were flying to a conference of the Society of Christian Ethics to deliver a paper about this book. After we took off, I gave him an e-mail concerning yet another murder of a person infected with HIV. It read: "Mrs. Gugu Dlamini of South Africa was HIV positive, an AIDS educator, and the mother of a thirteen-year-old child. She was beaten to death by members of her own community because of her efforts to bring education and enlightenment to them regarding HIV/AIDS. She made her HIV status known to her community last month on December 1st, World AIDS Day."

Fuller responded that though there are three million South Africans who have the HIV virus, only thirty of them have publicly stated that they have the virus. This reminded me of the words of the late Jonathan Mann, the pioneer in the international campaign against AIDS and a founder of the movement that linked health issues with those of human rights. He said many times that the way we define a problem will determine what we do about it. Thus in the face of HIV/AIDS, he defined the problem not only as a terrible viral disease, but as a social problem to be solved.

Recognizing HIV/AIDS as a social problem was the foundational insight that led to this book. Several years ago, Fuller was invited by Fr. Michael Buckley, S.J., director of the Jesuit Institute at Boston College, to sponsor a seminar that would explore the relationship between the AIDS epidemic and the Catholic Church. A "spinoff" of that seminar became the Catholic Theological Coalition on HIV/AIDS Prevention (CTCHP) whose members include Lisa Sowle Cahill, Jon Fuller, James Keenan, Kevin Kelly, Enda McDonagh, and Robert Vitillo.

Our coalition has worked now for eighteen months on this project to address the problematic that certain moral positions adopted by church personnel are at odds with some relatively effective HIV-prevention measures favored by Catholic health workers involved in the pandemic. We believe, however, that our common Catholic moral tradition can help us to mediate constructively the apparent clash of values occurring in these situations. To demonstrate that belief we have recruited thirty-five international moral theologians to address this claim.

After the introduction, the book is divided into two parts. The first presents twenty-six cases from around the world highlighting the complexity of HIV prevention, illustrating the relevance of local issues and concerns, but demonstrating the ability of the Catholic moral theological tradition to address HIV prevention. We present in the second part seven essays that address transglobally the fundamental moral issues that theologians recognize in HIV prevention.

As it goes to print, we realize that this is the first book in moral theology to engage Catholic ethicists from around the world in addressing a singular moral issue. It is the first time that moral theological questions about HIV/AIDS are being addressed on a global level. Finally, this book responds to one of the major methodological challenges of our day: it begins from and respects local cultural concerns but integrates them into a transglobal discussion that crosses cultural frontiers.

In our introduction, Fuller and I reflect on the essays that were written over the last fifteen years by several moral theologians who invoked the resources of Catholic moral theology to address the moral liceity of important HIV prevention methods in general and condom distribution and needle exchange in particular. There we conclude that, worldwide, moral theologians have argued convincingly and positively that the promotion of these preventive methods is morally licit. In fact, we note that the type of moral argumentation that these theologians advance is a very traditional method invoked precisely to allay conservative Catholic concerns. Likewise, we reflect on the changing face of HIV/AIDS after its first generation and consider the enormous promise and the even greater obstacles that social structures pose in meeting the problems of the pandemic.

As we face the second generation of HIV/AIDS we recognize that addressing effective HIV prevention is not simply finding good arguments for HIV prevention, but more importantly addressing the social problems that inhibit HIV prevention measures. In order to raise up those social problems, as an editorial board, we made a strategic decision: rather than encouraging our contributors to respond to questions or cases that we predetermined, we asked contributors to offer their own cases. Thus the actual agenda of the book was set by the local cultural problems that developed due to the outbreak of the virus, the patterns of social behavior found in these particular localities, and the different ethical presuppositions shared in these places.

Though as editors we originally thought that we would present the essays according to geographical regions, we find, instead, that our contributing moral theologians want to promote HIV prevention through similar ways. Acknowledging this overlap, we present the cases according to the particular methodological concerns that moral theologians have. Many want to provide a strong narrative that conveys the social, cultural, and ecclesial marginalization experienced by those infected by the HIV virus and those who serve them. As moral theologians, these writers see their task both to bring forth the experiential narratives of rejection and abandonment, and to summon believers to stand with these suffering and courageous persons. Another set of moral theologians focus precisely on the need to appreciate and address local cultural concerns. They describe the distinctive traditions of a particularly affected population and contend that Catholic beliefs are not compromised by this encounter with culture but rather become alive and effective.

Though almost all writers mention in their cases deep underlying biases that unjustly affect the vulnerable and marginalized, several moral theologians believe that their task is to focus precisely on revealing and critiquing these inequities. Another group writes about attempts to educate and to develop educational programs on HIV prevention. Because these are almost all written from firsthand experiences, the reader can sense from these writers the difficulties they encountered. Several writers explicitly invoke the principle of cooperation as a way of serving, while others make the case that many conflict-oriented situations in HIV prevention require good ethical counseling. Here, the practice of confidentiality comes under considerable scrutiny.

Though we present the cases according to methodological concerns, we do not want readers to miss the extraordinary overlap of substantive themes that we also found among the cases. Here, let me mention five. First, women do not have adequate power in the face of HIV/AIDS. Many cases describe women lacking the social structures, religious support, and psychological self-understanding to refuse to engage in risky sexual relations. The cases by Leonard Martin in Brazil, James Good in Kenya, Gerry Gleeson and David Leary in Australia, and Orlando Navarro in Costa Rica, among others, highlight this. But they also acknowledge that alongside the lack of structures empowering women is a prevailing ethos that endorses machismo. This insight became quite explicit in the essay by Gina Wolfe that looked at American university campuses. Other than young gay and lesbian students, the most vulnerable population on American campuses are many young women who are not yet empowered to avoid sexual situations made risky by a machismo as alive on an American campus as it is in Brazil, Kenya, or Costa Rica.

Second, religious scrupulosity inhibits so much effective prevention work. Some cases present a near neurotic anxiety among pastoral leaders who are more worried about preserving seventeenth-century teaching about sexual mores and marital dues than responding in justice and charity to the values and persons in front of them. This came out in the cases of Clement Campos of India, Kenneth Owens from Scotland, Linda Hogan from Ireland, Peter Harvey from England, and Eileen Flynn from the United States. But the case from Stuart Bate from South Africa catches it the best. There he discusses the case of a confessor who refuses to recognize that a woman whose husband is HIV positive has the right to demand that he use a prophylactic in their marital relations. In many ways, this case among others shows how women are particularly affected by this religious scrupulosity.

Third, the integrity of religious traditions that existed prior to Christianity and still exist today needs to be respected. Mark Miller from western Canada shows how the religious beliefs of First Nation people were not and are not engaged either by Christian evangelizers or by contemporary health care workers. The same myopia is discussed by Laurenti Magesa from Tanzania, Nader Michel from Egypt, and Gervas Rosario from Bangladesh.

Fourth, after twenty years living in an era of AIDS, homophobia remains virulent and vicious. Across cultures and churches, people simply do not know how to respect gay men as gay men. We are too familiar with how universally prejudicial views against gay men (and lesbian women!) are supported by a variety of religious and cultural practices as well as by social and legal structures. Through these practices and structures shame is especially used to inhibit the basic sexual orientation of millions of people. Inasmuch as this ethos promotes the "closet," addressing the fundamental issues of prevention, especially to young people, becomes an extraordinarily complicated matter. John Tuohey and Eileen Flynn from the United States, Jorge Peláez from Colombia, and Peter Black from Australia describe a variety of possible approaches to these situations.

Finally, there is a profound difficulty in protecting children. From cases regarding pregnancy and neonates to the children of intravenous drug users, moralists highlight the universal challenge of protecting our progeny. Moreover, the wishful thinking of many parents and church leaders also obfuscates the real issues of teenage sexual conduct and drug use, and becomes an enormous obstacle to HIV prevention. This recurring theme appeared in cases from Australia, North and South America, northern Europe, and east Africa.

The essays of the second part of this book were specifically commissioned by the editorial board. The issue of the progressive development of the moral tradition underlies each of them. Vidal and Gallagher present the issue in magisterial teachings about moral theology and medical ethics, respectively. Cahill argues that AIDS is a justice issue and demonstrates that the central themes of the Catholic social ethics tradition urgently need to be applied to HIV prevention. Odozor argues that casuistry is a traditional method of moral argumentation designed to lead communities forward as they face new moral challenges on the horizon. Until recently, casuistry was considered a method that promoted specious arguments or legalistic loopholes, but recent studies show that those arguments and loopholes were an abuse of casuistry. In the past, communities used casuistry or the case method to better apply moral principles. Moreover, sometimes the application of a principle to a case led ethicists to reformulate the principle in light of new insights that were discovered from the case. For example, when vaccinations first appeared, some ethicists argued that the principle prohibiting direct harm to another meant that one could not inject a person with a vaccination. But after doing casuistry, ethicists realized that the principle had to be amended, especially when the intended harm to the person was for the sake of preventing a much greater harm to the same person.

Burggraeve examines progress in the lives of children and offers an ethics of growth to accommodate a developmental approach to moral teaching. McDonagh puts the reign of God before us to invite us into the challenge of following Christ by fully entering into our human condition and fully emptying ourselves as well. Finally, Kelly concludes the book by looking to the future and offering us insights about what may lie before us.

We hope that this book promotes insight and discussion that move into action for HIV prevention. In particular we hope that it fosters among Catholics an understanding that our two-thousand year old tradition has resources to address the pandemic that affects especially the least empowered in our society. Likewise, as many of these essays try to do, we hope that the arguments we employ from our tradition foster unity among Catholics precisely as we try to promote social change to further accomplish HIV prevention.

We recognize, however, that we are not suggesting an overall grand or universal plan. This work is not about formulating universally held principles, but rather about applying long-held traditional insights. As a work of application, it does not pretend to speak for every Catholic or for every dimension of Catholic moral teaching. In fact, readers will find that the writers are extraordinarily diverse in their presuppositions, in their insights into the moral tradition, and in their approach to HIV prevention. One writer, for instance, claims that the tradition itself is "frozen"; another talks about how moral prophets have "unfrozen" important principles. For this reason, each essay ought to be seen as the singular contribution of its author and not necessarily of the editors.

The diversity of applications captures the richness of the Catholic moral tradition in the face of HIV/AIDS prevention. Hopefully, then, this collection will engender similar moves: prompting people to address their own local needs by applying the long-held beliefs that we all share.

Thus we present this book as an invitation to engage our colleagues and their students in ethics and moral theology to face the greatest pandemic in human history. We also want to encourage our local church leaders to think positively and constructively in the face of HIV/AIDS, drug use, and diverse sexual relations. Moreover, we want to encourage theological organizations and conferences around the world both to reawaken to the call to be concrete and practical, and to apply our traditions to answer specifically and practically, and not abstractly and speculatively, the urgent moral problems before us. Finally, we want to support those Catholic educators, social workers, church leaders, and medical personnel around the world who have been convinced from the start of this pandemic that Catholics can be actively involved in the work not only of serving HIV infected persons but also of promoting HIV prevention. The cases from Ireland, Tanzania, the United States, and Scotland particularly testify to this important work.

In closing, as editor, I want to acknowledge two major shortcomings: the lack of women contributors and the absence of contributors from certain parts of Europe and Asia. In both instances we suffered because church needs and the pandemic are claiming more and more time from such potential contributors. Due to their enormous workloads, two African women writers active in HIV prevention (one from Uganda and the other from Nigeria) had to decline belatedly their participation in the project. Three different Philippino writers were originally among the contributors, but each became the major superior of their religious congregations. A widely respected theologian in Thailand backed out of the project one month before the deadline due to illness and work. After a year of asking five different German theologians and five different French writers, including three who were involved in the drafting of the French bishops' statement, we had to give up on getting any of the ten, though all had written on the topic. Hopefully as the discussion goes forward, women and Asian voices will be more explicitly expressed and other European positions will appear in English.

On behalf of the editorial board I want to thank Fr. Michael Buckley, S.J., for his original vision, invitation, and active support of this project. We are grateful to Sue Perry for her early interest in the book and to Frank Oveis of Continuum for taking us on board. We are indebted to Angela Senander, Karen Enriquez, and especially Laura Richter for their help in putting this volume together and to José Carlos Coupeau, S.J., Mario Alberto Torres, S.J., and Andrea Vicini, S.J., for their work in translating three of the essays. Finally, though three of the authors are not moral theologians, their experience, training, and competency made them natural contributors along with our other colleagues. To all the contributors we acknowledge our appreciation.

As we present this work to you we believe that our contributors have put human faces on the topic of HIV prevention: Nomusa in South Africa, Andrew in Australia, David in Colombia, Laura in Italy, Sr. Mary in Ireland, Marcellus in Tanzania, or Agnaldo in Brazil. We hope that the book captures the humanity of the issue that we are inviting you to consider. On that human note I close with a quote from Jonathan Mann, to whom our book is dedicated:

> In the last few years we have gained confidence that as individuals and all together we are not condemned passively to allow the disease AIDS or the fears and forces which it can unleash to dominate us. Against AIDS, we will prevail together, for we will refuse to be split, or to cast into the shadows those persons, groups, and nations that are affected.

INTRODUCTION: AT THE END OF THE FIRST GENERATION OF HIV PREVENTION

Jon D. Fuller, S.J., and James F. Keenan, S.J.

A S WE LOOK back at the first generation of HIV prevention, we see progress on two important fronts: one in moral theology, the other in medicine.

Moral Theology

CATHOLIC MORALISTS AROUND the world have established two extraordinarily strong consensuses regarding condom distribution and needle exchange. They achieved these agreements by invoking the long-standing Roman Catholic tradition, and by trying to educate both local Roman Catholic communities and their leaders that the tradition has many resources for addressing the AIDS pandemic. In fact, Roman Catholic moralists throughout the world have been at pains to inform their episcopal leadership that in a variety of ways Catholics can respond to the AIDS pandemic, not only by serving those who are HIV infected, but also by working to prevent the spread of the disease.

An early attempt to work for prevention appeared in a case in the letter document from the United States Catholic Conference (USCC) Administrative Board, "The Many Faces of AIDS."[1] In that case, a health care worker urges a person who has tested positive for HIV "to live a chaste life." But, the letter added, "if it is obvious that a person will not act without bringing harm to others," then a health care professional could advise a form of conduct to minimize harm. Presumably, the health care professional could recommend the use of prophylactics. This position reflected in many ways

---

1. USCC Administrative Board, "The Many Faces of AIDS: A Gospel Response," *Origins* 17.28 (1987): 482–89.

the same type of casuistry that was found in an important pastoral letter by Cleveland Bishop Anthony M. Pilla.[2]

The USCC solution invoked the principle of toleration. This was the same principle that the American bishops invoked when writing their letter "The Challenge of Peace." There, when the American bishops discussed nuclear weapons, they rejected the validity of nuclear deterrence. They believed, however, that since the Soviet Union would not negotiate disarmament, that American unilateral disarmament would result in significant global political instability. Believing that they had no viable alternative, the bishops argued that they should not oppose but simply tolerate nuclear deterrence.[3]

Thus, in a good casuistic move, the USCC appropriated the earlier logic and made an important distinction: they were opposed to the promotion or advocacy of condoms, but when faced with a person who could further spread the disease and whose conduct would not be altered, they tolerated the advice that the patient should use a condom to prevent the spread of the disease. This position allowed the bishops both to resolve the new case and to protect the material principle that sex is illicit outside of marriage. It was a typical casuistry, the same one used on nuclear deterrence.

When this document was published, however, other bishops rebuffed the logic. Bishop after archbishop registered a double concern: first, the solution could be construed as approving or promoting illicit sexual activity and therefore could compromise Catholic teaching and confuse the faithful; and, second, condoms do not work effectively enough.[4]

After the USCC statement, many theologians attempted to respond to the bishops' first concern of compromising Catholic teaching.[5] These theologians invoked traditional methodological principles to address bishops' anxieties that existing moral teachings regarding contraception and illicit sexual activity would be undermined or made confusing. For instance, in addressing the case of the health care worker, Charles Bouchard and the late James Pollock[6] presented a history of the principle of toleration to

---

2. Most Rev. Anthony M. Pilla, "Statement on Developing an Approach by the Church to AIDS Education," *Origins* 16 (1987): 692–93.

3. "The Challenge of Peace," *Origins* 13.1 (1983).

4. "Reaction to AIDS Statement," *Origins* 17.28 (1987): 489–93; "Continued Reaction to AIDS Statement," *Origins* 17.30 (1988): 516–22; "Cardinal Ratzinger's Letter on AIDS Document," *Origins* 18.8 (1988): 117–21.

5. I discuss this casuistry at length in "Applying the Seventeenth-Century Casuistry of Accommodation to HIV Prevention," *Theological Studies* 60 (1999): 492–512.

6. Charles Bouchard and James Pollock, "Condoms and the Common Good," *Second Opinion* 12 (1989): 98–106.

highlight how traditional the USCC statement was. Later, David Hollenbach made a similar argument from common sense logic.[7] Then, Michael Place, one of the principal writers of "The Many Faces of AIDS," invoked the principle of toleration to demonstrate that the USCC statement did not jeopardize but as a matter of fact protected the church teaching on the exclusivity of marital relations.[8]

Because I believed that the USCC letter should have invoked the principle of cooperation instead of the principle of toleration, I published a long essay on the former, arguing for the same conclusion as the USCC did: the healthcare worker's advice was morally right.[9] The Irish theologian Enda McDonagh also proposed a casuistry in a time of AIDS, again arguing that though no one endorses or approves either illicit sexual activity or the "quick-fix approach" as it had been dubbed, still we may be involved in HIV prevention work.[10] The Austrian moral theologian Hans Rotter wrote along similar lines.[11] David Kelly looked not only at Catholic health care workers offering advice to those who are HIV positive, but also at married couples where one spouse is HIV positive; Kelly discussed how the use of a condom in their context was preventing infection, not conception.[12] James Drane looked at Thomas Aquinas's writings on the object of an action and again developed a casuistry of accommodation for the cases of both the patient and the spouse who are positive.[13]

For married couples, Béla Somfai invoked the principle of double effect and Dennis Regan subsequently endorsed this position.[14] Elsewhere I, too, argued for life-giving ways to interpret the law so as to protect both the law

---

7. David Hollenbach, "AIDS Education: The Moral Substance," *America* 157 (1987): 493–94.

8. Michael Place, "The Many Faces of AIDS," *America* 158 (1988): 141.

9. James Keenan, "Prophylactics, Toleration, and Cooperation: Contemporary Problems and Traditional Principles," *International Philosophical Quarterly* 28 (1988): 201–20.

10. Enda McDonagh, "Theology in a Time of AIDS," *Irish Theological Quarterly* 60 (1994): 81–99.

11. Hans Rotter, "AIDS: Some Theological and Pastoral Considerations," *Theology Digest* 39(1992): 235–39.

12. David Kelly, *Critical Care Ethics* (Kansas City: Sheed and Ward, 1991), 204–9.

13. James Drane, "Condoms, AIDS, and Catholic Ethics," *Commonweal* 189 (1991): 188–92.

14. Béla Somfai, "AIDS, Condoms, and the Church," *Compass* (November 1987): 44; Dennis Regan, "Perspectives from Moral Theology," *Dossiers and Documents; The Pandemic of AIDS: A Response by the Confederation of Caritas International* (February 1988): 58–67.

and people's lives. My position was that recommending condoms in a time of AIDS was not an endorsement of contraception, but rather prophylaxis.[15] In a more thorough way, John Tuohey argued that *Humanae Vitae* is not undermined at all when one acknowledges the moral liceity of using prophylactics in a marriage where one spouse is HIV positive.[16] Finally, Josef Fuchs reminded us of the importance of the principle of *epikeia* which helps us to do the casuistry of accommodation that moral theologians are called to develop.[17]

I have found very few theologians who differ significantly from the positions in this list. The philosopher Janet Smith argued that the use of the principle of toleration in the "Many Faces of AIDS" was unclear.[18] Mark Johnson argued that David Kelly's use of double effect was incorrect.[19] Neither author subsequently argued that advising on the use of prophylactics was itself wrong; they simply questioned a particular application of a particular principle. Only one writer objected to such advising and he argued simply that the advising was scandalous.[20] One wonders whether he thinks that the church's positions on ectopic pregnancies, pain relief for dying patients, and artificial insemination by husbands are also scandalous.

Despite this consensus of moral theologians offering traditional research for a casuistry that protects long-standing teaching while accommodating the value of protecting those at risk for the virus, the American bishops still feared that they could cause confusion and wrote another letter on AIDS, entitled "Called to Compassion and Responsibility." While not negating "The Many Faces of AIDS," the bishops resisted addressing infected persons who do not abstain from sexual activity.[21]

In the new pastoral letter, the bishops raised their second concern as well, the effectiveness of condoms. This objection appeared several times in two national Catholic newspapers, *Our Sunday Visitor* and the *National*

---

15. James Keenan, "Living with HIV/AIDS," *The Tablet* (3 June 1995): 701.

16. John Tuohey, "Methodology or Ideology: The Condom and a Consistent Sexual Ethic," *Louvain Studies* 15 (1990): 53–69.

17. Josef Fuchs, "Epikie—Der praktizierte Vorbehalt," *Stimmen der Zeit* 214 (1996): 749–50.

18. Janet Smith, "The Many Faces of AIDS and the Toleration of the Lesser Evil," *International Review of Natural Family Planning* 12 (1988): 1–15.

19. Mark Johnson, "The Principle of Double Effect and Safe Sex in Marriage: Reflections on a Suggestion," *Linacre Quarterly* 60 (1993): 82–89.

20. Joseph Howard, "The Use of the Condom for Disease Prevention," *Linacre Quarterly* 63 (1996): 26–30.

21. NCCB, "Called to Compassion and Responsibility: A Response to the HIV/AIDS Crisis," *Origins* 19.26 (1989): 421, 423–34.

Catholic Register, which published a series of essays claiming simply that condoms were not safe, employing such titles as "Sex, lies and latex: study busts condom myth."[22] There and elsewhere, Catholics cited a variety of studies about the effectiveness of condoms.[23]

In considering the second objection, we should realize that in the past four years studies have shown that condoms are very effective. The Jesuit physician Jon Fuller presents at length three studies that demonstrate the dramatic effect that condom use has had in stemming the spread of HIV.[24] One study appeared in the *New England Journal of Medicine*; it included 124 couples in which only one partner was HIV positive. Consistent use of condoms showed not one infection after a period of two years and an estimated 15,000 acts of intercourse. Studies in Uganda and Thailand also reported that preventive programs which urged abstinence and if not that, then condoms, had significant drops in infection rates.

In sum, moral theologians provided a very modest traditional casuistry to allay the bishops' first concern about confusing the faithful and compromising traditional principles.[25] They also offered substantial empirical data to address the second objection. Despite these moves, workers in Catholic health care facilities know that adoption of this casuistry can still result in considerable sanctions from many local chanceries.[26]

---

22. Julie Hoffman, "Bennett and Carey Rap Condom Plan," *National Catholic Register* 68 (31 May 1992): 1; Russell Shaw, "Condom 'Cure' Questioned by Top AIDS Researcher," *Our Sunday Visitor* 82 (23 January 1994): 3; Russell Shaw, "The Great Condom Con," *Columbia* 74 (June 1994): 5; Jean-Marie Guenois, "Sex, Lies and Latex: Study Busts Condom Myth," *Our Sunday Visitor* 86 (2 November 1997): 21.

23. Beverly Sottile-Malona, "Condoms and AIDS," *America* (21 November 1991): 317–19; New York Bishops, "Statement on Public Schools' Condom Distribution," *Origins* 22 (1993): 553–56.

24. Jon Fuller, "AIDS Prevention: A Challenge to the Catholic Moral Tradition," *America* 175 (28 December 1996): 13–20.

25. They did not question the concern about condom distribution in the schools without parental consent, which a variety of Christian spokespersons, including *Commonweal* magazine, attacked. Reed Jolley, "The Condom War on Children," *Christianity Today* 38 (1994): 19; "Statement on Public Schools's Condom Distribution," *Origins* 22 (1993): 553–56; "Condom Sense," *Commonweal* 118 (1991): 499–500. Whether the program is morally right is one question, but recent studies suggest that condom distribution in schools does not promote sexual promiscuity. See Lynda Richardson, "Condoms in School Said Not to Affect Teen-age Sex Rate," *New York Times*, 30 September 1997, A1, 33.

26. See Mireya Navarro, "Ethics of Giving AIDS Advice Troubles Catholic Hospitals," *New York Times,* 3 January 1993, 1, 24. "Vatican Intervenes to Stop HIV Pack," *The Tablet* (18 November 1995): 1489.

In their second AIDS document, "Called to Compassion," the American bishops also argued against needle exchange using basically the same two arguments as they did regarding condom distribution: people might perceive the bishops condoning illicit moral activity; and, the program is not effective.[27]

Regarding the concern about confusion, Jon Fuller has applied the principle of cooperation to the issue of needle exchange.[28] Fuller argues in favor of protecting the teaching that drug use is morally wrong, while at the same time providing an accommodation for the present crisis. Fuller's proposal prompted a strong editorial endorsement by *America* magazine as well as support from the well-known moral theologian, Richard McCormick. McCormick proposed some commonsense casuistry that again highlights the traditional accommodation of a case in the face of chaos. Invoking the case of drunk-driving and the possibility that someone drunk could compound their irresponsibility by driving, McCormick made a comparison to the needle exchange program and wrote, "We say, don't drive while drunk; let someone else drive. But supporting the designated driver doesn't mean we support over drinking; it simply means that we don't want the irresponsibility doubled."[29]

To Fuller's and McCormick's positions, we need to recognize also the claims of Jorge Ferrer whose essay in this collection applies the principles of cooperation and the counsel of the lesser of two evils to the case of needle exchange. Ferrer's article will undoubtedly become a major contribution in establishing the moral liceity and acceptability of needle exchange programs.

Regarding the bishops' second concern, studies of needle exchange programs provide two important, complimentary sets of data: one on their efficacy for HIV prevention; the other on the nonincrease of drug use resulting from needle exchange programs. In 1995, an advisory panel of the National Research Council and the Institute of Medicine declared that "well-implemented needle-exchange programs can be effective in preventing the spread of HIV and do not increase the use of illegal drugs."[30] Studies by the National Academy of Sciences, the

---

27. See also Joseph Doolin, "The Trouble with Needle Exchange Programs," *The Boston Pilot* (8 May 1998): 8; New Jersey Catholic Conference, "Statement on the Establishment of a Demonstration Needle and Syringe Exchange Program in the New Jersey Department of Health," November 1993.

28. Jon Fuller, "Needle Exchange: Saving Lives," *America* 179 (18–25 July 1998): 8–11. On the other hand, see Peter Cataldo, "The Ethics of Needle Exchange Programs for Intravenous Drug Users," in the newsletter of the Pope John Center, 1997.

29. "Needle Exchange Saves Lives," *America* 179 (18–25 July 1998): 3.

30. Cited in Fuller, 10. See Jacques Normand et al., eds., *Preventing HIV Transmission: The Role of Sterile Needles and Bleach* (Washington, D.C.: National Academy Press, 1995).

General Accounting Office, the Centers for Disease Control, and the University of California at Berkeley all found that needle exchange programs substantially lowered the spread of HIV and led to no increase in new drug use.[31] The programs are backed by the American Medical Association and the United States Conference of Mayors[32] as well as the National Institutes of Health.[33] Outside of the United States, similar reports of success come from many diverse studies, from Glasgow[34] to New Zealand.[35]

These programs could have significant impact: preventable disease, illness, and deaths. But the U.S. federal government continues to refuse to fund these programs and the American bishops' opposition to needle exchange programs remains unchanged. The failure to endorse needle exchange programs has caused scandal. In the British medical journal *The Lancet*, Peter Lurie claims that by 1997 up to 9,666 HIV infections would have been prevented by needle exchange programs and adds that "if current U.S. policies are not changed . . . an additional 5,150–11,329 preventable HIV infections could occur by the year 2000."[36] In 1998, *The Lancet* wrote an editorial urging the Clinton administration to lift the ban on federal funding of these programs. They noted that the United States remains one of the few industrial countries that refuses to provide access to clean needles and that injection drug misuse is now the leading source of pediatric HIV/AIDS.[37]

After a generation of this continuous work, moral theologians, having marshaled evidence by both applying traditional principles to the HIV prevention issues while communicating the results of important empirical

---

31. "Federal Funds for Clean Needles," *New York Times*, 22 February 1997, 16.

32. Katharine Seelye, "A.M.A. Backs Drug-User Needle Exchanges," *New York Times*, 27 June 1997, 15. See also Lawrence Gostin, "Prevention of HIV/AIDS and Other Blood-Borne Diseases Among Injection Drug Users," *JAMA* 277 (1 January 1997): 53–62.

33. "NIH Panel: Politics Hurting Fight Against AIDS," *The Nation's Health* (March 1997): 5; Warren Leary, "Panel Endorses Disputed Study of Hypodermic Needle Program," *New York Times*, 15 December 1996, A41.

34. Martin Frischer, "Direct Evaluation of Needle and Syringe Exchange Programmes," *The Lancet* 347 (16 March 1996): 768.

35. Bronwen Lichtenstein, "Needle Exchange Programs: New Zealand's Experience," *The American Journal of Public Health* 86 (September 1996): 1319.

36. Peter Lurie, "An Opportunity Lost: HIV Infections Associated with Lack of a National Needle-Exchange Programme in the USA," *The Lancet* 349 (1 March 1997): 604–8.

37. "Needle-Exchange Programmes in the USA: Time to Act Now," *The Lancet* 351 (10 January 1998): 75.

data, are beginning to have significant impact on church leadership. Now, as we enter a second generation in this era of AIDS, many in Catholic leadership realize that they can be both protective of existing teachings regarding contraception, illicit sexual activity, and drug use and at the same time advance the interests of HIV prevention. For these reasons, we should expect to see Catholic leadership loosening its resistance and returning to its traditional ways of addressing cases while upholding existing teachings. We have every reason to believe that in time, more bishops will not directly censure health care workers in Catholic facilities who in conscience recommend to their clients that they protect the common good by abstinence and, failing that, by prophylactic measures. Likewise, we should not expect the censure of moral theologians who assert the liceity of spouses protecting one another from infection. Moreover, we can reasonably expect to see Catholic hospitals becoming progressively involved in needle exchange. Finally, we should be able to see educational programs published with imprimaturs.

In fact, several bishops around the world are turning to this work of the moral theologians to address HIV preventive measures. In 1996, Bishop Rouet of the French Bishops' Social Commission issued a statement on AIDS which, through an appeal to the principle of the lesser evil, recognized the preventive function of the condom. This statement received a cautious but considered acceptance from many bishops, archbishops, and cardinals around the world.[38] Similarly, as Diana Hayes comments in her essay in this book, the Rochester Catholic Family Center in New York has promoted the first Catholic-supported needle exchange program in the United States. Moreover as Jon Fuller reported, three Catholic agencies support extensive needle exchange programs throughout Australia. For instance, in the state of Southern Australia alone we find fifty-five needle exchange programs for a population of only 1.2 million people. In that state, no new HIV infection has occurred from needle sharing in the last three years.

---

38. Craig Whitney, "French Bishop Supports Some Use of Condoms to Prevent AIDS," *New York Times*, 13 February 1996; Pamela Schaeffer, "Condoms Tolerated to Avoid AIDS, French Bishops Say," *National Catholic Reporter* (23 February 1996): 9; "Caution Greets AIDS Statement by French Bishops," *The Tablet* (24 February 1996): 272; Hubert Cornudet, "AIDS and Humanity," *The Tablet* (24 February 1996): 256–57; "Church Leaders Mix Condoms and Caveats," *National Catholic Reporter* (15 March 1996). See also "Dutch Cardinal Says Condoms OK When Spouse Has AIDS," *Catholic News Service* (16 February 1996); "Vienna Archbishop Says Condoms Morally Acceptable to Fight AIDS," *Catholic News Service* (3 April 1996). See also Robert Vitillo, "HIV/AIDS Prevention Education: A Special Concern for the Church," presentation for discussion at Caritas Internationalis, CAFOD Theological Consultation on HIV/AIDS, Pretoria, South Africa, 14 April 1998.

Bishops are able to take these steps because the tradition provides them with a way, as we have attempted to show, both to protect existing teachings and to simultaneously engage new problems creatively. We do not need to construct an entire new moral system, even at such a critical time as this one. Rather, the Catholic tradition is a supple and balanced legacy that we need to recognize, appreciate, and utilize.

Nonetheless as we look at the next generation a variety of new questions are arising. Richard Smith, for instance, asks how the church's teaching on homosexuality affects both the gay community and pastoral workers serving people infected with HIV.[39] More recently Kevin Kelly asks the overarching question: Why does Christian sexual ethics so often hamper rather than assist humanity as it faces the AIDS pandemic? Looking at the effects of Catholic Church teachings on two particular groups of persons, women and homosexuals, Kelly suggests that these teachings have a significant role in HIV prevention. Searching to empower these people with the deep theological resources of Christianity, he offers new directions that sexual ethics needs to pursue in order to be at the service of all human beings.[40]

As we now face the second generation, the structural issues that we noted earlier that are so important for HIV prevention must be open to examination. In terms of moral theology, we hope that these essays provide some sure guidance in that examination.

Medicine

IN REFLECTING ON the importance of related basic science, public health and clinical developments to the analysis of HIV/AIDS from the perspective of moral theology, it strikes me that St. Ignatius's "composition of place" is particularly appropriate. Our reflection is not speculative, but rather focused on engaging concretely with a life-threatening challenge of increasing proportions. For the sake of such reflection, we propose to preface these remarks on ethical issues with a brief discussion of the current state of the HIV phenomenon. After describing our understanding of whence and how HIV was introduced into the human population, we will review trends among HIV-infected populations, the impact of the epidemic on

---

39. Richard Smith, *AIDS, Gays, and the American Catholic Church* (Cleveland: Pilgrim Press, 1994). See also Eileen P. Flynn, *AIDS: A Catholic Call for Compassion* (Kansas City: Sheed and Ward, 1985).

40. Kevin T. Kelly, *New Directions in Sexual Ethics: Moral Theology and the Challenge of AIDS* (London: Geoffrey Chapman, 1998).

development, and briefly review the state of therapy and vaccine development, and close looking at ethical issues from clinical perspectives.

The Epidemic in Review

As this book goes to press in the late summer of 1999, we look back on a remarkable eighteen-year history since the HIV/AIDS epidemic was first reported in June 1981.[41] In the next six years three major milestones were achieved: first, the discovery (in 1983) of the human immunodeficiency virus (HIV) as the causative agent of AIDS; second, the licensing of an antibody test (in 1985) to diagnose the presence of HIV infection; and third (in 1987) the licensing of AZT (Retrovir, also known as zidovudine) as the first specific anti-HIV therapy.

Origins of HIV

After years of speculation, the source and timing of the introduction of HIV into the human community appear now to be fairly clearly established. There are actually two HIV virus families and two HIV epidemics caused, respectively, by human immunodeficiency virus type 1 (HIV-1) and human immunodeficiency virus type 2 (HIV-2). HIV-2 infection, however, accounts for a vanishingly small proportion of the global AIDS epidemic. It leads to AIDS in a smaller percentage of persons and over a longer period of time than does the dominant strain, HIV-1.

HIV-1, which accounts for up to 99 percent of the global AIDS epidemic, is most closely related genetically to a simian immunodeficiency virus (SIV) strain endemic in a subspecies of chimpanzees (SIVcpz) indigenous to western equatorial Africa. SIVcpz has been present in this chimpanzee species for several hundred thousand years, but with human encroachment on previously uninhabited territories, and with the increasing capture and butchering of chimpanzees for "bush meat," contact between humans and

---

41. Michael S. Gottlieb, Robert Schroff, Andrew Saxon, et al., "Pneumocystis Carinii Pneumonia and Mucosal Candidiasis in Previously Healthy Homosexual Men: Evidence of a New Acquired Cellular Immunodeficiency," *New England Journal of Medicine* 305 (10 December 1981): 1425–31; Henry Masur, Mary Ann Michelis, Susanna Cunningham-Rundles, et al. "An Outbreak of Community-Acquired Pneumocystis Carinii Pneumonia: Initial Manifestation of Cellular Immune Dysfunction," *New England Journal of Medicine* 305 (10 December 1981): 1431–38; Alvin E. Friedman-Kien, Linda J. Laubenstein, Susan Zolla-Pazner, et al., "Disseminated Kaposi's Sarcoma in Homosexual Men," *Annals of Internal Medicine* 96 (June 1992): 693–700.

chimps has led to three independent transmissions of SIVcpz into the human community as HIV-1. These three "moments of encounter" account for the three documented HIV-1 subspecies. The first, HIV-1 group M ("Main"), represents the vast majority of HIV-1 infections. Group O ("Outlier") has been identified in relatively few persons in western equatorial African countries, and the third subpopulation (group N, for "Non-M/Non-O") has been documented in only four persons living in Cameroon.[42]

One critical research issue is to understand how SIV in chimpanzees does not cause disease, whereas the same virus, when transmitted to humans (who are 98.5 percent genetically similar to chimpanzees), is nearly always fatal in the absence of therapy.

Changing Demographics

Over the past eighteen years the demographics of the HIV epidemic in the U.S. and globally have changed rather remarkably. In the United States, men who have sex with men have contributed a declining percentage of total cases, declining from more than 98 percent in 1981 to 35 percent of cases reported in 1998.[43] Sharing of drug injection equipment accounted (directly or indirectly) for 31 percent of AIDS diagnoses reported in 1998. Women account for 32 percent of U.S. AIDS diagnoses in 1998, a 50 percent increase from their 21 percent share in 1987.

In the early years AIDS in the U.S. was perceived as largely involving gay white males, but the epidemic has continued to gravitate toward members of minority communities. Despite dramatic reversals in U.S. AIDS mortality because of new treatments, AIDS is still the leading cause of death among African-American men aged 25–44, and the second leading cause for African-American women in the same age group. The Centers for Disease Control and Prevention (CDC) estimates that only 12 percent of the U.S. population are African-American, but 62 percent of women diagnosed with AIDS in 1998 were from the African-American community, and 85 percent of diagnosed children were from communities of color.[44]

Worldwide, we have watched an epidemic that initially spread in east and central Africa more recently move rapidly across southern Africa (where up to 25 percent of adults may be infected in Namibia, Botswana,

42. Feng Gao, Elizabeth Bailes, David L. Robertson, et al., "Origin of HIV-1 in the Chimpanzee Pan Troglodytes," *Nature* 397 (4 February 1999): 436–41.

43. Centers for Disease Control, *HIV/AIDS Surveillance Report* 10, no. 2 (1998) 1–43.

44. Ibid.

Zimbabwe, and Lesotho). At the same time, the epidemic is poised to spread rapidly in Asia (most especially in India and China), as well as in countries of the former Soviet Union (especially Russia and Ukraine). It is now estimated that since the beginning of the epidemic fifty million persons have become HIV-infected (thirty-four million in Africa), with twelve million having progressed to AIDS and death (5,500 AIDS funerals occur in Africa each day). New transmissions numbering sixteen thousand occur daily (one every 5.5 seconds): 90 percent in developing countries, half among women, and more than 75 percent from heterosexual contact.[45]

Impact on Development

Despite the relatively short history of interaction between HIV and the human community, in less than two decades HIV has surpassed tuberculosis and malaria as the (previously) no. 1 and no. 2 leading infectious killers in the world. Besides being the leading cause of death by infection, AIDS is now the fourth leading cause of all deaths worldwide.[46] Decades of painstakingly achieved improvements in infant, child, and adult mortality are now being reversed, with the life expectancy in some sub-Saharan African countries now being reduced by twenty or more years because of HIV/AIDS.[47] In some locations up to 40 percent of pregnant women are infected with HIV, with 1,800 HIV-infected infants being born daily on a worldwide basis.[48] As Peter Piot (executive director of UNAIDS) has observed, "AIDS has been with us for just twenty years and already it is killing more people than any other infectious disease. It is the most formidable pathogen to confront modern medicine, with the potential to undermine this century's massive improvements in health and well-being of people around the world" (14 May 1999).

As compared with other major epidemics in human history which particularly affect the elderly (most notably the 1918 global influenza epidemic), more than 50 percent of new HIV infections occur in persons under the age of twenty-five, causing death for individuals who are still raising children, who are often the sole or principal sources of income for their families, and who represent one of the most productive sectors of any country's economy.

---

45. World Health Organization, *World Health Report, 1999*, Geneva.

46. Ibid.

47. Youssef M. Ibrahim, "AIDS is Slashing Africa's Population, U.S. Survey Finds," *New York Times*, 28 October 1998, A3.

48. Lynn Mofenson, "Short-Course Zidovudine for Prevention of Perinatal Infection," *The Lancet* 353 (6 March 1999): 766–67; UNAIDS.

Advances in Treating Infected Persons

Our capacity to treat HIV-infected patients has expanded significantly since the early eighties. Fourteen anti-HIV drugs are now licensed in the United States, with many more in research and development (some of which attack novel stages in the viral life cycle). Where these drugs are available, mortality rates have dropped by up to 45 percent, and the number of new AIDS cases has similarly been reduced.

While developments in anti-HIV drug therapy are exciting and clearly provide hope for those who have access to these drugs, they are also a mixed blessing even to those able to appreciate their benefits (due to toxicities, side effects, and quality of life issues required for adherence to strict drug regimens). Though these medications can stabilize symptoms and slow the approach of death, they are also responsible for sometimes serious complications which include the development of insulin-dependent diabetes, increases in blood lipids (such as cholesterol and triglycerides) which can be associated with heart attacks and strokes, as well as the redistribution of body fat stores leading to increased deposits in the abdomen and breasts, while extreme loss of tissue can be seen in the extremities and in the face.

Taking HIV medications can be complex and time consuming. As compared with drugs which treat high blood pressure or diabetes, they are relatively unforgiving. Drug resistance can develop rapidly in patients who are unable to adhere to sometimes strict regimens which may require dosing with or without food, at times different from other anti-HIV medications, on strict schedules, and so forth. Even when used properly, there is no cure: viral eradication is not achieved by even the most stringent of regimens taken for years.

Unfortunately, for 90 percent of HIV-infected persons around the world, access to such expensive regimens is simply out of the question. In addition to their rather high cost (ranging from $12,000–$18,000 per year for drugs, not counting the cost of clinic visits and laboratory monitoring), the rational use of these medications requires the availability of moderately sophisticated and expensive laboratory testing. HIV drugs and the laboratory tests for monitoring their use are available in most industrialized countries, but introducing combination therapies in circumstances where the per capita budget for all health care needs may be less than $10 or $15 obviously raises important questions regarding the allocation of scarce resources, especially when other fundamental health needs such as nutrition, clean water, sanitation (and HIV prevention) are not fully funded.

An AIDS Vaccine

Efforts to develop a vaccine which would be preventive (for patients not yet infected) or therapeutic (to stimulate the immune response of already-infected individuals) are moving slowly. It is still not clear what kind of immune response in a vaccine recipient is necessary for protection against HIV infection. All the mechanisms which have been used to develop effective vaccines against other infectious diseases have proven unfruitful in the case of HIV. Trials of a vaccine candidate which contains subunit proteins of HIV are under way both in industrialized and developing countries. Although this vaccine is not expected to be highly effective, it is hoped that it might prevent infections in a few individuals at the same time that it makes contributions to a basic understanding of HIV vaccine development. Nevertheless, most observers anticipate that it will probably be ten to twenty years before vaccines will make a real difference in preventing HIV infections, if this is ever possible.

In summary, only 10 percent of the world's HIV-infected population have access to HIV treatments and to their laboratory monitoring. Even in the best circumstances treatment does not achieve viral eradication, and lifelong treatment appears to be necessary. Vaccine development is slow and will not play a significant role in preventive strategies for several more decades. In this context, primary prevention of HIV infection must remain our first priority.

Ethical Issues from the Clinical Perspective

In the world at large heterosexual contact is the dominant mode of transmission, and prevention efforts must be targeted at this population first and foremost. Studies demonstrate without doubt that when consistently and properly used, condoms are an effective means of preventing HIV and other sexually transmitted diseases (STDs), including hepatitis B.[49] In the "first generation" of ethical discussions regarding the prevention of HIV

---

49. Anne M. Johnson, "Condoms and HIV Transmission," *New England Journal of Medicine* 331 (11 August 1994): 391–92; Antonia C. Novello, Herbert B. Peterson, Jeffrey A. Perlman, et al., "Condoms Used for Prevention of Sexual Transmission of HIV Infection," *JAMA* 269 (9 June 1993): 2840; "Drug and Sex Programs Called Effective in Fight Against AIDS," *New York Times*, 14 February 1997, A27; Marie Laga, Michel Alary, Peter Piot, et al., "Condom Promotion, Sexually Transmitted Diseases Treatment, and Declining Incidence of HIV-1 Infection in Female Zairian Sex Workers," *The Lancet* 344 (23 July 1994): 246–48; Robert S. Hanenberg, Wiwat Rojanapithayakorn, Prayura Kunasol, and David C. Sokal, "Impact of Thailand's HIV-Control Programme as Indicated by the Decline of Sexually Transmitted Diseases," *The Lancet* 344 (23 July 1994): 243–45.

transmission in the heterosexual context, the conversation focused on the efficacy of condoms (now not disputed), as well as the concern that education to increase the use of condoms could increase illicit sexual behavior. It has now been well demonstrated that education which includes information about the appropriate use of condoms does not increase the rate of sexual intercourse, and in fact can lead to a delay in the age of first intercourse.[50] Numerous studies (from Uganda, Senegal, Thailand, among others) have demonstrated that educational programs which discuss condoms and which also encourage a delay in age of first intercourse and a reduction in the number of sexual partners can make enormous strides in decreasing new HIV infections as well as other STDs.

However, there has at the same time been a legitimate concern that focusing solely on condoms as an effective preventive method can diminish the focus on as-important behavioral and cultural issues which must be confronted if we are to make real progress. How much have we accomplished if we teach a wife to use a condom to prevent her becoming infected by her husband, who is continuing to engage in sexual intercourse with commercial sex workers, if we pay no attention to the culturally based support for such behavior on his part? Analogously, while we clearly want to protect the lives of women who for whatever reasons are engaged in prostitution, we must also examine the double standards which exist for men and women in societies around the world which place wives at risk and which lead to the trafficking of women and children as sex objects.

Although injecting drug use is not a major cause of HIV transmission in sub-Saharan Africa, it is an important means of the spread of HIV across countries of the former Soviet Union, in China, in northern Africa and the Middle-East, and certainly in western Europe and North America. With the scientific community now virtually unanimous in its support of the efficacy of needle exchange programs in decreasing HIV transmission, in bringing persons who are addicted into general health care and drug recovery, and in not increasing the number of persons who inject drugs, it is clear that the rhetoric surrounding policies which prohibit needle exchange programs has little to do with scientific data and more to do with the concern that "we

---

50. Sally Guttmacher, Lisa Lieberman, and David Ward, "Does Access to Condoms Influence Adolescent Sexual Behavior?" *The AIDS Reader* 8 (November/December 1998): 201–5, 209; Deborah E. Sellers, Sarah A. McGraw, and John B. McKinlay, "Does the Promotion and Distribution of Condoms Increase Teen Sexual Activity? Evidence from an HIV Prevention Program for Latino Youth," *American Journal of Public Health* 84 (December 1994): 1952–59; Douglas Kirby, Nancy D. Brener, Ron Harrist, et al., "The Impact of Condom Distribution in Seattle Schools on Sexual Behavior and Condom Use," *American Journal of Public Health* 89 (February 1999): 182–87.

don't want to send the wrong message." In attending international conferences and advisory meetings on HIV/AIDS, it is a frequent occurrence that persons from other countries look at the United States' stance on this issue and simply shake their heads. Most of the world's citizenries view needle exchange programs in the same way that we in the U.S. look at methadone: both are practical means of diminishing harm to individuals and to society, and are cornerstones of the public health approach to narcotic addiction. Nevertheless, given the still strong reticence in the United States for supporting these programs, we observe a continual increase in the proportion of new AIDS diagnoses which are related to sharing injection equipment.

Ethical Policies

Many of the ethical issues raised by the AIDS epidemic have initially been at the level of rights and responsibilities of the infected individual: access to care; confidentiality; access to health insurance, housing, public transportation and employment. However, as we cross into the new millennium a new set of ethical questions which are more communitarian in nature are being observed. For example, at least in the industrialized nations the majority of vertical HIV transmissions (from an infected, pregnant mother to her developing fetus) are transmitted during the time of labor rather than during the nine months of intrauterine development. Standard protocols for prevention of vertical transmission in the industrialized West call for oral therapy for the mother during her final two trimesters of pregnancy, intravenous therapy during labor, and six weeks of oral therapy for the infant. While this protocol reduces HIV transmission by 67 percent (from 25 percent to 8 percent), it also costs approximately $850 per treated mother and child. (This estimate is based on using AZT as a single drug, which in industrialized nations has now been largely superseded by two and three drug regimens because of the increasing prevalence of resistance to AZT.) Even this AZT-only protocol is economically out of reach in most developing contexts, but data now indicate that briefer, simpler monotherapy or dual-therapy trials may be able to reduce transmission risk by 35 to 50 percent by treating the mother only during labor, and by treating the infant not at all or for a very brief period, all for a cost ranging from $4–$250 per mother/infant pair.

For such simple monotherapy regimens to be effective, HIV must be sensitive to the drug being used. However, if anti-HIV drugs are made available for treating adults in circumstances where continuity of drug supply, appropriate prescribing, and the technical tools needed for rational use are not available, resistance may increase rapidly among treated persons. One recently reported study from Brazil examined increases in drug resistance where combination therapy was made available in the absence of tests to measure the viral response, or to properly target patients for treatment.[51] At baseline the level of resistance to two different classes of drugs were 0 and 5 percent, repectively, while after treatment resistance levels had increased to 65 percent and 30 percent, respectively. Obviously the effectiveness of brief, inexpensive monotherepy protocols to prevent vertical transmission would be doomed if resistance to the single drug being used had already become highly prevalent in the community.

Impact on Research Ethics

Experience with the AIDS epidemic has also led to a re-evaluation of certain ethical principles for research which have previously been firmly established. In many circumstances these principles were developed to prevent the recurrence of abuse which had been historically documented, most notably during medical research by Nazi doctors. For example, in order to prevent industrialized nations from using subjects in developing countries as "guinea pigs" in research that will eventually not benefit them, it has been a firmly established principle that subjects in trials which are comparing two therapies should be treated either with the current state-of-the-art therapy, or with the putatively better regimen which is being tested. Stated formally, "in any medical study, every patient—including those of a control group, if any—should be assured of the best proven diagnostic and therapeutic method."[52]

What if we take the case of a sub-Saharan Africa country which is attempting to research anti-HIV drug protocols which might not represent the state-of-the-art in an industrialized setting, but which would nevertheless present a real advance over currently available local treatments at a price which might be affordable? Rather than being driven by a policy which is intended to protect against previously observed abuses, we now observe conversations among researchers and ethicists who are exploring the possibility of restating these ethical considerations for the sake of achieving what is possible in a given country's setting. Thus it has been proposed that the principle described above be modified to allow for research when the "gold standard" may not be possible, especially when holding

51. C . D. Pilcher, M. D. Perkins, S. A. Fiscus, et al., "Genotypic resistance and the treatment of HIV-1 infection in the Espirito Santo, Brazil," *Journal of Infectious Diseases* 179 (May 1999): 1259–63.

52. *Council for International Organizations of Medical Sciences (CIOMS)*, Guideline 14, Article II.3 (cited in Barry R. Bloom, "The Highest Attainable Standard: Ethical Issues in AIDS Vaccines," *Science* 279 (9 January 1998): 186–88.

researchers to this standard might make no trials accessible to a given population: "Study participants should be assured the highest standard of care practically attainable in the country in which the trial is being carried out."[53] In addition, it has been proposed that it may not be ethical to initiate research in a developing country if there is no feasibility that the treatment, if proven beneficial, could ever be made available to the local populations on whom research was being conducted.[54]

Conclusion

THE DEMOGRAPHICS OF the spreading HIV/AIDS epidemic increasingly draw our attention to the developing world, to women and children, and their status in society, to injection drug users, and to minority groups and other marginalized and vulnerable populations. Ethical questions are moving from an analysis of the individual set against social forces to those which weigh the balance of goods and benefits for various groups in society. Ethicists and moralists will need to take into consideration the fact that even the most sophisticated HIV treatments do not cure this infection and, therefore, primary prevention of HIV infection must become the focal point of our discussions. This reflection must occur with adequate attention to the concrete realities which shape the day-to-day experience of vulnerable populations. While some have doubted whether HIV/AIDS would mature into an epidemic of global proportions, the facts before us leave no doubt in this regard. They must galvanize our efforts toward applying the traditional principles of our Catholic tradition in the context of this unprecedented biomedical, social, and cultural challenge.

---

53. Participants of the Perinatal HIV Intervention Research in Developing Countries Workshop, "Science, Ethics, and the Future of Research into Maternal Infant Transmission of HIV-1," *The Lancet* 353 (6 March 1999): 832–35.

54. George J. Annas and Michael A. Grodin, "Human Rights and Maternal-Fetal HIV Transmission Prevention Trials in Africa," *American Journal of Public Health* 88 (April 1998): 560–63.

Part 1: The Cases

1.
STANDING WITH THE MARGINALIZED BY BRINGING FORTH THEIR TRUTH

AN IRISH NUN LIVING WITH CONTRADICTIONS: RESPONDING TO HIV/AIDS IN THE CONTEXT OF CHURCH TEACHING

Linda Hogan

SR. MARY WORKS *with a church-funded HIV/AIDS prevention and education service in an urban diocese in Ireland. Her work involves traveling to Catholic-run secondary schools both in her own diocese and around the country to educate the students on aspects of the virus, including prevention. In the Republic of Ireland the Catholic Church, with substantial state funding, runs most secondary schools. The church has a constitutional guarantee that the Catholic ethos of schools will be protected. Religious and moral education takes place in this context, and teachers are expected to promote the magisterium's teachings on all aspects of relationships, sexuality, and sexual relationships. However many teachers believe that much of this is rejected by their students as being out of touch with the reality of young people's lives. Sr. Mary recognizes that there is a great richness within the Catholic tradition and she is committed to promoting these values. However she also believes that this richness is often not evident in many of the official pronouncements on sexual behavior.*

This is the context in which Sr. Mary educates students about HIV prevention. She is convinced that if she simply repeats the official church line on HIV prevention and if she tries to avoid or ignore the difficult questions, then her message too will be dismissed as being unrealistic. She has given serious thought to her approach and has taken advice from many people.

From this she has constructed a program which she believes is both appropriate and ethical. Although this program does not follow explicitly church teaching on HIV prevention, it is faithful to the essentials of the Catholic approach to sexuality. In the program she talks frankly about sexual relationships, about HIV prevention and condoms, and about a range of related issues involving sexual health. She does so in the context of discussing the importance of moral values and virtues and the nature of relationships. She advises the students to take decisions about entering into sexual relationships very seriously, to try to resist peer pressure, to respect their own bodies, and to avoid alcohol and drug abuse. She tries to gain a balance between being realistic about young people's behavior and promoting the values implicit in church teaching on sexuality.

Over the years she has realized that it is pointless for her simply to give a lecture about abstaining from sex until one is married. She knows that if her message about HIV prevention is to be successful, then she must acknowledge that many young people have active sex lives. She is adamant that she must deal with that reality. Of particular concern to her is the issue of condom use. Having thought long and hard about this she decided to include a section in her talk that deals explicitly with it. She talks honestly about the benefits of using condoms, especially in situations of casual sex. She talks about the effectiveness of proper condom use in limiting the risks of contracting HIV, and of course about the failures of condoms as well. She hopes to provide an honest and balanced overview of the issue.

Unsurprisingly she has encountered hostility from her peers, from school authorities, from her religious superiors, and from Catholic parents. They insist that, if she is engaged in this kind of work at all, then she should be educating the students in the formal teaching of the church on HIV prevention. Many of her co-religious believe that she should be admonishing young people to abstain from all sexual activity until marriage and that she should only be promoting the clear teaching that the way to prevent HIV infection is to abstain from sex. She is often accused of promoting promiscuity, of undermining church teaching, and of acting against the religious ethos of the schools. One parish priest even ordered her to stop visiting schools in his parish until she changed the content of her teaching.

However she also gets positive feedback, especially from pupils, but also from teachers and parents. She occasionally worries that her critics may be right about the effects of her work. Although she does gain positive support privately, she often feels very alone and vulnerable in her work. Sr. Mary's dilemma is whether or not she should be engaged in this kind of work. Is her duty, as a religious sister, simply to explain and defend official church teaching on this matter? Or is she right to draw on different aspects of the Catholic tradition to forge a new approach to HIV education? Despite being marginalized by many in her community, Sr. Mary has

resolved to continue. In doing so she appeals to many aspects of the
Catholic tradition. First she looks to the church teaching on conscience in
order to explain her approach, one which may be regarded as contrary to
recent church instructions on HIV prevention. Second, she appeals to the
positive valuation of sexuality within some aspects of the Catholic tradi-
tion, which she believes is often missing in the church's formal teaching on
HIV/AIDS. Third she applies another neglected aspect of the tradition to
the ethics of sexual activity—that is, the aspect which stresses the impor-
tance of circumstances and intentions in assessing the morality of decisions.

The Dignity of Conscience

IN THE COURSE of her work Sr. Mary encounters criticism from many quarters. The criticism tends to be the claim that she is not obedient to church
teaching on HIV/AIDS prevention. As a result she is acting and encouraging others to act in an unethical fashion. She is also occasionally accused of
undermining the whole edifice of church teaching and church authority.
She has encountered personal abuse and hostility. She has also been the
subject of anonymous complaints to her religious superiors. Many of these
complaints are vague and inaccurate, and as a result are difficult to respond
to. In essence her critics claim that Sr. Mary should only be explaining official church teaching on HIV prevention, that she should insist that all
extramarital sex is immoral, and that condom use is forbidden. This should
be the extent of Sr. Mary's education on HIV prevention.

After serious reflection Sr. Mary has concluded that her approach is
right. It is a cause of concern to her that she ignores and occasionally disagrees with church teaching on the matter. However she resolves this concern by appealing to the church's long tradition of upholding the dignity of
conscience. This is not merely a political maneuver or strategy, rather it
forms the basis of her rationale for her work. She reminds herself and her
accusers that from the earliest centuries Christianity has promoted respect
for each person's conscience. A celebrated passage from *Gaudium et Spes*
summarizes this tradition when it suggests that:

> Deep within their consciences men and women discover a law
> which they have not laid upon themselves and which they must
> obey. Its voice, ever calling them to love and to do what is good
> and to avoid evil, tells them inwardly at the right moment: do this,
> shun that. For they have in their hearts a law inscribed by God.
> Their dignity rests on observing this law, and by it they will be
> judged. Their conscience is people's most secret core, and their
> sanctuary. There they are alone with God, whose voice echoes in

their depths. . . . Through loyalty to conscience, Christians are joined to others in the search for truth and for the right solution to so many moral problems. (no. 16)

This is really a summary of Catholic teaching on conscience. It reminds us that conscience is both a gift and a challenge. Conscience refers to the inherent capacity of people to know and do good. The gift aspect highlights the fact that this is innate, the challenge is to develop and tune it so that one's conscience is a sensitive and judicious instrument of choice and action. In the context of the current dilemma, Sr. Mary's concern is to help young people to come to terms with this tremendous moral responsibility and to learn how to make good and honest moral decisions. In this context she believes that the best way to do this is not by repeating uncritically, official teaching on HIV prevention, but by finding a more nuanced and pastorally sensitive approach to the issue.

Within the church, conscience is not regarded as a free-floating and independent ethical sense, but rather is an aspect of the person's character that is shaped within the context of the moral teaching and tradition of the church. As such the church has an important teaching function. Its task is to enable individuals to recognize the moral truth in each situation. It does this in many ways: through moral formation, through the witness of exemplary figures, and through preaching and formal teaching. Each of these forms of moral education is important, although the formal teaching through magisterial pronouncements and doctrine tends to be given most attention. To be a Catholic means one is always in dialogue with this multifaceted tradition. Sr. Mary conducts her work in dialogue with this tradition. She shares the values and concerns that underlie church teaching although she disagrees with the educational strategy that it advocates. And so she draws on the tradition of respect for conscience in order to justify her departure from official church teaching.

Over the centuries the church has attempted to balance these different aspects of ethical discernment. However, there is now and there has long since been confusion regarding the relationship between conscience and tradition, especially between conscience and the teaching of the magisterium. Problems arise when the individual, in good conscience, comes to a decision which is not in accord with what the church teaches. This is precisely the situation in which Sr. Mary finds herself. In an ideal world decisions of conscience and the teaching of the magisterium would be in harmony. Yet history and personal experience indicate that there is often disagreement between serious minded Catholics and the magisterium. However, although the teaching of the church has an important role in determining the direction in which any dilemma should be resolved, it can never replace the individual's decision of conscience.

The issue of the relationship between the individual conscience and the teaching of the institutional church continues to be contentious. Indeed in recent decades the debate has been even more polarized and has led the church into internal conflict and crisis. Although she is concerned about this, Sr. Mary has no ideological or political agenda to promote. Indeed she is deeply upset by suggestions from those who oppose what she does, that she is contributing to the present crisis within the church. Sr. Mary is a loyal Catholic. She in no way wants to undermine or detract from the authenticity and integrity of the church. In fact it is because she believes such things that she has chosen her present course of action, at great personal cost.

The Positive Valuation of Sexuality

ONE OF THE things Sr. Mary has discovered is that young people perceive the church's teaching on sex to be overwhelmingly negative. When asked what they know about church teaching, they list a series of prohibitions; "thou shalt not do anything" is how one student put it. Sr. Mary is aware that the church's formal response to the issue of HIV prevention could be seen in this light also. She is constantly surprised by the degree to which students think that the church regards sexuality with fear and loathing. She is aware that this is only a partial view of the church's approach to sexuality and tries to communicate the positive aspects as well. She reminds students that the Christian tradition is based on the belief that human beings are created in the *imago Dei*—that is, in the image and likeness of God. As such, Christians believe in the sacredness of human persons in all their dimensions, including the corporeal and sexual ones.

Christianity has frequently struggled with this. There has been a tendency to prioritize the spiritual aspects of human beings and to dismiss the value of the flesh. However the traditions of *imago Dei* and of incarnation attest to the value and importance of the body. Christians should recognize that the body is not merely an accessory. It is the ground of our subjectivity and the medium of all our experiences. Furthermore our bodiliness mediates our connectedness with the world and with other embodied subjects. A central aspect of this connectedness for many people is their sexual relationships. These too can be a truly sacred and highly ethical expression of their humanity. This approach to the body is significant. It reminds Christians that the manner in which we treat our own bodies and those we encounter has ethical implications. If the body is the way we mediate our connectedness, then we must have reverence for the body. We must nourish and care for the body with as much attention as we would nourish the spirit. Respect and care for the body and one's sexuality is not an optional extra, but is one of the ways in which the value of each person is affirmed.

However Sr. Mary believes that this central aspect of Christian teaching is often neglected when the church teaches on certain issues. In particular the language of condemnation detracts from the positive message on the human body and sexuality. Of course it is important that the morality of particular acts is discussed and that the church's insistence on respect for one's own and other's bodies is heard. However, if condemnation is the only aspect of the church's teaching which is given attention, then Christianity's positive approach to the human body and sexuality will be completely undermined.

The Importance of Circumstances and Intentions in Morality

OVER THE YEARS many people have told Sr. Mary of their dissatisfaction with church teaching on sex. Their most serious complaint is that the church holds an absolutist line, without much attention being given to the particular circumstances in which couples, for example, may use condoms to avoid conception or to protect a partner from contracting HIV. However Sr. Mary is aware that although many of the pronouncements on sex seem rather black and white, there is another aspect of the tradition which promotes a more nuanced approach to morality in general. In her own teaching she attempts to draw on this tradition and extend it into the field of sexual ethics and so present a context-sensitive evaluation of sexual relationships.

Within the Christian tradition there have been many debates about how to properly assess the morality of specific decisions. Especially in the past thirty years many theologians have reasserted the significance of circumstances and intentions in each moral evaluation. Moral acts are not isolated single actions that can be separated from the context in which they are performed. They must be recognized as a complex and unique combination of factors including context, intentions, circumstances, and consequences. This implies that a particular action can have a different meaning in two separate contexts. Circumstances and intention can be included in the moral evaluation of an action to change its meaning. Using this tradition, Sr. Mary asks her students to consider two cases. One is of a person who engages in casual, protected sex regularly, the other is the case of a couple who use condoms to protect the wife from contracting HIV from her infected partner. In each case condoms are used; however, in the second case one might say that the reason for using condoms is to protect from HIV infection and not to prevent conception. As a result in this case the choice to use condoms may be a positive and good one.

Some traditional views disregarded context and intentionality in determining the morality of the act and proposed that each act could be either good or evil in itself. However, within the tradition there are also many theologians, such as Aquinas, who sought to include the intention of persons and the circumstances in which they were acting in the moral description of the act. They insist that it is not possible to describe any moral act in itself, independently of the context in which the act is performed. Of course this is not a simple matter. It requires that attention be given to the particular context to ensure that one is describing it honestly and accurately. One must also be able to determine which features of a situation are morally relevant and which are irrelevant. Sr. Mary draws on these reconceptualizations of the relationship between actions, circumstances, and intentions. She encourages her students to see that the Catholic tradition can respond to the particularities of situations and is not as absolutist as it may appear.

This approach has long been an important part of the Catholic moral tradition. In the years since Vatican II it has gained a renewed impetus as a way of approaching ethical dilemmas. Indeed, the importance of circumstances and intentions has always been appreciated in assessing the morality of public and social issues such as war. However, much church teaching seems reluctant to extend the same degree of subtlety and discrimination to the sexual arena. In her discussions of sexual relationships Sr. Mary teaches that circumstances and intentions alter cases, that no two choices about sexual activity are the same, and that blanket condemnations fail to appreciate the complexity and indeterminacy of real life situations.

Conclusion

SR. MARY'S SITUATION will be familiar to many Catholics who attempt to live their lives in a spirit of respect and obedience to the church. Although unity is important, the complex and ambiguous nature of moral decisions in real life means that there will inevitably be disagreement among serious and honest individuals regarding the right course of action. Although not strictly in accordance with certain teachings, Sr. Mary's approach draws on many central and essential aspects of Christian theology. Indeed, it is precisely because she believes that she is true to Christian values in the midst of human confusion that she continues her work. She is confident that in her role as educator she is promoting the spirit of the gospel in the contemporary world.

A WOMAN CONFRONTS SOCIAL STIGMA IN UGANDA

John Mary Waliggo

THE MYSTERIOUS AND *most dreaded epidemic which much later came to be known as AIDS or locally as Silimu (from the abnormal slimness it caused to its victims) first appeared in the southern district of Rakai which borders with Tanzania in 1982. Once it was established by medical doctors that the so-called mysterious epidemic was none other than AIDS caused by sexual contact with an infected partner or through infected blood transfusion, and that it has no cure, the stigma on persons with HIV/AIDS began to build up very quickly. Anyone identified to be HIV positive was looked on as having engaged in irresponsible, extramarital, excessive sex.*

AIDS was perceived as the disease for perpetual prostitutes, persons with very loose sexual morality, people who slept with anyone they could find. Many "judges" of the morality of others, including many religious leaders and self-righteous people, began to point fingers at groups of people who would be wiped out by AIDS. These included fornicators, adulterers, prostitutes, and any other persons of loose sexual morality. Such moralists had no sympathy with persons sick with AIDS. For such people AIDS had provided the opportune occasion to preach against sexual unfaithfulness, marriage infidelity, promiscuity, and sexual liberalism.

I attended one Catholic service where the priest warned people in these words: "We have been telling you for several decades now to know how to control your sexuality and use it only in accordance with the Christian doctrine but you have refused. It is time now for you to reap the fruits of your stubbornness."[1] The preacher seemed to take "joy" in the increasing deaths of the disobedient members of his church. I took courage to talk to him after the service, to challenge his ungodly sermon. He was not pleased by what I said.

In the absence of any meaningful initiative from any of the major Christian churches in Uganda, Noerine Kaleeba as an individual Catholic, together with her seventeen colleagues, courageously went along and founded TASO (The AIDS Support Organization).[2]

---

1. On 1 January 1986 in one of the parishes within Masaka diocese. The good news is that a few years later that priest radically changed his mind and attitude. He is now a prophet of hope to persons with HIV/AIDS and their families.

2. Noerine Kaleeba, Sunanda Ray, and Brigid Willmore, *We Miss You All: AIDS in the Family* (Kampala: Marianum Press, 1993); M. H. Merson, *TASO Uganda: The Inside Story* (Kampala: Marianum Press, 1995).

To know the origins of TASO is to know something special about Noerine and her family. Noerine married Chris in December 1975. They had four daughters before Chris received a scholarship to do a postgraduate degree in Britain. Noerine was a Catholic and from a staunch Catholic family. Chris was a member of the Anglican Church in Uganda. Chris left for Britain in July 1985 to do his masters in sociology and social administration at Hull University. On 6 June 1986 the fateful telex arrived through the British Council informing Noerine that Chris was seriously sick and was admitted into a London hospital. Nobody could tell Noerine the sickness of her husband. The best they could say was meningitis. When Noerine talked on the phone to the doctor in London, the response came that Chris had been tested for AIDS and found to be positive. Shocked by the news but still not fully aware of the stigma around AIDS, Noerine told her friends, daughters, and in-laws that Chris was sick with AIDS. She was soon to regret that she ever told anyone. From that moment her life changed, and so were the attitudes of her friends, workmates, and some family members. This was the first experience in Noerine's life which would eventually lead to the founding of TASO.

She had her second experience in the London hospital where she went to look after Chris. Here, Noerine found a loving and caring medical staff and Catholic chaplain. Individually and as a group, they assisted, comforted, and counseled her. They provided her with the moral strength she needed. She now accepted the predicament of Chris having AIDS and approaching death. She took two positive actions: to read everything that she could on AIDS and to undergo an AIDS test herself. When she returned to Uganda she came with that experience of love and care for AIDS patients. The initial results of her test indicated that she was negative, a result she did not fully believe but which she placed before God.

Soon after her return, Chris also returned to Uganda in November 1986. The entire family and relatives were at the airport to receive him. He was feeble, slim, and very sickly. He was taken to Mulago hospital. Despite the fact that both Chris and Noerine worked at this hospital, the stigma did not diminish. Several doctors and nurses seemed not to care much about Chris and Noerine. They were looking at both with accusing and condemning eyes. The stigma was powerfully felt.

It was soon decided to remove Chris from the hospital and place him in the loving and caring atmosphere of his family. Genuine friends frequently came to the family to offer their moral and religious support. Several persons with AIDS also began to come to provide support to each other. It was in this atmosphere that TASO began. Chris died in January 1987. In November of the same year, Noerine and her colleagues decided to form TASO to provide *the support that seemed to be absent from medical staff and society as a whole. Noerine says four factors were crucial to this founding: her strong belief in God's love and power; the fact that she was still healthy and therefore had a mission to realize; the gift of her four daughters whom she wanted to grow up as caring people; and the gift of friends with whom she wanted to be committed to a special mission.*

The TASO Movement[3]

TASO WAS REGISTERED as a nongovernmental organization and soon received the backing of both government and foreign donors. Its mission is to contribute to the process of restoring hope and improving the quality of life of persons and communities affected by HIV infection and the AIDS disease. Its widely known motto is "living positively with AIDS and dying with dignity."

TASO is both a movement and an organization. As a movement, TASO invites all individuals and groups in Uganda to unite with it in the struggle to contain the spread of AIDS through massive sensitization of communities, especially the young. It calls on all persons and communities to respect the dignity and rights of infected persons and to give them support for positive living. Employees with HIV/AIDS should be supported to continue working. They should be assisted to meet the medical expenses and allowed rest whenever they need it. Medical and professional confidentiality should be kept, and employers should be caring and understanding in order to respect the dignity of their infected workers.[4]

In turn, people infected with HIV/AIDS have responsibilities, too. They are encouraged to cultivate self-esteem, hope, respect for life, protection of their communities, and care for self through abandoning dangerous habits such as drinking, smoking, and engaging in unsafe sexual practices. They have a responsibility to their dependants. Moreover, the community has the right to protect itself from the spread of AIDS through means that are designed to curb the epidemic.

This philosophy of compassionate care, mutual support, and elimination of any trace of discrimination or stigmatization has characterized the work of TASO since its inception. Although not specifically mentioned, from its founding up to now TASO operates on a strong faith in

---

3. TASO, *Taso Movement Philosophy* (booklet), Kampala, 1997.

4. The Uganda AIDS Commission founded in 1992 has advocated for the rights of persons with HIV/AIDS, especially employees. The Uganda Human Rights Commission established in 1995 is also paying special attention to the protection of the human rights of infected persons and their affected families.

a loving God, creator of all. Uganda is predominantly composed of Catholics, Protestants, and Muslims. They all share in the faith of a loving God who controls the destiny of people and is the source of their hope and strength. The counseling services of TASO recognize that belief. Members of all religious backgrounds go to TASO. TASO invites religious leaders from all churches, mosques, and other faith communities to come regularly to TASO centers and meet the infected and affected people in order to give them moral support and counseling. This is an extra strength of TASO. Given a very high religious prejudice in Uganda, if TASO had operated on an exclusive religious heritage, it would have never made the impact it has.

I noted earlier that Noerine is a Catholic and that her faith has been instrumental in directing her to found TASO, but Noerine can be said to be a "liberal" Catholic who has a strong personal faith and conviction to guide her, but without taking every teaching of the Catholic Church on such matters as the use of condoms as part of her belief. She married Chris after living with him for some years and having their first daughter. The opposition she received from her parents on learning that Chris was a Protestant made her more open to Protestants and members of other faiths. TASO, therefore, is a unique example of an ecumenical, interfaith movement and organization. It helps to bring out the common denominators of all believers in God. The issues of human dignity, human equality, human rights; preferential care for the vulnerable, disadvantaged, marginalized, those in special need; issues of the compassion of God, God's loving care and forgiveness; the need for human solidarity and concern; the challenge against self-righteousness and judging others rashly all come to the fore in TASO. TASO, therefore, is a challenge to AIDS organizations based on a single religious faith.

TASO's Organization

As an organization, TASO has a board of trustees of thirteen people which sits at least once every year. Its director is the executive officer of the organization. It has heads and staff for each of its major services both at the headquarters and in the districts. These are the people who plan the work of TASO and supervise its implementation.

TASO activities can be placed under five categories: sensitisation and advocacy; training counselors at various levels of society; giving counseling to people infected and affected by AIDS; providing medical services; and, carrying out social welfare services.

Sensitization and Advocacy

Since its foundation in 1987, TASO has succeeded in sensitizing government, religious bodies, schools, hospitals, and the general public on matters related to AIDS and the positive action to take. As a result, the Uganda AIDS Commission was established and is doing commendable work in coordinating various organizations and activities on AIDS. The Uganda government, since the coming to power of the National Resistance Government in 1986, has been one of the most open and transparent African government on AIDS. President Yoweri Museveni and his ministers talk about AIDS wherever they go. All major presidential speeches contain a section on AIDS, calling on society and especially the youth to fight the epidemic positively and responsibly through behavior change. Although promotion of the use of condoms is the most vigorous policy of the government and the AIDS Commission, Museveni prefers to advocate abstinence from unsafe sex and commitment to loving faithfully in marriage.

Numerous associations, groups, and clubs have mushroomed throughout the country with the singular aim of sensitizing people on AIDS. Several schools, primary and secondary, have developed educational material and exercises for this sensitization and they are part of the curriculum. *Youth Alive* was founded by a missionary Franciscan Sister, Dr. Miriam Duggan. Its philosophy is to change behavior among youth. Members use songs, drama, poems, and art to carry the message all over the country. Composers of music (*kadongokamu*) daily come up with new messages on AIDS and most renowned drama groups have produced at least one play on educating the public about AIDS. What most people feared to hear or speak about eleven years ago is now readily communicated and welcomed by most Ugandans. This dramatic change from negative to positive, regarding the mentioning of AIDS or relating with people infected or affected by AIDS, is indebted to the courageous action taken by TASO.

Training Counselors

Although sensitization and advocacy must continue vigorously and reach every corner of society, TASO in its eleven years of existence has played its prophetic role of initiating and promoting what most others feared then and still fear now.

TASO developed a library on AIDS, joining all possible regional, continental, and world AIDS organizations. TASO is convinced that knowledge is power, and in respect of AIDS, knowledge is life. TASO counselors are introduced to the knowledge about HIV/AIDS in great detail. They are trained in positive attitudes and communication skills. Counselors themselves need support and are given insights on anti-HIV drugs and the ethics of research.

Given the absence of a medical cure for AIDS so far, African medicine men and women are having a field day. One after another declares he or she has the cure for AIDS, and multitudes of people rush there, only to be disappointed later on. Diviners, "witch doctors," and sorcerers continue to connect AIDS with witchcraft. People with AIDS spend much of their time convincing themselves and trying to be convinced that they are bewitched.[5] They struggle to find out who did it and how the spell can be removed. It is usually much later that they turn to TASO medical units and other AIDS organizations for assistance. By this time it may be already too late to do much for them.

So far TASO has trained 993 counselors in and outside Uganda.[6] But what number of counselors are needed for a population of twenty-one million people? If all medical units, religious organizations, and social welfare organs had responded positively to this training, Uganda would have now thousands of trained counselors. This specific training would have become a regular course for all medical personnel, religious leaders, social workers, and elected leaders. China succeeded in training one million barefoot "doctors." Uganda cannot afford to ignore the need for trained counselors who can reach every village and community in the country. An excellent organization of the country in villages, parishes, subcounties, counties, and districts does exist. It should be maximally used to train counselors in the struggle against AIDS. Christians and Muslims are also well organized countrywide. They should also take the challenge to train counselors using TASO and other related organizations. Only then can we say we have done what is required of us amid the terrible AIDS epidemic.

Counseling Infected and Affected Persons

This is the central work of TASO, the heart of its mission and vision. This counseling provides basic knowledge of AIDS in simple terms and

---

5. The Ganda philosophy and worldview is that no one ever dies of a merely natural disease. Each sickness and death is attributed to an evil cause and person. The natural reaction is to seek to establish that external evil cause, that person who hates you. This is where traditional medicine and medicine men and women play a major role. AIDS is identified as an endemic disease without a cure in scientific medicine. Thus, on their deathbeds, persons with HIV/AIDS are given traditional medicine.

6. Merson, *TASO Uganda*, 5.

explanations. This counseling has helped many people accept testing, live positively after the test, and continue to work as normally as possible while taking precautions and better care of themselves. Counseling is prolonging the life and usefulness of many infected people.

Many infected people work until they are fully bedridden. They inform some of their family members and relatives. They plan for the future of their dependants: making proper wills, preparing an income-generating project, discussing support for their dependants with relatives and friends, and preparing themselves spiritually to meet a happy and dignified death. Proper counseling helps to remove any bitter feelings in the infected and affected persons against God, neighbor, and society as a whole. It replaces despair with hope; self-condemnation with re-assurance; fear of having been bewitched with proper facts about HIV/AIDS; and, fear of contracting the disease through casual contacts with the sick with facts on how such care should be provided.

Provision of Complementary Medical Services

Uganda's health services are still very inadequate for the rural population. Medical units are unevenly distributed in the country. Where they do exist, they too often lack essential drugs. This has prompted private dispensaries to provide their services, but these private units are profitable businesses. Drugs or any types of treatment are paid for by cash, which many people with HIV/AIDS cannot afford. TASO, through its eight district centers, freely supplies some drugs to clients. They distribute low-cost drugs to treat usual diseases such as fever, TB, hypertension, loss of appetite, and so on. These are donated by many international organizations. This service needs to be strengthened since it is essential to the prolongation of life.

Provision of Social Welfare Services

These services include the promotion of a balanced diet for people infected with HIV/AIDS. On special days at each of the eight centers of TASO, clients are given a balanced meal and are taught to prepare for themselves a balanced diet. Another service provides clothing, bedding, utensils, and the like. Another offers both educational training for particular income-producing skills—sweater-making, for example—as well as loans for the purchase of equipment, like sewing machines and other tools for any skilled work, to generate small-income projects. Still another service pays school fees to orphans left behind.

TASO's Expansion

Until 1995, Noerine was the director of TASO, but in August 1995 she stepped down to enable the organization to grow, though with her in the background. Mrs. Sophia Mukasa Monico was appointed director. This was a clear indication that TASO had achieved maturity.

The expansion of TASO from one center in Noerine's home to eight fully-fledged district centers in eleven years is a sign of its positive impact on society. Three of these centers are in the eastern part of the country (Jinja, Mbale, and Tororo), three are in the central area, Buganda (Kampala, Masaka, and Entebbe), one in the west (Mbarara) and one in the north (Arua). TASO has therefore covered the four major regions of the country.

In 1996 Noerine was given a UN job in Geneva to promote the same vision she had in founding TASO. With her appointment, TASO philosophy and vision became international and Africa, a continent of usually bad news to the world, became the light and hope to the rest of the world in the struggle against HIV/AIDS. It became a shining example of loving care and support for people infected and affected by HIV/AIDS.

In 1998 TASO got a real home six kilometers from the capital city, Kampala. There TASO is doing greater work and giving more rest and care to its clients. Arua TASO center at Arua hospital is being developed as a model which all other centers throughout the country will follow.

Small is indeed beautiful, not only in economics but in all other endeavors. TASO is another biblical story of the mustard seed and the leaven. One small seed has grown into a huge tree which now encompasses the entire world.

Moral-ethical Challenges from TASO

FROM MY CASUAL contacts with TASO centers, talking to clients of TASO, and hearing comments on TASO, I offer several ethical-moral considerations for reflection. Through its philosophy and work, TASO has emphasized the human dignity of every person, created in the image and likeness of God. Life is sacred and every attempt should be made to preserve it with dignity, equality of persons, and respect for the fundamental human right to life. For TASO, as it is for Christ and his true followers, this divine image in every person appears most clearly in those who are most vulnerable, wounded, marginalized, despised, sick, lonely, and helpless.

From the Scriptures we find the duty of every human person and community to protect, promote, heal, and sustain life. What is prolife is good and godly. Whatever is antilife is evil and to be avoided. This message is alive in Christianity and in African religion as well.[7] The African, Christian challenge TASO poses to all our human organizations is to be prolife, propeople, and proliberation.

Human solidarity is an important ethical-moral requirement. Other people expect from us not things primarily, but personal relationships. We have an obligation to journey to our final destiny without abandoning anyone by the wayside. TASO is an example of the Good Samaritan who sacrificed in order to be in solidarity.

The liberation or empowerment we give to people should be integral: addressing not only the spiritual-religious dimension but also the social-cultural, economic-political dimensions. Empowerment based on values and personal convictions enables people to make personal decisions on such matters as whether to use condoms or not. Instead of setting standards, oftentimes in idealistic ways, much energy should be put on empowering people to judge situations in their own way, guided by their consciences and personal relationship with their God. TASO has never imposed moral rules on the people it serves. It provides education, values, and sensitization necessary for all persons to make their personal decisions.

What anyone infected and affected by HIV/AIDS needs to hear most is that life, goodness, health, and right will eventually defeat death, evil, sickness, and wrong. It is the theology of hope, worked by grassroot Christians that has made TASO what it is today.[8]

Noerine herself provides another challenge. Every person is called to a mission. Everyone should identify that mission. Everyone can have a vision to direct the mission. Everyone has the means, however limited, to carry out both the mission and vision. This is a purposeful and positive living realized in solidarity with others. It challenges us to move from the me-center to others-as-the-center of our mission.

I conclude with Noerine Kaleeba's message for the future:

> My message to all people in the world is one of hope. Hope for a future world without AIDS. This hope comes out of a realization that the whole population, the infected, the affected, and the uninfected, need to join the fight against AIDS. This hope also hinges on each one of us, as individuals, taking up the fight against AIDS. The responsibility to curb the spread of HIV lies with each person as an individual. Collective efforts by government and nongovernment

---

7. See Laurenti Magesa, *African Religion: The Moral Traditions of Abundant Life* (Maryknoll, N.Y.: Orbis Books, 1997), especially chapters 3, 4, 5, and 6.

8 John Mary Waliggo, "African Christology in a situation of suffering," in Jesse Mugambi and Laurenti Magesa, eds., *Jesus in African Christianity* (Nairobi, 1989), 93–111.

agencies rely on each individual's determination to refrain from the type of behavior which puts them at risk of contracting HIV infection.

To everyone living with HIV infection or disease the message is of hope, and the courage to fight until a cure is found. We triumph over the view when we do not allow it to spread! We do not, however, have to fight alone, in isolation. There are increasing numbers of friends willing to share with us and accompany us through this difficult period.[9]

ENCOUNTERING A BRAZILIAN MAN ABANDONED IN HIS ILLNESS

José Antônio Trasferetti

I HAVE INTERVIEWED *a man, Agnaldo da Silva. He is twenty-five years old and lives in Campinas, which has about a million inhabitants and is located in the southeastern part of the state of São Paulo. Agnaldo has been married for five years and has two children, a five-year-old and a one-year-old. Lately he has been helped by an AIDS support group, "Hope and Life."*

He suspected that he was infected because of strong diarrhea and high fever. He decided to take an exam and subsequently learned that he was positive. The situation was very difficult and he thought his life had ended. He started to drink and smoke. He was not addicted, but due to his pain, he had a wish to destroy himself. He was supported by his close family; however, most of his kinfolk discriminated against him and many no longer speak to him. When he arrived at the house, "Hope and Life," he was underweight. After a period of treatment, he is healthier and happier. His life changed radically after the sad news.

Agnaldo does not know exactly how he contracted the virus. He always had a behavior considered "normal." He had not slept with women of "bad reputation" and he had never taken nor injected drugs. He believes (and he is very convincing) that he contracted AIDS through a tattoo that he got from a store in a slum. He is not absolutely sure, but he thinks that the needle with which he was tattooed was contaminated. Agnaldo also argues that one of his friends who has been tattooed is also infected.

---

9. Kaleeba, *We Miss You All*, 99.

Before being infected, Agnaldo had no knowledge about AIDS. His presence at "Hope and Life" helped him get over his initial shock and provided him with an education about the meaning of AIDS. When he visits his friends or attends a social club, he addresses people about AIDS. Before being HIV positive, he was a Catholic, but his attendance at church was not assiduous. Today, however, his religious life has a new paradigm: every moment he thinks about God, thanking God night and day for everything he has been given. Agnaldo still visits "Hope and Life" and lives with his family trying to lead a "normal" life.

In responding to this case, I want to focus on three issues: the need to be more concretely aware of self-care and, in particular, care for one's body; the need to develop a medical and moral education that communicates well with the reality of people's lives; and, third, the need to develop a sexual moral teaching that constructively engages the world in which we live and promotes an integrated anthropological vision.

Nowadays, it is necessary to pay attention to life in its smallest details. If during the nineteen fifties and sixties, children could play in the streets without seriously risking their lives, care must be taken during the nineties. Any fault can be fatal. It is not necessary to belong to the "risk group." According to the latest research published in Brazil by the Ministry of Education, AIDS has infected a great number of women and heterosexuals. This data indicates that "risk group" has no real meaning.

In Brazil in 1981, the notion of "risk group" designated mainly homosexuals. In 1982 hemophiliacs were included. The original idea of divine punishment began to be scrutinized and a certain hypocrisy started to develop as society sought to label HIV-infected people on the one hand as guilty, and on the other as victims. Afterwards in 1985, intravenous drug users entered the "risk group." In 1987, AIDS reached heterosexuals, whether they were promiscuous or not. In 1990, women became the most infected group. Up to then, for every thirty-six infected men, there was only one woman.

From 1990, the concept of "risk groups" no longer makes any sense. Now, we use the term "risky behavior." "Risky behavior" would be to have unsafe sexual intercourse any time during the last ten years with someone whom one does not know sufficiently. Even that concept suffers, since many persons note that many young women are contracting AIDS from their boyfriends whom they have known for years.

In the age of AIDS, can we state that a relationship is safe? Some years ago the public propaganda said: "Reduce the number of partners," but AIDS kept contaminating people. Cannot a wife get AIDS from her husband?

AIDS does not discriminate, does not recognize social constructs, and does not observe boundaries. According to the World Health Organization, there are no "risk groups" anymore; every person must be treated as potentially HIV-infected. Care must be taken inclusively!

As mentioned above, in 1990, there was only one woman infected for each group of thirty-six men in Brazil. Nowadays, for each three men there is one woman infected, and in São Paulo, these figures are already even. Many people believe that women may even exceed men in AIDS contamination and transmission. It may be necessary to study more about the structures of society and the way women think in those structures in order to understand why many women seem to act as if they are not at risk for HIV. According to the World Health Organization, sixteen thousand people are infected everyday and we can ask: "Do these sixteen thousand people belong to the group of risk?" No, they are common people, heads of family, housewives, teenagers. Nowadays most of the people are infected through sexual intercourse with unfaithful partners.

Many married persons have an extramarital relationship, but are not per se promiscuous. Agnaldo's case is different, but his case reinforces the thesis that it is necessary to take care of our bodies. If moral theologians want to contribute to HIV prevention, they must educate the population— particularly women—about self-esteem, self-love, self-care, love of neighbor, and health. The gospel preaches the idea of loving others as much as oneself. Thus, one has to first love oneself, not in a selfish way, but through a co-responsible love that conveys safety for oneself and for others.

Nowadays, we live in our big cities treating life as if it were worthless. Life can lose its sacredness, its true religious value. We can regard life as a banal thing in every aspect, especially overlooking its moral value as God's gift that calls for a response. In this context, especially, moral theology must put aside its abstract speech and get into the social tissue, promoting the re-education of people, helping them into loving themselves and taking care of their bodies as if they were taking care of a holy temple. We must take care of our bodies with the same love we adore Christ, because it is also a divine sanctuary, a religious altar, God's house. Moral theology could provide a great contribution with this issue, recovering the corporeal dimension of the gratuity of God.

Second, it is necessary to develop a real moral education of society in two ways. First, we must train both infected persons to avoid self-exclusion, and close family and friends to accept the loved one who is HIV positive. The infected person must be treated with love. Agnaldo related to us that when his friends learned that he was infected, they immediately moved away from him, fearing to be contaminated likewise. He also thought that way before contracting the disease. A long process of education was necessary for him to understand what the virus is, how we become infected and how we can transmit it. It was difficult to understand and accept. However, after he understood and accepted his situation, he started to speak publicly about AIDS and HIV education.

Second, we must educate society into sheltering without prejudice persons who are HIV positive. However, self-exclusion of infected persons makes this education difficult. Even nowadays in my own country, infected people tend to be seen and to see themselves as guilty sinners. Familiar groups, schools, factories, and religious communities still discriminate against these people and treat them hypocritically. Ignorance about HIV/AIDS is still a reality in my country.

For this education to take place, it is necessary to create cultural and social mechanisms in which the infected people and their allies are the main characters of the effective education. The president of "Hope and Life," Roberto da Silva, cites from his experience that many people acquire the virus through extramarital sexual relations. Often husbands, from apparently "good" marriages, have extramarital affairs and acquire the virus in this way. In most cases, people are surprised because they did not expect that they could be infected by HIV through a simple "adventure." In fact, they were not morally educated for AIDS prevention. They acted in a spontaneous way, unaware that carelessness can be fatal these days.

It is worthwhile to remember that in my country, prematrimonial relations and marital fidelity are not always respected. The challenge for moral theology gets tougher here, when we theologians are inhibited from developing a moral education that in some way includes education regarding safer sex. Some church leaders' teaching about condoms makes our task more difficult. In order to make a serious contribution to AIDS prevention, moral theology must get in direct contact with the population, educating for sexual abstinence before marriage and marital loyalty within marriage. Since we are aware that this guidance is often not taken seriously, we must offer a sexual education as moral as possible, including medical advice about both contraceptives and condoms. For this, it is necessary to acknowledge and face ignorance, fear, and taboos. In this globalized world where moral values are in constant change, respect for life and a safe sexual education should guide our behavior and moral attitudes.

When it comes to homosexual couples, the work of moral theology is even more difficult. Although it is a reality in our country, the doctrine of the church does not accept love and sexual union between persons of the same gender. The situation of the homosexual is particularly burdensome in Brazil. It is almost impossible to develop a pastoral support, due to prejudice and the moral charge of sin. For moral theology to contribute to HIV prevention, it must first ban prejudice, fear, and judgments which destroy human beings. Moreover, we must offer a spirituality, where homosexuals, transvestites, transsexuals, prostitutes, and so many others, with their real and painful lives, have an equally central place in theological discussion.

Finally, I believe that the struggle for HIV/AIDS prevention is a great challenge for religious institutions and Catholic moral theology.

Unfortunately, we are out of date. My country is apparently very liberal: we have carnival, beautiful beaches, beautiful bodies exposed everywhere, but sexuality is still regarded as a great unknown. Educated for a long time by the traditional Catholic moral teaching that cast our behaviors with an irresponsible casuistry, we are still searching for a sexual education that is really effective and liberating. We have gone through sudden changes: we abandoned a rigorist morality for a lax one. This passage followed no known rules of a praxis that developed maturely and efficiently. Instead, church leaders were bewildered by the changes and, under the guise of rules and laws, never learned how to dialogue with growing globalization. Catechists tried to offer guidance, but like church leaders, they eventually repeated old dogmas that could no longer be applied to the reality of most Brazilians. As a result, Catholics no longer had meaningful direction.

When the pope was in Brazil in October 1997, he registered this plea: "The Brazilian families should be united around the resurrected Christ." He defended the indissolubility of marriage, preached fidelity between couples, attacked abortion, defended the use of natural contraceptives, and pointed to the responsibility in children's education. Research shows, however, that there exists a great distance between official teachings of Catholic morality and the daily behavior of Brazilian Christians.

According to research in *Datafolha* (in *A Folha de São Paulo*, 13 June 1997) entitled "Catholics and Behavior," 90 percent of those interviewed stated that they are for the use of condoms as a means of contraception, 96 percent support it to avoid diseases such as AIDS, 47 percent said that masturbation is not a sin. For 68 percent of the interviewed, conscience was more important than church rules, and only 27 percent obey these rules. Finally, 64 percent do not regard religious marriage as mandatory.

We can observe furthermore that the difficulty in following Catholic moral teaching is real, especially among the poorest families. In Campinas alone, a city with one million inhabitants, there are one hundred thirty-six thousand living in the slums. Barely able to survive, they do not have the social structure that would encourage them to follow church rules. How can moral theology contribute to HIV/AIDS prevention in a reality as dramatic as ours? Many rules and moral guidance that we have in ecclesiastical documents are not followed due to the brutality of our social reality.

Thinking about Agnaldo and so many others, we can see the need for moral theology to contribute to HIV/AIDS prevention through a solid education that integrates the totality of human life. In my country, we have several enterprises of sexual education, restricted solely to anatomy and the physiology of the genitals. But sexual education must have its perspective not on genitality, but sexuality, a sexuality that involves the human being as a whole. This integral vision of the human being must be the starting point. If we lose this anthropological view of humanity, we are not educating nor enlightening nor promoting behavioral change; we are merely passing technical information.

Our starting points must be: knowledge, responsibility, respect, honesty, sincerity, and fidelity. Would that the Ministry of Education included within the required curriculum, a subject called "education for love." Clearly, we need to teach principles for the affective life. In Brazil, teenagers are led to sexual experiences without having any education for dealing with feelings. Pregnant twelve-year-old girls and nine-year-old boys with an active sexual life are common in my country nowadays. Why is it so? Because they have been stimulated before the right time and many stages of affective development have been skipped.

Thus, moral theology must be closer to the Brazilian family if it is to contribute effectively toward HIV/AIDS prevention. Christian families are suffering a lot in our country. We can see the need for a total revolution in both Catholic moral theology and in society as a whole, if we want to find plausible moral means of education in HIV/AIDS prevention. In this way, Agnaldo and many others can lead life in the plentitude that the creator gave them.

As AIDS Just Emerges in Bangladesh

Gervas Rozario

ON 24 JANUARY 1997, a popular Bengali daily Janakantha reported a pathetic news item regarding a married woman, her husband, and two children. The woman, named Khadija Begum, had been burnt to death as she was suspected by the people of the village of having AIDS.[1] The incident took place in a remote village of the Faridpur district.

Khadija Begum was happily married about ten years ago to Abul Kashem of the village next to her own. It was an arranged marriage but still she was happy. Abul Kashem was a small trader in the local market place. In 1993, when their two children, a boy and a girl, were born, Abul Kashem decided to go abroad to earn more money for his family. He managed to go to a Middle Eastern country to find a job. Everybody was very happy.

---

1. *Janakantha*, 24 January 1997, 7.

In 1996 Abul Kashem came home for a vacation. The joy of Khadija and her two children knew no bounds. After two months Abul Kashem left home for his workplace. Six months later Khadija fell sick.

She visited the local doctor several times but there was no improvement. The doctor could not tell her what was the reason for her continuous fever, headache, anemia, and weakness. She was not diagnosed as being HIV positive. However, suddenly a rumor was spread in the village saying Khadija had AIDS.

The people knew from the newspapers that some of those who go abroad for work in the Middle East have contracted this deadly disease. However, they have no idea about this disease and believe that anyone who contracts this disease suffers the curse of God for some past sins and that there is no remedy for this. Others also might contract this disease from the person and the result will be sure death. People panicked and in order to stop the spreading of this mortal virus they set fire in the house where Khadija was sleeping. She was burned to death only to satisfy the superstitious attitude of the illiterate people.

In Bangladesh the knowledge and awareness about HIV/AIDS is very recent and often inaccurate. Although the deadly disease has been detected here, it is in its early stages and the country still continues to be an area of low prevalence. Yet, a recent survey indicates a rapid spread.[2] Considering the situation of AIDS in neighboring countries like India and Thailand, many concerned experts predict a high risk area. Bangladesh is the eighth most populated country in the world with a population of about 120 million in an area of 147,570 square kilometers.

Although almost 85 percent of the population lives in rural areas, frequent internal migration to urban areas causes overcrowding in unhygienic slums. Bangladesh is a country that is already riddled with many health-related problems, such as infection, malnutrition, poverty, ignorance, and superstition. Infectious diseases and immune deficiency problems predominate among children. A study directed by Abdullah H. Baqui has found that about 10 to 12 percent of children were having cell-mediated immune deficiency. It was also observed that these immuno-deficient children experienced 50 percent increased incidence of diarrhea in comparison to their immunocompetent counterparts.[3]

The English language newspaper *The Daily Star* reported that at least 20,000 people are carrying HIV and a total of 120 people have so far died

---

2. M. R. Chowdhury, Nazrul Islam, and Golam Rasul, eds., *Meeting the Challenges of HIV/AIDS in Bangladesh* (Dhaka: ICDDR, B, 1996), viii.

3. Ibid., 14.

of AIDS in Bangladesh. The International Center for Diarrhea Diseases Research, Bangladesh (ICDDR,B) situated in Dhaka, has found in its study that one percent of expectant mothers in most parts of Bangladesh are infected with HIV, implying the possibility of giving birth to millions of AIDS-infected children in the country.[4]

In a recently held seminar of the Islamic clerics and religious leaders about "Creating Consciousness on HIV, AIDS and STDs," the speakers expressed their concern about the overall situation. Organized by the Islamic Medical Mission, the three-day seminar was the first attempt to build awareness among the religious leaders of the Islamic society. It was revealed that people living in different slums and squatter areas across the country cover around 11 percent of the total victims of HIV; about 50 percent of the STD victims are young. The participants in the seminar stressed the urgency of making awareness programs available among the youth.[5]

In another recent study "Women and AIDS in Bangladesh" conducted by Afroza Parvin of Nari Unnayan Shakti, an NGO among the rickshaw-puller (tricycle drivers) community in the slum areas of Dhaka, sexual abuse has been identified as the main reason for HIV and STD infections. Though Bangladesh is a predominately Islamic country which claims to have a strict sexual morality, promiscuity and sexual abuse are still very common. In most cases, sexual abusers are also promiscuous. Hence, they are the most dangerous medium to spread STDs and AIDS.

Polygamy is sanctioned by the religious norms of Islam which allow a man to have up to four wives at a time, whereas a woman cannot have such a right. Many educated people now consider polygamy legalized promiscuity. In addition, prostitution is legally sanctioned by the law of the country which issues licenses for this purpose. Bangladesh officially claims to have only about 60,000 women engaged in prostitution, but according to the assessment of CARE-Bangladesh, an NGO, there are more than 100,000 commercial sex workers.[6]

Data from Studies Related to HIV/AIDS

1. Promiscuity

(a) *Premarital Sex.* Several studies indicate that the incidence of premarital sex is quite widespread in Bangladesh. The studies by Aziz and Maloney

---

4. *The Daily Star*, 10 July 1998, 4.
5. Ibid.
6. Afroza Parvin, "Women and AIDS in Bangladesh," unpublished handout, 1998.

reported that 50 percent of the youth had experience of sex before marriage. They found that the incidence of this was more prevalent in the lower socio-economic class than in the higher. They also found that in premarital sex among their respondents, 29 percent of them use condoms.[7] Other studies reported almost similar findings with occurrences of induced abortions among unmarried girls.[8]

(b) *Extramarital Sex*. A survey of long-distance truck drivers revealed that 60 percent of those under study had extramarital sex with a prostitute about twice a month, and that they had no knowledge about HIV/AIDS.[9] These studies also observed that extramarital sex was quite common, particularly in rural societies. Instances of adultery were also not uncommon, especially when the husband was away for a long period.

(c) *Homosexual Practices*. The above-mentioned studies clearly indicated some instances of homosexual activities, especially among the youth.[10] An increasing number of college and university students who live in hostels engage in homosexual activities.

(d) *Prostitution*. There are about 100,000 commercial sex workers in Bangladesh. They are generally illiterate and divorced or separated women.[11] They are organized in brothels or "free-floating."[12] The customers are usually businessmen, students, rickshaw-pullers, and truck drivers. STDs are widespread among the prostitutes. Some customers use condoms, but most do not. And there is a considerable amount of drug addiction both among the prostitutes and their customers.

2. Intravenous Drug Users

The exact prevalence of intravenous drug users in Bangladesh is not known. Various studies carried out so far do point to the existence of drug

---

7. K. M. A. Aziz and C. Maloney, *Life Stages, Gender, and Fertility* (Dhaka: ICDDR, B, 1985), 50–85.

8. S. Islam, *Indigenous Abortion Practices in Rural Bangladesh* (Dhaka: Women for Women Research Study Group, 1981), 47–65, and C. Maloney, K. M. A. Aziz, and P. C. Sarker, *Beliefs and Fertility in Bangladesh* (Dhaka: ICDDR, B, 1981), 38–56.

9. E. Arco, "Personal Communication," 1993 (lecture handout). See other studies with similar facts: Aziz et al., *Life Stages*, 51–71, and Maloney et al., *Beliefs and Fertility*, 35–60.

10. Ibid.

11. Maloney et al., *Beliefs and Fertility*, 87.

12. A. Z. M. Islam, "Ulcerative Genital Disease in Male" (1993) and "Prevalence of STDs amongst Commercial Sex Workers in a Brothel in Bangladesh" (1996) (lecture handouts).

addiction. Data about substance abuse remain curiously silent about the methods of use. Findings, however, indicate that heroin addiction is the most predominant drug. It is generally believed that the main method of use is by inhalation ("chasing the dragon"). Another popular drug of abuse is "phensedyl." Since Bangladesh is one of the conduits of the "Golden Triangle" and "Golden Crescent," heroin is quite easily available and it is feared that presentday "inhalers" will, in the course of time, be converted to "injectors." There is an increasing number of users injecting drugs.[13]

3. Blood Transfusion Services

The existing system of blood transfusion is fraught with the danger of transmission of HIV. Therefore, it is in urgent need of overall improvement. It seems that the Health Ministry of the Government of Bangladesh is aware of this problem and steps are being taken according to the advice of the National AIDS Committee.[14]

4. Bangladeshi Migrant Workers and Foreign Tourists

The most prominent mode of entry and spread of AIDS in Bangladesh is through foreign contact. One way of entry and spread of HIV in the country occurs when Bangladeshi expatriate workers come home for vacations, especially from the Middle East. Every year about 74,000 Bangladeshi go abroad to earn their livelihood. Another way is the visiting of foreign tourists every year. A large number of tourists involve themselves with sexual activities during their sojourn in Bangladesh.[15]

5. AIDS Patients in Bangladesh

Because of the superstitious and discriminating attitude against AIDS patients in Bangladesh, people living with HIV/AIDS try to remain anonymous. If their names become known, they may be the victims of various biases. Therefore the exact number of AIDS patients in Bangladesh is not known. At present the reported number is only ten of which four are already dead. One died of persistent diarrhea, the second of malaria, the third of encephalitis, and the fourth of tuberculosis. The remaining six are

---

13. Choudhury, *Meeting the Challenges of HIV/AIDS in Bangladesh*, 19.
14. Ibid., 20.
15. Ibid.

alive but suffering from tuberculosis and other complications.[16] One can be thankful for the intervention of the government and of several NGOs, that there are relevant programs toward building awareness about HIV/AIDS among the people.

Love and Compassion Is the Answer

THE ATTITUDE OF seeing a disease as a curse and the result of sin is not new. There are such instances in the Bible. Lepers faced discrimination and were sent away from society. We read in the Book of Leviticus: "The leper who has the disease shall wear torn clothes and . . . cry, 'unclean, unclean.' He shall remain unclean as long as he has the disease; he is unclean; he shall dwell alone in a habitation outside the camp" (Lv. 13:45–46). The same restrictions are also found in the Book of Numbers: "Command the people of Israel that they put out of the camp every leper, . . . every one that is unclean through contact with the dead" (Nm. 5:2).

The social attitude is almost the same for those who have AIDS. They face unfair discrimination and this mortal disease becomes a cause of shame and humiliation. They have to hide themselves in fear of the unfavorable reaction of the public, at exactly the same time when they need love and compassion of people, especially the loving care of their dear ones.

The Scripture notes that Na'aman, commander of the army of the King of Syria, was fortunate to have such a loving wife who sent him to Prophet Eli'sha of Israel for a cure (2 Kgs. 5:1ff). Jesus, who came to free humanity from all sin and bondage, manifested the fullness of God's love and compassion. He healed sick people, including lepers (Mt. 8:2, 11:5; Lk. 7:22, 17:12). He visited the houses of the lepers (Mt. 26:6). This challenges us to recognize an urgent need to change the attitude of people about those infected by HIV.

The Christian answer to this problem is love and care for those who are infected by HIV. However, the issue of HIV/AIDS is very much connected with the sexual and moral lives of people. Christianity advocates and allows sex only within marriage and condemns all extramarital sexual relationships. Whereas the secular institutions and organizations advocate and promote condoms as a means of prevention of HIV/AIDS, official Catholic teaching does not.

---

16. Ibid., 25.

A Call to Authentic Sexual Ethical and Moral Norms

THERE CAN BE many possible reasons for AIDS in a person. Yet it is widely accepted that promiscuous or homosexual activities and drug abuse are the most obvious reasons for the spread of HIV/AIDS. It is most important in our times to be ever-more attentive to the human and spiritual dimensions of the gift of human sexuality over and above its mere physical dimensions. It is also very important to insist on the interpersonal relationship in matrimony as the final goal of sexuality. The Catholic moral tradition will play a very authentic and significant role in safeguarding the spiritual values of sexuality.

In particular, the mass media need to be challenged. The unlimited advertisement of every type of sexual pleasure has been undermining age-old authentic moral behavior. This is especially true in Bangladesh, where people have been used to more sober sexual practices, but are now being caught up in the deluge of a totally licentious presentation of these matters. It is important to pull together the valid sexual norms of the different religions in Bangladesh in order to restrain the present situation.

A culture of correct sexual behavior is required to inspire, guide, and enable individual persons toward moral correctness in sexual matters, while avoiding the dreadful disease.

Love and Compassion for the Afflicted

WHILE PASTORAL MINISTRY for persons with HIV/AIDS requires that our people be formed correctly in sexual matters and that we insist on the sinfulness of certain behaviors leading to the disease, it is important that we treat with love and compassion persons undergoing the long physical, mental, and spiritual suffering because of HIV/AIDS. It needs to be recognized that beyond one's personal responsibility, one is also prey to social sinfulness: this disease leads one to social ostracizing. Christ has given ample examples of the love and compassion we must exercise for the sinner, and more so for the person caught up in the sinful situation of society, making a clear distinction between the fact of sin and the person of the sinner. Comparison can be made to the ostracizing of lepers in the Bible (Lv. 13:45–46; Nm. 5:2) and the solicitude for them through care and love and compassion (2 Kgs. 5:1ff; Mt. 8:2, 11:5, 26:6; Lk. 7:22; 17:12). There is also the need to develop a more hopeful future in the line of education and job opportunity for the young in our society, so that they can be inspired to love life to the fullness of it, instead of oppressive despair leading to destroying life through use of drugs.

AIDS and Islam

BANGLADESH IS A predominantly Islamic country, and so Islam has a major influence on the social attitude of the people here. Two of the NGOs working for HIV/AIDS awareness and prevention, HASAB (HIV, AIDS, STD Alliance of Bangladesh) and CAAP (Confidential Approach to AIDS Prevention), have found out that Islamic society of Bangladesh is not yet favorable to their work. Dr. Halida Hanum Khandaker of CAAP writes:

> Prevalence of misconception, superstition, discrimination, and exploitation in the cover of religion and Islam complicates the exposition of religious teaching. In order to have behavioral and attitude change of people in AIDS prevention, an education program with open discussions on reproductive health and reproductive behavior is necessary. Unfortunately . . . many religious leaders discourage or even prohibit such discussions with the argument that this will generate and promote promiscuity.[17]

She mentions that the Holy Quran values marriage and sexuality within marriage (30:21) but prohibits all extramarital and unnatural sexual relations (26:164–66). In the present-day context she feels that there is need of a sex education program in view of building an awareness about HIV/AIDS. Such programs will effectively help AIDS prevention activities in Bangladesh. This is also necessary to safeguard young people against sexual misbehavior.

Conclusion

THE ISSUE OF AIDS is urgent and needs to be addressed without delay. The world has been struck by this deadly disease harder than before. Bangladesh is not an exception. The situation is turning worse day by day. The good news is that the government and a number of NGOs are already organizing awareness and prevention programs with regard to HIV/AIDS. But the effort is too small. While the country is fighting the battle against HIV/AIDS on many fronts, it is unfortunately also fighting against many other odds. Principal among them is perennial poverty. In order to develop an effective HIV/AIDS prevention program, Bangladesh must find funds. In addition, adequate effort must be made for an effective education program, including moral and religious teaching with regard to HIV/AIDS.

---

17. Dr. Halida Hanum Khandaker, "AIDS and Islam" (handout).

LISTENING IN ENGLAND TO A WOMAN'S LIFE EXPERIENCE

Nicholas Peter Harvey

APPROXIMATELY FOURTEEN YEARS ago, at the age of about twenty, a woman whose lifestyle was at that time permissive but not promiscuous became infected with HIV. She and her partner, together for over two years, used contraceptives but not condoms, and shared intravenous drugs. Neither seems to have given a thought to HIV infection. His hospitalization after they had split up alerted her to the possibility, and in 1994 she was diagnosed.

She was brought up as a Catholic, but at the time of this relationship, she was only conscious of a persistent guilt at behaving in a way she knew to be forbidden. But she "couldn't not go to Mass" on the anniversaries of the deaths of relatives and close friends. In the area of sexual morality she had received nothing from the church except two clear prohibitions: on sex before marriage, and on any use of contraceptives. These she associated with her parents' generation, understood them simply as rules, and saw no wisdom in them.

Yet her reaction to the diagnosis when it came was that she deserved the disease. She associated this with an experience at the age of six, when a catechist told her that it would be better to die young because this would mean the avoidance of grave sin and consequent damnation. Thereafter she was afraid of darkness because that was where the devil was, she couldn't sleep, and she told her mother she was afraid of going to hell. Her mother had a word with the catechist, but did not remove her from the class. God's love, she says, was "not the predominant theme" of her religious upbringing.

From one point of view this history exemplifies the destructive consequences of a sin-centered approach dominated by the image of a punishing God. But this is not the story of someone bitter and angry against the church. Her Catholicism has revived. She has joined a Catholic HIV/AIDS support group because she needed support, and in particular because she "needed to feel she wasn't being punished." The most interesting aspect of the story for our purposes is that a rule-based and sin-centered theology, if taken sufficiently seriously, makes irresponsible behavior more likely.

It is worth adding that there is no "happy ending" in respect of this person's dealings with the teaching church. She recently questioned a priest, involved in her support group by hierarchical appointment, about the possibility of marriage for someone in her situation. His answer was that if she were now to marry with the intention of using contraceptives, the marriage would be invalid. This response, she said afterwards with remarkable restraint, did not do much for her self-esteem!

It is not possible to make any direct causal link between church teaching and this woman's HIV, because she was not following church teaching and would, had she done so, have been a different person. Instead, I draw attention in what follows to one effect of church teaching on her and others' attitudes: it promotes irresponsibility among those falling on the wrong side of its very narrow boundaries. For instance, the concept of safe sex is a moral one, but church teaching makes it amoral. The church fails to provide a culture in which people like our subject are encouraged to think about these aspects.

It is commonly said, or at least assumed, that the church has always taught the same thing, especially in the field of sexual ethics. Yet to read the church fathers on matters of sex alongside the statements of most modern church leaders, even where the moderns quote the fathers, is to find oneself in different mental worlds. Looked at over time, the church has managed to contain quite different and sometimes contradictory starting points and conclusions in this sphere, as indeed in others. The appeal to tradition to validate any form of moral absolutism in the present is always selective, and in that sense oversimplified. A hermeneutic of suspicion is always in order toward such claims. In any case the primary source for moral theology is not usually texts from the past, but engagement with the present. An example is the readiness of contemporary church leaders to acclaim the role of sexual intercourse in building up the marital relationship. This insight does not come from past texts, with most of which it is comically at odds!

What is to be said and done in the face of new questions such as those posed by the spread of HIV/AIDS? One kind of answer is to treat the documents of the past, or rather a careful selection of them, as oracular. In these terms the documents of Vatican II are just as much past as Augustine, and have already been abundantly quarried for oracles in support of a great range of opinions and practices. The conciliar documents are especially apt for such treatment, for they are the result of a series of political compromises between differing interest groups and emphases among the participants. These documents therefore lack intellectual coherence, not infrequently juxtaposing conflicting outlooks as if they could be held together. The most obvious example is the major change of mind on religious liberty.

This example also makes the further point that the process of appeal to tradition as an oracular source is in any case inconclusive. The past cannot tell us what to do or what to think, for moral living is itself creative. There is no alternative to taking responsibility. "You search the scriptures, because you think that in them you have eternal life; and it is they that bear witness to me" (John 5:39). These words stigmatize the oracular approach, directing the hearers' attention instead to present reality.

To come more directly to our theme, the sexual morality on which our subject was reared is one of boundaries, prohibitions, and threats of damnation for any transgression. Only in monogamous, lifelong hetero-sexual marriage is any genital sexual behavior permitted, and that only when every such an act is open to the possibility of procreation. In this mentality prohibitory and condemnatory elements predominate at the expense of notions of human growth and development. If it is already known what should be the case—a world of chaste, faithful, lifelong, pro-creative marital relationships—then we are prisoners of what is seen as the ideal, with no scope for other possibilities. If all other forms of sexual rela-tionship are ruled out in advance, the usual developmental process of trial and error—and indeed of the discovery of vocation—cannot proceed.

Appearing to strike a severely cautionary note about the use of sex, this morality in fact encourages irresponsibility. It does so by putting in the wrong those who engage in any form of sexual activity outside an explicit-ly marital context. Very many people for considerable periods of their lives, and for all sorts of reasons, either cannot aspire to such a relationship, or do not feel called to do so, or find that the ideal has betrayed them. Such people discover a great variety of ways of relating sexually to one another. Rigorous allegiance to the ideal of marriage wrongs them from the start. However sensitively and honorably they seek to relate to one another and in particular to express the sexual dimension of their communion, this the-ology, having already condemned them, cannot offer them any encourage-ment in discerning what behavior might or might not be appropriate in this or that relationship.

Thus serious questions about, for example, exploitive and dishonoring behavior are not addressed, because the relational settings in which they arise are given no moral status. Either you are single or you are married! The vast variety and potential for good in much that lies "in between" can-not be recognized. There is no honoring of the resilience and resourceful-ness of people who find ways to relate to each other, sexually and otherwise, against the odds, while not conforming to the "ideal."

We need to ask what are the forms that faithfulness is actually taking in our world, instead of assuming that all forms of nonmarital sexual activ-ity are deviations. Old-fashioned casuistry could and did live with such "deviations," but it never sought to deny that that is what they are. We need to go much further, beyond talk of the lesser evil or of the avoidance of promiscuity as grounds for condoning forms of relationship still seen as morally questionable.

When one moral framework is in dissolution, people commonly crave another. I can offer no such thing, but only a very different starting point, that of attentive listening to and honoring of what is proceeding in our own and others' lives, particularly in the relational dimension. One contrast between this and more established ways of thinking about morals is that we cannot know in advance where such listening and honoring may take us.

Our subject was ill-served by her religious and moral upbringing in that she was given no resources to enable her to think in ethical terms of any way of relating sexually other than procreatively-intended marriage. What this education had succeeded in doing was in effect to trivialize in advance her moral choices, and indeed her relationships, by putting them in the category of sin.

In our distress at stories of this kind it is easy to hold the church uniquely responsible for the inculcation of destructive attitudes to sex, as if getting rid of or away from the church would solve all such problems. A more balanced perspective comes from the observation that in all known cultures sex is a focus of acute anxiety; in which case all that needs to be said about the church is that, for all its high claim to revealed wisdom in these matters, it has failed to transcend this endemic human anxiety. In other words, the church does not originate uptightness about sex but has often propagated its own version, as in the moral frame of reference being criticized in this article. To place this teaching in the wider setting of the analysis of cultures is not to deny its tragic consequences.

The point about anxiety is easily misunderstood by those who suppose that the permissiveness of modern western societies means that they are unanxious about sex. To be permissive is not at all the same as to be at ease with our sexuality. There is every reason to think that there is still plenty of this kind of anxiety about, as much outside the church as within. At the same time it is only fair to add that the church has not made any significant contribution to creative thinking in this sphere. This is especially notable in this century, when so much original thought has emerged about sexual behavior, sexual identity, and psycho-sexual development. Some of this has been gradually colonized by the church, more or less uneasily, but it all derives from elsewhere. In this sphere the church has been on the defensive for a very long time, and so has not felt free to explore new possibilities.

It would be difficult to exaggerate the significance of the reason for Pope Paul VI's condemnation of the use of contraceptives. It was not that he disagreed with the arguments in favor of change, but rather that a minority of his commission persuaded him that it could not be the case that the papacy which had condemned contraception for so long could have been mistaken. At least, it would not be reasonable to expect large numbers of the faithful to be other than scandalized by such a volte-face. These commissioners did not know enough history, but the pressing point for us is that the overriding concern was not the rights and wrongs of contraception as such but the identity of the church, imagined as signified by unchanging teaching.

The interweaving of the sexual theme with a compulsion to defend a supposed continuity of teaching at all costs meant that dispassionate consideration was not given to the matter in hand. This is a familiar story, and not only about contraception. But it is important here as helping to explain the dearth of constructive thinking by church leaders about sex, and the concomitant poverty of resources on which to base contemporary reflection and pastoral/ethical advice.

A baneful consequence of *Humanae Vitae*, no doubt unintended, is a tendency to examine all questions of sexual morality through the lens of an absolute prohibition of artificial contraceptives. The distorting effect of this on other debates is at times surreal, exemplified in the chilling advice already mentioned as having recently been given to our subject: that if in her present state she were to marry with the use of contraceptives in mind to avoid spreading the infection, her marriage would be invalid. Thus a condemnation designed to apply in one context, that of healthy marriage partners, is arbitrarily transferred to another, that of a prospective marriage partner with HIV. So a person now eminently prepared to think and act responsibly as a result of her own infection is again confronted with condemnation. Monsignor Caffarra takes this logic to its *reductio ad absurdum* by saying that it is better to risk death than to use forbidden devices.

It might be objected that these reflections are not about traditional resources. But theological resources are never simply past, any more than in the Catholic sacramental tradition the death and resurrection of Jesus are simply in the past. Tradition is not effectively invoked merely by repeating formulas, whatever their status. A living tradition functions as a reality in the present, by way of an ongoing, open conversation. In the case of sexual ethics in the Catholic Church such reflective, interpretative, free-flowing conversation is blocked by the combination of factors just outlined. Meanwhile a great variety of conversations on this subject, some of them very productive, are pursued in society at large.

It is always possible to excavate texts from scripture and other documents of the past which can be made to bear on our questions. It is a procedure which strains credulity, and in any case such texts of their nature cannot speak with any degree of incisiveness to the painful particulars of the spread of HIV. The work is being done elsewhere, and we must be humble enough to acknowledge this. To the extent that HIV/AIDS is a new phenomenon, old answers have no power over it. They merely obfuscate.

The proper and urgent concern with HIV prevention of publications like this book needs to recognize the ineffectiveness of drawing attention to Catholic tradition at the moment, for this tradition is unable to operate. All we have is a frozen tradition. When a tradition has become frozen, it has ceased to be a tradition. This is one of the most dramatic aspects of the HIV/AIDS phenomenon: it demonstrates the theological paralysis of a large and ancient church in face of what is happening.

The paralysis described in this chapter is systemic. It is not that no bishop or moral theologian has anything pertinent to say about sexual morality, but that there is no free flow of thought. Questions and considerations that need to be in play make their appearance obliquely if at all, and are not followed through in any open forum. Conferences tend to be rallies for the like-minded rather than of a genuinely exploratory character. The focus is so much on pronouncements from the center or, more subtly and silently, on what the center might think of our possible pronouncements, that discussion cannot develop in a healthy way. On two recent occasions I invited different non-Catholic friends to attend a meeting of moral theologians. Each was struck, quite independently, by a note of fear in our discussions. This made me realize how desensitized I had become!

This state of affairs is corrupting, for it inhibits theological thinking, which to that extent ceases to be theological. It is not primarily a matter of individual bishops' and theologians' conscious choice, but rather of an entrenched habit of mind, a corporate climate which declares largely unspoken limits to what can be called in question. Such an ethos is very bad news indeed for someone like our subject, who looks again to accredited Catholic spokespersons for guidance. Not only can no sensible teaching develop in these conditions, the powerful witness of someone like her cannot be heard.

Listening to those who have firsthand experience of HIV is indispensable to the rejuvenation of Catholic tradition in the proper sense. In other words, people like our subject are a major resource for the work of HIV/AIDS prevention. To say this is of course to turn the entire argument on its head. The view of tradition which starts from documents, and looks within the corpus for enlightenment, is misguided. The primary source of this moral tradition is Catholics with HIV/AIDS. It can even be said that such people are the tradition. Those readers inclined to think that this approach ignores or belittles the past overlook the fact that our corporate past is inescapably caught up in all present exploration. We are all necessarily carriers of our past.

2.
TAKING CULTURE SERIOUSLY

RECOGNIZING THE REALITY OF AFRICAN RELIGION IN TANZANIA

Laurenti Magesa

O N 23 MARCH 1998, *I visited Marcellus Okinyi Amemo for what would be the last time. I am a Catholic priest in charge of a small parish in northwestern Tanzania and Marcellus was one of my parishioners. He was dying of AIDS. During a previous visit I had administered the sacrament of the sick to him. He had then been lying on a wooden bed in a mud and thatch hut built some years previously. Those present told me when I inquired about it that this house was not properly Marcellus's; it belonged to his relative's widow whom he "inherited" in 1990. On this visit, scarcely two weeks later, I found Marcellus placed on the floor of a newly built hut. Someone standing there informed me when I asked him the reason for the move, that this house was built for Marcellus's own (first) wife, Jeni Aoko Zakayo, who passed away in 1992. Custom dictated that this also was therefore properly Marcellus's house, in which he should die and out of which his body should be taken for burial.*

Marcellus was born around 1963; he wasn't quite sure. He belonged to the Luo ethnic community of Tarime district in northwestern Tanzania around Lake Victoria. The Luo people form a big part of the population in this region and spill over across the border into neighboring Kenya to the north. Since 1974 when he was just about eleven years old, Marcellus had lived across the border at Muhuru in Kenya, fishmongering. While his first wife, Jeni, was still alive he had, as already mentioned, "inherited" as caretaker Wilfrida Ogallo, his late relative Nyaonye Oloo's widow, as prescribed by Luo custom in such circumstances.[1] It was Wilfrida together with the village neighbors who cared for Marcellus since he was taken ill in 1996 and returned here to Nyamirende, an outstation of Bukana parish and his village of birth.

---

1. Michael C. Kirwen, *African Widows* (Maryknoll, N.Y.: Orbis Books, 1979).

It will be easily appreciated that I could not inquire too closely from Marcellus himself or his close relations into the circumstances of his illness, although it was evident beyond all doubt that he was suffering from full-blown AIDS. His Kaposi's sarcoma indicated that. In Muhuru, where he had lived for about twenty-two years, HIV/AIDS is very prevalent among fishmongers. Furthermore, Wilfrida's husband Nyaonye Oloo had, I was told, died with similar symptoms as Marcellus. Wilfrida herself complained to me of experiencing what sounded to be too much like pneumocystis carinii pneumonia *(PCP), an HIV/AIDS related opportunistic disease. This was all circumstantial evidence, of course, but in many rural areas of Africa, and certainly in Bukama, it is often all we have to go by in the way of prognosis.*

On my visit of 23 March, Marcellus could still recognize me, even though he was very weak and quickly ran out of breath. We conducted a brief conversation during which he made clear to me a number of things. First of all, he attributed his illness to a "bad wind" (upepo mbaya in Tanzania's lingua franca, Kiswahili), and ascribed its cause to persons who did not wish him well (mazingara, kuchezewa) . Consequently, he was convinced that no "European" (meaning western-type, scientific) medicine could help him in any way. If the persons responsible for his situation could be known, he thought, which at this stage seemed impossible, the "African" medicine (dawa ya kienyeji) would probably help.

In spite of his physical suffering Marcellus seemed quite composed, even resigned to whatever fate would befall him. He gave me instructions on how he would like to be buried that he insisted he wanted honored. He instructed me that he wanted no casket (caskets being increasingly the practice now all over this area); he only wanted to be wrapped in a white shroud (sanda). To prevent sand from directly hitting his body, he wanted his body placed in a special hole-section dug at right angles on the bottom of his grave (mwanandani). He hoped that none of this contradicted Catholic teaching, and I assured him that it did not.

Marcellus made it quite clear that he would die a happy man since his most serious concern had been taken care of: he now had a house he could call his own, because it was his first wife's, in which he would die and out of which he would be buried. A week later he died and, as I was away from the parish, one of the catechists presided over the burial ceremony in full accordance with what he had instructed. Marcellus died believing that evil people (wachawi, witches) had caused his illness and eventual death.

The Cultural World

MARCELLUS AS A case is merely a microcosm of a macrocosm; he illustrates a situation prevalent across sub-Saharan Africa where injunctions to abstain from sexual relations, or to be faithful in monogamous unions, or even to use condoms as protective and preventive measures against HIV/AIDS transmission, will not much succeed in the African person's cultural context. This context includes the perception of disease aetiology and the understanding of the meaning of sexuality and sexual relations. Current socio-economic and political aspects affecting the status of the disease in Africa must also be seen from this context if they are to be appreciated properly as contributing factors.

When the AIDS epidemic broke out and began to spread throughout the world, the scientific community soon discovered that it was a viral disease transmitted from one person to another through body fluids (especially semen and blood). Its origin was of course initially politicized, linking it to central Africa, but the scientific, biological facts of its transmission could not be contested. These facts were published quickly by the mass media all over the world, and most Africans, as much as anyone else, soon became aware of them, as well as how to protect themselves against the epidemic. Still, by and large, the African people interpreted the disease in terms of their cultural world as a breach of a taboo and witchcraft and, as the case of Marcellus above shows, largely continue to do so today.

Let us cite an example. In the early 1980s, AIDS was killing scores of people in Kyotera village in southern Uganda, right across the north-western Tanzanian border. In spite of the scientific information just cited, the residents of Kyotera village asserted that the disease had erupted there on account of a breach of a taboo. Some Ugandan traders, it was claimed, had reneged on their promise to buy certain goods for the Bakerebe, of the neighboring Tanzanian island of Ukerewe, who had given them money for this purpose. But the Bakerebe had the reputation of being powerful witches; there was therefore no doubt in the Ugandans' mind that they had wreaked vengeance by causing this disease. The Kyotera medicineman asserted the same thing and confessed that they were powerless to counteract the witchcraft since they could not find the Bakerebe concerned so as to repay them and reconcile with them. The Kyotera villagers thus accepted the fact that they would continue to fall sick and die for breaking the taboo of not swindling an unknown person (or visitor).[2]

One may call this mentality by whatever name, including "primitive" if one so fancies, but it doesn't help to address the issue. The real issue is that the mentality exists and influences very much HIV/AIDS epidemiology in Africa. And it is not the rural "ignorant" and poor alone who are

---

2. C. Bawa Yamba, "Cosmologies in Turmoil: Witchcraft and AIDS in Chiawa, Zambia" in *Africa* 67:2 (1997): 200–223.

affected by it, but also the educated and urban well-to-do. Among the supposedly farthest removed from this perception of illness causality are arguably African Catholic priests and nuns. Their training, which is up to now thoroughly Western in style and content, involves vigorous denial of and active campaign against this worldview. Yet evidence shows that the mentality is not completely obliterated from the majority of them at the end of the day. Accusations of witchcraft and suspicions about casting the "evil eye" still occasionally surface in the parishes and convents. This alone should make one think twice about facilely dismissing the influence of this aspect of culture, mistakenly thought to be dead or dying, on the great majority of African people.

Let us cite another example. An American missionary in Kenya, Dr. Carol Narkevic, reports about an AIDS training session for nurses which another missionary was offering. The audience were all community nurses, trained in an accepted school, and had experience in a hospital. And when she asked them, there were several in this particular group who still believed that AIDS was a curse. They knew the medical, technical part of it but still in their hearts thought, "Well, I can't say it's not a curse, regardless of what I've seen and know." And these are probably some of the most educated people in the area.[3]

In a different cultural setting the scientific, biomedical explanation would predominate, if it were the only one. In Africa, however, an AIDS patient (fully aware of that fact) will have recourse to the hospital first. When his/her health continues to deteriorate, he/she will in all likelihood consult some diviner healer. The diviner healer will most likely confirm what the patient and his/her relatives already suspect; namely, that there is a witch or an evil spirit behind the affliction, and appropriate steps will be prescribed to pacify or neutralize the forces in question. This is a matter of belief, and one may wonder if it is relevant here to inquire into its practical efficacy.[4]

If we appreciate that in Africa, disease aetiology or disease causation is often considered an external (and most often malevolent human) agent, an understanding of African perception of the meaning of sexuality and sexual relations is just as important. Sexuality and sexual activity are in Africa ultimately geared toward marriage and procreation. Procreation preserves the individual's and clan's life force, and therefore their immortality. Consistent with this, Marcellus, and the Luo in general, tend to be polygamous in the sense of direct polygyny, widow inheritance, leviratic unions, and surrogate or ghost marriages and unions. They also practice rituals

---

3. Cathy McDonald, "*Maryknoll and the AIDS Pandemic*" (unpublished), 7.
4. Yamba, 208–16.

such as widow-cleansing, in which a widow is required to have sexual relations with one of her deceased husband's male relatives. In terms of HIV transmission, all of these are of course "high-risk" practices. Despite widespread knowledge of this fact they continue to be practiced (as in Marcellus' case). Why is this so?

The reason lies in African culture's fundamental view, which is ultimately religious, that all forms of sexual relationships have their legitimate purpose only in the formation of kinships and kinship-solidarity, "and the bonding of the visible and invisible worlds that is effected through the birth of children."[5] To disturb this purpose in any way means to tamper dangerously with human life, God, the spirits, and the ancestors. If the lineage is to die because a person refuses to fulfill his or her responsibility in this regard, the person in question commits a grave offense against God and the ancestors. Such behavior can bring about untold calamities, not only for the individual concerned, but often also for the entire community. For this reason, the requirement to observe these sexual customs is in many cases weightier in the eyes of the people than the risk of acquiring HIV/AIDS which arises from these customs. Specifically among the Luo of Bukama, "wife inheritance" and levirate unions have two purposes which make the people very reluctant to avoid or change custom. One of the purposes is social, the other is religious.

Inheritance and levirate unions are meant to be permanent and stable institutions whose intention is to protect the widow by taking care of her material and sexual needs. Perhaps more importantly for the Luo, the custom also is meant to assure the continuation of the life of the clan on the one hand, and the "ancestorship" or immortality of both parents on the other, through the continuing birth of children. Very few Luo men and women dare in practice to overlook this expectation.

A Contextualized Approach

As I HAVE pointed out above and as Yamba also concisely notes, Africans who "are now the target of HIV/AIDS prevention messages, find themselves drawn toward the orbits of three competing and contradictory forms of discourse, all of which claim to tell them how to lead safe lives, free from AIDS."[6] To recapitulate, there is the biomedical paradigm which says "Treat your Sexually Transmitted Diseases (STDs), use condoms and

---

5. Laurenti Magesa, *African Religion: The Moral Traditions of Abundant Life* (Maryknoll, N.Y.: Orbis Books, 1997), 136.
6. Yamba, 200.

change your sexual behavior in order to survive." There is, secondly, the Christian-missionary approach which preaches against the use of condoms and insists on abstinence. Then there is "the third discourse" which, as Yamba shows:

> centers upon traditional ideas and perceived tradition; particularly, notions of how things are and were. This type of discourse is in the ascendant because its proponents have perceived that, although the biomedical discourse claims certainty and has usually the backing of the authorities, it is able neither to cure AIDS nor to explain why a particular person has chanced to catch it. Nor is it able to explain the conjunction of events which may lead to tragic consequences. Indeed, biomedical discourse is perceived as reverting to concepts such as chance and accident to explain what all people know to be due to infractions of traditional norms, inevitably resulting in evil through sorcery or witchcraft. Proponents of the missionary discourse are aware of this, although they would not admit that they were wrong to have declared such beliefs "primitive" in the past.[7]

Both the biomedical and missionary discourses have to admit this and begin "to grapple," as Yamba says, "not only with the idea of disease aetiology and causation that are peculiar to the local [African] context but also with appropriate strategies for prevention that are likely to be effective."[8] Such strategies must avoid what Jennifer L. Walters, Renee Canady, and Terry Stein call "homogenization," the tendency not to be "culturally sensitive," so that one fails to "recognize cultural differences between cultural groups." Even in other areas, they argue, "prevention messages with a middle-class bias (for example, advocating monogamy) may not speak to significant numbers of working poor women who are unmarried. Similarly, directives to be 'honest with your partner' may be inappropriate for people in relationships where there is inequality or hidden information about a partner's behavior."[9]

In trying to change high-risk practices and behavior in the African environment, it is important to recognize the fact that "the message must be delivered in a fashion that is culturally relevant" or "culturally responsive."[10]

---

7. Ibid.

8. Ibid., 216.

9. Jennifer L. Walters, et al., "Evaluating Multicultural Approaches in HIV/AIDS Educational Material," *AIDS Education and Prevention: An Interdisciplinary Journal* 6:5 (1994): 448.

10. Ibid., 450.

This means that the motivation for change must be found within, and be based on the cultural beliefs in question themselves: in our case, belief in witchcraft as the primary cause of illness and the use of sexuality as a means to enhance life. Substitute or alternative beliefs, practices, and forms of behavior that are culturally relevant, comprehensible, and acceptable need then to be proposed and introduced.

With reference to disease causality, "an important first step toward behavioral change," Yamba points out, "lies in whether people accept that the illness they have contracted results from their own behavior or whether they believe it is due to some agent(s) outside themselves. If the former, then it is likely that such people will be receptive to the idea that altering their behavior will reduce their chances of being infected. If the latter, then obviously behavioral change will be perceived as having no consequence whatsoever."[11]

How, then, to tackle the belief that HIV/AIDS is not so much due to the malevolence of external witches but rather the witchcraft ("evil") that is within each one of us? For in African belief, all persons, inasmuch as they have propensity to wrongdoing, are potentially witches. The human task, which is unending, is for every person to control this propensity or inclination to fundamental waywardness as much as possible so that no harm is done to oneself or to other persons. To give in to promiscuity in an age of HIV/AIDS means to risk the ultimate wrong to oneself—that is, suicide. Victims of suicide are until today seen as witches in many African communities, and so they do not receive a proper burial among the Bukama Luo. HIV/AIDS, therefore, in this context must be understood, like suicide, as the result of one's own behavior which can, and by cultural expectation, must be changed if one's own life force and that of the community are to be maintained and grow. This strategy here is not to deny witchcraft or to deride it as "primitive," but to take it seriously and use its ethical demands in the struggle against HIV/AIDS.

Appreciation of different culturally conditioned approaches to sexuality and sexual relations must similarly be grounded in cultural perceptions if anti-HIV/AIDS strategies and campaigns are to make any headway in Africa. Once again, the point is not to deride African marital institutions and sexual rituals as high-risk practices, though they may be. The point is rather to transform and change them from within, realizing the fundamentally important role they play in African society. This can only be done not only on an individualistic level but on a communal basis. As Bénézet Bujo has explained, "Only a communitarian examination of conscience, only

---

11. Yamba, 216.

communitarian thought and action, can help master the problem of AIDS in Africa."[12]

If the use of sexuality in African culture is oriented toward solidarity of the community, that is, by enhancing the life force of the living, the dead, and the yet to be born through procreation, anything or any behavior that obstructs this contradicts the sense of life and cannot be encouraged by the community. When African communities, therefore, are made to realize that some of their marriage institutions and sexual rituals do in fact diminish rather than promote the life of the community, because they are agents of death, they may more easily be persuaded to transcend and change them. But "if an information campaign is satisfied with advertising condoms, without exposing . . . [these] deeper causes and ignoring . . . [this] ethical question, then one is merely treating the symptoms."[13] Merely advertising condoms effectively separates the use of sexuality from its communal dimension; it "rather promotes the consumer mentality, reducing sexuality to a commodity." A new approach to fighting HIV/AIDS in Africa is needed "whereby [each] sexual encounter has to be viewed in its communal dimension instead of stressing a one-dimensional and individual oriented self-realization as the highest value."[14]

Insofar as African culture succeeds in persuading the community or the individual in question to live by its code, or to guarantee punishment of one sort or another to those who don't, it is an ethical system. Of course, the relationship between the code and the ethics is inseparable. The code points out in more or less clear terms the way the ethics ought to go and enforces it with physical or spiritual measures. The ethics in turn validates and strengthens the code.

What must be underlined is the fact that, in the final analysis, the ethical life is more or less the result of a communal choice or decision. Admittedly, this choice is always situated in a place, environment, and time as well as a host of other variables that constitute the identity or "being" of the human being in the group. But in spite of, or perhaps because of all this, it remains true that the possibility of the community deciding otherwise is not neutralized, even though such a decision may cause a great deal of trauma and socio-structural readjustment. As a matter of fact, cultural worldviews develop and cultures change and grow probably as the result of choices and decisions (some of them nearly

---

12. Bénézet Bujo, *The Ethical Dimension of Community: The African Model and the Dialogue between North and South* (Nairobi: Pauline Publications Africa, 1998), 187–88.

13. Bujo, 186.

14. Ibid., 187.

imperceptible) which are different from the rule. Kraft argues in a similar vein:

> The worldview of any culture presumably originated in a series of agreements by the members of the original group concerning their perception of reality and how they should regard and react toward that reality. This, like all other aspects of culture, has undergone constant change so that it now differs from the original worldviews that have developed (in related cultures) from that common-ancestor worldview.[15]

While keeping in mind, therefore, that ethical practices do not always correspond to dominant cultural religious codes, we must not forget either that they are most fundamentally based there. Any effective change begins with addressing people's worldview. In the case of HIV/AIDS in Africa, this appears to be the approach that could achieve results, a healing from the roots.

UNMAKING A HIDDEN EPIDEMIC AMONG FIRST NATION COMMUNITIES IN CANADA

Mark Miller, C.Ss.R.

A PHONE CALL *from a healthcare worker in a northern Canadian, mostly aboriginal community sought my advice on a strategy to deal with the spread of the human immunodeficiency virus. An initiative from outside the community advocated safe sex and a number of people wanted the local Catholic hospital to provide free condoms. Some of the health care workers agreed with this approach and there was a bit of an uproar when the Catholic hospital simply refused on the basis of its Catholic values. As the hospital was the only one for many miles, there were voices suggesting that the Catholic sponsors give up the facility and "not impose" their values on the whole community. Was there a way that the hospital could make condoms available for the community?*

---

15. Charles H. Kraft, *Christianity in Culture* (Maryknoll, N.Y.: Orbis Books, 1979), 53.

Catholic hospitals in Canada are expected to follow the *Health Care Ethics Guide* of the Catholic Health Association of Canada, supported by the Canadian bishops. Issues around contraception and sterilization usually comprise a delicate topic because the Canadian health care system is paid for by the government, whose respect for Catholic moral principles in their delivery of health care has always been tentative. The *Guide* explicitly prohibits formal cooperation in the use of artificial contraception.

There is a perception in many corners of modern society, including some within the church, that clear moral prohibitions require obedient and unquestioning implementation. If condoms for contraceptive purposes are immoral, then condoms will not be used or made available. End of discussion.

However, the Catholic tradition is much richer than such a perception would allow. To begin with, and following all good ethical processes, the moral situation and the moral issue must be clarified. If the prevention of AIDS is the context, then perhaps the main issue is not condoms at all. For Catholic moral theology to make good practical moral judgments, all the data must first be gathered and correctly understood. As we shall see, the actual relations of aboriginals among themselves and with the larger society, based on their own experience, were crucial to understanding the true moral issues at hand.

Furthermore, Catholic moral theology has always understood the role of virtue in the making of moral judgments, particularly in those areas where prudential applications of moral teaching must be made. Aquinas in his *Summa Theologiae*, for example, outlines his understanding of moral theory by first discussing virtue and only then law. Entering into the experiences of the First Nations' peoples began to reveal a set of virtues that were appropriate to aboriginal communities. So many of the wise members of the community, in their deep desire to do good for their communities, found solutions in such "quiet" virtues as good listening, respect for all opinions and experiences, and the prudent fashioning of practical solutions.

Finally, the use of moral imagination played an enormous role in overcoming the confrontational narrowness presented by posing the wrong question. Moral imagination has not always received its due in a Catholic tradition that tended to depend upon the law as arbiter and judge. Nonetheless, its place in good moral decision-making has been emphasized in the past thirty years as essential to the best of the Catholic moral tradition. This creative imagining allows people to see broader contexts, and actively and creatively to seek possible solutions in these contexts.

The experience (pursued principally through conversation), the virtue, and the moral imagination of the native peoples made their solutions to the issue of condoms and safe sex an explicit example of good Catholic moral reasoning and resolution. The details of their story follow.

In concert with the hospital administrator, a native social worker and several concerned members of the community, we first disposed of the condom issue. The pharmacy was independent of the hospital and if it chose to dispense condoms, that was its business. The underlying issue of who pays for them could have caused some problems because people are presumably much more apt to be aware of and make use of condoms which are freely available. An additional argument was put to me by one person who favored the involvement of the hospital, "People will use them if they are free and supported by the hospitals!" (Ironically, I think this would be called "moral support"!) It was, however, suggested that if members of the community thought that condoms should be free, then it would not be hard to find a few sponsors or even solicit community donations in order to make them available.

Of far more importance was the question that occasioned the condom flap. Are First Nation communities in danger of an epidemic of AIDS, and if so, how can this be prevented? The condom-for-safe-sex raised many problems that were very difficult to talk about. What are the sexual practices among the people of this community? This question challenged a great many hidden assumptions about natives and sexuality. The majority of the members of this community were committed to their spouses and struggled to raise their children in awareness of the responsibilities of adulthood.

Nevertheless, problems arose in four distinct areas. First, there were those in the community who abused drugs and alcohol, often severely. A high level of promiscuity existed in these circles. Travel between this community and the cities exacerbated the drug, alcohol, and sexual problems. Second, there were occasional extramarital affairs which endangered unknowing partners. Third, marriages and common-law relationships were not always stable, particularly among those under forty. After a break-up, liaisons before entering into another union were not uncommon. And, finally and most thought provoking, was the level of sexual activity among the teenagers and young adults.

Part of the strategy that had originally been in place concerning "safe sex" was a strong educational program about the deadly nature of HIV, the manner of contagion, and some forms of protection, of which the use of condoms was primary. Learning something about the community, especially those who were at higher risk, allowed for a redesigning of the educational program. Targeting the teens and young adults increased their awareness but did little to combat the teenage myth that AIDS was a gay disease or found only among older people. That another teen might be infected seemed beyond consideration. In conjunction with the local school, a visit was arranged for the young people. Two young men and a very young woman (none, unfortunately, aboriginal) who were HIV positive told their stories in person. No amount of education or moral suasion could have accomplished more.

More problematic was the educational program for those in the middle age group, those who had entered into marriages or common-law unions from high school to their mid-forties. Most of the men were not interested in anything anyone had to say, with the exception of the elders who would hopefully have an eventual longer-term effect on younger men willing to listen. The First Nation social worker began to target the women. Of interest was the process whereby the social worker finally got the women to talk. It was only in small coffee-klatsch gatherings. Anything larger meant no one wanted to reveal sensitive information.

Stories of loving, responsible sex between loving partners were rather rare. The enormous complications of sex as a language of communication began to surface. Women had some say in the matter of sexual relations; indeed, in some situations their word was final. Troubling stories began to surface, however, of sex being forced upon them by belligerent husbands. Even more serious were the occasions when alcohol fuelled the men's desires and no "escape" was possible. Passive cooperation was often the only alternative to violence. One particularly striking comment arose a number of times: "You think he's going to stop and take time to put on a condom when he's like that?" A sense of sexual intimacy as a mature, respectful, mutually shared experience of loving union was a description that raised ironic eyebrows while also touching a deep longing.

Gradually, and not surprisingly, a picture began to emerge of underlying issues that would make the use of condoms almost a moot point in the existential reality of these people's lives. Poverty and chronic unemployment, boredom especially for the young males but increasingly for the young women as well, drug and alcohol addiction, abuse "resignedly accepted" within the community, and a peculiar aboriginal pride added instability and cycles of abuse to the daily life.

The word "pride" used in the previous paragraph requires an explanation. Pride is not arrogance in these communities; it is closer to the notion of "face" in Oriental cultures. Psychologists might call it self-esteem, but it is more than a lack of self-esteem which asserts itself in aggression. I would suggest that the word refers to a sense of self-dignity as a human being and as an aboriginal. This pride plays itself out on two levels—within the community, it has to do with how others see you, talk about you, respect you (or not). Within the community this pride is highly susceptible to damage in love relationships. People who are hurting because of rejection or feeling slighted or laughed at will sometimes do very stupid things. Few mechanisms, as it turns out, are in place in aboriginal communities today to deal with such hurt. Perhaps in centuries gone by, a young male could take out his rejection in the hunt and prove himself on that level. Or the sweat lodge could provide a spiritual respite. Many of these community devices disappeared in the face of the colonialism by Europeans (including an uncomprehending Catholic Church).

On the second level, pride as dignity comes from one's standing as an aboriginal in an overwhelmingly white world. The values that sustain a person on the reserve are incomprehensible to most whites, such that life in the cities can be a cultural "de-nuding." The compensations of drugs and alcohol accompanied by welfare and poverty erode a person's dignity. Education must be a very specially directed tool to overcome such degradation. The brutality often experienced by natives from natives is an enormously sad commentary on the re-victimization of the victims. As aboriginals re-discover their profound values of community, sharing, harmony, interdependence, humour, and their sense of extended family, their place in the world of whites will change (and, hopefully, change the larger society); until then, their road is steeply uphill.

Sound discouraging? Well, it is if everything has to be solved at once. However, there were enough clues in the stories triggered by the condom debate to offer considerable hope for this First Nation community to face some of its problems, only one of which was the danger of AIDS.

The life-and-death urgency of the AIDS menace stirred many of the most responsible members of the community to seek out creative ways to counter the danger. Formal educational sessions were mostly ignored. As noted, informal conversations began to draw more and more members of the community into the concern. Interestingly, while I had been consulted about the issue of condoms and the Catholic hospital, I was not invited into the daily conversations. Once in a while I was consulted about ideas and directions that surfaced, and I was able to make some suggestions which the community used. "Outsiders," who have often tried to "solve" native problems, were consciously excluded, except where some kind of expert advice was needed. (The Catholic principle of subsidiarity could describe this activity.)

In short, the following results emerged from our facing the original controversy. First, the conversations proved the most helpful because they were occasions for a new honesty, openness, and self-respect among many of these people, even if the struggle to involve the men has, to date, produced only modest success. In turn, these conversations led to the willingness of women to set up support groups (my phrase, not theirs) when women were having problems. These groups gave many of the women a support that they had never had before, both for advice and for comfort.

Secondly, the groups began to catch the interest of some of the younger people, mostly older teenagers. A sense of working/being together, of solidarity, and of mutual responsibility grew within the community.

Third, resolving the chronic lack of employment was recognized as the most critical, underlying issue. Young people, right out of school, literally had nothing that they could do for gainful employment. There was only so much that the community could offer to keep the young people busy and "a right to work" remains the number one issue that three levels of government have been unable to resolve.

Fourth, a subtle part of the conversation groups was an effort to teach responsible, loving sexuality. Instead of sex being a "male conquest" or a "who's-connected-with-whom" event, the notion of a sexual relationship as an enduring gift of love within a loving relationship was emphasized. (The Catholic tradition around love, marriage, sexuality, and family was very helpful in this re-imaging.) Sexual attitudes in this community had, until this point, been mostly caught rather than taught. A genuine effort was made to encourage the young people to discipline themselves, not just as individuals, but for one another. Needless to say, the theory and the practice still do not coincide perfectly.

Fifth, the deeply religious nature of many of the elders brought to the attention of the community a phrase from one of St. Paul's letters. "Say only the good things people need to hear" (Eph. 4:29) became a challenge to the negative down-grading and jealous ways people employed in struggling with self-esteem. "Going white," for example, was a phrase that struck at another aboriginal's dignity when that person tried to "get ahead" in the white man's way. Most of these attitudes expressed a bitterness which in turn kept the whole community on guard and effectively trapped by native customs. Some of the most beautiful traditions—for example, that of hospitality by which anybody who came at meal time was fed without question—meant that long-range planning for one's own family was not possible because too many shirkers took advantage of the hospitality. Discussing such blatant injustices was very helpful for some of the community, although the native values are deeply ingrained and very few dramatic changes took place.

Finally, an interesting discussion with the social worker almost a year later about condoms produced some thoughtful insights for both of us. First, she noted that condoms were really not a major issue. They were available, but seemed quite ineffective as a strategy against AIDS. And when I noted how easily it would have been to terminate the Catholic sponsorship of the hospital around this issue, she responded that the community was only now realizing how much the sisters loved these people and how much that added to the health care there. She had been in a number of other communities where the problems of northern health care are exacerbated by constantly changing personnel as well as by the lack of understanding of the aboriginals. Second, she mused on how easily the hospital had been made a scapegoat. In the anxiety around the AIDS scare, a simple solution was sought. This, she noted, allowed everyone to avoid the deeper and much more complicated issues at the root of the problem.

I then pointed out two issues that troubled me as an ethicist. One was the campaign to reduce "safe sex" to condoms. The attitude that underlies this campaign betrays the understanding of sex as a stable, loving, and procreative relationship. Often I have been laughed at and told that such definitions are pie-in-the-sky and I need to be more realistic about what is really going on. Realism, however, is not the problem; what we ask and expect of people is. Getting people to be realistic about who they are as sexual beings is not only a more noble goal, it may well be the only way to make people morally responsible for their sexual selves. Condoms without responsible people are not nearly as safe as portrayed. They appear as a "technological fix-it" device when the real issues are human relations and attitudes.

The other lesson that struck me was that moralistic solutions are not very helpful. For a Catholic facility to say that the use of condoms is against our moral principles and then wash its hands of the underlying issues, would be to miss an opportunity to do much needed good. The purpose of moral teaching (in an antiauthoritarian era) is not to polarize issues, but to assist in finding good resolutions. Unless we are willing to look actively and creatively for ways to deal with the problems raised by others, then we will find that fewer and fewer will even listen to us. Only with such creativity can Catholic health care truly serve the poor.

Looking to the internal resources of this community bore much fruit. The desire to do good, to look after the vulnerable, and to protect the health of the community led to a further plumbing of community wisdom about how to plan and make changes. Open, honest discussions proved very helpful, but only after the obstacles to such dialogue were faced. Communal responsibility for problems was acknowledged as was communal responsibility for solutions. And a communal pride in facing these issues began to develop. Among other things, correct information about protection, the building of communal responsibility for the meaning and place of sex in the aboriginal community, and a healthy, growing self-respect became the "aboriginal friendly" approach of these good people. To draw a theoretical note, I would suggest that an ethic of rules, which sought "an answer concerning condoms," was overtaken by an ethic of virtue—and virtue in a communal even more than in an individualized sense in this close-knit community.

A final word, as told to me by the social worker, goes to an anonymous member of one of the coffee groups discussing the problems of the community. Outlining the often overwhelming difficulties faced in First Nation communities and the numerous efforts of governments, social agencies, schools, and community activists to deal with them, one woman made this insightful comment, which I paraphrase. "Condoms keep everything in place; they allow every problem to remain. What we need is to fix our hearts."

HIV/AIDS AMONG DESERT NOMADS IN KENYA

James Good

MICHAEL K[1] WAS one of the first generation of the Turkana tribe to complete secondary education. With numerous foreign agencies operating in his tribal territory, he had no problem getting himself a post as clerk in one of the larger agencies. Soon he was head of the agency at a local level.

Promotion brought a salary around ten times the income earned by the rest of his fellow tribesmen. His higher salary enabled him to increase the number of his wives and to widen the circle of lady friends who were paid liberally for their favors. Soon he contracted tuberculosis (it was thus referred to by everyone). But when he died, everyone knew he had died of HIV/AIDS.

The Turkana tribe numbers about 300,000—mostly nomads who wander around their desert land in northwest Kenya, seeking pasture for their flocks of goats and fat-tailed sheep. The civil district of Turkana covers about 72,000 square kilometers of sand and rock. Until very near the date of Kenyan independence (1963), British colonial policy was aimed at keeping the Turkanas boxed inside their tribal boundaries. Turkana was declared a "closed area!"—a policy directed mainly at halting the aggressive advances by the tribe against British colonial settlements to the south, as well as against neighboring tribes.

Turkana morality was clear-cut and strict especially in sexual matters. Heavy fines were imposed for breaches of the sexual code. Young men went on cattle raids to provide the bride-price required to purchase the lady of their choice. The basic bride-price was about 120 goats, payable in installments. But failure to pay in full meant that the bride's father could reclaim his daughter, plus any children she might have at the date of reclaim.

A major famine in Turkana in 1960 changed all that. Herds were wiped out and cattle raiding was severely dealt with; theft of a goat carried a mandatory sentence of seven years. Bride-prices could not be paid and, so, marriage could not be undertaken. Sexual morality broke down, the process being speeded up by the example and practice of "down-country" officials who left their wives at home and established relationships with Turkana girls unable to find a partner. Marriages were few and far between, and soon even the concept of marriage began to be devalued. Young men, who in the past had to risk their lives in cattle raids to earn the

---

1. The name has been altered to preserve confidentiality.

bride-price, now found that they could have short-term relationships with Turkana girls who by tradition produced children as soon as they reached puberty. While some relationships were stable and long-lasting, many girls found themselves—through no fault of their own—with a series of short-term partners who, as soon as the baby was born, moved on to another and similar relationship, leaving mother and baby to fend for themselves.

There were other problems. Even where a stable relationship existed, it was generally accepted that the man retained his freedom to have other relationships. This was particularly true of times when the wife was breast-feeding—usually for two years and more—or otherwise sexually inactive. It is on record that prostitutes from outside tribes arrived in Lodwar as early as 1943, introducing a pattern of life which was, apparently, unknown in the desert in earlier times.

The result was inevitable: the general spread of sexually transmitted diseases throughout the whole of Turkana with—as could be expected—a heavy concentration in the small centers of population which developed rather quickly. Increased numbers of police, civil servants and other outsiders arrived into Turkana in the 1970s with the building of the 300-kilometer tarmac Fish Road connecting Lake Turkana (formerly Lake Rudolf) with the outside world. The Turkana desert could no longer be retained as a "closed area" as it had been in colonial times. It was now open to the influences, both good and evil, from the outside world.

The Arrival of HIV/AIDS

IT IS ACCEPTED that in many parts of Africa (and perhaps elsewhere) the spread of HIV/AIDS has been mainly along the highways joining major towns. While there have undoubtedly been a few cases of HIV being introduced into the desert by Turkana men going "down country" to places like Nairobi and Mombasa and associating with infected women in these areas, the principal route of HIV into Turkana has been via truckers delivering goods to southern Sudan. Due to the civil war being waged by the Sudan People's Liberation Army (SPLA) against the Khartoum Islamic government, there is no access to southern Sudan from the north: access is either through Turkana or through northern Uganda. The route through Turkana had the advantage of having a highway crossing the border into southern Sudan. It was also safer than the Uganda route, not being open to rebel groups like the Lord's Resistance Army in northern Uganda.

Even before the arrival of HIV, Turkana was not well equipped medically. While Lodwar town had its district hospital and a few health centers and dispensaries scattered around the desert, these units were generally under-staffed and lacking in basic medical facilities. As a recent report stated:

The government health care infrastructure in Turkana is one of the weakest in Kenya, 60% of all health facilities are run by nongovernment organizations (NGOs) and if they would pull out, there would be no health care for the majority of the people in Turkana district. At the moment, the government does not even have the capacity and resources to maintain the few government facilities that exist. Lodwar District Hospital is in a poor state of repair, Ministry of Health staff frequently make an appeal to NGOs to assist them when they run out of drugs or when they need transport to specific activities.[2]

In view of this, medical care was one of the first undertakings of the Catholic missionaries. Within a decade of the arrival of the first Catholic priests and sisters in 1961–62, a well-equipped mission hospital had been built at Kakuma, along with a large number of ancillary units around the desert. In these early years, the Catholic Mission—which evolved into the diocese of Lodwar in 1978—was delivering about 85 percent of the medical care available to the Turkana people.

Desert illnesses included all the expected ones—malaria, typhoid, and tuberculosis, along with the life-threatening disease of hydatid cysts, endemic in the northern half of the desert. As has been noted above, sexually transmitted diseases were also high on the list and the mission medical units did their best to deal with those patients who came for their free services. They were, however, fully aware that a very large proportion of the population was not being reached, so the health centers developed a mobile unit which brought medical care to the nomads. This was a most valuable but difficult undertaking.

Unfortunately, the elimination of harmful traditional medical practices among the Turkana will not be easy. The causation of disease as understood by the desert people is that all illness is something evil (in Turkana terms "hot") inside the body, usually put there by a spirit. Cure is affected by "letting the evil out," thus returning the patient to a healthy or "cool" state. The first attempt at a cure is undertaken within the family: the mother cuts the flesh of the sick person in certain areas in a kind of ritual blood-letting in order to "let the evil out." If this fails (as it generally must) the patient has to be taken to the medicine man, who will perform a very complex ritual sacrifice aimed—like the simpler "domestic" ritual—at restoring the patient from his sick or "hot" state to a healthy or "cool" one. It is hardly necessary to point out that as long as the authority of the medicine man or witch-doctor is recognized, the possibility of getting the patient proper medical care does not exist. A long and difficult process of education will be necessary.[3]

---

2. *Diocese of Lodwar, Diocesan Health Programme,* July 1998, 2.

3. See Anthony Joseph Barrett, *Sacrifice and Prophecy in Turkana Cosmology* (Nairobi: Paulines Publications Africa, 1998).

The last few years have brought to the fore another element which operates against underdeveloped peoples in their efforts to combat disease and specifically to handle HIV/AIDS. This is the simple fact that while many useful drugs are available in the developed world to ameliorate the condition of HIV/AIDS victims and slow down the development of the disease, lack of finance makes these drugs absolutely unavailable to patients in underdeveloped countries. Until more finance becomes available for treatment of Third World patients, the diagnosis that they are suffering from HIV/AIDS will produce only statistics of sufferers—without offering them adequate treatment and without taking any really effective measures to prevent the disease from spreading further. The arrival of HIV in Turkana did not take the mission medical personnel entirely by surprise. The main medical team in Turkana were the Medical Missionaries of Mary, whose colleagues were already doing heroic work for HIV sufferers at Kitovu Hospital in Masaka, Uganda. Unlike most African leaders who stubbornly denied the existence of HIV in their countries, President Yoweri Museveni of Uganda proclaimed openly to the world that a disastrous epidemic was devastating his country. He asked for, and got, massive international aid which put Masaka in the forefront of world centers dealing with the HIV/AIDS epidemic. The Uganda experience was of great assistance when HIV made its first appearance in Turkana.

It is well known that when an individual becomes aware that he is suffering from a fatal disease, the first reaction is frequently one of denial and disbelief. Many governments have reacted similarly to the discovery of widespread HIV/AIDS among the general population. The Kenyan government was initially no exception, though eventually a program was undertaken aimed at publicizing details about HIV and recommending a relevant sexual morality. However, in a country which has serious problems in providing a basic minimum health service for its fast growing population, it was only to be expected that the finance available for dealing with the HIV outbreak was inadequate. As with other areas of health care, the Catholic dioceses of Kenya tried to fill the gap, organizing mobile teams of health advisers to disseminate information about HIV. This project was aimed at schools, factories, and any organized groups that were prepared to listen to the message. Early results suggest that despite much publicity, the message did not get through—the usual individual reaction being "it won't happen to me." It is now felt that the topic will have to develop a broader approach, underlining the necessity of a deeper understanding of human relationships in general and of sexual relationships in particular. There is no easy way or short cut to a solution of the HIV crisis.

In addition to denial, another and related defense mechanism became common in the desert. Tuberculosis is a common illness in Turkana, and AIDS sufferers were described as having TB. Tuberculosis was a "respectable" disease in Turkana and carried no social stigma. So HIV/AIDS sufferers were listed as TB patients, many of the medical symptoms being common to both illnesses. In fact many AIDS sufferers could rightly be classified as TB patients. The word commonly used to describe HIV/AIDS in the Swahili language was *Ukimwi,* a readily understandable term which side-stepped the difficulty of translating terms like HIV and AIDS into the Turkana language. At the same time it covered or removed the social stigma attached to a new and potentially fatal sexual disease. Deaths from AIDS are still reported as TB-related deaths, despite the growing fund of knowledge about HIV/AIDS, and statistics of HIV/AIDS are rendered incomplete and at least to some extent unreliable.

In the light of what has been said, it is clear that dependable statistics of HIV/AIDS-related diseases are hard to come by. As with similar figures of HIV elsewhere in the developing countries, the reported cases are almost certainly only a small fraction of the actual number of sufferers. This will be particularly true of a largely nomadic people like the Turkana, many of whom are born, live, and die without ever being touched by professional medical care, and who in any case will turn first to the witch-doctor, coming for professional medical supervision only in the last stages of the disease—that is, if they come at all.

Whatever way one looks at the available statistics, the problem is an ever-growing one in Turkana. Every year since 1991 has shown an increase in the number of AIDS cases in the district (55 in 1991 to 98 in 1996). The number of HIV-infected persons is also increasing every year. In 1996, only 22 out of 186 persons (12 percent) screened for HIV were positive, while in 1997 68 out of 215 (32 percent) screened were HIV positive.[4] And we emphasize once again that due to the nomadic way of living common to most Turkanas, this is only the tip of the iceberg

The Catholic diocese of Lodwar, which is coextensive with the civil district of Turkana, has for some years past provided an AIDS educational service. This has been integrated as far as possible with other health and health education activities, such as prenatal clinics, family planning, and Community Based Health Care programs. The diocese offers its AIDS educational service at every location where it is acceptable, including schools and women's groups, and for nomads at desert watering places. While the service has been generally well received, concern has been raised as to whether the message is really being interiorized by the general body of listeners. Much ignorance still exists, especially among the nomads, concerning the origin and spread of HIV/AIDS. Widespread addiction to local alcoholic brews makes the problem even more intractable. Many drinking sessions are but the preliminary steps to irresponsible sexual encounters in which the fear of HIV/AIDS ceases to be an effective deterrent.

How effective is the work of the church in its HIV/AIDS operations? The negative factors already described guarantee a negative answer. The

---

4. *Diocese of Lodwar, Diocesan Health Programme,* 23–24.

social complexity outlined here shows the enormous problems facing us in Lodwar: the denial of HIV/AIDS reporting; the shift in economic structures that affect, in turn, sexual and marital practices; the neighboring military conflicts; and the deep division between the authority of the medicine man and the physician. Beyond this, getting to the nomads is itself a major deterrent. Mobile units operating out of the various health facilities provide partial access. Blanket coverage of the whole desert is a physical impossibility.

Catholic leadership in the desert area has a fully positive approach to the HIV/AIDS project. No leaders censure or interfere with the information provided. In a word, thankfully, we have been doing most things rightly. But the response is pretty universal: "It won't happen to me."

What can be done to alter this situation? Frankly, very little. Many initiatives have been undertaken—perhaps the most hopeful is a week-long marriage workshop in which Christian sexual values are inculcated. It is significant that the scope of participants in these workshops had to be widened to include couples not married but living in stable relationships. Church married couples are a rarity in the Turkana desert. While this situation continues, and while existing patterns of sexual activity remain the way of life for a large number of the nomads, the further spread of HIV/AIDS is inevitable.

Probably a change of heart will come eventually when the desert community at the grassroots level realizes the destructive nature of the HIV/AIDS pandemic and takes appropriate remedial steps. The solution will come not from outside but from within the community. We outsiders may point the way to solutions, but we cannot impose them from outside. Hopefully, when they are ready, so will we.

COME, YE DISCONSOLATE: AMERICAN BLACK CATHOLICS, THEIR CHURCH, AND HIV/AIDS

Diana L. Hayes

UNLIKE THE OTHER *contributors to this first part, I told the editors, "give me a case." Jon Fuller responded, "What resources are there from within the Black Catholic Church to address needle exchange programs?" So that's my case.*

Today, the Catholic Church finds itself in a situation of paradox as it attempts to deal with the issue of HIV/AIDS and its corollary concerns. The emergence of this epidemic and its rapid spread has created a challenge to the church's social and doctrinal teachings, leading it to take often contradictory stances.

In the United States, HIV/AIDS was first seen as a disease resulting from homosexual activity to which the Catholic Church is categorically opposed. This resulted in a number of often conflicting statements which attempted to blame the sin but not the sinner, a stance rooted in a neo-Platonist dualistic understanding of body and spirit which historically has condemned the sexual activities of the former, unless they resulted in new life, while sanctifying the spiritual aspects of humanity. However, humans cannot and do not live in this bifurcated way. Body and soul are intimately connected, are equal in importance to the maintenance of human integrity and, especially in the African American community, form an indivisible whole which sustains life and the Spirit that dwells within.

Thus, the church's dualistic and, at times, parochial stance has created obstacles to efforts to control the spread of HIV/AIDS not just among the homosexual community but also among heterosexual communities which are becoming the largest infected group at the end of the twentieth century. In fact, African Americans and Latino/as make up a disproportionate number of new AIDS cases, not because of their homosexual populations, but because many are intravenous drug users or have relationships with them. Women who have these drug users as sexual partners—and their children—are the most vulnerable, followed by women married to men who are ostensibly heterosexual but engage in same-sex relationships as well. Thus, today the majority of the new AIDS cases being reported occur among African Americans and at least 30 percent of these cases involve Black women of child-bearing age.[1]

The Church: Black and Catholic

THERE IS A Black Catholic Church which dwells within the Roman Catholic Church. It does not differ in doctrine or beliefs, but in understanding of community, faith, and worship styles. Although numbering almost three million persons, it is often overlooked and marginalized by the dominant members of the church body just as African Americans as a whole, more than thirty million, find themselves marginalized and silenced in the United

---

1. See Emilie Townes, *Breaking the Fine Rain of Death: African American Health Issues and a Womanist Ethic of Care* (New York: Continuum, 1998), chap. 6.

States. Yet they have persevered in their Africentric value system which upholds the individual as part of an all-embracing community grounded in a faith belief which enables all, not just a few, to prosper. Less willing to separate "body and soul, spirit and material, spiritual and physical nourishment . . . it (the Black Roman Catholic Church) has historically and presently been available and supportive when the community and its most valued entity, the Black family, has been threatened."[2]

The historical role of the Black Church which crosses denomination and often religious boundaries[3] "has been the one place which has not been able to forget the fate of its suffering and struggling members."[4] Until now:

> The church has been the central authenticating reality in their lives. When the world has so often been willing to say only "no" to these people, the church has said, "yes." For black people; the church has been the one place where they have been able to experience unconditional positive regard.[5]

Ironically, in the face of AIDS, the Black Church, known as the source of liberation, refuge, education, and spiritual upliftment for the Black community, finds its voice muted and its usually aggressive stance on behalf of its own is strangely hesitant when dealing with issues of sexuality (especially homosexuality), substance abuse, and sexual promiscuity. This reticence to address these issues, especially among Black youth, coupled with the lack of or restricted availability of financial and medical assistance, medical insurance, and educational programs ignores a growing crisis in their midst.

The issue of sexuality is a very difficult one for the Black Church to deal with, mainly because of the stereotypical way in which Blacks have been portrayed in the United States. Often depicted as immoral, promiscuous, deviant sexual beings, fattening on the public trough while producing little of value in return except for more children, they have found themselves in the paradoxical situation of being victimized and therefore marginalized as unwanted or unneeded members of society to whom little is

---

2. Toinette Eugene, "How Can We Forget: An Ethic of Care for AIDS, the African American Family, and the Black Catholic Church," in Emilie Townes, ed., *Embracing the Spirit: Womanist Perspectives on Hope, Salvation and Transformation* (Maryknoll, N.Y.: Orbis Books, 1997).

3. Black Bishops of the United States, *What We Have Seen and Heard: A Pastoral Letter on Evangelization* (Cincinnati: St. Anthony Messenger Press, 1984), 159.

4. Eugene, "How Can We Forget?" 259.

5. Wallace Charles Smith, *The Church in the Life of the Black Family* (Valley Forge: Judson Press, 1985), 56.

offered to provide for their medical, psychological, educational, and other needs.[6] The church, in an effort to counter the negative attributes projected upon the Black community, has sought to restrict open discussion of sexuality, homophobia, and heterosexism as well as other issues of critical importance to the survival of both church and community today. Kelly Brown Douglas locates this reticence in a reaction to what she calls the development of "white culture" and its necessary perpetuation at the expense of those who are different. She notes:

> It is necessary for White society to control Black people's sexuality, meaning their bodies and reproductive capacities, so as to control them as a people. It is also necessary to impugn Black sexuality in order to suggest that Black people are inferior beings. . . . White culture exists primarily as it is contrasted with that which is non-White. It is a culture maintained by an ideology of White supremacy while at the same time it secretes this ideology. If this ideological foundation were to be authoritatively refuted, then the foundation of White culture would be deeply shaken. With the fall of White culture would come the collapse of white patriarchal hegemony in America.[7]

Rather than fighting against these stereotypes, too often the Black Church has perpetuated them within their midst. Some assert "that the refusal to engage in public sexual discourse is a form of Black cultural resistance to the corrupting influence of white culture, or a survival strategy against white cultural attacks."[8] Although this may be a way of looking positively at the situation, the final truth is that the Black community has been significantly harmed by its reticence.

> White culture's sexual characterization and exploitation of Black people has had a far-reaching and deleterious impact on Black lives. This attack has provided a gateway for the contamination of all of Black sexuality, from Black people's relationships with themselves to their relationship with God. But perhaps the most insidious result of the White cultural attack upon Black sexuality is that it has rendered the Black community practically silent in terms of sexual discourse.[9]

---

6. See Eugene article as well as Kelly Brown Douglas, *Sexuality and the Black Church: A Womanist Perspective* (Maryknoll, N.Y.: Orbis Books, 1999), esp. chapters 1–4.

7. Douglas, *Sexuality*, 23.

8. Ibid., 68.

9. Ibid., 85–86.

Yet, it is emphatically the Black, and in this instance, Catholic Church which must respond to these needs as it has in the past:

> In practice, the African American Church has proved adaptable, pragmatic, and even crafty when need be. . . . Time and time again, the church has demonstrated its awareness of the variability of human existence and the fragility of the soul under siege. Time and time again, the Church has been responsive to the needs, spiritual and nonspiritual, of the community.[10]

Such a time has once more arisen as the Black Catholic Church is being called upon by its members to help them deal with the scourge of HIV/AIDS in their midst which is a threat to their continuing existence. Eugene affirms that, "being infected with the HIV virus is a spiritual, physical, emotional, mental, and socio-political reality. Perhaps more than any other form of oppression or disease, it is all-encompassing. Hopefully, the Black Church in all of its dimensions and denominations will not forget that its families are dying from AIDS and that because of this, the whole body suffers."[11]

An Ethic of Justice

THE AIDS EPIDEMIC is having an unforeseen negative impact on the African American community such that its very existence as a viable, cohesive community is threatened. This is not because all Blacks have AIDS or engage in behavior that could lead to AIDS, but because of the still closely-knit nature of the community:

> AIDS, in many ways, is like every other health, social, and economic crisis that black people have faced for generations. What is alarmingly different about AIDS is the severity of the infection and the particularly repressive political timing of the emergence of the disease. The combined effect of all of these elements leaves the black community in an extremely vulnerable position. AIDS has the potential to cripple black people in a way that few other health or social forces have since slavery.[12]

---

10. Harlon L. Dalton, "AIDS in Blackface," in Nancy F. McKenzie, ed., *The AIDS Reader* (New York: Meridian Books, 1991), 127.

11. Eugene, "How Can We Forget?" 260.

12. Beth Richie, "AIDS in Living Color, " in Evelyn C. White, ed., *The Black Women's Health Book: Speaking for Ourselves* (Seattle: Seal Press, 1990), 183.

The major negative impact has been on the Black family. Unlike the nuclear-family of middle-class America, Black families have always been comprised of persons, linked by blood ties or not, of several generations and genders. These extended families reach back to the villages of their African ancestral homes, but were uniquely shaped and strengthened in the fiery furnace of slavery in the United States. The family unity which was the foundation of the Black community is now under serious threat as mothers die from crack cocaine or AIDS, and fathers die or are rendered incapable of caring for their children because they are incarcerated in greater numbers than any other racial or ethnic group in the United States.

Grandparents, especially grandmothers, and aunts continue to take up the slack but are too often stymied by the red tape of an unfeeling bureaucratic system which stigmatizes all Blacks as dysfunctional and prefers to place their children as far away from relatives or persons known to their families as possible. In addition, although the numbers are dropping, young women are still having children by young men, neither capable of being parents, who see their sexuality as signs of maturity and prowess, placing even greater burdens on the usual family caretakers who themselves are also often physically, emotionally, and financially overwhelmed.

Emilie Townes discusses these issues in greater depth and clarity in *Breaking the Fine Rain of Death*. Affirming that the "Black body has long been a site of contention," so much so that the "health of the Black body as cultural production, then, becomes extremely problematic,"[13] she discusses in detail the "repercussions" of the Tuskegee study which have left a legacy of mistrust of institutional medical care among Black Americans.

> Because of the persistence of structured social inequality and its attendant stereotypes, phobias, and hatreds, many African Americans see a conspiracy against Black life that is lodged not only in individual acts of terror and hatred, but also within governmental structures. These conspiracy theories run a chilling gamut—from the belief that the government promotes drug abuse in African American communities to the belief that HIV/AIDS is a human-made weapon of racial warfare . . . the word "genocide" is often linked with HIV/AIDS in the Black community.[14]

For many of this community, the AIDS epidemic and the nation's and churches' reaction and response to it present an excellent, albeit often chilling, perspective of the problems confronting African Americans with regard to health care issues and needs today:

---

13. Townes, *Breaking*, 122, 123.
14. Ibid., 125–26.

> The historic Black Church has often been the one and only institution which sees the problems of its people yet does not cast its people out. It is often the one and only institution which remembers that all people are made in the image of God and are thus worthy of respect. If drug users are simply written off and cast out by the Roman Catholic Church (as they are by nearly every other institution), AIDS will continue to be an epidemic in the African American community. Rather, by accepting and giving all African Americans a sense of belonging, by recognizing and being clear about the connections of drug abuse to a much larger and more powerful systemic racism, the Black Church will continue its tradition as an adoptionist church, a church that provides family when there seems to be none.[15]

The African American community is disproportionately represented with respect to HIV/AIDS as the disease is growing faster there than among any other racial or ethnic group. African Americans have been found to be six times more likely to have AIDS than whites. Since 1990, AIDS has been the leading cause of deaths for Black men between 35 and 44 and second for Black men and women between 26 and 36. The risk for Black women has also increased, accounting for 57 percent of newly reported cases among adult females; 32 percent were the result of intravenous drug users, while heterosexual contact caused 38 percent. The numbers continue to grow as more children are born to HIV positive women who are often unaware until too late that their sexual partners were infected and that they, too, as a result of his or her behavior, were infected as well.[16]

As Townes notes, "there is still no systematic, structural, and effective antidrug program in communities of the dispossessed in this nation."

> The colored folks are laboring under a mighty curse that is larger than HIV/AIDS. African Americans as a group receive lower levels of routine and preventive health services than other racial-ethnic groups. When poverty is added to this mix, it becomes even more lethal. Poor folks have higher rates of HIV infection than middle-class and wealthy folks. When resources are scarce, poor folks may not have the money to purchase protection. And this becomes more than simply a matter of abstinence at this point . . . a plethora of gender codes and roles and issues of self-esteem are here at work in a system of structured social inequity.[17]

---

15. Eugene, "How Can We Forget?" 265.

16. Statistics are taken from both Townes and Eugene as well as the *HIV/AIDS Surveillance Report* 9:2 (1998) and the *Journal of the American Medical Association* 277:1 (1 January 1997).

17. Townes, *Fine Rain*, 122–23.

Moreover, Evelyn Hammond notes:

> By focusing on individual behavior as the cause of AIDS and by set-
> ting up bisexuals, homosexuals, and drug users as "other" in the
> black community, and as "bad," the national black media falls into
> the trap of reproducing exactly how white society has defined the
> issue. But unlike the situation for whites, what happens to these
> groups within the black community will affect the community as a
> whole. . . . If people with AIDS are set-off as "bad" or "other"—
> no change in individual behavior in relation to them will save any
> of us. There can be no "us" or "them" in our communities.[18]

Needle Exchange Programs

EUGENE SEES THREE areas in which the church can overcome this harmful,
painful, and artificial dichotomy, by serving as caretakers, educators, and
prophets to those in need in their midst. I will use the example of a Needle
Exchange Program (NEP) as a means of addressing these roles. NEPs have
been successfully developed in several major urban areas at state and local
levels. One of the few Roman Catholic programs was instituted in 1992 by
the diocese of Rochester, New York, the result of a growing concern within the diocese at the significant rise in HIV/AIDS among heterosexuals,
especially women. Upon investigation, they found that much of the rise
was caused, not by homosexual activity, but by the sharing of needles by
intravenous drug users and by sexual activity among intravenous drug
users and their partners. For those who entered and stayed with the program of needle exchange and drug treatment/rehabilitation, the program
was successful in reducing the number of new cases of HIV/AIDS, while, at
the same time, not increasing the spread of substance abuse.

The goals of the Rochester program which enabled its success were
threefold: to change behavior that will save human lives by preventing the
spread of the HIV virus; to serve as a bridge to treatment for intravenous
drug users in the program; and to send a message to the spouses, lovers,
and children of substance abusers that their lives should not be lost because
of someone else's behavior.

The question of whether an NEP would send a mixed message about
drug use to the Catholic and wider community was addressed. The significance of the lives at stake was seen as more critically important, especially
since it was shown that substance abusers were not being encouraged and

---

18. Evelyn Hammond, "Race, Sex, AIDS: The Construction of 'Other',"
Radical America 20 (1987): 32.

that their numbers did not increase as a result of the program. The program, in other words, was not simply an exchange of clean needles for dirty ones, but rather an effort to educate and rehabilitate intravenous drug users so that their entire lifestyles would change. The belief that this was possible was supported by the success of similar programs in the US and Europe. The significance of the Rochester case, however, is that the Catholic Church took an overt, active stance with regard to HIV/AIDS in a way which helped to transform the lives of many, thus fulfilling its prophetic stance in the lives of its people.

The success of the Rochester program reveals that an NEP can work, but only if, from the outset and at every level of its development and implementation, the affected communities are actively involved. In this case, the Black and Latino communities whose needs, impacted upon by the multiplicative oppressions of race, class, and gender, had to be particularly and openly addressed.

The church, thus, served as *caretaker* in providing much needed resources to help those already infected; as *educator*, in establishing programs which taught the community about the inherent dangers of using "dirty" needles and engaging in unprotected sex; and as *prophet*, in that it was able to look beyond the disease to the persons affected by the disease and hold out the promise of breaking free from their self-destructive behaviors while giving them hope for a better future with less loss of life.

Church Teachings, Practice, and Intravenous Drug Users

TRADITIONAL CHURCH TEACHINGS on HIV/AIDS have too often addressed the issue within the context, as noted above, of homosexuality. With its dualistic emphasis on condemning the sin while caring for the sinner, the more critical perspective of prevention is often overlooked, especially among poor Blacks and Latinos. Already overwhelmed by poverty, racial prejudice, and discrimination, finding little or no support from overstretched government agencies, they turn to their church only to find that it is more interested in how they contracted the disease than in how they can be helped in their efforts to take care of themselves while not passing on the disease to others around them, especially their wives and children.

Efforts to educate Catholics, especially African American and Latino/a Catholics, about the scourge of HIV/AIDS in our midst have not been as forceful or pervasive as the church's efforts to deal with issues of economic justice or peace in our world. The need for such education is weighed against the "appearance" of condoning what is seen as a moral evil, promiscuous sexual behavior, or substance abuse. In addition, the fear of scandalizing the faithful often seems to overcome the equal, if not greater, scandal of a church turning away from its own by doing "too little, too late" that could have saved human lives, especially in the face of studies which show the viability of life-saving programs such as the NEPs. Those ill and dying with AIDS or at great risk of exposure to the disease need more than the promise of an afterlife with God; they need the very present comfort, protection, and proactive acceptance of their church and its members who are their family.

NEPs answer such a need. Yet few Catholic dioceses in the US have addressed the issue and those, when they do, usually oppose NEPs as contributing to a greater evil: the promotion of substance abuse. Yet study after study, including those of the program in the diocese of Rochester, show that the opposite is true. Persons do not become substance abusers because of the availability of clean needles. They become substance abusers because of addictive personalities, poverty, poor education, hopelessness, and despair.

Addiction to heroin or "crack" cocaine is not seen as an acceptable medical need despite the fact that such addictions prevent a significant proportion of the Black and Latino/a population as well as whites from attaining meaningful employment, maintaining family commitments, and living decent lives. Few questions are raised regarding the causes behind substance abuse as most programs simply emphasize self-control for a group suffering from an illness whose manifestation is lack of control over their lives and their actions. Like gay men, the abuser is seen as a volunteer in his/her own addiction and subsequent illness.

The Rochester program clearly shows that access to such programs enables intravenous drug users to work toward overcoming their addiction, while those without access to such programs revert to substance abuse. Objections to NEPs and to the provision of bleach to clean needles reflect an attitude which, as previously noted, sees substance abusers as solely responsible for the spread of HIV/AIDS rather than seeing the AIDS virus itself as culpable.

At the same time, this does not mean that the church should not be advocating sexual abstinence and the avoidance of drugs. That message should be at the heart of any church-related program. It does, however, require the church to recognize an already existing reality: the growing population—not only in our inner cities but increasingly in rural and smaller urban areas—of persons who are already infected with HIV who will, indisputably, infect others with whom they share needles if they do not have access to clean needles:

> Placing the ethical responsibility for AIDS squarely on the shoulders of those who are likely to contract it certainly has distinct advantages. Blame is assigned; the effect of enormous suffering

usually issues from culpable conduct; and the virtue which keeps the healthy well is in sharp contrast to the vice which yields the terrible affliction. . . . Whether the person afflicted by AIDS contracted the syndrome through irresponsible conduct or the curse of fate, the AIDS patient remains a person who is the bearer of rights. As such she/he makes claims on other persons, and those who are well should not justify turning their backs on those who are ill.[19]

Who, if not the church, will speak for them and prevent their further decimation not only as individuals but as members of a living community? Jesus and his followers gathered grain on the Sabbath, an act for which they were chastised by the Pharisees and for which, under Mosaic law, they could have been condemned to death (Ex. 31:15). Yet Jesus replied that the action was necessary in order to prevent hunger, saying "And if you had known what this means, 'I desire mercy, and not sacrifice,' you would not have condemned the guiltless" (Mt. 12:1–7). A NEP coupled with access to treatment programs and to culturally sensitive education which addresses the underlying reasons and causes of substance abuse can only have a significant, positive effect on this population. As church, we should be engaging in acts of mercy, not requiring the sacrifice of those least able to fend for themselves.

We are all moral beings, created in the image and likeness of God. We all, ostensibly, have the freedom to choose lives of good or evil. We can place the ethical responsibility for AIDS on those most likely to contract it, but least able to receive the necessary medical care and treatment because of their societal status, and thereby free ourselves from complicity. But is that really the case? For many in our society today, that freedom has been restricted by factors that are not of the person's choosing. A person's freedom becomes apparent in the act of choosing from among several viable alternatives. Are these alternatives truly available to substance abusers, their sexual partners, and their children? HIV/AIDS exploits contemporary societal weaknesses and proceeds along the fault-lines of inequity and discrimination: belonging to any marginalized or stigmatized social group creates an increased risk of receiving inadequate care and support. Therefore, to approach the individual as if her or his behavior were independent of economics, culture, and politics, as independent of human rights and dignity, would be to deny the reality that we know.

Unequal access to care, to education, to employment and to a future with dignity makes societies more not less vulnerable to HIV/AIDS. Once

---

19. Eileen P. Flynn, *AIDS: A Catholic Call for Compassion* (Kansas City: Sheed and Ward, 1985), 3.

we have understood that AIDS exploits the fundamental weaknesses in society—inequity and discrimination—is it not essential for us to confront those issues, as deeply rooted and difficult as they are? In addition to our education-based prevention, we need to identify and join with others to change the critical features of the social environment in our communities and in this country which fuel the spread of HIV/AIDS.

In the last analysis, is this not our mandate from God: to establish justice and care for the widowed and orphaned, those who are the "least among us"? The issue is not, then, merely how successful the NEPs are in terms of large or small numbers. The issue is how many lives are we willing to forfeit in order to maintain a rigid act-centered moral stance which does not allow for the fallible nature of fallen humankind? Surely every life saved leads to many lives saved, for that one substance abuser has a circle of contacts within which he or she interacts. Jesus left the ninety-nine to seek out one lost sheep (Mt. 18:12–14). Can the church do any less?

3.
REVEALING AND CRITIQUING INEQUITIES

CONDOMS, COUPS, AND THE IDEOLOGY OF PREVENTION: FACING FAILURE IN RURAL HAITI

Paul Farmer, M.D., and David Walton

IN THE CITY of Jérémie, at the far end of Haiti's southern peninsula, one can sit in the town's main square and see two opposed images. Both, curiously enough, soar into the sky. One is the town's cathedral, built in a previous century. The other, on a billboard directly across from Our Lady's sorrowful gaze, is a giant condom.

This first level of complexity—the facile opposition of church and condom—has been much commented upon. But this opposition masks far deeper contradictions. The billboard condom is, as modern condoms so often are, animated: standing erect on a tranquil beach, the condom sports sunglasses and a cellphone. In the background, a couple hold hands. Her hair is silky and falls over her shoulders in a manner distinctly unusual in southern Haiti; he is robust and fit. The central message is in English: "Panther Condoms: It's cool!" The impression conveyed is hip, urban, transnational, and worshipful of the accouterments of modern life.

The cathedral, on the other hand, is dilapidated. No longer erect, the brick structure is sliding into the soft earth of Jérémie's central square. Inside, the message is one of sorrow, pity, and recourse to a deeper courage. "I have suffered," reads the writing over Our Lady's gently inclined head. "But I am strong." There are no cellular phones.

The billboard, we learn, is the product of PSI, a social-marketing firm based in Washington. It is part of a project funded by the United States Agency for International Development (USAID). The cathedral is the parish seat of Bishop Willy Romélus, who stood firm in a different manner: during the coup d'état against Haiti's first democratically elected government—a government led by another son of the church, Jean-Bertrand Aristide—Romélus was alone among the church hierarchy to speak out

*against the military regime that controlled Haiti from 1991 to 1994.
Romélus's "preferential option for the poor" brought him what it brought
Aristide: death threats and harassment (Romélus, frail and elderly, was
once beaten by thugs in front of the cathedral after a mass on behalf of
thousands of Haitians lost at sea). Like many Haitians, Romélus regards
this coup as having been supported, at least initially, by certain representatives of U.S. officialdom, including some within USAID; the historical
record supports this assertion.[1]*

*The church-condom complexities run deeper still. As Penny Lernoux
pointed out in her magisterial work, The People of God, progressive forces
in the church in Latin America are, like Romélus and Aristide, concerned
largely with social and economic rights for the poor; progressive forces in
the church in affluent countries have been more concerned with individual
liberties and with sexual freedoms of one sort or another.[2] The opposition
of the Haitian church to condoms has been, to coin a phrase, under-
whelming. Concerned with repression against the poor, local clergy and
religious have had little to say against condoms. The battle, it is felt, is
being played out on a different field.*

This essay will attempt to bring into relief the large-scale forces structuring
HIV risks for the poor—and poor women in particular—in Haiti's central
plateau. In attempting to identify the distal and the proximal forces that
promote the transmission of HIV in rural Haiti, we seek to cast doubts on
the "ideologies of prevention" that drive much AIDS work. We will also
lay bare our own HIV/AIDS-prevention failures.

Our stance on condoms may be summarized as follows: *of course* barrier methods are critical to HIV/AIDS prevention in a setting such as Haiti.
But while the distal interventions so ardently desired by those who erect
billboards in public spaces are important, we will argue that more proximal interventions are critical too. We conclude that the promotion of social
and economic rights for the poor—central to the magisterium of the
church, in the view of these two Catholic physician-writers—is the key
missing ingredient in the struggle against a pathogen that makes its own
preferential option for the poor.[3]

---

1. The case for U.S. complicity in the coup d'état of 1991 is outlined in Paul
Farmer, *The Uses of Haiti* (Monroe, Maine: Common Courage, 1994).

2. Penny Lernoux, *People of God* (New York: Viking Press, 1989).

3. This topic is explored in Paul Farmer, "Medicine and Social Justice: Insights
from Liberation Theology," *America* 173 (1995): 14.

Haiti's Health

PUBLIC HEALTH EXPERTS and physicians can agree that Haiti's population suffers from poor health. For the past few decades, Haiti has had the worst public health indices of the hemisphere: an infant mortality rate between 80 and 160 (depending on the study), a maternal mortality rate of up to 1,400 deaths per 100,000 live births, and a life expectancy at birth of forty-eight to fifty-six years. Gastroenteritis is the leading cause of infant and juvenile mortality, with measles and neonatal tetanus not far behind. Most Haitian children are malnourished, and it is these children, by and large, who fall ill with terminal infections. Adults, too, are vulnerable to infectious complications of undernutrition. If we are to believe autopsy series of both urban and rural Haiti, tuberculosis has long been the leading killer of Haitians between twenty and fifty years of age. In recent years, as the case is in many parts of the Third World, tuberculosis has been upstaged—in urban Haiti, at least—by death from AIDS.[4]

The excess mortality reflects Haiti's extreme poverty. Income is about $300 per year, a catastrophic figure in an agrarian country marked by landlessness, ecological degradation, inflation, and a growing reliance on food imports. When in 1991 international health and population experts devised a "human suffering index" by examining several measures of human welfare ranging from life expectancy to political freedom, 27 of 141 countries were characterized by "extreme human suffering." Only one of them, Haiti, was in the Western hemisphere. In only three countries on earth was suffering judged to be more extreme than endured in Haiti; each of these countries was in the midst of a recognized civil war.

Living in Haiti is such a difficult proposition that some, following the example of Latin American bishops, have been led to write of its "structural violence." Sickness here may be thought of as a result of structural violence, because it is not nature, geography, or pure individual will that is at fault, but rather historically given (and, often, economically driven) processes and forces that conspire to constrain individual agency. Structural violence is visited upon all those whose social status puts them at heightened risk of disease. At the same time, it denies them access to the fruits of scientific and social advances. The poor bear, of course, the brunt of that violence, just as they bear the garden-variety political violence of more recent vintage.

These, then, are the numbers; these are the forces, large-scale and local, arrayed against those who would work to improve the status of the Haitian poor, the majority.

---

4. These data are reviewed in Paul Farmer, *AIDS and Accusation: Haiti and the Geography of Blame* (Berkeley: University of California Press, 1992).

AIDS in Haiti: The Last Straw

THE HISTORY OF the Haitian AIDS epidemic reveals a great deal about the dynamics of HIV transmission. Prior to 1979, when a Port-au-Prince dermatologist diagnosed Kaposi's sarcoma in a young woman, AIDS was not known to exist on the island. In the first years of the epidemic, the majority of Haitian cases were clustered in Port-au-Prince, the capital city. Most of the early patients were men, a number of whom reported sexual contact with North American tourists. Risk factors for AIDS in these years— 1982 to 1984—strongly resembled those noted by the U.S. Centers for Disease Control in regards to patients in the United States. In fact, it would be safe to qualify these years as representing the "American" phase of the Haitian epidemic.

Some of the sexual exchanges between the Haitians and North Americans involved financial transactions. Indeed, the role of economic inequalities in promoting HIV transmission was obvious, if unacknowledged, from the outset. As the virus was introduced into local networks of sexually active young adults, heterosexual transmission rapidly became the rule. Poverty and gender inequality became the motor forces of the Haitian epidemic. By 1987 some surveys of asymptomatic adults living in slums revealed that up to 10 percent of the urban poor were infected with HIV.[5]

Although AIDS became widespread in urban Haiti during the early eighties, the disease was then virtually unknown in rural areas, where the majority of Haitians live. The public health challenge was to prevent HIV/AIDS from becoming a leading cause of death among rural adults. But this challenge was posed at the same time that political turmoil led to the paralysis of an already weak public health sector. During the last four years of the eighties, Haiti knew more than half a dozen governments, none of them elected and, consequently, none of them particularly interested in public health. Unimpeded, HIV continued to spread.

Although the moment had been lost in much of Haiti, more remote areas remained low-prevalence zones well into the nineties. AIDS was diagnosed in clinics throughout the country, but cases registered in rural Haiti tended to be young people who had lived in the city, and were returning to their home villages because they were sick. This, at least, was the pattern in the central plateau, where we have worked since 1983.

Haiti's central plateau is home to several hundred thousand people. Although all of Haiti is poor, the Péligre basin may be especially so: in

---

5. For an overview of HIV's first decade in Haiti, see Jean Pape and Warren Johnson, "AIDS in Haiti: 1982–1992," *Clinical Infectious Diseases* 17 (1993): S341-45.

1956, thousands of families in this region were flooded out by a large hydroelectric dam. The displaced persons were all peasant farmers, and they received little or no compensation for their land. The hilltop village of Do Kay was founded by refugees from the rising water. Initially a dusty squatter settlement of less than 200 persons, Do Kay has grown rapidly in the past decade and now counts about 2,500 inhabitants. In spite of the hostile conditions—Do Kay is stony and steep—most families continue to rely to some extent on agricultural efforts. Many more are involved in a series of development projects designed to improve the health status of the area's inhabitants.

Most of these services are provided where we work at the Clinique Bon Sauveur, a medical facility receiving over 30,000 visits per year. A complementary health-surveillance project is conducted in large part by the village-based community health workers from over thirty nearby communities and provides preventive and primary care to more than 50,000 people.

Over the past decade, we have diagnosed scores of cases of HIV disease among people coming to the clinic with a broad range of complaints. With surprisingly few exceptions, those so diagnosed shared a number of risk factors. Risk for many of our patients lies not with the number of sexual partners, but rather with the degree of social inequality between partners. Many women with HIV infection had histories of sexual contact with soldiers or truck drivers; extended residence in Port-au-Prince and work as a servant were also strongly associated with a diagnosis of HIV infection. We came to conclude that sexual unions with nonpeasants—salaried soldiers and truck drivers who are paid on a daily basis—reflect these women's quest for some measure of economic security. In this manner, truck-drivers and soldiers have served as a bridge to the rural population, just as North American tourists seemed to have served as a bridge to the urban Haitian population.

In other words, research in rural Haiti suggested that poverty and inequality serve as the most virulent co-factors in the spread of HIV.[6] It is possible to identify several factors enhancing rates of HIV transmission among rural Haitians:

- *Gender inequality, especially concerning control of land and other resources;*
- *Emerging patterns of sexual union, such as the serial monogamy described by most of our patients;*
- *Lack of timely response by public health authorities, a delay related not merely to lack of resources but the persistence of a political crisis;*

---

6. This thesis is explored in Paul Farmer, *Infections and Inequalities: The Modern Plagues* (Berkeley: University of California Press, 1999).

- *Social upheaval and political violence, much of it state-sponsored and directed at the poor;*
- *High prevalence of other genital-tract infections and, perhaps more significantly, lack of access to treatment for them;*
- *Traditional patterns of polygamous sexual union;*
- *Lack of culturally appropriate prevention tools.*

These were the factors and forces relevant to the lives of most of our patients. Although the reigning ideologies of prevention meant that most of these factors would not be the focus of HIV/AIDS prevention, addressing them should be central, we felt, to effective HIV prevention among the poor. But how to do this in the midst of political chaos and repression against the poor? It was not until December 1990, when the country's first free and fair elections brought to power Aristide's progressive government, that we could fully integrate HIV/AIDS-prevention efforts in order to reconcile our analysis with our actions.

Shifting the Paradigm of HIV/AIDS Prevention

THE ADVENT OF a democratic government was the moment many had long awaited. Here, it seemed, was a chance to have strategies of HIV/AIDS prevention match analyses of HIV risks. Our project, as initially conceived, was to design AIDS-specific interventions that were resonant with the larger project of democratization designed by the Haitian people and implemented in December 1990. Our goals were to restore the concept of equity to HIV/AIDS-prevention and care through a series of linked projects:

- *To create a series of culturally-appropriate educational materials and to launch a large public awareness campaign around AIDS issues, including the pathogenic role of social inequality;*
- *To train healers and health professionals—including village health workers, voodoo priests, nurses, and physicians—to better prevent, detect, and treat HIV infection;*
- *To undertake research that would bring into relief the factors promoting or retarding HIV transmission, and share these with the new public health authorities and others engaged in efforts to prevent HIV/AIDS;*
- *To improve the quality of care available for people living with both HIV disease and poverty;*
- *To make condoms widely available to those who sought them.*

Immediately after the elections, two community-based organizations, one based in North America and the other based in the central plateau, began planning an HIV/AIDS-prevention project based on these principles.

Each of these two organizations had experience in either HIV/AIDS prevention or in the delivery of comprehensive health services; we had worked together fruitfully in the past. Furthermore, both organizations were eager to undertake a project that might be replicable throughout Haiti and perhaps other poor countries as well.

In the summer of 1991, we received word that funding would be made available over the course of two years, beginning in January 1992. At the same time, a strong letter of support was received from both the Ministry of Health and the Prime Minister of Haiti: the social-justice approach to HIV/AIDS prevention received strong endorsement from the Aristide government. Our small team was euphoric. Well before the first disbursements were received, we were hard at work, designing curricula, meeting with women's groups, church and community leaders, and area health providers. Ties with local community-based organizations were forged or tightened. By late summer 1991, plans for training all levels of health-care providers were well underway. Agreements were reached with research laboratories in Port-au-Prince, and a study group was formed in order to plan a community-based research initiative. These activities were organized, in large part, by two coordinators, each representing one of the organizations involved in designing and implementing the project.

All euphoria evaporated at the close of September 1991, when a military coup unseated the Aristide government. According to most estimates, the coup led to over 8,000 deaths, the totality of them among civilians killed by military or paramilitary forces. But outright killing was merely the tip of the iceberg of increased morbidity and mortality. The coup brought immediate increases in rates of interpersonal violence ranging from rape and torture to arson. It also brought massive dislocations: hundreds of thousands of refugees fled their homes, some by sea and some by land. The number of lives lost at sea is unknown; U.S. estimates ran into the thousands.

Still other deaths ostensibly had more mundane causes—the interruption of medical services—but were nonetheless linked to social unrest. The Pan-American Health Organization and the WHO issued dire reports, suggesting that millions of Haitians were at risk of adverse health outcomes due to "environmental stresses." But can any quantitative estimates be made? Given the absence of major studies, our own experience may be instructive. We too were unable to continue communitywide surveys and have no reliable vital statistics for these years. They were marked by threats and, at one point, forced closure of the clinic (regarded by local military authorities as strongly supportive of the Aristide government). In spite of our inability to conduct research, we were able to discern three main types of effects of the coup: on programs, on morale, and on patterns of morbidity and mortality—or, at least, on the nature of presenting complaints to the clinic.

Each had an enormous impact on HIV/AIDS prevention efforts. First, the coup's direct effect on programs was dramatic. There were material problems. Paper, medications, electricity, gasoline, HIV tests—all were scarce. More significant were security problems: community organizing was forbidden; adult literacy efforts were suspect. Soon, the Haitian project director was forced out of the country by threats; the U.S. coordinator was briefly declared *persona non grata* as well. One of the chief collaborating organizations, based nearby, was forced to close. It has not since reopened. The region's leading peasant movement, which had already solicited the assistance of our team in planning a major primary-care initiative, was violently repressed. Several key leaders were killed or expelled. With brief exceptions, our clinic remained open, although there was a drop in the number of patients and an increase in the gravity of presenting complaints.

Second, there was a marked demoralization of the medical staff, with several resignations during the years of the coup. There seemed to be a paralysis among all the members of the staff, a lassitude that could not always be linked to direct constraints on activities. For example, even when it became possible to resume community-based activities, temporization was often the order of the day. Furnished with a ready supply of excuses, staff meetings were missed or canceled, research projects abandoned, and poor health outcomes shrugged off. This marked lowering of expectations endured well beyond the coup. Indeed, of all its symptoms, demoralization has proven the most persistent.

Third, there were the presumed effects of the coup on the health of the population. Our patients were sicker and had traveled greater distances to obtain care. Delays in seeking care were popularly attributed to widespread "insecurity" due to the violence of the military coup. It was during the coup that we treated our first reported rape victims, and the number of assaults increased dramatically. During the coup years, we also noted a marked increase in the percentage of patients with measles, tuberculosis, typhoid, and complications of HIV infection.[7] It would not be difficult to show that a coup d'état that dislodges hundreds of thousands of persons from a high-prevalence area and sends them fleeing to low-prevalence rural regions will have an effect on the rate of HIV transmission.

But the HIV/AIDS-prevention efforts did eventually continue, if somewhat timidly. The project's scope was much reduced geographically, but the proposed format was to a large extent followed. We took our messages to villages and towns throughout the region, developing, in the course of work, innovative teaching tools. We also trained community workers, nurses, and physicians from other nongovernmental organizations. We attempted to

7. These data are reviewed in Paul Farmer, "Haiti's Lost Years: Lessons for the Americas," *Current Issues in Public Health* 2 (1996): 143–51.

keep social and economic rights—again, the proximal factors in AIDS risk—central to our prevention efforts. One of the project's most important products was created by a group of poor women, most of whom did not read or write prior to their involvement with the project. They wanted to create a video that would, as one of the participants (herself HIV-positive) later put it, "explain how our situations have led us to fall into certain traps." In soap-opera format, the video tells the story of a young woman who, out of economic necessity, takes up with a succession of men perceived to have access to resources—the first two, truck drivers and, finally, a soldier. At the end of her trials, the woman has four children and AIDS. The story, based on the real life experiences of women from the region, is a powerful tool for raising consciousness about HIV and the threat it poses to poor women.

But efforts to use this video were often thwarted. It was an anxious moment for all involved when we were prevented by soldiers from showing the video to a large group of villagers not far from the project's home base. A group of soldiers interrupted the showing by shutting off the power and threatening the group. The video was, they said, antimilitary and subversive. And so it was.

The soldiers' aggression halted HIV/AIDS-prevention activities for months. "What have we gotten ourselves into?" asked Lilia, the film's narrator and the facilitator of the ill-fated session. "What would happen to our children if anything happened to us? Being dead from a bullet is almost as bad as being dead from AIDS. It's just that the bullet gets you quicker."

Facing Failure in Rural Haiti

ALMOST A DECADE later, we look back on this project—deemed successful by its funders and in our own reports—and ask harder questions. What are the best criteria for defining success in a setting in which structural violence ensures that the poorest each day face increased risks of HIV? How might we, as people of faith, incorporate a preferential option for the poor in our HIV/AIDS-prevention activities? How might we alter our strategies in the face of failure?

The more we have asked such hard questions of ourselves and our own work, the more we marvel at the lack of such introspection in the medical and public health literature. After all, successful HIV/AIDS prevention is rare in any setting, as a few honest assessments have noted. After ten years of effort, note the authors of a major overview, "the course of the pandemic within and through global society is not being affected—in any serious manner—by the actions taken at the national or international level."[8]

---

8. Jonathan Mann, Daniel Tarantola, and Thomas Netter, eds., *AIDS in the World* (Cambridge, Mass.: Harvard University Press, 1992), 1.

But the dominant ideology of prevention—that holds that education and condom promotion are the answer—has not yet been subjected to critical appraisal. We would argue that, as important as such AIDS-focused activities such as condom promotion might be, they largely attack the symptoms of a deeper malaise. Such distal interventions must be linked to efforts to empower women living in poverty. The much abused term "empower" is not here meant vaguely; it is not a matter of self-esteem or even parliamentary representation. Those choosing to make common cause with poor women must seek to give them control of their own lives. Control of lives is related to the control of land, systems of production, and the formal political and legal structures in which lives are enmeshed. In each of these arenas, poor people are already laboring at a vast disadvantage; poor women's voices are almost unheard.

What have been the chief health-related outcomes of our own HIV/AIDS-prevention efforts? Certainly, the prevalence of condom use increased—condom promotion was controversial to neither the army nor the church hierarchy. The level of community dialogue about AIDS was enhanced. The number of adolescents receiving formal sexual education went up from nil to thousands. Rural Haiti's first culturally appropriate prevention tools were developed. A coalition of nongovernmental organizations in the central plateau was formed in order to prevent HIV/AIDS. The project was eventually replicated in Port-au-Prince, using the tools and approaches developed in rural Haiti. Finally, the project is still functioning years after its inception.

But can this project be termed a success? Can we prove that new cases of HIV infection have been averted by our efforts? Are measures of condom prevalence a better gauge of success than a reduction of structural violence? In short, the answer to these questions is no. We cannot document decreased rates of HIV transmission in rural Haiti. We can, however, point to our efforts—thwarted by a military coup—to promote the social and economic rights of those we sought to serve.

Other questions follow: Are physicians and nurses and community-health workers responsible for the more equitable distribution of land and power? For many health care professionals, the answer to this question is also no. These tasks do not fall under the purview of medicine and public health. But those working within the institutions of the church and those adopting a faith-based approach to HIV/AIDS prevention have to answer to a more stringent mandate.

Our failure serves as a reminder of the significance, to health outcomes, of forces beyond the control of medicine and public health as traditionally conceived. But can the efforts of those committed to public health slow the advance of an epidemic whose chief co-factors seem to be poverty and inequality? It is imperative that HIV/AIDS prevention be linked to efforts to diminish the poverty and inequality that serve as the most virulent co-factors for this epidemic. This means offering "pragmatic solidarity" to women's groups, which in turn means putting resources directly into the hands of poor women. This means protecting certain adolescents from the risky situations to which they are heir even before emerging as fully sexual beings. This means innovations in methods to protect sexually active persons from HIV (for example, woman-controlled protection instead of methods that depend on male approbation). Pragmatic solidarity means, in the final analysis, more just distribution of the resources that might be marshaled to fight HIV/AIDS. It means addressing structural violence.

Conclusions: Good News and Bad in HIV/AIDS Prevention

OUR EXPERIENCE CALLS for a certain humility, at least among public health and medical personnel. Throughout the world, AIDS offers the same humbling rebuke to those who have relied overmuch on conventional approaches to preventing HIV transmission among the poor. This collective failure to respond to one of the great health challenges of our times is not due merely to bureaucratic sloth or, in settings such as Haiti, the ill will of the powerful. Increasingly, AIDS is a symptom of poverty and inequality, and local efforts to address AIDS need to be linked to large-scale efforts to address the forces that promote the transmission of HIV. Looking back over a decade's experience in rural Haiti, where structural violence has hampered our best efforts to prevent HIV transmission, we discern three central lessons:

If poverty and gender inequality conspire to increase HIV risks for poor women, then the promotion of social and economic rights must be central to HIV/AIDS prevention. The press for fulfillment of these rights falls squarely within the magisterium of the church, which has to date failed to incorporate social-justice perspectives into its HIV/AIDS-prevention activities—such as they are. Just as the Haitian bishops have by and large failed to underline the connections between social inequality and HIV transmission, so too have they failed, with notable exceptions, to back the Haitian popular movement. Yet support for this movement—and for the social and economic rights that are its centerpiece—remains strong within the base communities of the church. There is thus reason to hope that support for a social-justice approach to HIV/AIDS prevention will find its leading protagonists within the church.

Condoms are necessary but inadequate. To push the metaphor, it is a mistake to put all of our eggs in the condom basket; condoms are not, in general, a woman-controlled prevention strategy, and will be ineffective wherever poor women's agency is constrained. Given the limitations of the technology, the impotence of the Catholic hierarchy to alter popular views on condoms—and on most matters pertaining to sexuality—is of limited significance. There was, as noted, a striking lack of objections to our HIV/AIDS-prevention materials, which featured condoms prominently and were used in parishes throughout central Haiti and beyond. Our own experience revealed the debate over condoms to be, in Haiti, a minor skirmish in the battle for a world in which structural violence no longer guarantees that some are slated for increased AIDS risks, while others are shielded from harm. In the midst of political violence, the debate over condoms was not so much a false quarrel—other chapters in this volume reveal just how central the condom question can be—as a secondary concern for those whose lives are so vulnerable to structural violence.

Faith-based responses must be technically correct and based on sound analyses. One of the obligations of accepting a faith-based mandate to serve is the obligation of speaking truth to power. As far as AIDS goes, this often means questioning the "immodest claims of causality" currently advanced to explain the failure of HIV/AIDS prevention among the poor. The default explanations have been the usual ones: the "noncompliance" of the poor, their cultural particularities, their cognitive deficits. Each of these essentialist explanatory gambits locates the problem squarely within the poor: the problem lies with the poor, so HIV/AIDS-prevention efforts should change them rather than their circumstances.

This exaggeration of agency has favored the emergence of HIV/AIDS-prevention projects built upon facile notions of education, "empowerment," and "self esteem."[9] But claims that we can alter HIV risks by altering the inner psychological states or cognitive skills of women living in abject poverty have not been buttressed by data. These claims reflect to a large extent ideologies of prevention. In fact, there is evidence to support a quite different hypothesis: the effects of such interventions will be negligible precisely where HIV/AIDS prevention is most needed. We need to ask what might be the likely yield of bringing to an end any official church tolerance of discrimination, any official condemnation of condoms. In Haiti, at least, the task before us is far more daunting: to ground our HIV/AIDS-prevention efforts in the broader struggle for social and economic rights for the poor.

The bad news, then, is that poverty and steep grades of social inequality—rather than patient ignorance or refractory church officials— are the motor forces behind high rates of HIV transmission. The good news might be that we had a mandate to work against such injustices long before HIV arrived to further complicate our task.

---

9. See Paul Farmer, Margaret Connors, and Janie Simmons, eds., *Women, Poverty, and AIDS: Sex, Drugs, and Structural Violence* (Monroe, Maine: Common Courage Press, 1996).

Preventing HIV Transmission to Neonates in the United States[1]

Maura A. Ryan

ANONYMOUS, ROUTINE TESTING *of newborns for antibodies to HIV has been in practice in New York state for more than a decade. In 1996, New York hospitals began disclosing test results to those mothers who agreed to be notified. But on 1 February 1997, New York became the first state in the U.S. to require hospitals to notify mothers when their newborns test HIV antibody-positive. While a positive test result always indicates that the mother is infected, only a third of U.S. newborns exposed to HIV in utero become infected. In the first three months of the program, 33 women out of the 57,000 who delivered in that period learned that they were HIV positive through mandatory disclosure. Twenty-nine lived in New York City. Public health officials say they hope that doctors will also notify mothers when their infants test negative.*

Critics of the policy cite concerns for confidentiality, difficulties in locating mothers after they have left the hospital, inadequate counseling and follow-up care. The director of one social service agency for HIV-infected women in East Harlem complained that mothers are just told that they are HIV positive and given a list of programs to contact. But some of the most vocal critics argue that mandatory disclosure simply does not go far enough in reducing the incidence of maternal-to-child transmission of HIV. Pointing to studies showing that the administration of AZT during pregnancy, labor, and delivery and then to exposed infants for six weeks after birth dramatically reduces the likelihood of perinatal infection—from 23 percent without AZT to 8 percent with it—they argue that public health emphasis should be on prenatal testing. As one New York hospital physician put it, "If you're going to mandate that all women be tested without their permission, then at least do it when you can make a difference. Postpartum is too late."[2]

---

1. The author wishes to thank James Ball for his assistance in research and the editors of this volume for helpful comments on an earlier draft.

2. Deborah Sontag, "H.I.V. Testing for Newborns Debated Anew," *New York Times,* 2 February 1997; Lynda Richardson, "Mandatory H.I.V. Testing for Newborns Draws Complaints," *New York Times,* 16 June 1997; Center for Disease Control, "Public Health Service Task Force Recommendations for the Use of Antiretroviral Drugs in Pregnant Women Infected with HIV-1 for Maternal Health and Reducing Perinatal HIV-1 Transmission in the United States," 30 January 1998.

In their 1989 statement, "Called to Compassion and Responsibility: A Response to the HIV/AIDS Crisis," the United States Catholic bishops argued that "with respect to HIV/AIDS, it is important to infringe as little as possible, in light of community needs, on individual liberty, privacy, and confidentiality." While allowing for exceptions, the bishops found no justification at that time for universal or mandatory testing policies.[3]

Mandatory testing for HIV has been hotly debated since the onset of the AIDS epidemic in the United States. Supporters argue that the devastating personal and social costs of AIDS warrant the adoption of whatever public health measures are necessary to encourage early diagnosis and intervention, and to prevent further transmission of HIV. Since universal, mandatory screening programs have proven effective in addressing other less urgent public health concerns (e.g., phenylketonuria in newborns), surely we should embrace them in the case of AIDS. Indeed, for some supporters, any measure short of mandatory testing for HIV is foolish and unethical: "To have a national or international policy that enables people at risk of being infected with HIV voluntarily to choose not to know whether they carry HIV, a fatal, sexually transmitted disease, is a perversion of human rights and a formula for HIV disaster."[4]

During much of the first decade of the epidemic, however, AIDS activists and public health officials successfully defeated most mandatory testing proposals.[5] Pointing to widespread discrimination against HIV-infected individuals and the risk of driving patients away from treatment, the leading voices in AIDS prevention argued for education and counseling of at-risk populations over universal or mandatory testing. As a result, many states adopted legislation reflecting the "least infringement" philosophy of the bishops' statement—requiring voluntary, informed consent for HIV testing and ensuring strict confidentiality of test results.

As James Childress observes, even liberal societies, which place high value on the protection of individual rights, sometimes protect public health through such measures as compulsory screening and testing, quarantine and isolation, and contact tracing. The difficult question for such a society is, "When does the public health justify overriding [personal] rights

---

3. National Conference of Catholic Bishops, "Called to Compassion and Responsibility: A Response to the HIV/AIDS Crisis," *Origins* 19/26 (30 November 1989): 430.

4. Robert T. Jensen, "HIV Testing of Pregnant Women and Newborns," *Journal of the American Medical Association* 265 (1991): 1525 (letter to the editor).

5. Some mandatory HIV-testing programs have been initiated, e.g., for immigrants; inductees into the armed forces; blood, organ, sperm, and egg donors; and incarcerated prisoners.

and liberties?"[6] In the United States, it is now taken for granted that competent patients have the right to make health care decisions in accordance with their own needs and interests. Health care professionals are obliged to enable free and informed decision-making, refrain from imposing unwanted testing and treatment, and protect confidentiality.

Policies which involve significant infringements on individual autonomy, such as mandatory testing policies, are generally defensible only under the following conditions: such measures are likely to be effective in preventing the transmission of disease or ameliorating its effects; the anticipated social or medical benefits clearly outweigh the harms, costs, and burdens to be imposed; there exists no morally preferable alternative for achieving the ends in question; only those infringements on individual liberty that are truly necessary for realizing those ends are permitted; and policies are clearly communicated to those who are most affected.[7]

For over ten years, opponents have argued persuasively that mandatory testing for HIV is unjust, ineffective, and unnecessary. No one has doubted the serious public health threat posed by AIDS nor the importance of identifying those at risk of transmitting or contracting the HIV virus. But critics have dismissed mandatory testing as a "knee-jerk" response which fails to give sufficient weight to the particular vulnerability of AIDS patients and maximizes the risks of disclosure for a population already socially marginalized. As a sexually transmitted disease, appearing first in the U.S. among homosexual men and intravenous drug users, AIDS quickly became in public consciousness a disease of "social deviance" as well as "sexual deviance." In that context, a positive HIV test is not only an indication of exposure to a contagious, fatal disease but also a stigma, further exposing individuals to lost employment and insurance benefits, marginalization within their families and the wider community, and discrimination even in the delivery of health care.

For HIV-positive pregnant women, most of whom are poor women of color, discrimination has included the loss of social and medical services, the erosion of personal and family relationships, loss of control over medical decision-making, and even the loss of their children.[8] AIDS advocates have insisted that the serious harms to individuals of forced disclosure

---

6. James F. Childress, "Mandatory HIV Screening and Testing," in *Contemporary Issues in Bioethics*, 4th edition, Tom L. Beauchamp and Leroy Walters, eds. (Belmont, Calif.: Wadsworth, 1994), 557–73, 557.

7. Ibid., 557–73.

8. Working Group on HIV Testing of Pregnant Women and Newborns, "HIV Infection, Pregnant Women and Newborns: A Policy Proposal for Information and Testing," *Journal of the American Medical Association* 264 (1990): 2416–20.

require proof that mandatory testing will yield equally compelling and obvious benefits.

Until fairly recently, the difficulty of definitively diagnosing HIV and the lack of effective therapeutic options for those exposed to the virus weakened the case for the benefits of mandatory testing. Where widespread compulsory screening programs were adopted (in states such as Illinois and Louisiana that passed mandatory premarital screening statutes) they quickly proved cost-ineffective and were abandoned. Since HIV infection is not widespread outside of groups engaging in high-risk activities, screening in groups or areas with a low prevalence of HIV positivity produces a high rate of false positives. Moreover, as the Illinois premarital screening program showed, many of those who are identified as HIV positive through universal screening would have been identified more efficiently through voluntary programs aimed at high-risk populations.[9] In circumstances where information regarding seropositivity would not alter public health practices—universal precautions and safe sex practices would be recommended whether or not one knew a partner's or patient's HIV status—identification and disclosure of HIV status does not directly translate into benefits for others.[10]

Even in target or high-risk populations, critics have argued that mandatory testing has no clear or independent prophylactic benefit and is ultimately counterproductive in reducing rates of HIV transmission. Mandatory testing programs for pregnant women and newborns are a case in point. The rising rate of HIV in women has repeatedly generated public interest in prenatal and neonatal screening programs similar to those aimed at the prevention of phenylketonuria (PKU) and sickle cell anemia. But unlike PKU, HIV infection is difficult to diagnose at birth. Even the best screening test available, the polymerase chain-reaction test, is not accurate until six to eight weeks, and not 100 percent accurate until closer to three months. Therefore, mandatory newborn screening exposes a certain number of infants to the risks of unnecessary treatment, as well as to the risks of abandonment, difficulty in adoption or foster care placement, and discrimination in access to day care.

Also unlike PKU, there has been no safe and effective therapy for AIDS, and unlike other conditions for which prenatal screening is routine, such as Rh factor, no effective intervention. Thus, abortion was long the only certain way to prevent the birth of an HIV infected newborn and discouraging future pregnancies the only way to slow mother-to-child transmission rates. At the same time, the threat of mandatory testing risks discouraging early

9. Childress, 564.
10. Ibid., 562.

detection and driving women from the clinical relationships which are most beneficial to their infant's health and most likely to foster the long-range changes in behavior important in preventing HIV transmission—adoption of "safe sex practices" or abstinence. Thus, critics have argued, more babies are likely to be lost to lack of prenatal care as a result of mandatory testing programs than to be helped by early detection of HIV.

In addition, there has been little evidence that mandatory testing programs are any more successful than voluntary programs at identifying infected individuals and reducing the number of new cases. A study of prenatal testing at Harlem Hospital, for example, showed that 90 percent of women who were counseled about HIV risks voluntarily accepted testing. Preliminary analysis of New York's program of voluntary notification showed that the overwhelming majority of women whose babies were tested agreed to receive test results (over 93 percent) and that most already knew their HIV status.[11]

But improved clinical options for those exposed to HIV are challenging the long consensus against mandatory testing, particularly prenatal testing. The 1994 study,[12] showing that giving AZT to HIV-positive women before and during childbirth and then to their newborns after birth, could decrease the chances of newborns becoming infected with HIV by some 67 percent, has forced a reassessment of the benefits versus burdens of mandatory testing.

If it is possible, not simply to ameliorate the effects of HIV infection by early diagnosis and intervention, but to *prevent* transmission by early diagnosis and intervention, should the freedom of pregnant women to choose not to know their HIV status continue to be protected? Many one-time supporters of voluntary testing are no longer convinced. Reversing its earlier position, the house of delegates of the American Medical Association passed a resolution in June of 1996 recommending mandatory testing of pregnant women. In May of that same year, U.S. Congress gave states a directive: reduce the rate of mother-to-child transmission by 50 percent through voluntary testing or enact mandatory HIV testing for pregnant women or newborns. States unable to show significant reductions in the incidence of HIV in newborns will lose federal AIDS emergency funding.

The ethical (and legal) question raised by mandatory prenatal testing is whether the harms to be prevented are serious enough, and the chances of preventing them good enough, to justify infringements on pregnant

---

11. Sontag, B 8.

12. Edward M. Connor, Rhodha S. Sperling, Richard Gelber, Pavel Kiselev, Gwendolyn Scott, et al., "Reduction of Maternal-Infant Transmission of Human Immunodeficiency Virus Type 1 with Zidovudine Treatment," *New England Journal of Medicine* 331 (1994): 1173–80.

women's liberty and threats to their well-being. But how might we think about prenatal testing *theologically*? Are there resources in the Catholic moral tradition for discerning the rights and responsibilities of those infected with HIV, for weighing the obligation to prevent HIV transmission to neonates against duties to HIV-infected women?

Three principles in Roman Catholic social teaching are helpful in an analysis of mandatory prenatal testing for HIV: the *priority of the common good, the preferential option for the poor,* and *subsidiarity.*

In "Called to Compassion and Responsibility," the U.S. bishops place the question of HIV prevention within the context of the common good. The Catholic social tradition presupposes that social institutions exist to serve the essential dignity of each human being, a dignity which can be realized and protected only in solidarity with others. What is required of individuals, of institutions, or of the social order is specified by the concrete, shared needs and potentialities of persons as they seek to achieve fully human participation in society. In order for the common good to be realized, individual liberty must be respected at the same time as individuals are held accountable to their responsibilities for the common life—for social conditions under which all have access to the means for human fulfillment. The common good is not achieved at the expense of personal liberty; rather, it becomes possible precisely when personal rights and duties are maintained.[13]

Two objectives, therefore, should frame our evaluation of just public policy: "first, preserving and protecting human dignity while guaranteeing the rights of all; second, caring for all who need help and cannot help themselves."[14] In addition, the preferential option for the poor requires that social arrangements and decisions be judged in light of their impact on those persons or groups who are most marginalized within the existing order.

Several things follow for assessing the place of mandatory testing programs in the prevention of HIV in neonates. First, the goal of preventing the transmission of HIV cannot be pursued apart from or at the expense of providing for the medical, emotional, and social needs of HIV-infected women. Even if they meet the goals of prevention, policies which pit the interests of women against the interests of their children, or which fail to attend to the health and well-being of babies as dependent upon the health of families, ultimately fail to serve the common good.

It is important, therefore, to take into account the long-term impact of intervention strategies on women's health—to take seriously concerns that

---

13. Pope John XXIII, *Pacem in Terris* (1963), no. 79.

14. NCCB, "Called to Compassion and Responsibility: A Response to the HIV/AIDS Crisis," 430.

AZT use in pregnancy may reduce the later effectiveness of new treatments for AIDS in women as well as concerns about the unknown side effects of AZT use in newborns.[15] It is also important to look at the social context in which a policy for mandatory testing would be implemented: Who are the women likely to be affected? What support is available to them? Do they have access to basic medical care and treatment in case of infection regardless of ability to pay, adequate food and housing, and help in keeping their families together? What provisions are in place for the protection of confidentiality and for counseling and follow-up care? Precisely because mothers and infants are *in relation*, policies will not serve the dignity and genuine well-being of neonates which expose HIV-infected mothers to social or institutional discrimination or which advance the rights of children without regard for the social conditions that are necessary for the good care of children.

It also follows that framing and implementing public policy for HIV prevention requires the *"balancing* of individual and community rights and interests."[16] This implies that the goals of HIV prevention cannot be pursued at the cost of pregnant women's human and civil rights, however much the needs of the common good might demand sacrifices of individuals. At a minimum, then, prevention efforts should not be incompatible with continuing efforts to secure equitable access to employment, housing, social services, and medical care for persons with HIV/AIDS. Neither should efforts to prevent transmission of the virus to newborns become new occasions for marginalizing infected persons or for deflecting attention, by "blaming the victim," from the social factors—poverty, drug abuse, and the economic and social dependency of women—that play a role in the rise of HIV infection in women.

In the context of medical care, to balance individual and social interests means that public health policies should override individual authority only where social responsibility truly requires it and that rights to bodily integrity, meaningful participation in the decisions affecting one's life, privacy, and due care continue to be moral priorities even where individual autonomy is constrained for the sake of the common good. The further question for mandatory prenatal testing programs, then, is not only whether interests in preventing transmission of HIV to neonates truly require overriding pregnant women's authority, but whether such policies

---

15. A recent French study reporting the deaths of two infants following prenatal AZT therapy raises serious questions in this regard, although, obviously, more data are needed. See "Babies Deaths Raise Fear Over AIDS Therapy," *New York Times*, 3 February 1999, 1.

16. NCCB, "Called to Compassion and Responsibility." Emphasis added.

can be developed and implemented in a way that continues to honor bodily integrity, the right to participate in decisions affecting one's own life, privacy, confidentiality, and due care.

Placing HIV prevention within the context of the common good also means that rights imply responsibilities. Because human society is intrinsically interdependent, rights are "mutual accountabilities"; we cannot claim for ourselves a right we are not willing to protect for all persons, nor defend our liberty without responsibility for what our freedom creates. Thus, the bishops argue, "if HIV-infected persons have rights which others must respect, they also must fulfill their fundamental responsibility to avoid doing harm to others."[17] The risk of transmitting HIV in utero or through breast feeding (at 30 percent) is not certain, but it is real. The possibility of averting infection through AZT is not guaranteed nor risk-free, but it is significant. It is fair to argue that pregnant women who believe they may be infected with HIV have an obligation to be tested and to use the resources available and morally acceptable to them to avoid knowingly transmitting HIV to their newborns. It is also fair to argue that the state has an obligation to act to protect the welfare of those at risk of harm who are unable to protect themselves. But the important issue for public policy remains how to most appropriately encourage and enable responsible reproductive behavior on the part of women infected with HIV.

A final principle from the Catholic social tradition is helpful here. *Subsidiarity* holds that "it is gravely wrong to take from individuals what they can accomplish by their own initiative and industry and give it to the community."[18] The care of children belongs properly to the family, not to the state, just as the teaching of faith belongs to the churches, and the establishment of professional standards to professional associations. Responsible government supports rather than absorbs the functions of various social agents, creating and sustaining conditions for the responsible exercise of their own capacities.

Using the principle of subsidiarity, we could argue that the role of public health policy in HIV prevention should not be to usurp individual decision-making, particularly in such an intimate area as reproduction, but to provide the means and support for responsible decisions by pregnant women. Only where it is clear that individual initiative cannot accomplish the goals of prevention might it be appropriate for the state to intervene in the right and responsibility of individuals to act on behalf of their own health and the health of their children.

---

17. Ibid.
18. Pope Pius XI, *Quadragesimo Anno* (1931), no. 79.

It is not obvious that individual initiative has failed in the goals of preventing HIV transmission to neonates. Indeed, between 1992 and 1995, the number of perinatal transmissions dropped 27 percent, a decrease the Centers for Disease Control attributed to Public Health Service recommendations that pregnant women be counseled about HIV testing. In addition, the use of AZT by HIV-infected pregnant women rose from 17 to 80 percent, also as a result of CDC recommendations. Once pregnant women were informed of the need to seek HIV testing and prophylactic therapy, they did it voluntarily. Voluntary action has led to decreases in perinatal transmission.[19]

Experience shows that voluntary HIV testing policies can serve the needs of newborns at risk while honoring the moral agency and protecting the civil rights of pregnant women. Voluntary prenatal testing programs are preferable to mandatory programs from the perspective of the Catholic moral tradition. But the real challenge of HIV prevention remains in enabling and empowering women at risk to make responsible and loving choices for themselves and their children.

"I FED YOU WITH MILK": A MISSIONARY MORALS IN BRAZIL IN A TIME OF AIDS

Leonard M. Martin, C.Ss.R.

MARIA DAS DORES, *a country girl, was brought to work as the live-in maid for a middle-class, Brazilian family whose residence is a high-rise apartment building in a major northeastern city. She is the seventeen-year-old colored daughter of a worker on one of the family's farms in the interior of the state. Her cash salary is a pittance, but she has guaranteed food and lodging, and a chance to go to night school in return for domestic duties every day, except Sunday, when she has a half-day off.*

She begins to feel unwell, to have bouts of nausea. The patroa, *the lady of the house, arranges for her to go to a doctor, a friend of the family. As*

---

19. Jennifer Sinton, "Rights Discourse and Mandatory HIV Testing of Pregnant Women and Newborns, *Journal of Law and Policy* 187 (1997): 215. It should be noted that not all pregnant women have meaningful access to treatment. Mandatory testing programs that do not include a commitment to insuring universal access to care would raise additional ethical problems.

suspected, she turns out to be pregnant. After further tests, due to her run down state, she is diagnosed as HIV seropositive. When questioned by the doctor and her employers, she is reluctant to say who the father is and insists that she has no idea how she got infected. The desirability of an abortion is discretely hinted at by the doctor.

Marco, the fifteen-year-old son of the house, when he hears the news, gets into a panic. He goes to a Catholic school, has made his First Communion, but has shown no interest in being Confirmed. He has the usual circle of friends and no special girlfriend but, for some time has been having sex with Maria das Dores when his parents are out at work. He finally confides in a school pal, telling him about his adventures with das Dores. Following his friend's advice, but without his parents' knowledge, he gets a blood test done, which also comes up HIV positive. Physically, he feels fine, but his mother notes that he has suddenly become withdrawn and seems to be worried.

Suspecting that Marco has followed the age-old custom of sexual games with the maid and fearing the worst, his mother badgers him until he blurts out that, in fact, he has been having sex with the girl. When his mother hears his story, she gets into a rage and expels Maria das Dores from the apartment on the spot. "The whole point in bringing into the house a nice, clean girl whose family we know is to avoid infection!"

"Such ingratitude," she storms. "We bring her into our home, treat her like one of the family, and this is how she repays us, getting pregnant and giving AIDS to our son."

What the mother doesn't know is that while Maria das Dores, a virgin on arriving in the big city, had provided Marco with the opportunity to explore the mystery of heterosexual sex; along with a group of friends of various ages, he was no novice in the world of homosexual experiences.

A case such as the one we have just described can be approached from various angles. One approach would be to develop an abstract discussion of themes and principles, and then try to apply them to a number of issues raised by the case. Another approach, which is the one I propose to follow, although not shy of abstract discussion, proposes to take as its starting point the lived experience of the main characters who appear in the story. Entering into their world, we try to understand their perspectives, their dilemmas, their values, their suffering, and their hopes. Starting from a basic posture of attentive listening does not, however, signify a subsequent posture of self-imposed dumbness. On the contrary, having listened attentively and having understood with both the head and the heart, there is far greater possibility of finding an adequate way to express the saving word of the gospel and an appropriate manner of transforming a situation of human suffering and disintegration, of *disgrace*, into a moment of *kairos*, of life-giving grace.

One of the first tasks facing moral theologians is to listen and observe, with a view to discerning the complexity of the situation we are called to deal with. The case in hand requires us to examine carefully the situation in which Maria das Dores finds herself. The story told from her point of view, the initial hopes, the magic of big-city living, her sexual experiences with Marco, her pregnancy, her isolation, her expulsion onto the streets, all form part of a wider picture which must be evaluated if moral theology is to make an effective contribution toward providing people with ethical tools for preventing AIDS.

Although our initial sympathies lie strongly with Maria das Dores, it is important that this not blind us to the very real suffering of other protagonists in this situation, nor lead us to an oversimplistic identification of victims and oppressors. Marco is neither an angel nor a demon. He is the not untypical product of an urban, Brazilian middle-class family, with roots in old rural wealth, but whose current financial security depends on both parents working long hours at their respective professions, leaving them with little time for more traditional forms of parenting. His sexual activity, whether with his male friends or with Maria das Dores, is totally incompatible with standard Catholic teaching on sexual morality. Undoubtedly, because of his Catholic up-bringing and schooling, he would have some awareness of that. Standard Catholic teaching, however, is but a small part of the cultural mix which conditions the Brazilian Catholic's choice of values and practices. Especially in the northeast, the impact of the Portuguese colonial slave culture on today's attitudes and practices should not be underestimated. Although slavery was abolished in Brazil well over a hundred years ago, the social roles and general situation of many salaried house servants still bear many of the traces, both positive and negative, of a family system sustained by slave labor. Similarly, we should not underestimate the impact on Brazilian middle-class teenagers of the postmodern hedonism found in pornographic material, especially videos and on the Internet, to which there is easy access.

Finally, Marco's mother would undoubtedly consider herself a good, traditional Catholic who had treated Maria das Dores extremely well, and who considers herself entitled to feel hurt by the young girl's betrayal of confidence (not, we may hasten to add because she had sex with her son, because Marco's mother seems to have expected that, but because she is believed to have allowed herself to be infected by a serious disease and then passed it on to the son of the house!).

One of the things that strikes us in this situation is that while the suffering of both Maria das Dores and of Marco is very real, the support structures available to each are different and unequal. It is important to note that in the initial stages of the drama, the girl is not left unsupported. The *patroa* arranges for her to see a doctor, who by all accounts treated her adequately, even if he does suggest that an abortion might be one way of solving a series of problems that are arising. When the girl is diagnosed as HIV positive, there is still a place for her in the family. The expulsion comes when she is perceived as having infected the son of the house, thus failing in one of the presumed, though not formally explicitated, social roles expected of her, the "safe" sexual initiation of the young man in question. While Maria das Dores finds herself pregnant and on the streets, Marco has the support of his school pal and continues to have a home, though his situation too runs the risk of complicating considerably when and if the truth of his homosexual activity becomes known. Though there is growing acceptance of homosexual activity, in traditional family circles the homosexual continues to be stigmatized.

At this stage in our reflection on the case two basic types of ethical questions arise: those that look forward to how to cope with the fact that both Maria das Dores and Marco are infected with the AIDS virus, and those that look back to what caused the situation and the possible contribution of moral theology toward helping avoid similar tragedies in the future. Since our concern at this time is principally with prevention rather than with the ethical demands of ongoing care for those already with AIDS, we will not delay over such questions as Marco's need to assume responsibility for his child and for the fact that he infected Maria das Dores, or the many other challenges arising from living with AIDS.[1] Instead we will focus our attention on the second type of ethical questions and the dilemmas that provoke them.

Sexual activity among young people outside marriage is certainly one of the broad areas which the case in hand raises as an urgent question. It is doubtful, however, that a straightforward enunciation of the traditional Christian teaching that sexual activity is only legitimate within marriage will make much impact on Marco and his friends, or even on Maria das Dores precisely because of the other socio-cultural factors that also influence them. The sublime ideal of total sexual abstinence before marriage for girls of a certain social class has always had strong acceptance in traditional Brazilian Catholic families. As far as boys and men are concerned, there is a widespread disbelief in the possibility of such abstinence and, indeed, such abstinence is treated with suspicion and even concern.

---

1. See Leonard M. Martin and Anísio Baldessin, *Conviver com AIDS: subsídios para o doente, sua família e grupos de apoio* (Aparecida-SP: Editora Santuário, 1990). In Spanish: *Convivir con SIDA: Ayuda para el enfermo, su familia y grupos de apoyo* (Buenos Aires: San Pablo, 1995). Leonard M. Martin, *A Ética Médica diante do Paciente Terminal: Leitura ético–teológica da relação médico—paciente terminal nos Códigos brasileiros de ética médica* (Aparecida-SP: Editora Santuário, 1993).

For the moral theologian who is anxious to propose an adequate understanding of sexuality for young people in this context as one of the means of preventing AIDS, an immediate barrier that needs to be overcome is the communications barrier. Insistence on a rigid proclamation of coldly true propositions, or even on an enthusiastic presentation of the sublime ideal of Christian chastity embraced for the sake of the kingdom of God, may result in either blank incomprehension or in running the risk of feeding the finest of red meat to people who have difficulty digesting even milk (see 1 Cor. 3:1–3).[2] When dealing with people who have not yet arrived in the promised land and who are still struggling for basic dignities in situations of captivity or desert wandering, ethical demands require a didactic presentation if we are to avoid turning life-giving wisdom into crushing burdens too heavy to bear. We need to develop a missionary morals geared to people who are in the process of becoming Christians.[3]

Marco's life as a schoolboy in a Catholic college is totally parallel to his life outside school, unsupervised by parents. As in many other areas of life, and not just in the area of sexuality, a veneer of Catholicism covers an enormous welter of postmodern values and countervalues mixed in with cultural elements of Afro, Amerindian, and European origins, all of which still await evangelization. It is an exercise in self-delusion to think that strengthening the veneer of Catholicism by reinforcing indoctrination, without any serious attempt to engage in dialogue with the underlying cultural expressions, will lead to behavior modification.

The minimalist approach favored by many government-backed AIDS prevention campaigns would be preparation to look on the homoerotic games of Marco and his friends as not particularly significant in themselves, provided condoms were being adequately used. Working on the basic assumption that teenagers are going to have sex anyway, the most effective way to prevent the spread of AIDS, from this point of view, is to make condoms widely available and to give clear instruction on how to use them. By the same reasoning, his heterosexual escapades with Maria das Dores would be discussed in terms of "safe sex" and mutual consent, rather than in terms of avoidance of genital contact, relationship, respect, and commitment.

When Christian moral theology questions this minimalist approach, it is often accused of being backward-looking, authoritarian, unrealistic and,

---

2. Leonard M. Martin, "Moral Sexual Missionária de Paulo (Subsídios para uma moral do matrimônio no Brasil)," *Revista Eclesiástica Brasileira* 50 (September 1990): 515–36.

3. Leonard M. Martin, "Moral Missionária para o Novo Milênio" *Vida Pastoral* (May 1997): 23–29.

even worse, responsible for the spread of AIDS especially among the young, because of its failure to endorse *condoms–for–all* style campaigns. Against this sort of background, breaking the communication barrier is but the first step. An even more demanding task is to have something to communicate. An authoritarian list of dos and an even longer list of authoritarian don'ts is no substitute for a moral theology thoroughly nourished by scriptural teaching and presenting the vocation of Christians to bring forth fruit in love for the life of the world (see *Optatam Totius*, 16). It is precisely this "something to communicate" which challenges us to produce a missionary morals which avoids disheartening rigorist demands on the one hand and, on the other, a laxism that is no challenge at all.

The veneer of cultural Catholicism to which I have already referred has obviously its limitations, but it also has its strengths in that it provides at least a starting point of shared Christian sympathies on some level. Its openness to religious experience and its deep-rooted devotionalism are elements that can be built on. People like Maria das Dores, like Marco, like his mother, if not sternly driven away by the newer brands of neo-Jansenism that are making inroads in some quarters, can be supported and guided through a less authoritarian and a more humanistic and scriptural presentation of the demands of Christian living. A faraway God who prohibits sex and who punishes wayward children with syphilis, AIDS, and unwanted pregnancies can gradually be dislodged from the popular mind through substituting a God who first loved us and who manifests the splendor of this love by sending us his Son to show us the way through life. The first step toward elaborating a moral theology geared toward saving the life of the spiritually and materially poor, building on traditional devotionalism, is the initiating of an experience of religion as a following of Christ where the paces are measured according to the strength of the legs that are trying to do the walking, and where the weaker are bolstered up by fraternal shoulders or are carried in loving arms as circumstances dictate.

This being bolstered up and being carried draws attention to a fundamental aspect of the following of Christ as a foundational moral category. The following of Christ, although it has an essentially personal dimension, where liberty and the conscious choice to accept an invitation play an indispensable part, also has a communal and social dimension that in recent times has been often expressed using the expression *solidarity*.

Awareness of the community and its social dimension opens up paths which may help to prevent other young people from repeating the tragic destiny of Maria das Dores and Marco.

In the case of young women like Maria das Dores, moral education geared toward AIDS prevention would need to be tackled on two fronts: in the interior, before ever they leave their family homes, and on arrival in the big city. There is nothing wrong with them heading for the city with high hopes of opportunities for work and study, being open to new experiences. It is important, however, that they are prepared for this and taught their own worth. Obviously there should be no question of creating a pathologically suspicious mentality, but they need to be made aware that sexual favors bestowed on the males of the family where they are staying and working is no part of any contract. As underage teenagers, as many of them are, they have the right to expect the respect and protection of the adults where they live.

They need also to be prepared to recognize friendship and genuine emotional involvement with boys of their own age and to distinguish them from situations of exploitation, often accepted because of a sense of loneliness and isolation. Maria das Dores's reluctance, for example, to reveal the identity of the father of her child is typical of the ambiguity of her feelings. Her silence is an ambivalent mix of loyalty to Marco, not wishing to cause him trouble, and of fear of the consequences for speaking the truth. One of the ways of overcoming the isolation which favors the type of relationship which she had with Marco, would be to encourage young women in her situation to become involved in Church youth groups and school activities. This is not always possible, however, because of the long hours they are required to work and because of the prohibition to leave the house or apartment during the week except to go on messages or to go to school. Part of the poverty of these girls is that their opportunity for education of any sort, and not just moral education, is severely limited.

Marco's case is marked by spiritual rather than material poverty. Theoretically, he should have had all the chances for a solid moral formation, attending a Catholic school, and coming from a respectable, traditional family. A veneer of cultural Catholicism, however, is no match for the swirling cultural undercurrents represented by postmodernity, with its closed condominium style apartment blocks and electronic pornography, on the one hand, and the remnants of Portuguese slave culture on the other.

One of the ironies of high-security apartment blocks is that while they lock one set of dangers out, they lock in another set: unsupervised youngsters left to their own devices by working parents. The challenge of moral education in these circumstances is not to do away with urban living but to prepare people to cope with it in a human way. It is necessary to question the contemporary myth that the pleasure principle is the primary sexual value. It is necessary to question the dual standard whereby there is one moral code for women and young girls and another for men and boys. It is particularly important to reintegrate the unitive, procreative, and re-creative aspects of sexuality and sexual relationships into a coherent system of values. It would be extremely difficult to convince the Marcos of this world to embrace all of a sudden the ideal of sexual abstinence until marriage. Within the perspectives of a missionary morals, the pedagogical strategy would be to present short-term, practical ideals that can be achieved. If boys like Marco could be taught to respect girls like Maria das Dores and to treat them not as sex objects, but as equal human beings with inherent dignity and feelings, a step will have been taken toward breaking with the old slave mentality and toward creating a new form of social relationships.

People like Marco's mother need also to be helped if moral theology is to collaborate effectively in the prevention of AIDS. They need to be assisted to rethink at least some of their presuppositions, especially in relation to the adequate sexual initiation of their sons. They need also to be helped to rethink in broader terms the role of the live-in domestic servant who is traditionally a mix between a god-child and a slave, part of the family, but always on the edges.

Moral theology can help prevent AIDS, but only if it learns to listen before it speaks, and only if it learns to discern when to offer milk and when to offer good, red meat.

WOMEN AND CHILDREN'S RISKS OF CONTRACTING HIV IN COSTA RICA

Orlando Navarro Rojas

IN CARRYING OUT an analysis of the risks of Costa Rican women and children contracting the HIV/AIDS virus, the moral attitudes of such sectors of the population must be contemplated.

The problem that Costa Rican society faces is the absence of any dialogue between everyday morals and Christian morals, for the latter tries to impose its principles without an understanding of the former's social reality. On the one hand, this situation has brought about a series of habits among Costa Rican citizens that has led them to a sexual culture and to family and community life that separates them from one another. On the other hand, the Catholic Church is alienated from this reality and from its role as mother and teacher, a task that could be realized if there existed a commitment of the church to women and children who face the risk of contracting HIV and developing AIDS.

The following account describes the situation of a woman of thirty-three years of age, the mother of eight children, one girl and seven boys, whose ages range from one to sixteen. When referring to her story as an HIV-AIDS patient, she says, "As a housewife, I never thought this would happen to me; I was at home with my one partner, believing he was faithful. Personally, I was totally ignorant about the disease because I believed that it could only happen to people living in the streets, perhaps sex workers, homosexuals or transvestites."

"My partner was a chauvinistic and alcoholic man who had hazardous sexual relations with women and with men too, I suspect today. During the beginning of his disease, I thought it was a cold; the physician confirmed it was a carelessly treated flu. However, he grew worse, lost weight, sweated too much, and suffered from influenza, until one day he was immobilized in bed. He was taken to the hospital and, because of his symptoms, he was examined for AIDS and the result was positive.

"As a woman, I felt the earth was swallowing me and a very strong pain took hold of me. The physician asked me to take the test too, so I could be treated in time, for my partner was suffering from all types of opportunist diseases, such as meningitis, candida, and others. When I picked up the results of my blood test, they told me I was positive. My reactions were to cry, to think about my children and my family, and at the same time to realize that I would soon die, in two weeks, at the latest.

"Three days later he died, and for three months, I sank into total depression, for due to my diagnosis, I lost my job, my house and my so-called friends. Besides, the person I loved the most was gone."

One of the most difficult aspects was breaking the news to her children: "The most impressive event was that one of my eldest sons helped me get out of my depression. He told me that he was alive and that he needed his mother to care about him, his food, and his adolescent problems. At that moment, I started looking for help and I found a social worker at San Juan de Dios Hospital."

"I was exposed to risks as a woman because I loved, believed, and trusted the person who I shared my life with; I assumed he was responsible because he looked endearing and did not appear to be sick.

"As it turns out, he had had an HIV test five years before dying, but even so, he was able to assert that what he suffered from was the flu, because our family doctor collaborated with him. It is important to point out the complicity of the physician, who not only concealed the truth, but never suggested testing until it was so late. This is the culture of deceiving and lying."

The Housewife's Risks

THIS CASE SHOWS the need for women to know about the symptoms of the disease because, in many cases, even though they have suspicions, men manipulate them through lying in order both to keep them by their side and to avoid losing their family's support and their social prestige.

It is necessary to note that this man's family knew about his licentious sexual behavior which they concealed. This turned into another risk not only for his partner but for other people with whom he had sexual relations. Normally, the housewife is ignorant of her partner's behavior outside the home, though his family, workmates, and friends do know about his double life, which seems to be a facet to admire in the men of this chauvinistic society.

Thus, the man lives three moments: one at home, where he has a definite authoritative role; a second one, which develops outside the home with his friends, mates, and family members; and a third one, in the religious environment, whose practice he usually shuns but whose duties he requires his wife to fulfill. Though on occasion he attends religious and social activities, he expects to compensate for his religious neglect at the end of his life by asking the priest for forgiveness.

His worldview generates an attitude toward sexual conduct in which his wife must respond submissively to his sexual wants and has no right to express what she feels. He believes his own interests as legitimate, just as he judges, for example, his children's education without being responsible for it. The man believes in this worldview without submitting it to any critique at all.

Opposite to the man, the woman keeps a more uniform behavior inside and outside the home, without much dissociation between her ethical-moral model and the religious morals promoted by churches. In other words, her worldview prompts her to live according to her husband's needs, to be faithful and believe in his fidelity, to respond to his sexual necessities without expressing her own, and to assume the responsibility for their children's education. She also lives according to the needs derived from her social relationships with her neighbors, and submits herself to the religious norms which impede her from rebelling in any way.

The Children's Risks

WHEN SHE DESCRIBES her children's father, she mentions that, just like her children, she faced physical and psychological aggression. "He had a very ambivalent disposition: he was nice at times, but the slightest error on the part of any of us led him to punish us severely; since he was a welder, he would burn the children's arms with fire and hot iron, which is proven by the marks they have today. This was one of his many punishing tactics."

An alcoholic and a womanizer, this man stayed away from home even for four days and came back later to claim his rights with violence and authoritativeness. He considered his wife his property; he did not let her leave the house, so he did the shopping. He was married very young and this was his second marriage. For her, living meant being at home and having children.

He opposed any kind of birth control methods. Because of his macho condition, he did not care about having many children, even though he usually forgot to bring them the necessary things for their survival. That was the reason why they grew up badly fed and in a troublesome atmosphere. And as if this weren't enough, the house they lived in was not finished and was in bad condition.

Moreover, the youngest child showed a number of allergies and bronchial and pulmonary infections. When it was finally revealed that the father had AIDS, the physician considered it pertinent to have the children take the blood tests, too. Unfortunately, the youngest son's tests turned out to be positive.

When they learned about the situation, the father's family promised they would never abandon the children and that they would be attentive to their needs, a promise they have not fulfilled up to the present.

Economically, the mother relies on a pension of approximately one hundred dollars monthly and on the little income she receives for the rent of the workshop which belonged to her late husband. And, though she receives sporadic help from organized groups, with the many needs that constantly arise, she does not know how to cover them.

After her husband's death, the only support came from her mother. However, at this moment, she is in the hospital because of an accident. Alone, between the disease and the work of looking after so many children, it is extraordinarily difficult for her to take herself and her son to their respective appointments.

The situation has become unmanageable, specifically because her children are mirroring their father's chauvinistic behavior of aggression not only toward her but also toward their younger siblings. She has only succeeded in protecting the youngest son from the aggression of his older siblings.

Presently, the child is being seen at Hospital de Niños (children's hospital). He is physically stable, but his psychological situation has not been evaluated by any professional. Because of his HIV status, he is not accepted in child care centers, he is rejected in his neighborhood, and mothers, out of fear, do not allow their children to play with him. As a result, it is hard for him to develop, for he is isolated from peers and siblings.

In a country like Costa Rica, high-risk cases like this one make it imperative to include the HIV blood test in prenatal care. Women are willing to take it, according to surveys that CECODERS (Centro de Coordinación de Evangelización y Realidad Social) has carried out, especially when the mother has been prepared for the help she might receive if her child were infected.

Another risk for the child is the family's extreme poverty, for his health may worsen due to a lack of food, clothing, and a pleasant environment. Nor can he count on the solidarity of his other relatives, who do not fulfill their promises and isolate the family instead. Besides, as it is well known, the incubation period of the virus in children is shorter than in adults, and the sooner he develops sickness, the worse the consequences of it.

The mother's bad nutrition, which did not let her enjoy a healthy pregnancy, and the violence suffered during that same period promoted other risk factors for the baby's infection. Moreover, she knows that had she been treated with AZT when it was originally learned that her husband was infected and that she was as well, she would have had a chance of not passing the disease onto her son.

The mother's character has been transformed. She has turned violent and has an attitude of loneliness and anguish which generates an atmosphere of roughness and insecurity that affects the HIV-positive child. The other children evade their brother's disease and do not talk about it, so there is no environment of family solidarity. The mother says she would like to leave her house one day and just forget everything.

This difficult situation shows up in a mother who spent her whole life raising her children. Her final burden is that one of them is HIV-positive and she cannot get the other members of her family to become more supportive.

Conclusion

AN ANALYSIS OF this case allows one to assert that the AIDS threat varies according to gender, age, and economic, social, and cultural factors. In relation to men, the disadvantage of women and children is much more compounded. Social and legal isolation, poverty, and the lack of higher levels of education are aspects which make women and their children more vulnerable.

Moreover, in the face of AIDS, women also face the disadvantage of their physical condition, for the vagina retains seminal liquids for a longer time and is prone to fissures, fungal infections, and easily transmitted sexual diseases. Finally, faithfulness to their partners protects neither women nor their children from infection, for the epidemic has been nurtured by a chauvinistic culture in which men have casual sexual relations without any protection and with various partners.

Ironically this culture inhibits men from developing their own masculine sexuality. All these experiences become a game where men conceal their own identity and look for harmful outlets for themselves. In the end, this generates very deep personal insecurities.

Furthermore, women are kept inside the home. They invest their lives in their children and their partner, bearing domestic violence, which further annuls their personality. The children are a consequence of these relations, through which men strengthen their chauvinism and children inherit their father's legacy.

Two very different worldviews are operative here. The only possible way of moving forward is to promote a dialogue between the chauvinistic culture and women's experience. This requires the church to support dialogue, acknowledge the social reality, and promote human dignity. Toward this end I suggest six steps of development, and then three very specific tasks for church leaders.

First, the basic needs of men and women must be identified. In turn, these people must be accompanied in their poverty. Finally, creative alternatives should seek to promote a sense of respect for the dignity of the human being.

Second, there must be the committed search to promote communal health, extending health to its amplest meaning: from hygiene, recreation, and drinking water to good relationships and mutual respect. This demands a commitment by the church to support efforts to reinforce among individuals and within society, the recognition that everyone is responsible for the health of all.

Third, through dialogue men and women must achieve a deeper knowledge of themselves and of how family life in turn influences them. Above all, there must be a context that promotes the ability to speak about reality as it is. Here the church must dialogue with everyday life, trying to understand it rather than to judge it.

Fourth, from that dialogue we must seek to improve interpersonal relationships and develop mutual responsibilities. At this stage of development the church must strongly promote Christian forgiveness, justice, and love.

Fifth, strong interinstitutional communication must occur on a variety of levels within society: education, health, artistic culture. Here again the church can be a stimulating agent insuring the recognition that the problem we are discussing is not solely between husbands and wives but rather a problem endemic to Costa Rica.

Finally, churches should promote pastoral work with children, youngsters, adults, senior citizens, and families through catechesis and a sexual education with the purpose of transmitting spiritual values that will enable men and women to respect and love one another.

For these to occur, the church has three specific tasks. First, to learn and understand people's everyday behavior and from this understanding to learn a new pedagogy for helping men and women to make ethical decisions generated by their own convictions. The church must consider everyday behavior without judging or—even less—censuring it, but instead, looking for a team solution and a more participative one.

Second, to propose solutions from the context of the dialogue itself. The validity of a solution must originate from the series of relationships that the dialogue engenders.

Finally, to create rites which will neutralize present chauvinistic rites. It is crucial that the church be creative and concretely introduce them.

The most important goal is looking for new horizons. The church must offer Costa Rican society a way of recognizing that each person is capable of creating new family modalities. Moreover, the church must do it not through sermons that promote guilt or judgment, but by sermons that provide guidance, information, and service. That will offer new liberating rites of family life.

4.

DEVELOPING EDUCATIONAL PROGRAMS

Educating for HIV Prevention in a Medical School in Colombia

Jorge H. Peláez, S.J.

FOR NINE YEARS I was the dean of student welfare at a school of medicine. My Ph.D. in moral theology permitted me to start participating gradually in ethical discussions that arose within the framework of our university hospital and, in turn, to develop ties of solid friendship and affection with teachers and students. This experience was so intense that it marked forever my activity as a university professor as well as my work as a priest.

One day I was in my office and was informed that David, one of our professors, had been hospitalized in our institution for examination because he was showing strange symptoms. At that moment David was thirty-four years old. He had carried out medical studies at our university and, after specializing in internal medicine, had traveled to the United States to pursue special training in infectious diseases.

Apart from his academic qualities, he enjoyed great prestige among his colleagues and his students considered him to be an excellent professor. His homosexuality was known; however this had not interfered with his teaching nor with his professional practice.

When I learned about his hospitalization, I went to visit him as I used to do with professors and students in the same situation. We had a nice conversation on general subjects: the political situation of the country, the reforms of the social security system, and their impact on the professional practice of medical doctors, and on the financial difficulties of our university hospital.

A week after this visit, the general director of the hospital telephoned to inform me that David was HIV positive. I was deeply moved by the news, though I was not completely surprised because some of his symptoms had suggested such a diagnosis.

I spent two days pondering over what I should do. Finally, I mustered enough courage and went to his hospital room. He was alone sitting on his bed when I arrived. When he saw me, he could not hide his distress and burst into tears. In the midst of his emotional upheaval, he said that he could not understand why he, a specialist in infectious diseases, had contracted the virus.

I let him speak for a long while. He needed to give vent to his sorrow and I did not want to interrupt him because I realized that he was expressing feelings he had not dared to show to his family or colleagues. When he finished talking, I gave him a warm embrace and expressed the affection and respect I felt for him. Since that visit a very strong relationship with him and his family started. Contact was interrupted two years ago when David traveled abroad. I have been told that he is in good condition at present.

In the Firing Line of the Laboratory

ONE OF THE ethical issues presented by David's case concerns confidentiality, as well as responses to HIV/AIDS patients that reflect social or class differences.

A few minutes after the results of the laboratory exams were obtained, all people working in the laboratory found out about them and this was the main topic of conversation for several days. The tone of the voices betrayed a sort of excitement that increased whenever the homosexuality of the patient was mentioned.

At the beginning I could not understand how a painful reality such as the one experienced by a member of our university community could provoke reactions of such a morbid nature. Then, little by little, I started to discover that, on the one hand, the excitement reflected social resentment, for status differences between doctors and lab workers are very great. Frequently doctors display arrogance and this hurts the feelings of other people working in health institutions. A positive HIV diagnosis in a doctor reminded others that demigods also get sick and die. Moreover, the homosexuality of the patient uncovered social prejudices which still exist in great sectors of our society.

People were not satisfied just with comments full of morbidity; their curiosity also led them to invent pretexts to visit the patient. What did they expect to find? I can imagine their disappointment when they saw a handsome young patient, in very good physical condition, who received his inopportune visits with the best of smiles.

Worried about the reactions of people, several meetings of the directors of the school of medicine and the hospital were called to reflect on the situation and undertake some action. Three priority subjects came up during our conversations: confidentiality, the human character—not exclusively the homosexual side—of the HIV virus infection, and the sanitary instructions for the management of such patients. Apart from giving priority to these topics, strategies were designed.

Confidentiality. The concept of professional secrecy is an essential element in the ethics of health professionals. Only with the assurance of confidentiality can doctors obtain complete information from patients, not only about their diseases, but also about their personal lives. This information is particularly important in HIV cases. If patients fear information leaks, they will not subject themselves to the required exams, thus producing disastrous consequences for them and society. This is why the observance of confidentiality constitutes a particularly delicate element in clinical laboratories. People must be educated to respect confidentiality, and administrative procedures must be created to guarantee it.

The human character—not just the homosexual side—of HIV. At the beginning it was thought that HIV was exclusively a disease that affected homosexuals and drug addicts who shared needles. This belief favored a sort of false security in the other groups of society, so they assumed they were safe from contracting it. At present, the term *risk groups* has given way to the term *risk behaviors.* Prevention against HIV demanded the change of such an erroneous concept. There is no social group exempt from this virus. Consequently, prevention requires great responsibility in the way people manage their private lives and marital relationships. Regarding the latter, people believe in the fidelity of their partners, so they do not take special precautions.

Instructions for the attention given to HIV patients. During the first years after the identification of HIV there was panic among health professionals. Physicians, dentists, and nurses did everything possible to avoid treating these patients, failing to meet their ethical responsibilities. As better knowledge of the virus was acquired, many of these fears and fantasies have disappeared. HIV prevention among health professionals has obliged clinical laboratories and hospitals to educate their personnel regarding the ways in which this infection is transmitted. It is better to assume that all patients are HIV carriers so as to prevent unpleasant discrimination. Therefore, all the required precautions must be adopted with every one of the patients in handling fluids. This nondiscriminatory prevention policy needs to be promoted in all health institutions.

The three priority subjects (confidentiality, human character—not only the homosexual side—of the HIV, and care of HIV patients) are being systematically dealt with in workshops and conferences. Pertinent actions must be periodically implemented. At the beginning such actions were only directed to clinical laboratory workers, but soon after they obviously were extended to all the nursing personnel and this is where we are at present.

HIV Prevention and Medical Students: Toward Teaching Accompaniment

THE POSITIVE DIAGNOSIS of David, an internal medicine professor, caused a deep impression on the students of the school of medicine, particularly on those who had been his pupils. However, their manifestations were far more discreet than those observed among the clinical laboratory workers.

The board of directors of the school of medicine became convinced of the urgency of designing a complete educational program regarding HIV prevention and accompaniment of persons with HIV. This task required the establishment of an interdisciplinary team, whose work has not been easy and there is still much to be done.

Naturally, many of the subjects analyzed with students are the same as those covered with the personnel of the clinical laboratory and with the nurses. However, there are particular subjects to which special importance is given, such as: the sexual life of students; the training for achieving an adequate communication with patients, their families, and the community; and the knowledge of feelings experienced by HIV patients so that they may be offered the most human accompaniment possible.

The sexual life of students. In spite of the epidemiological knowledge they possess, many students still think—against all logic—that HIV is a matter restricted to homosexuals and drug addicts who share needles. This is why they believe themselves above possible infection and, therefore, do not change risky behaviors.

Like many young people of the same age, medicine students have a very active sexual life. Generally, they are faithful to the affective relationship of the moment, but their affections are of a short-term nature. Consequently, affections and sexual encounters occur throughout their university life. Also, as young people's mentality makes them feel immortal and immune to all dangers, they do not take adequate precautions.

Another element that casts a darker shadow on the prevention horizon is alcohol consumption. Our exploratory studies suggest that drug consumption is very low among medicine students, but this is not the case with alcohol, since they release the stress caused by their studies and practices by drinking on the weekends. Alcohol lowers inhibitions and preventive measures are forgotten. Therefore, responsible sexuality is incompatible with alcohol abuse. The university is well aware of this problem. Activities promoting reflection on different types of dependencies (alcohol, drugs, tobacco) are organized every year.

Training to enhance communication. Medical schools strive to train medical professionals in the best possible way. But when the curriculum is closely analyzed it may be discovered that in most cases professional competence is identified with specific medical knowledge and skills, neglecting other formative aspects pertaining to the social sciences. In this field I shall specifically consider the communication aspect.

Medical practice requires particular communication skills since physicians must interact with patients, their families, the community, government officials, and others. Doctors must interrogate patients concerning signs and symptoms; afterwards they have to tell them the diagnosis, and finally propose a therapy to them (medicines to be taken, routines to be followed, and precautionary measures to keep in mind). They must do the same with the families of their patients. At the community level, they must inform people about risks and promote health campaigns. It is clear, then, that to be a good doctor, purely scientific abilities are not enough. It is also necessary to be a good communicator able to find the right expression— timely and tactful—according to the cultural level of the interlocutor.

The clinical and socio-cultural characteristics of HIV make it even more urgent to offer training in communication to doctors and to all health professionals in general. It must be realized that communication is a two-way affair: communication given and communication received. This exchange requires learning how to decode verbal and nonverbal language.

Prevention campaigns require highly professional knowledge of communication regarding messages, motivations, and image management. Let us now consider accompaniment processes for HIV patients for whom the generosity of some volunteers is not sufficient, since specific training is required to accompany them. When such specific training for communicating with HIV carriers is lacking, their sensitivity and dignity may be deeply hurt.

These experiences have compelled us to take the first steps in the design of educational strategies for communication and we have requested the cooperation of some departments of the university: social communication. education, psychology, psychiatry, anthropology, and theology. The purpose is to train doctors within the perspective of these sciences.

Exploration of the personal world of people with HIV. If a truly human accompaniment of HIV carriers is sought, it is necessary to know, in the best possible way, their personal, unique, and unrepeatable world. It is equally necessary to know the behavior characteristics common to them.

Before continuing with this reflection, it is necessary to understand thoroughly the type of relationship existing between accompaniment and prevention. The case of HIV carriers who do not modify their risky behavior, thus becoming propagators of disease and death, is rather frequent. We know cases of HIV carriers who, blinded by their personal tragedy, react by taking revenge against society through the spread of the virus. Therefore, the adequate accompaniment of these carriers constitutes an excellent prevention strategy. This is why we have considered that students in our school of medicine must not only know HIV's epidemiology, they must also explore the complex and frequently distressed world of virus carriers.

From the moment persons learn that they are seropositive, they feel trapped in an irreversible situation. Even asymptomatic persons feel the sword of Damocles upon them. This case is similar to that of other hopeless patients in the sense that HIV carriers die within a time lapse which is relatively short (in our developing countries new drugs are prohibited because of their high prices). Nevertheless, their anguish in the face of death is usually more lucid, intense, and clairvoyant. It frequently stems from an environment marked by cultural, moral, and social segregation that makes them feel surrounded by hostility. They also know that they might be rejected by the very health professionals who must take care of them.

One of the most important common denominators is the need these patients have to reinvent their lives. All HIV carriers must reinvent their position regarding life and death, the future, sex, the family, and friends, since they experience an abrupt alteration in all relationships.

On the more or less long path of HIV carriers, the wishes to know and not to know alternate in a pendular manner. These feelings are exacerbated with the proximity of a new medical or laboratory exam. Must I take the exam or not? Must I see the results or ignore them? This alternation of feelings may also be observed in the hope-hopelessness duality: on the one hand, HIV carriers know that at present there is no cure for their condition but, on the other hand, they are aware of the great research efforts made and of new treatments being tested which offer them quality of life and permit them to gain time. However, they are out of reach for poor people due to their high cost. This oscillation between hope and hopelessness makes these patients highly vulnerable to the message of illusion-filled salespersons who offer magic substances to fight the virus.

Although I have stated above that there are some common denominators in HIV carriers, there is not just one accompaniment pattern. Accompaniment must be diversified and this requires a good deal of creativity. An adequate personal relationship between the patient and those around them is necessary to build the accompaniment process. The relationship must be of a close and continuous nature, not distant or sporadic, including mutual respect, openness, listening, material help, and support in finding sense in life.

Accompaniment must be given by an interdisciplinary team that includes different competencies: doctors and nurses, psychologists and social workers, and the chaplain or minister. The team rendering this service has to be willing to attend to the family or the affective partner (homosexual or heterosexual) because these relations may give rise to great conflicts, similar or worse than the ones experienced by the diseased person.

Questions about the reasons of the HIV infection are inevitable during the accompaniment process. Beware of false religious or moralistic interpretations! Beware of showing God as an avenger who enjoys the suffering and death of creatures! God is not an avenger; God is love and shelter.

The twisted interpretation of HIV as a punishment must be overcome. Instead it must be considered as a human disease equally threatening for women and men, children, young people and adults. It is a human disease that deserves the same cares and the same interest as any other disease.

In the accompaniment process, aspects of the intimate life of patients must inevitably come to the surface. When dealing with such delicate matters, the moralizing discourse ranging from fear to alarm must be avoided. It is natural for the HIV pandemic to raise questions about the permissiveness of a consumer society. Such questioning must not be based on fear; instead it should be a call for responsibility. Fear only produces short-term effects. On the contrary, responsibility transforms behavior patterns and this constitutes the best guarantee for an efficient prevention.

David was the first of our professors. Other members of our university community have had the same fate. We have walked together, we have laughed, we have prayed. HIV's presence in our midst has shattered old schemes and is requiring the creation of new expressions of solidarity, of new education and prevention patterns from us.

TEACHING ABOUT HIV PREVENTION IN AN AMERICAN CATHOLIC COLLEGE CLASSROOM

Eileen P. Flynn

I INCLUDE A segment about AIDS in an introductory college course on morality which I have been teaching for the past fifteen years. I begin the segment with facts about AIDS and a description of what life is like for people living with HIV. This coverage precedes classes which focus on Christian religious insight and Catholic social teaching as these pertain to AIDS.

An aspect of the factual picture is preventative strategies—how the virus is transmitted and what can be done to eliminate or lessen the possibility of infection. Addressing the issue of HIV prevention could be an easy task. Since it has been almost two decades since the first halting media references to a frightening cluster of symptoms which proved fatal to those afflicted, the stories of AIDS have been told and retold in the media as well as in school auditoriums. I could make it simple for myself and say that I know my students are aware of prevention transmission, so I will not be redundant. But this is not necessarily the case and, therefore, I cannot *justify avoiding the subject. As recently as spring semester 1998, a student wrote that the first classroom discussion she ever participated in on AIDS was as a college sophomore, in my course. Another student in the same class wrote, "In (high) school I mostly got the lecture on safe sex, hardly anything on abstinence." Add to this the fact that most students still report little to no discussion at home about sex-related topics, and I find myself believing that it is important to cover everything.*

By avoiding the nitty-gritty of prevention transmission, I am putting myself in a sensitive spot and leaving myself open to possible penalties. By not short-changing my students and advising them of the merits of condoms, I become vulnerable to disciplinary action from the hierarchy which, over the past dozen years, has censured theologians for deviating from the letter of magisterial teaching. How do I resolve the case of "the professor skating on thin ice"?

When I address the topic of HIV prevention, I could just inform my students that by avoiding all contact with HIV-contaminated blood or body fluids people are at zero risk of becoming infected. Since condom use, which reduces, but does not eliminate the possibility of infection, is not foolproof, and since usage for contraceptive purposes goes against the teachings of the magisterium of the Roman Catholic Church, reliance on condoms should not be considered a technically dependable or morally defensible preventive strategy.

As it happens for me, however, the topic of AIDS prevention does not play out so simply. I do not think that teaching is a form of indoctrination. Instead, it is an interactive endeavor in which the viewpoints of students ought to be heard and, as far as possible, honored for the cogency they evince. And, unfortunately, the ideal world in which behavior is governed by rules dictated by reason and reinforced by authorities (religious or otherwise) bears little resemblance to the real world inhabited by my students, the world in which the ranks of those infected by HIV grow by two young people between the ages of thirteen and twenty-one, every hour of every day.

When I begin discussing the topic of AIDS prevention by advocating abstinence from premarital sex (my wont), my students inevitably raise the issue of *reality*, a reality which I must acknowledge actually exists. This reality consists in the fact that lots of people, especially traditional college-age students, are sexually active in either promiscuous or serial-monogamous contexts. There is no reason to think that this pattern of behavior is going to change any time soon. Additionally, while there is awareness about risks related to unprotected sex, use of condoms is sporadic. Given this situation, this "reality," many of my students argue that church leaders as well as classroom teachers, anyone with a soap box, should give up on trying to impose morally based sexual restrictions and concentrate, instead, on encouraging practical prophylactic measures in the interest of curbing the pandemic.

In responding to this contention I find myself facing a dilemma. I am a Roman Catholic moral theologian, teaching a theology course in a theology department of a Catholic college. Catholic theology, especially as manifest in sexual and medical ethics, tends to be extremely precise and detailed in its prescriptions and proscriptions. On the one hand, keeping the act of heterosexual intercourse within marriage and open to the transmission of human life and not engaging in any homosexual genital acts are staples of official hierarchical doctrine.

On the other hand, HIV prevention is important because prevention is a human good which ought to be pursued so that people can maintain good health, a necessary precondition to being able to perform their duties. I need to resolve how I can honor loyalty to my students, adherence to my belief system, and exercise of my professional competence while maintaining residence in the real world. What should I say about condoms?

By loyalty to my students I mean fidelity to them, conveying truth to them, and supporting their intellectual, moral, and spiritual development. Based on what they have confided in me, I know that students in a typical class are likely to be in one of three places. First, there are reassuring exceptions to the "everyone is doing it" generalization. For the most part these students are from strict Catholic, evangelical Protestant, Muslim, or Hindu backgrounds, and are convinced that sex apart from marriage is wrong. Their conduct corresponds to their beliefs. Second, there are students who are "in a relationship," a code which means that they are sexually intimate with their boyfriend or girlfriend. Many of these young people naively believe that they are not at risk of AIDS. Hence, they acknowledge having sex without protection. And, third, there are young people who have had an AIDS scare and an HIV test. These students will probably not be careless again. Neither will they be willing to practice abstinence.

Knowing what I do about Catholic moral teaching as well as the behavior of my students, how should I respond to the majority who insist that, as far as AIDS is concerned, being practical and realistic—promoting the use of condoms—is the only approach which makes sense?

This question backs me up against the wall and calls for considerable soul-searching. From the outset I have understood that my concept of God is the foundational element in my decision-making. The God in whom I believe is creator, mother and father. In these modes God is understanding and compassionate. This God knows that young people desire acceptance and want to be attractive and to fit in. God understands, too, the hormones which God created, the powerful passions and desires which well up in human flesh and which can result in foolish actions. I trust that God understands and makes allowance for young people as they progress toward maturity. This trust is in marked contrast to the cringing fear many religious people feel as they imagine the lengths to which their vindictive God will go in punishing sexual transgressions. Honestly, I am glad I do not share this kind of terror. And, as a teacher, I hope that I am not passing it on.

In resolving moral dilemmas, I employ natural law, broadly construed. By this I mean that I consider it possible to use reason to determine proper human conduct and to exercise volition in order to effect morally appropriate choices. My satisfaction with natural law methodology does not extend as far as biologism—the tendency to equate the dynamics of heterosexual coupling and possible conception following therefrom as God's will—making normative only noncontracepted sex which is open to procreation. The magisterium of the Catholic Church on the other hand emphasizes this biologistic premise in its corpus of teaching on sexual ethics. From this foundation come the absolute prohibitions of both artificial contraception and homosexual genital acts. These prohibitions have been the subject of significant dissent, and some dissenting theologians have suffered significant penalties.

Since I do not concur with a biologistic interpretation of natural law, my thinking on homosexual acts and artificial contraception is not open and shut. And my responsibility as a moral theologian is to pursue rationality, rather than unthinking obedience to hierarchical authorities who may be mistaken. In respect to homosexual genital acts, the question of why God would create approximately ten percent of humankind homosexual and then, as it is argued, will celibacy and frustration for them, is especially perplexing. It could be that the search to discover in what truly moral sexual conduct consists has not yet been completed.

Beyond this, there is no dispute that, to be happy, people need to attain spiritual, psychological, and emotional maturity. This is true regardless of sexual orientation. The fear and guilt which gay people experience in conjunction with their orientation and sexual conduct inhibit attainment of this goal. Therefore, it might make sense to reformulate moral teaching so as to counsel a compromise approach: that gay people accept and esteem their sexuality and live it out in committed same sex unions. If hierarchically based moral theology were to dispense such advice, it would constitute a radical departure from advocacy of abstinence. Abstinence is 100 percent effective, when it is practiced. From what homosexual persons disclose, however, achievement of total abstinence is seldom the case. Since lapses by gay men who are committed to celibacy are usually spontaneous and promiscuous, putting them in grave danger, this issue is of far more than theoretical interest. It is a matter of life and death. Recognition of the fact that prophylactic use of condoms reduces transmission of HIV might just be the spur which prods development of doctrine in this area.

As far as artificial contraception is concerned, there are several reasons why the teaching of the magisterium has been questioned by moral theologians. Equating a biological process with a normative requirement is problematic because circumstances and intentions are not considered in moral evaluation. Beyond this, mandating that each and every act of intercourse be open to the transmission of human life puts the focus in the wrong place. It would be more reasonable to teach that married people should be open to children whom they would lovingly raise, a relational and intergenerational responsibility, rather than investing a biological process with ultimate meaning.

In addition, the lack of assent to *Humanae Vitae* from bishops, priests, and laity alike continues to undermine the authority of the papal magisterium which holds fast to this encyclical. This situation requires resolution through honest dialogue which is open to the possibility of revision. It will not disappear based on the threats of academic or ecclesial penalties.

Which position is morally correct on contraception and homosexual acts? Obviously, being in opposition to the magisterium puts professors in a vulnerable place. But this is where I find myself. When I hear my students clamoring "be real," my reservations in this regard strike me as especially germane because, if use of a condom can be considered a lesser evil or a tolerable means to a desirable end, such usage might be reasonable in situations where the goal is to prevent infection with HIV. And, if all instances of homosexual genital activity were not *absolutely* prohibited, then, perhaps, allowing for committed gay relationships in view of AIDS might be a responsible step to take.

A word on dissent is in order here. A significant function of moral theology is to provide rationale and guidance about what are and what are not proper human actions. What a person ought to do or refrain from doing is an extremely crucial matter. During the 1960s and 1970s moral theologians and the Roman Catholic magisterium found themselves at odds in respect to such moral issues as artificial contraception and homosexual genital acts. Since the early 1980s, the magisterium has become increasingly intolerant of dissent, and has moved to put a stop to it. Conformity of teaching has been encouraged in seminary preparation and in Vatican publications such as *The Catechism of the Catholic Church*. Few people today pursue advanced studies in moral theology, and those in the field who teach and write tend to be "careful" so as to avoid penalty. The resulting false calm, however, has not yielded a desirable situation. The fundamental concerns around which dissent took place a generation ago have not had a thorough airing with both sides at the same table, and hence remain unresolved. There is an underlying tension with which I must contend as, over and over, I am questioned, "Since people aren't going to change their behavior, why won't religious leaders, like the pope and bishops, support protection during sex as a means of curbing the spread of HIV?" The issue I face is how to present strategies which conflict with the views of many church officials but which could be of practical benefit to my students. When the needed dialogue finally does occur, hopefully during the next papacy, I think a broadening, deepening, and nuancing of moral theology will take place. In the meantime, it is up to me whether or not I allow myself to be tongue-tied. Since I need to choose between my students' well-being and specific teachings which the magisterium has placed beyond reevaluation (most likely on political rather than rational grounds), I opt to provide information which may prove life-saving.

While my concept of God and my take on natural law lead me to be somewhat accommodating to students who would have me join them in preferring safe sex to unsafe sex, a considerable obstacle prevents me from being enthusiastic. This obstacle is the fact that I have serious reservations about accepting the *reality* they repeatedly describe as a situation which cannot be changed. My reservations stem from the insight that since we have created our culture, we can change it. It goes without saying that if we were to do so, we would change the sexual mores which are currently operative. In so doing, we would alter the nature of reality as we experience it today.

One of the major issues in regard to culture is whether we belong to culture or culture belongs to us. Since culture is such a complex phenomenon, incorporating so many beliefs, attitudes, and practices, it is understandable that we seldom give thought to how culture came to be or how it could be changed. It is important to recognize that culture is a human construct; it is what we have made, not how our society *must be*. People have fashioned all the elements that comprise culture, and people can retain, revise, or discard these components. Altering sexual mores would not be easy because recently established patterns of sexual behavior have become deeply rooted. Change, nevertheless, is possible. This insight figures largely in my thinking because I am convinced it is reasonable and germane.

In the wake of the sexual revolution of the 1960s, genital sexual intimacy lost its meaning as a profound bond uniting loving partners and serving as the means of propagating the human species. Instead, sex became casual, devoid of deep meaning, and most taboos surrounding it disappeared.

This change happened at the same time feminism was making an impact and feminists were arguing against gender-based inequality in sexual relations. There is no question that women and men are equal and have equal rights in regard to sex. However, this advance in awareness needs to be appreciated simultaneously with the recognition that contemporary culture has lost an understanding of the seriousness and significance of sexual intimacy.

To the extent that young people assume that sex is trivial, they deceive themselves about the physical, emotional, and spiritual harms which follow upon recreational sex. Add to this the fact that subjectivism and relativism characterize much of moral reflection, leading to an alarming decline in moral standards, and one begins to comprehend the enormous problems attendant on the confusion about sex and responsibility which pervade our culture.

I believe that people who believe in God or people who are concerned about the well-being of the human community should take up the work of fashioning a different kind of culture. The sexual revolution went too far. There is too much permissiveness and sexual intimacy has been stripped of its sacred meaning. These phenomena need to be corrected through recognition of the problems, consciousness-raising about their perniciousness, and a coordinated plan to correct the overall laxity.

Taking on the culture would be an enormous undertaking. But, for Catholic Christians, this seems to be precisely the nature of the challenge which requires response. Since it is the mission of the baptized to work to accomplish the reign of God on earth, I think that believers do not have the option of doing nothing.

What does God have to do with culture? According to Catholic theology, at least two things. One is that Scripture conveys to us an idea of a just and holy social order in which people have dignity and sex has meaning. The social order is a reality tainted by sin, corrupted by self-deceit, license, and licentiousness, but ultimately God's grace will triumph over sin. Thus, with the help of grace, believers can shake off their lethargy and accomplish the work which needs to be done. God would be partner and facilitator in the task of transforming culture

Practically speaking, this tremendous project needs leadership and coordination. The intransigence which has settled into the church and the in-fighting over political issues need to be overcome. A first step would be to move beyond the climate of fear and incivility, and a willingness to tackle disputed issues of sexual morality. After that, forward movement could take place, not by an army of righteous vigilantes, but by humble, caring believers who fear for young people who are growing up in dangerous times.

WHEN I STAND before a class and raise the issue of prevention of HIV, I am a teacher, a person who has influence, but not someone who dictates what students think or do. I wish there were no HIV, no pandemic, no chilling nightmares. And I wish the sexual climate were restrained; I would even welcome a return to the way it was when I was their age. If wishes were horses, beggars would ride.

But wishes are not horses. HIV is not going to vanish and cultural change is not going to sweep over society like a blizzard in winter. And so I keep plodding. I reluctantly agree with my students that it would be preferable for those who are sexually active and unmarried to use condoms every single time than to have unprotected sex. I also maintain that it would be much better to wait for sex until after marriage and to be faithful to one's partner for an entire lifetime. Above all, I try to convey the message that sex should be reconceptualized as a life-giving blessing from God, not as a threatening encounter which could become the locus for transmission of a deadly virus.

FIGHTING AIDS IN A SOCIETY WHERE WE EGYPTIANS DON'T TALK ABOUT IT

Nader Michel, S.J., M.D.

IN EGYPT AIDS is a taboo. The sexual modes of infection are judged contrary to the religious traditions of a country where Muslims constitute the majority (94 percent) and a Christian Orthodox community, the Copts, makes up most of the remainder population (6 percent). The Egyptian Catholic community represents only 200,000 people of the 63 million people in Egypt.

In this society, AIDS is considered a foreign disease which is contracted outside Egypt. Health officials declared that the few patients who have the HIV infection had been infected most probably during their stay abroad. Foreigners who come to work in Egypt are subjected to AIDS tests, and those who are infected are firmly asked to leave the country. There are no departments in public or private hospitals to treat AIDS patients. They are instead treated in the Hospital of Infectious Diseases in Cairo, where six beds have been reserved for them. Moreover, though the latest statistics of the Ministry of Health declared only six hundred HIV-infected Egyptians, the WHO estimated that there are about six thousand patients in Egypt. No specific anti-AIDS treatment is delivered in Egypt, only for secondary diseases caused by AIDS. The real number of AIDS patients and their condition are practically speaking kept secret.

AIDS is more than a syndrome of immune deficiency: it destabilizes the impression of an intact society that people want to keep; it puts forward the images that society wants to ignore or repulse. It reveals a part of humanity that society has difficulty assuming and integrating.

A Unique Case of AIDS Prevention

IN THIS CONTEXT, *only five governmental and nongovernmental organizations work in AIDS education and prevention. No place really gives care directly to the patients. A Catholic organization, Caritas-Egypt, which has worked thirty years in social development and health promotion, was the first organization to take up the challenge and develop a program of AIDS prevention in Egypt. A lay crew formed from specialized centers for AIDS prevention has expanded this program. Since 1995 it has annually sponsored more than 150 lectures at youth centers, high schools, sport clubs, mosques, and churches throughout Cairo, Alexandria and other parts of Egypt. In addition, Caritas administers a telephone help line for anonymous calls, information, and counseling. Caritas has also published two books on both the modes of infection and prevention of AIDS and general sexual education on a large scale. The installation of a medical laboratory for anonymous AIDS tests is under study, together with free administration of specific anti-AIDS treatment for patients.*

Caritas-Egypt began to prepare a film for information about AIDS and asked an international Catholic organization to finance it. The film would have been the only one in Arabic in the Middle East. The organization agreed and began to help the project. After the film was completed, the representatives of this international organization in Cairo noticed that in one scene a doctor advised the use of the condom as a method of protection from HIV. He suggested this to the wife of a man who had accidentally been infected by the AIDS virus during a blood transfusion. The financing organization threatened to abandon the project if the scene was not changed and asked to remove its name from the film. It was a moment of real panic. Not only was the project of the film stopped, but also Caritas-Egypt was implicitly accused of not following Catholic moral teaching—and even worse, of diffusing a contrary teaching. Negotiations began between Caritas-Egypt and the international Catholic organization, and I was asked to counsel Caritas-Egypt on how to reply to these objections to the film and on the position of the Catholic Church concerning AIDS prevention.

As we address this case, it must be noted that Caritas's work in Egypt is mainly addressed to non-Catholics—that is, the 99.7 percent of the population who are either Muslim or Coptic Orthodox, and who permit the use of condoms as a means of contraception as well as for protection against AIDS. In such a society a Catholic social organization, such as Caritas, can not ignore sensibilities different from its own. If it does not mention the use of the condom, it would have to justify and explain this serious omission.

The Catholic moral teaching in a pluralistic society has to draw from its own tradition and resources. It has to take into consideration the different components of society and their moral references to see how to dialogue with them. In this way, the Catholic Church may find its place in society and show the specificity of its moral contribution. In the case of this Caritas film, then, we have first to examine whether the use of the condom represented a drift from Catholic moral teaching, and second to point out the specificity of the Catholic moral teaching in this society.

Can a Married Couple Use Condoms for AIDS Prevention?

IN THE CATHOLIC moral tradition many elements helped answer objections to the use of the condom in this precise situation. First, the advice to use the condom was given for three primordial values: to preserve life, a supreme good, and to protect the dimensions of love and of unity in this stable married couple. The contraception that results from the use of the condom is not the aim, but a secondary effect of that which is pursued—namely, the protection of life. Unwanted contraception can also occur as a secondary effect of hormonal treatment for some diseases of the reproductive system. The intention and the objective of this couple's actions are directed to protect their lives; they are not for contraceptive purposes. Even if contraception is the foreseen consequence of the use of condoms, the aimed-at objective of protection of life has without any doubt a greater beneficial effect. Moreover, to advocate abstinence as the unique method of AIDS protection for this couple could hurt their love in its greatest and most intimate expression, and condemn them to neuroses and their marriage to dissolution. Saint Paul warned couples against prolonged abstinence and counseled instead wisdom and prudence in these things and not to lose self-control (see 1 Cor. 7:5).

In the case of this film, the makers did not mean to choose the lesser evil (contraception) to avoid the greater one (death). Rather, they were trying to promote resolutely the greater good—that is, the values of life, love, and conjugal unity. Here we can listen to the words of Jesus to the Pharisees: "Is it lawful to do good or to harm, to save life or to kill?" (see Mk. 3:4). AIDS prevention is about that same responsibility for one's own life and for the life of others. This responsibility is love and love begins with responsibility for another's life. Thus, there is no love that does not take responsibility for its actions. Respecting other people's lives is the most elementary and essential act of love.

For HIV/AIDS patients, the use of the condom helps protect life. Certainly it is not the only way because prevention begins by responsible love, which means that one has to give an explanation for one's acts and a meaning to them in a durable relationship. Prevention begins by the development of a love that implies a control of one's own sexuality and behavior. For those who fail in this aspect, we should not refuse them the possibility of becoming responsible for and protective of their lives and those of others. These have not yet achieved the ideal of life that they are asked to reach. Until they do, we should help them stay alive so that one day they would be able to achieve this standard. Thus we must take into consideration the weakness and the vulnerability of the human condition and its fundamental historic dimension. We must reach people where they are, help them to protect their lives, and then help them to move forward toward a more responsible humanity.

This was the same position of the French bishops, which was published on 12 February 1996, a year before the problem of Caritas-Egypt with the international Catholic organization. The social commission of the French episcopate admitted for the first time in a document on AIDS that the use of the condom is necessary for AIDS prevention; they recognized that the relative decline of the number of infected people in France is due to the use of condoms. But the French bishops judged this means of protection insufficient in itself, for we have also to study the causes of AIDS, including those like banal sexual acts or multiple and diverse sexual relations.

In the face of death, the church can't act for death. While the use of the condom is a means of protection, it provides no education of love or adult sexuality. The church offers, then, something greater, a global love education that essentially helps people discover the quality of life.

Catholic Morality in a Muslim and Orthodox Society

IN A CONTEXT like Egypt, we have to demonstrate clearly the main points of Catholic moral teaching. If we only speak about its opposition to the use of condoms, we take a serious risk of obscuring what is most essential in its teaching. Non-Catholics could see this position as a refusal to help people who are in real danger, a refusal that is difficult to understand or realize. The Catholic Church in helping these patients, through the action of Caritas-Egypt, revealed its courage in breaking the bonds of silence and in fighting the negative moral judgments and condemnations of AIDS patients. The church looks at everyone personally without any discrimination of race, religion, or personal convictions, and recognizes their dignity as children of God, a dignity revealed in the weakness and wound of sickness. At the heart of Catholic moral teaching concerning respect for every human being, especially the most impoverished and the most marginal, is the call to welcome these people, to reassure them, to orient them toward the places of care, and to educate them to both protect their partners and grow day after day in more responsible love.

The specificity of the Catholic moral teaching has been revealed in the commitment of Caritas-Egypt to change an unjust situation to the better, by accompanying AIDS patients, and by acting against sickness, death, ignorance, fanaticism, and obscurantism. It puts into action Catholic moral values: solidarity, attention to the poorest, and promoting awareness and responsibility.

In a context like Egypt's where the danger of ignoring and refusing AIDS patients is great, the social dimension of Catholic moral teaching is powerful. In a society where infection by the AIDS virus disturbs society's self-image, a Catholic organization looks at those who are at the margins of this society and works to protect the members of the society from the dangers that it wants to repulse and hide. A healthy society is able to care for those who are rejected, to exorcize its taboos, to heal its wounded and protect its members. The action of a Catholic organization in Egypt should be at the same time an incarnation of these values and an appeal for their implementation. It should be directed toward the social solidarity and the protection of the common good. The health of a society must be measured by its capacity for respectful welcome of its sick members and protection of its healthy members, which is precisely the mission of the Caritas-Egypt prevention program.

The global vision of human love and dignity that Catholic moral teaching advocates implies self-control, responsibility, and fidelity; it prophetically proposes this ideal. The love that the Catholic Church calls us to is a horizon to reach, but it can remain a difficult task to achieve at a particular moment in some people's lives. Nevertheless, this ideal is not utopian; it continues to act as a mobilizing force upon people's lives, since it questions and challenges the authenticity and the truth of their real life engagements both personally and socially. In its prophetic aspect also, the Catholic moral teaching appears to be concise and incisive, with no intention of giving a systematic presentation of its resources or to detail all the dimensions of its moral thinking. Instead, like a prophetic word, it may stress one point more than others. For instance, it insists on the ideal that abstinence is the only means of AIDS protection, independently of any human context (psychological, demographic, or sociological conditions). The implementation of this special point by some people could be considered as a vocation to become a sign or a reminder of the ideal that others might forget or ignore.

In the Egyptian context, where the body and sexuality are often considered hindrances and obstacles for the spiritual life, the Catholic moral teaching fights this duality by announcing that a true spiritual life does not renounce sexuality or despise it, but acknowledges the real life conditions of people's lives and manages sexuality in such a way so that a true relation to God can be developed. There is no duality between the spiritual and the corporal, but the spiritual is in the heart of the corporal.

In the Egyptian context where moral teaching is limited to a legalism which defines what is allowed and what is forbidden, what is licit and what is not, if we don't announce the complexity of Catholic moral teaching but merely a prohibition of condoms, we don't do justice to the resources of the Catholic moral tradition and its global vision of humankind. True, the human act is important in itself. But also we have to examine the various aspects that are involved in it and connected to it, and we have to understand the different elements that condition it and that are revealed through it. We have to look at its inscription in a larger framework and in a greater context—that is, the whole history of a human life.

A dissolute act may reveal a dissolute social structure economically and culturally, and if we remain in our judgment at only the level of the act, we ignore the evil structure that led to it and generated it, and that needs to be considered in order to respond to moral evil. An unjust structure generates and contributes to dissolute acts. In order to remedy these behaviors, we have to confront the dissolute individual and social structures. And until an individual and social ideal is established, we have to take the realistic and concrete measures to move forward toward this ideal. The first condition to achieve this goal is to maintain people in life.

We have to work rigorously for greater social justice at all levels—in education, health services, cultural and economical areas—and to accept the distance that separates the real human conditions of today from the ideal of tomorrow. We have to learn to deal with the real situations of people with courage and inventiveness, without any complicity with evil, and without any hypocritical pretension of purity. We have to learn to soil our hands while stretching them out to those we think have soiled hands, to learn to be present to those who really and deeply suffer.

Conclusion

REPEATING THE PROHIBITION of the use of condoms or advocating abstinence as the only means of AIDS protection only partially presents Catholic moral teaching. This teaching also recognizes the historicity of human life and the advancement of human beings toward the ideal of their lives through numerous roads on which they are sustained and consoled by divine mercy. Catholic morality has always fought injustices and the deficiencies of human life, and has displayed its inventiveness of helping people in all their needs. Catholic morality has always recognized the interrelation between the individual behavior and the social structure that conditions and modifies it. Catholic morality has known that one has to work on both dimensions at the same time. Catholic morality has always announced a prophetic ideal to achieve, and at the same time has known how to meet people where they are, and to propose to them concrete ways to progress toward this ideal.

From a film and a conflict around a particular question, the use of the condom by a couple where one partner has contracted AIDS, we could explain that this case is a real exception to the rule prohibiting the use of condoms. But beyond this we could show the relevance of Catholic morality in a Muslim and Orthodox context. This approach insists on a global vision of humankind, respect of human dignity, especially of the poor, attention to the common good, and efforts for an efficient solidarity. In other words, we stand before a true situation of Catholic casuistry, where the global and ideal vision of Catholic morality is considered in its particular context (Islamo-Orthodox), taking into account its singularity (stable married couple). Fighting AIDS in a society where we don't talk about it, Caritas-Egypt knew to take up the challenge of the truest Catholic moral teaching, and to get out of the trap of legalism which does not address the complexity of the situation nor the values at stake. Catholic morality appeals to responsibility. Caritas-Egypt opted for life, solidarity, and human dignity, by educating and clarifying modes of AIDS infection and prevention, and by fighting with audacity and creativity the sickness that kills in the midst of the silence of hypocrisy and ignorance.

THE STRUGGLES OF THE EDINBURGH HIV PREVENTION PROGRAM: LOCAL THEOLOGY AND EXTERNAL PRESSURE

Kenneth Owens

EDINBURGH IS A *beautiful and historical city that is soon to be home to the new Scottish parliament. On a more somber note it has also been described as the "AIDS capital of Europe" because of the high numbers of the population, particularly drug-users, living with HIV infection. Toward the end of the 1980s there was an identified need to produce a resource pack that could be used in the Catholic community by clergy, teachers, and youth workers. This work was undertaken by a Salesian priest with considerable expertise in the HIV/AIDS field and a community worker engaged with a wide spectrum of young people.[1] This case study will examine how the resource pack came into existence, the underlying methodological issues, and the consequences for HIV/AIDS prevention work when it was forced to be withdrawn on instructions from the Congregation for the Doctrine of the Faith.*

The resource pack was launched with high-profile media coverage in January 1993 at Archbishop's House and was generally well received by educators. The first edition sold out and a second run was printed. It was a resource pack that would sit alongside other resources in the religious, moral, personal, and social development of young people. At its heart it had a vision of the human person which sprang from Scripture, prayer and reflection, moral wisdom, as well as factual information. It was an invitation to draw on the rich traditions of the Christian community and an opportunity for formation and discussion through a diversity of resources. It comprised six sessions of input, fifty-four pages of text, twenty transparencies, one game, eleven resource sheets, six pages of glossary, seven fact sheets, and eight work sheets. The resource pack was the fruit of education and formation shared with young people in the post-sixteen age group. The purpose of publishing it was to make a need-ed resource more available. It was not seen as a text book, a manual, a compendium of all that had been said by the Catholic community, or a radical document challenging the church. It was a loose-leaf folder to allow additions, updating, deletions, and materials to be added from other sources.

A whispering campaign was orchestrated by a small number of people, with angry letters to Archbishop O'Brien, archbishop of St. Andrews and Edinburgh, as well as to the media. They were dismayed that the pack carried the imprimatur of the local bishop. At issue was the fact that the resource pack represented a liberal interpretation of how education and formation should be taught in the Catholic community.

Three copies of the resource pack were requested by the nuncio in London to be forwarded to the Congregation for the Doctrine of the Faith. There was complete silence after those resource packs were sent. Six pages of comments were sent from the congregation to the diocesan bishop which remarked about the insufficiency both of its content and presentation. The material was subjected to an inquiry that was well beyond the project's scope. It was a resource pack, not an encyclical. Subsequently a letter from

---

1. Tom Williams and Rhona Hutchison, *HIV Prevention: A Christian Response*, 1993.

Cardinal Ratzinger, prefect of the Congregation for the Doctrine of the Faith, stated: "Notwithstanding the validity of the program's intention, as well as certain pedagogical qualities, it is gravely deficient and ambiguous on the level of moral teaching, and thus may well cause harm to the young people entrusted to the care of the Catholic Church."[2] Faced with such pressure the diocesan bishop had no other option but to accede to the wishes of the congregation. At the time of writing this essay, the Catholic community in Scotland has offered no other resource.

The core problem for the congregation was that individual conscience was presented as the sole, unquestionable criterion of moral decision-making. Then the congregation highlighted four principal difficulties: the importance of living a chaste Christian life was not presented as the ideal; the resource pack did not provide a moral evaluation of the case studies but placed that crucial role on the teacher; the presentation of sexuality was treated in a reductive manner; and the existence of definite moral norms which are binding on individuals was not stated.

Hindsight is a wonderful gift that allows the past to be reviewed and critiqued. From this experience there are a number of methodological insights that creators of the resource pack could have better employed. I will examine those insights and then turn to two other issues: the need for a true appreciation of the task of local theology and an acknowledgment of the problematic assumptions held by opponents of the resource pack.

Methodological Insights

1. The resource pack was a local resource for young people in the diocese. Yet requests were made from all over the world for copies. This highlights that there is a need for accessible material that can be used with young people. Our principal mistake was to seek and receive the *imprimatur* for the resource pack. Carrying such an official endorsement meant that it became the subject of a political debate in the church between conservatives and liberals. This deflected energy and resources away from HIV prevention. It could have served its purpose equally well without the *imprimatur*.

2. The purpose of the resource pack was for young people to encounter a God and a Christian tradition that was loving, compassionate, and merciful. More emphasis should have been focused on the different images of

---

2. Letter from Cardinal Ratzinger to Archbishop O'Brien (Prot no. 5/87-00960), 6 September 1995.

God presented in Scripture which have more to say about justice than about sexual morality. The text of the resource pack should have presented a deeper appreciation of the Christian message about human persons in relationships, grounded in a more adequate portrayal of the many different ways that God has been revealed in human history.

3. The particular difficulties in articulating an adequate theology of sexuality, the morality of the human person in relationship, and the pastoral care of people in difficult situations soon became apparent. Sufficient depth was not given to developing these areas fully.

A whole range of people began taking interest in and commenting on the strengths and weaknesses of the resource pack. It was not the fruit of academic research, nor presented as a compendium of all that the Catholic tradition had to say. It was the fruit of education and formation work done with young people. Thus, it aimed at developing a bond of trust with its young readers and so the resource pack only aspired to be a contribution to the ongoing debate, and not a definitive conclusion.

4. Similarly, the resource pack did not attempt to communicate every aspect of the complexity of every moral situation in life. The modesty of the attempt needed to be more clearly stated. At its core was a desire to promulgate a preventive strategy that would equip young people with information and skills to deal with issues related to sexuality, choice, assertion, and lifestyle. Particularly it tackled the area of peer pressure and how to deal with life situations. It was offered as one resource among many and should not have been viewed as standing alone. A better developed understanding of the complexity of the decision-making process in the moral life would have helped.

5. The realism and the language of the case studies shocked some people. Many stated that they thought it was inappropriate for young people. Yet the response from young people was very positive. Perhaps the lesson was that it needed an accompanying handbook for parents and other concerned adults. If that was the case, then more resources would need to have been allocated to support the program.

6. The resource pack introduced a complex area of moral education and formation because it dealt with the fragmented life experience of many. Hopefully the moral, social, and religious education programs helped to present the Christian ideals in a broader context. It was a common false methodological conclusion that, because the resource pack offered material from the lives' of people whose behavior was at variance with church teaching, the authors were advocating such lifestyles. They were not. Their intention was to educate, discuss, and inform through the real life dilemmas that many face.

7. The appendix of the resource pack included material from other secular agencies. This was again misinterpreted as an attempt to undermine

the church's position. It was not. At its heart, it was a gesture to try to embrace dialogue with other traditions and agencies working in the field. A lesson here would have been to explain more clearly to readers why those secular agencies were included.

Local Theology

1. *The Pastoral Constitution on the Church in the Modern World (Gaudium et Spes),* paragraph 1, states that the concerns of the poor and the vulnerable are at the heart of the Christian community. An authentic theological response to their concerns must value their experience and listen to their heartfelt needs. The local community has to be empowered and enabled to make a contribution. Theology is not the preserve of academics or professional clerics. It is a tool and a resource that has to be available to the whole community. The actions of the Spirit are evident in the local community and their experience must be valued by the tradition. The struggle of the local faith community in living with and ministering to those living with HIV must inform the formulation of the response to this pastoral issue. Those whose hearts experience the closeness of God in their lives' should be heard.

2. The wisdom of those most closely involved in working with men and women living with the virus is a worthy starting point in formulating a prevention strategy. Much suspicion and prejudice has been stirred up in the wider society through fear and ignorance. The lived praxis of the local community must be seen as a source of revelation of God's love for all people. Those most vulnerable must feel loved, respected, supported, and encouraged to voice their experience in the midst of suffering. Their voices should not be suffocated by the universal church. The power and the prestige of the institutional church should be at the service of eradicating the causes of poverty, discrimination, and hardship.

3. The Christian community needs to be able to articulate the gospel message to those who are most in need. The tone and vocabulary of the way that message is communicated matters. When individuals are suffering or ill, they want to be comforted by words and gestures that are familiar. Those who are most in need benefit from a theological and pastoral response which helps them to encounter a merciful God in their all-too-real situation.

4. Pluralism reflects the God-given diversity of the world. To insist that this can easily be reduced to one point of view or one way of seeing reality is wrong. Within the Catholic tradition in the recent past we have struggled to articulate an objective pluralism in the area of sexual morality that respects the diversity of life experience. This continues to be a challenge

which we need to meet as a Christian community. The HIV/AIDS crisis has made this all the more urgent. We need to rediscover the diversity within our own tradition in this arena.

5. Perhaps our attempt at local theology may have been more successful if we had embarked on it with other Christian traditions. The stated aim of the resource pack was to provide Catholic material. The conclusion of the Vatican was that the resource pack was not Catholic enough. A good Christian response may have been the best we could have achieved when our own tradition has been afraid to enter into dialogue about sexual morality. The support of other Christian traditions in this instance may have helped in our local setting. This may have kept others from seeing our position as exhausting the Catholic tradition.

6. To educate and form young people we need to be able to offer a broader approach. We need to draw on the resources in Scripture and in our tradition to show that there is not one uniform solution but a variety of legitimately different ways to know God and how God is revealed in the lives of individuals, particularly in the midst of suffering. The vulnerable need to have their experience valued and their difficulties understood. The compassionate Christ embraces all, irrespective of their life situations, and calls them to the ways of the gospel.

Methods of Opponents

1. The resource pack was for use in Edinburgh. When it was published, it began to have a life of its own. As an educational resource, it became a test of orthodoxy for those opposed to it. This highlights how an initiative with good intentions became portrayed as a vehicle which could erode all things Catholic. The resource pack represented liberal views within the Catholic tradition. It was a plea for dialogue and openness which never took place. With the banning of the resource pack, a void has been created. People are also fearful about sharing resources. There needs to be an opportunity for acknowledging diversity with respect and openness.

2. Doing theology in the time of HIV/AIDS also highlights areas of wider debate in the church. These are particularly pertinent to the issues of sexual morality, relationship, and diversity. Many would oppose the realism demanded for engagement in this debate. Some experience a climate of fear at the present time. There needs to be a sufficient breadth in the church to embrace the diversity and pluralism that is part and parcel of the objective human condition. A fuller debate needs to take place between our church tradition and the human sciences. To understand adequately the human person we must draw from the resources of philosophy, psychology, and theology.

3. The Vatican instructed that the resource pack be removed without any dialogue with the local bishop or the authors. This caused both hurt and confusion. The discussion was abruptly brought to an end without the interested parties even meeting each other. This was a lost opportunity. There needs to be a forum where there can be an honest exchange of differing views. A church that cannot dialogue among its members cannot promote a dialogue beyond its borders.

4. The recent *General Directory for Catechesis* acknowledges that young people have different levels of commitment and that their faith has matured to different levels. There appears to be an internal inconsistency that on the one hand an official document of the church recognizes this, but on the other it does not allow for this diversity at the local level. Young people are called to live according to the ideals of the gospel. They must be helped along the way to develop both their spiritual and their faith lives.

5. Many critics of the resource pack took individual case studies, particular examples, or salient facts out of context. Care would need to be taken so that the message of the educational teaching could be treated fairly and not distorted. The complexity of both helping young people make moral judgments in the area of life choices and sexuality, and calling them to a life of conversion takes time.

6. Those who were the most severe critics came from a predominately deontological stance. They feared that the resource pack did not sufficiently underscore the transcendental nature of the human person. Yet there needs to be a variety of approaches which reflect the diversity of the human reality. Contemporary ethical writing, particularly the contribution of feminist and liberation ethics, tries to help us capture new ways of viewing reality. One of the challenges of our experience must be to find ways in which there can be a meeting of different mindsets for the good of the community.

7. One of the saddest aspects of the silencing and withdrawal of this resource pack was that the voices of those living and working with individuals affected with HIV/AIDS were not listened to or valued. The Catholic community's response to the HIV/AIDS crisis was impoverished through this experience. A very small minority of people, most of whom had no interest or expertise in the issues, were successful. Neo-orthodoxy was prized above all else.

Conclusion

I MUST REPEAT, the investigation of the resource pack as well as the instruction to withdraw it took place without dialogue. There was no opportunity for either the *congregation* or the authors to meet and exchange views. There must be a forum for differing positions and perceptions to be discussed and debated. The authors were left demoralized and a vital area left without resources.

As the issue of HIV/AIDS emerged and touched the lives of individuals and families, there was a need also to find an adequate theological resource. As with any new crisis a certain tolerance in the way in which issues are handled is needed. At heart, there must be a concern to allow individuals the opportunity to be comforted by God's love.

The complexity of the issues of HIV/AIDS cannot be isolated within the Catholic community. Individuals are part of the wider society. As a Catholic community we need to be able to share our resources and insights on the issues of health, education, and social being in order to contribute to the common good.

At the core of the mission of the Catholic community should be the desire to mobilize our energies for those who are needy and vulnerable. We should work to promote human dignity and an authentic quality of life. The scandal of division diverts attention away from the issue at hand, namely HIV/AIDS, and highlights wider theological tensions in the church.

ESTABLISHING U.S. CAMPUS-BASED HIV/AIDS AWARENESS AND PREVENTION PROGRAMS

Regina Wentzel Wolfe

FOR A NUMBER *of years now, Joanne had been among the faculty and staff calling for some type of HIV/AIDS awareness and prevention program on campus. From her perspective, it was imperative that students be made aware of the seriousness of HIV/AIDS and the manner in which it is contracted in order that they might better be able to protect themselves from the disease. It seemed incongruous to her that an institution of higher education, which prided itself on providing a quality education, chose not to address the issue directly.*

When she approached the administration about this she was informed that when circumstances warranted it—in or out of the classroom—students were made aware of any risk of transmission and provided with appropriate information on eliminating or reducing that risk. But she found that, for the most part, this referred to a brief lecture on high-risk behaviors given during new student orientation and to the universal precautions for training nursing students preparing for clinical rotations. She remained frustrated that nothing further was being done.

Having heard Joanne express her views on the issue, the dean asked her to be the school's faculty representative to a working group of representatives from Catholic colleges and universities whose brief was to focus on the design and implementation of campus-based HIV/AIDS awareness and prevention programs. Joanne accepted immediately. She felt both challenged and excited about the prospect of being involved in formulating responsible ways of addressing the topic. And she was pleased that the nurse practitioner from the university health center had also agreed to be part of the working group.

The twenty or so people in the working group represented the spectrum of Catholic higher education in the U.S., from small liberal arts colleges to large research universities, from urban to rural settings. Faculty, staff, and administrative areas were all represented. For the most part, the approaches that individuals took to the topic fell into one of three categories. There were those who emphasized the Catholic character of the institutions and were primarily concerned that any proposed program be compatible with church teaching, particularly teachings in the area of sexuality. Then there were those who focused on the students and emphasized the institutions' responsibility to act in the best interests of their students both in and out of the classroom. Finally, there were those who were primarily concerned with the relationship and responsibility of student health center staff to the institutions that hired them and to the students who were their patients.

Though the group met only a few times each year, the members communicated with each other on a regular basis, sharing their research findings and discussing appropriate responses to them. One of the most valuable aspects of the group was its interdisciplinary character. This enabled Joanne to look at the challenge of developing an HIV/AIDS awareness and prevention program from an interdisciplinary perspective. When she first began, her primary concern—based on her assumption that students had little knowledge about HIV/AIDS—had been to ensure that students had the facts about HIV/AIDS. She learned, however, that nationwide slightly more than 40 percent of students have been taught about HIV or AIDS in college classrooms and almost 50 percent report having received information about HIV/AIDS prevention while attending college.[1] Furthermore, almost 40 percent of college students have had a

---

1. "Youth Risk Behavior Surveillance: National College Health Risk Behavior Survey—United States, 1995," *Morbidity and Mortality Weekly Report*, Centers for Disease Control and Prevention, vol. 46, 14 November 1997. At http://www.cdc.gov/epo/mmwr/preview/mmwrhtml/00049859.htm.

blood test for the HIV infection.[2] *She began to realize that it wasn't simply a matter of dissemination of facts, a realization that was corroborated by many of the people whom she interviewed in the process of doing research.*

Voices

STAFF AND ADMINISTRATORS working in student life were emphatic that while presentation of clear and accurate information is necessary, it is not sufficient. To be effective, prevention education must take into consideration students' developmental stages as well as behaviors that put students at risk for becoming infected. Concern was expressed over the relationship between alcohol use and risky sexual behavior. This relationship is particularly troublesome, not only because it increases the risk of contracting sexually transmitted diseases (STDs), including HIV, but also because it reflects an inability to form healthy intimate relationships. It highlights underlying issues of identity and self-confidence. Other considerations are the sense of immortality and the "it won't happen to me" attitude prevalent among college-age students.

Much of this was corroborated by the medical practitioners. They are worried that some young people are unaware of the basic facts about the manner in which the HIV/AIDS virus is spread. The medical practitioners fully recognize the need for those who are sexually active to take appropriate precautions against the spread of HIV as well as other STDs. However, they have serious misgivings about the false sense of security that the safer sex message provides many of their patients. These misgivings are coupled with a desire to see that the message is spread that the only certain way of ensuring against contracting the HIV infection is to engage in sexual activity only in the context of a faithful monogamous relationship with a noninfected partner. In this the medical practitioners echo the 1993 surgeon general's report that states, "the surest way to protect yourself against HIV infection and other STDs is not to have sex at all, or to have sex only with one steady, uninfected partner."[3]

The medical practitioners were also troubled by emerging trends in new HIV infections. Among their concerns are the fact that about half are in individuals who are age twenty-five or younger,[4] that a disproportionate number of African-Americans are becoming infected, that rates of

---

2. "Youth Risk Behavior Surveillance."

3. Marian Segal, "Women and AIDS," *FDA Consumer Reprint*, October 1993, revised September 1995 and September 1997. At http://www.fda.gov/opacom/catalog/womanaids.html.

4. "Facts about Youth and HIV in the United States." Fact sheet published by *Health Initiatives for Youth* (hi-fy), San Francisco, November 1997.

HIV infection are increasing faster among women than men, and that while there is a one percent female-to-male transmission of HIV, the male-to-female transmission rate is twenty percent.[5] The medical practitioners attributed some of these trends to issues of identity, self-worth, and self-confidence.

Women are particularly vulnerable. In discussing the mode of exposure to HIV or other STDs, medical practitioners often found that women patients knew both how the infection was contracted and how to reduce the risk of becoming infected. The problem was their inability to say no to their partners or to insist that their partners use a condom or other reliable barrier.

In some cases this inability was due to loss of control as a result of alcohol or drug use, but in many others it was related to a desire to please their partners despite being fully cognizant of the fact that to do so would be to place themselves at risk. In some cases the patient mistakenly believed a partner who claimed to be a virgin or who claimed to be uninfected. In other cases the patient acquiesced in response to a partner's insistence that the experience of safer sex would be less sensually pleasurable for the partner, or that it would be less intimate and thereby diminish the relationship.

Regardless of the reason given, from the medical practitioners' perspective the root cause is understood to be an inability to assert oneself and to put legitimate concerns for the health and well-being of both self and partner before the physical or emotional needs of the partner. That this lack of assertiveness or power to control the situation was particularly true of women patients is disconcerting for medical practitioners, particularly in light of the fact that among women the rate of infection through heterosexual sex is rising and is now significantly greater than the infection rate through injection drug use.[6]

Also vulnerable are young men who in college begin to face the immutability of their homosexual orientation. Fear of possible social rejection, a negative self-image from internalized homophobia, and the desperation for companionship might prompt them toward anonymous sexual encounters. Such impulsive behavior would, of course, put them at great risk of infection with HIV.

A further complication is the structure of health care delivery systems which increasingly limits the development of long-term, personal doctor-patient relationships. Without such relationships it is difficult for medical

---

5. Segal, "Women and AIDS."

6. Table 29, *HIV/AIDS Surveillance Report*, Centers for Disease Control and Prevention, vol. 9, no. 2. At http://www.cdc.gov/nchstp/hiv_aids/stats/hasrlink.htm.

practitioners to go beyond treating physical symptoms. Thus, their attempts to assist patients with identity issues and with modifying their patterns of behavior are hampered. Campus health centers are subject to these same structures, which often hamper attempts to build appropriate relationships with students who seek medical care.

Students were clear that they had been given the facts, not only in college but also in high school and, in some cases, elementary school as well. However, knowledge of the facts does not necessarily change behaviors. Students reported that they often "tune out" when presentations are in the context of mandatory events, such as residence hall meetings, or when the presenter is an authority figure. Such messages are usually viewed as "preachy" or moralizing. Students often come away with a sense of being told no, and they reported that among their peers there was great resistance to being preached at and told what to do. In addition, they reported that there is frequently a sense that it is the "same old" message, so there is no reason to pay attention to it.

Students also noted that though they talk to one another, particularly their partners, about everything else, they don't talk about sex.

A Fuller Picture

FORMAL STUDIES SUPPORTED the anecdotal information that Joanne had gathered and filled out the picture for her.[7] Reflecting patterns in their own practices, the medical practitioners with whom she had spoken focused on women's identity issues. Studies revealed that identity problems—particularly living up to some stereotypical masculine ideal— were also a factor in male students' choices to engage in behaviors that put them and their partners at risk.[8] This was reflected in studies that found that male athletes were among the most sexually active students, while female athletes were among the least sexually active, a behavioral difference which in part is attributed to self-image and identity.[9] Also of significance was the correlation between behavior that put college students at risk for becoming infected with HIV and those students'

---

7. See the *Journal of American College Health* 46, no. 6 (1998) and 47, no. 1 (1998).

8. Richard P. Keeling, MD, "Men, Masculinity, and Health Behavior," *Journal of American College Health* 46, no. 6 (1998): 243–46.

9. Patricia K. Kokotailo, MD, MPH; Rebecca E. Koscik, MS; Bill C. Henry, PhD; Michael F. Fleming, MD, MPH; and Gregory L. Landry, MD, "Health Risk Taking and Human Immunodeficiency Virus Risk in Collegiate Female Athletes," *Journal of American College Health* 46, no. 6 (1998): 263–68.

moral reasoning skills: the more developed students' moral reasoning skills, the lower the incidence of risky behaviors. It is also worth noting that the number of college age students who are not sexually active is increasing.

Joanne had begun the project with the naive view that there needed to be some campus-based program that would give students the facts so that they would be better prepared to make informed decisions. She came to realize that, in general, they were aware of the facts. She found that the church's call for genital sexual activity to be in the context of a committed, faithful, marital relationship was similar to that of the medical practitioners who call for genital sexual activity to be in a committed, faithful, monogamous relationship. In effect, the message to those engaging in sex outside such relationships is simply "don't do it." Joanne realized, however, that such a simplistic, one-dimensional response would be woefully inadequate given the social and cultural environment found on college campuses and the developmental stages of students. What is required is a comprehensive and integrative campus-wide HIV/AIDS awareness and prevention education program—a program that draws on the strengths of Catholic higher education.

Contribution of the Catholic Moral Tradition

THE CATHOLIC MORAL tradition, grounded in the threefold command to love God, neighbor, and self, has much to contribute to the task at hand. It is a rich tradition which calls people to respond positively to God's gift of love, and challenges them to become people of virtuous character. Acting out of that response, they lead lives of love and justice through active participation in the transformation of society. Clearly it challenges students, heterosexual and homosexual, to become morally mature people of faith. But in this instance it goes well beyond that. It also challenges colleges and universities not only to assist students in their search for appropriate sexual expression, but also to use their many institutional resources in the work of transforming the social systems and structures—both internal and external—that either hamper or preclude students from growing and developing into morally mature persons of faith.

If Catholic institutions of higher learning are to be faithful to their missions, those involved in and responsible for the way these institutions are structured must strive to ensure that the environment—which forms and shapes those who are affiliated with such institutions—not only is grounded in the gospel values which undergird mission statements, but also fosters the creation of a community of moral discourse.[10] In this way these institutions will be moving toward the creation of campus communities whose cultures will provide alternative visions of what it means to be human and how to relate to an ever-changing world.

In particular, in a time of HIV/AIDS, there are three challenges that must be taken seriously. First, there is a prevailing ethos on college campuses that promotes aggressive and risky behavior by men as they struggle with understanding and expressing their manhood. Second, there is no safe place for gay men and lesbians to talk about sex and sexual identity. This leaves these students isolated, uninformed, and vulnerable. Finally, despite all the purported advances women have made in our society, as a group young women still have not learned to be assertive, to speak in their own voices, and to trust their own selves.

Meeting these challenges requires, first, that attention be given to campus culture, which can either impede or foster meeting the above challenges. Second, the claims made in college and university mission statements need to be reflected in practice. At a minimum this would require establishing processes that put the values inherent in those mission statements at the core of decision-making. Here, Catholic institutions of higher learning have much to learn from Catholic health care systems and their emphasis on mission integrity. Seriously attending to mission integrity can go a long way to creating a respectful environment in which open and honest dialogue can take place as young women and men grow not only intellectually, but also physically, emotionally, and spiritually. This involves commitment from faculty, staff, and administration who, in the best of the Catholic moral tradition, have as their starting point compassion and respect for students as they are, and yet who challenge students to expand their horizons, and thus to grow and develop into more mature moral beings.[11]

In keeping with its primary purpose, the faculty's principal focus is on curricular concerns. Emphasis should be placed on facilitating students' development of critical, analytical skills, and on enhancing their ability to apply those skills in various scholarly disciplines. These are the same skills needed to engage in mature moral reasoning. As noted above, this has a

---

10. For a discussion of the place of a community of moral discourse in training individuals to engage in moral discernment, see James M. Gustafson, "Moral Discernment in the Christian Life," in *Christian Ethics: A Reader*, ed. Ronald P. Hamel and Kenneth R. Himes (New York: Paulist Press, 1989), 583–97.

11. For a discussion of the compatibility of authentic representation of objective norms of morality, and compassionate and respectful acceptance of persons who in all sincerity cannot accept the teaching, see Richard M. Gula, *Ethics in Pastoral Ministry* (New York: Paulist Press, 1996), especially 56–59.

direct correlation to choices about risky sexual behaviors. But these skills are not simply to be exhibited in the classroom. An integrated approach to education accepts the task of aiding all students, regardless of their sexual orientation, in applying these skills to their own lives as they struggle to grow into morally mature persons. Facilitating this, particularly as part of an effective HIV/AIDS awareness and prevention program, calls for changing the compartmentalized nature of many institutions of higher learning. Faculty and development staff, particularly those directly concerned with student health and well-being, must adopt a collaborative approach to teaching and learning, an approach that reflects the holistic nature of the educational enterprise and models it for students.

Encouraging all voices to participate requires that adequate and appropriate consideration be given to all constituencies. Thus, students' claims that an effective program is one that relies in significant ways on peer-education, is multidimensional, and is ongoing must be heeded. Respecting these claims will assist in facilitating broader participation.

All participants must adopt a respectful listening stance, which is necessary in order to ensure that all voices, heterosexual and homosexual, are heard and that the wisdom which students bring to the discussion informs program design and implementation. In addition, attention ought to be given to the voices of the sizable number of single students who are offended at the presumption of many of their peers and of nonstudent members of campus communities that the vast majority of students are sexually active. Based in the joys and struggles of living a chaste celibate life, they too have wisdom to share, a wisdom that is eloquently captured in "Chastity as a Creative Strength: An Open Letter to Students at Georgetown University."[12] To move in this direction is to begin to create an environment in which students can consider and discuss sex and sexual self-understanding in an atmosphere that both respects the dignity and uniqueness of each student and challenges each student to engage in serious reflection on these critically important issues.

Conclusion

CATHOLIC INSTITUTIONS OF higher education in the U.S. are well placed to respond to the HIV/AIDS pandemic. Their mission, to provide an integrated educational experience that is grounded in gospel values, provides a context

12. Mary Patricia Barth Fourqurean. "Chastity as a Creative Strength: An Open Letter to Students at Georgetown University" (Washington, D.C.: Office of Campus Ministry, Georgetown University, 1993).

that fosters a comprehensive response. Their challenge is to be faithful to that context by creating communities of moral discourse. Such communities will enable the development of strong and effective HIV/AIDS awareness and prevention programs. They will provide a campus environment that fosters ethical reflection in the context of faith in order to assist all members of the community in their spiritual and moral formation and growth, with particular emphasis on the needs of the students whom it serves.

5.
USING THE PRINCIPLE
OF COOPERATION

NEEDLE EXCHANGE IN SAN JUAN, PUERTO RICO: A TRADITIONAL ROMAN CATHOLIC CASUISTIC APPROACH

Jorge J. Ferrer, S.J.

PUERTO RICO IS *known to many in the United States as a tropical holiday destination, with sunny beaches and plenty of piña colada with Puerto Rican rum. That is, of course, part of the picture, the part understandably presented and promoted abroad by the U.S. tourism office. But there is also a darker side to the story of sunny Puerto Rico. Both the city of San Juan and the island of Puerto Rico have a very high prevalence of HIV infections and AIDS. On 30 April 1998, there had been a total of 21,805 reported cases of AIDS in Puerto Rico, since cases began to be registered in the early eighties.[1] For cases reported in 1993, Puerto Rico had the second highest seroprevalence in the U. S.: 112.7 cases per 100,000 population. San Juan was one of the five cities with the highest seroprevalence rates in the U.S. that year: 103.4 cases per 100,000 population.[2]*

Since its inception in Puerto Rico, the HIV epidemic has been tied to the use of intravenous drugs. The use of contaminated needles and syringes for injecting drugs has been the main route for the transmission of the AIDS virus in our country. In over 50 percent of registered cases of AIDS, both in Puerto Rico and among persons of Puerto Rican descent in the U. S., HIV transmission has taken place through the use of infected equipment to

---

1. Centers for Disease Control, *Puerto Rico AIDS Surveillance Report* (30 April 1998).

2. Jacques Normand, David Vlahov, and Lincoln E. Moses, eds., *Preventing HIV Transmission. The Role of Sterile Needles and Bleach* (Washington, D.C.: National Academy Press, 1995), 32–35.

inject illicit drugs. A significant number of cases of heterosexual HIV trans-mission also are drug-related.[3] The virus is transmitted to sexual partners of intravenous drug users (IDUs)—who are mostly women—and, not rarely, to their offspring. This situation does not come as a surprise to any-one familiar with the drug situation on the island. For years, it has been said that Puerto Rico is one of the favorite entrance points to the U. S. mar-ket for illegal drugs coming from South America. Being an island, there are ample borders which are difficult to control at all times. Moreover, the lin-guistic and cultural affinity with the rest of Latin America seems to make Puerto Rico more attractive to drug dealers from further south. As in other places, repressive measures—mano dura (a "heavy hand") in the present governor's lingo—have proven to be ineffective to stop both drug traffick-ing and drug abuse.

Needle Exchange in San Juan

GIVEN THE SERIOUSNESS of the drug problem in Puerto Rico and the obvious failure of repressive measures to create a drug-free society, it is surprising how little attention risk-reduction programs have received in our society, outside of the all but forgotten methadone program. As Ethel A. Nadel-man, director of the Lindesmith Center, has recently written, risk-reduction models acknowledge that "criminal justice responses can be costly and counterproductive, and that single-minded pursuit of a drug-free society is dangerously quixotic."[4]

Advocates of harm reduction strategies do not deny that a drug-free society is a desirable goal to strive for. The abuse of drugs—both legal and

---

3. Rafaela R. Robles et al., *Proyecto de intercambio de jeringuillas. Vol I: Evaluación del impacto* (Bayamón P. R.: Centro de Estudios en Adicción, Universidad Central del Caribe, 1998), 2–3. From now on I will quote it as *Evaluación*. The researchers who authored the evaluation quote several studies to back up this statement: M. Selik et al., "Birthplace and Risk of AIDS among Hispanics in the United States," *American Journal of Public Health* 79 (1989): 836–39; T. Díaz, J. W. Buehler, and K. Castro, "AIDS Trends Among Hispanics in the United States," *American Journal of Public Health* 83 (1993) 504–9. As of 30 April 1998, 52 percent of the cases of AIDS reported in Puerto Rico since the begin-ning of the epidemic are directly related to the use of injectable drugs. Many others are indirectly related to the use of injectable drugs, such as the infections reported in sexual partners and offspring of drug users who do not inject drugs themselves. See Centers for Disease Control, *Puerto Rico AIDS Surveillance.*

4. Ethel A. Nadelman, "Commonsense Drug Policy," *Foreign Affairs* 77, no. 1 (1998): 111–26.

illegal—has damaging effects not only on the lives of individuals, but also on the lives of their families and neighbors, and on society as a whole. It is enough to think of the large number of automobile accidents, with their toll of death and suffering, caused by drunk drivers alone in Puerto Rico or in the United States, not to mention the high rate of crimes directly or indirectly connected with the use of illicit drugs, to realize how much harm drug abuse causes in our society.

But drug-free advocates also recognize that many people will not refrain from the use of drugs, licit or illicit, no matter how much information is given to them about the harmful effects of drug abuse for the individual as well as for the community as a whole. It is important to add that the use of illicit drugs is frequently associated with other social problems, including poverty and marginalization. It is true that the abuse of illicit drugs—such as cocaine—also happens among members of the upper middle class, but it is no secret that drug trafficking and drug abuse more severely affects the poor and the marginalized who live in our public housing projects and in our poor communities in the big cities and towns throughout the island. They are also the ones who most frequently end up behind bars for drug-related violations.

It is not enough to send a message calling for abstinence. Drug users must be empowered through adequate social and behavioral interventions if they are going to move to abstinence or at least to reduce risks to their health and safety, and that of their partners and children.[5] Risk-reduction models strive to minimize the harms that persons who use drugs inflict upon themselves. Persons are accepted in a nonjudgmental way and instructed on the health risks of their behavior and in the ways to reduce such risks, including the use of clean needles and syringes every time that

---

5. Psychologists know well that willpower usually is not enough to change deeply ingrained behaviors, no matter how pathological or incapacitating they might be. In a book about scrupulosity, J. W. Ciarrochi, a behaviorally oriented psychologist, writes: "In western society and in many religious cultures willpower is oversold. Many believe that most, if not all, habits can change through an act of the will, i.e., through a decision to change. Research and life experiences tell us otherwise. . . . Almost all behavior change . . . require[s] several different skills to accomplish" (*The Doubting Disease* [Mahwah, N.J.: Paulist Press, 1995], 66). Among the ingredients that people need if they are going to change successfully are cognitive and behavioral skills to establish alternative behaviors and social supports which will enhance the new, more constructive behaviors. And, of course, a person needs a lot of motivation and a healthy love of self. Therefore, it is not enough to preach abstinence from the pulpit, in the classroom, or through the media to obtain behavioral changes in users. Moreover, drug using behaviors are pleasurable and many users have already developed an addiction which in many cases implies a physical dependency.

they inject drugs. Risk-reduction strategies include the establishment of a friendly relationship between professionals or activists doing education and their clients. Usually the possibility of referral to a treatment program is one of the services offered by harm reduction programs, but clients are only referred when they are ready for the referral.

Iniciativa Comunitaria (IC) is a well-known community organization, recently developed in Puerto Rico, based on the philosophy of risk-reduction. The organization works with intravenous drug users in the San Juan metropolitan area. The main objective of IC is to offer health education and services to persons living with HIV infection and AIDS. It focuses its attention on those populations which are most deprived of services in our society, such as drug users, sexual workers, women, and youth. These groups, particularly in lower socio-economic environments, are the objects of prejudice and rejection. They have difficulty receiving social and medical services of high quality. It is especially difficult to find such services in an environment where they feel respected as persons, without judgment or condemnation.

IC was born in 1990, funded by a grant awarded by the American Foundation for AIDS Research. Its programs have continued to develop and it has become one of the principal providers of primary health services for persons living with HIV in our city. The organization's programs have also received the support of many entities public and private throughout the years, including the Centers for Disease Control (CDC), the House of Representatives of Puerto Rico, Hoffman Laroche, and Borroughs Wellcome Corporation, among others.

One of IC's services is a needle exchange program, the only one, as far as I know, presently functioning in San Juan. This program was instituted as a pilot project in 1995, with the support of Puerto Rico's health department. The pilot project was established under two different modalities: stable and mobile. The stable program was entrusted to *Oasis de Amor*, a nonprofit organization devoted mainly to the treatment of HIV-infected drug users. IC took responsibility for the mobile modality. The pilot project was observed and evaluated for a period of eighteen months by the Center for the Study of Addictions of the *Universidad Central del Caribe* in Bayamón. A final report related to this project was published by the center.[6] IC still continues to operate the needle and syringe exchange program.

IC has received some public criticism from different groups. The main criticism, whether from police, conservative religious groups, or neighborhood protests, has been that the program promotes drug addiction. The criticism, if I understand it correctly, has *an explicit factual claim and an*

---

6. *Evaluación*, 4.

implicit moral claim. The factual claim—that syringe and needle exchange actually promotes addiction—cannot be resolved on the level of general moral principles. It requires that we take a look at the empirical evidence at hand. The moral claim could perhaps be construed as saying that "promoting addiction to illegal drugs is morally wrong." This claim could be brushed aside if we can show that needle exchange programs, in general, and IC's program in particular, in fact do not promote drug addiction. But the moral claim could be construed in a somewhat different way, at least from a Catholic perspective: the distribution or exchange of clean needles and syringes is a form of cooperation in an evil behavior, and we should not enter into any kind of compromise with moral evil. For the sake of this paper, I will construe the moral objection in these latter terms. I will now examine both of these claims—the empirical claim and the moral claim—and see if they stand up after the critical scrutiny of empirical evidence and traditional moral principles.

The Empirical Claim

THE SCIENTIFIC EVIDENCE at hand does not seem to support the "empirical claim" advanced by the Puerto Rican police force and by many others: that syringe and needle exchange programs promote the use of intravenous drugs. If "promoting" has any meaning, it should mean that the number of addicts grows or that the persons who would have withdrawn from drug use continue using them. Indeed, these were among the principal objections advanced by the U. S. bishops in their 1989 letter on the AIDS epidemic, "Called to Compassion and Responsibility." The bishops opposed the exchange of needles because: 1) it could bring about an increase in drug use; 2) it could discourage addicts from seeking treatment; 3) if the programs lack adequate supervision, HIV transmission through the use of infected needles could actually be increased; and 4) the distribution of clean needles and syringes would send the false message that it can be safe to inject illicit drugs.[7] It must be kept in mind that when these objections were presented, very little empirical data about the results of needle and syringe exchange programs had been documented. These episcopal misgivings were probably warranted given the information available at that time.[8] The

---

7. U.S. Bishops, "Called to Compassion and Responsibility," *Origins* 19, no. 26 (1989): 421–34.

8. It is, however, fair to comment that, in 1989, the data were scarce but not totally lacking. The first results published by the pioneering Amsterdam program, as early as 1987, were indeed quite encouraging. See Charles F. Turner, Heather G.

question is whether they continue to be reasonable with the knowledge that we have today.

A number of studies, including six reviews sponsored by the U. S. government, have shown that needle and syringe exchange programs reduce the incidence of HIV infection among intravenous drugs users and do not contribute to an increase in the use of drugs by habitual users or in the number of addicted individuals.[9] In response to a legislative directive from the U. S. Congress, the National Research Council (NRC) and the Institute of Medicine (IOM) of the National Academy of Sciences organized the panel on needle exchange and bleach distribution programs within the Commission on Behavioral and Social Sciences and Education. Although the panel recommended that the present ban on federal funding to support needle exchange programs be rescinded, the federal government has not been persuaded by the recommendation of its own scientists.[10] As I write, three years later, the ban continues to bar the use of federal money to fund needle exchange programs in the U. S. and its territories.

In August 1997, *AIDS Information Exchange (AIX)*, an official publication of the United States Conference of Mayors HIV/AIDS Program, presented a good summary of research results on needle exchange programs up to the first half of 1997.[11] According to the information published in

---

Miller, and Lincoln E. Moses, eds., *AIDS: Sexual Behavior and Intravenous Drug Use* (Washington, D.C.: National Academy Press, 1989), 202–3. This book presents an ample bibliography about AIDS and drug use, at pp. 240–55.

9. I take the reference for the six U. S. government-sponsored reviews from Peter Lurie and Ernest Drucker, "An opportunity lost: HIV Infections Associated with Lack of a National Needle-Exchange Program in the USA," *Lancet* 349 (1 March 1997): 604–8. Besides the book edited by Jacques Normand, David Vlahov, and Lincoln E. Moses, *Preventing HIV Transmission,* already quoted above, Lurie and Drucker give the following references: Peter Lurie and Arthur L. Reginold, eds., *The Public Health Impact of Needle Exchange Programs in the United States and Abroad,* vol. I (San Francisco: University of California Press, 1993); General Accounting Office, *Needle Exchange Programs: Research Suggests Promise as an AIDS Prevention Strategy,* GAO/HRD-93-60 (Washington, D.C.: U. S. Government Printing Office, 1993); National Commission on Acquired Immune Deficiency Syndrome, *The Twin Epidemics of Substance Use and HIV* (Washington, D.C., 1991); D. Satcher, *Note to Jo Ivvey Boufford, December 10, 1993* (available from the Drug Policy Foundation, 4455 Connecticut Avenue, NW, Suite b-500, Washington, D.C., 20008); Office of Technology Assessment, *The Effectiveness of AIDS Prevention Efforts* (Washington, D.C., 1995).

10. Normand, Vlahov, and Moses, eds., *Preventing HIV,* 253.

11. *AIX* is available from the United States Conference of Mayors, 1620 Eye Street N.W., Washington, D.C., 20006.

that issue of *AIX*, research evidence continues to strongly suggest that needle and syringe exchange programs significantly reduce injection drug users' risk of HIV infection without having an adverse impact on communities. Syringe exchange does not increase the number of users and does not increase the number of publicly discarded syringes. Moreover, the cost effectiveness of implementing a national syringe exchange program in the U. S. significantly exceeds the cost effectiveness of providing treatment for persons living with HIV infection and AIDS (putting aside the enormous amount of human suffering and disease that could be avoided).[12] The cost effectiveness of needle and syringe exchange programs has been studied, using statistical methods, by Peter Lurie and Ernest Drucker in an article published in March 1997.[13] According to their estimates of needle exchange programs efficacy, the number of HIV infections that could have been prevented, between 1987 and 1996, ranged from 4,394 (if we attribute a 15 percent incidence reduction to needle exchanges) to 9,666 (33 percent incidence reduction). The cost to the health care system of treating these preventable HIV infections ranges between US $244 million and US $538 million. This cost is equivalent to operating between 161 and 354 needle exchange programs. There were sixty-eight such programs in the U.S. in 1994.

In 1997, the National Institutes of Health (NIH) convened a *Consensus Conference on Interventions to Prevent HIV Risk Behaviors*. The conference focused on the identification of behavioral interventions that are effective for risk-reduction for the two primary modes of HIV transmission: unsafe sexual behavior and unsafe injection practices. An independent panel of experts weighed the scientific evidence presented at the conference and developed a draft for a consensus statement. The panel reviewed data on the efficiency of needle and syringe exchange programs. It concluded that needle exchange is *demonstrably effective in preventing transmission of HIV: consistent use of sterile injecting equipment is almost 100 percent effective in preventing HIV infection among injecting drug users*. Moreover, it: 1) does not increase syringe-injecting behavior among current drug users, 2) does not increase the overall number of drug users, and 3) does not increase the number of discarded syringes or drug paraphernalia in communities.[14]

---

12. *AIX* (August 1997): 1. The article presents new research released during the first half of 1997. Unfortunately, it does not give references.

13. Peter Lurie and Ernest Drucker, "An Opportunity Lost: HIV Infections Associated with Lack of a National Needle-Exchange Program in the USA," *Lancet* 349 (March 1997): 604–8.

14. *AIX* (August 1997): 1–3.

These conclusions are compatible with the results of the pilot project evaluation carried out in San Juan: 1) although only 40.3 percent of the total number of syringes distributed by the program came back, the number of syringes returned to the program rose significantly during the eight-month evaluation period: from 12.4 percent during the first month to 32.5 percent during the last month.[15] 2) There was at least a 40 percent reduction in the sharing of needles and syringes.[16] 3) There was no evidence of an increase in injecting behavior among participants.[17] 4) The program was not as successful in getting participants into treatment programs for drug addiction; only 9.4 percent of the participants entered a treatment program.[18]

According to this evidence it seems warranted to conclude that the "empirical claim" is groundless. The *onus probandi* rests, in my opinion, on the shoulders of whoever advances it. Having shown the lack of empirical evidence precisely for what we have called "the empirical claim," we can turn to the strictly moral argument. It could be articulated as follows: the distribution or exchange of sterile injection equipment, that one knows will be used for injecting illicit drugs (moreover, one intends it to be used precisely for that purpose), represents a morally untenable cooperation in evil.

The Moral Claim

IT SEEMS TO me that the usefulness of needle exchange programs from a public health perspective is reasonably well established on the basis of the scientific evidence that we have just reviewed. It is true that these conclusions could be proved to be wrong in the future, but they represent the most solid grounds for responsible action today. We do not have to wait for absolute and irrefutable evidence to act responsibly. Such evidence might well never come. Moral action requires neither mathematical nor metaphysical certainty. If such were the case, it would be impossible to act with responsibility in most human affairs. Still, it could be argued that by providing injection equipment to an intravenous drug user, we are cooperating in a morally evil action, becoming ourselves guilty of the same evil. By providing clean syringes and needles we would become, according to this line of argument, promoters or, at least, accomplices of the moral evil of drug abuse. We are never allowed to engage in the deliberate commission of moral evil.

---

15. *Evaluación*, 11, 15.
16. Ibid., 12–13, 15–16.
17. Ibid., 16.
18. Ibid.

Are there any principles in our Catholic moral tradition that would allow us to find an answer to the moral objections advanced against needle and syringe exchange programs? It must be kept in mind that our endeavor here is to search for traditional arguments in the Catholic tradition, even when some of them are not commonly used in contemporary moral theology.

Two closely connected traditional principles come to mind: the principle that allows us to counsel the lesser evil *sub specie boni* and the principle of cooperation (*cooperatio ad malum*). Both principles were discussed and developed for centuries by Catholic theologians in the so-called manualist or casuistic tradition. I will take up first the principle of cooperation. Even though these principles are different from the traditional principle of the double effect, they are, nonetheless, its first-degree relatives. All three are signs of the realism and common sense present in much of the classical tradition of moral theology.[19] In a finite world we cannot be expected to act in such a way as to avoid all possible evil effects. Therefore, although to cooperate in the wrong action of someone else is regrettable and should be avoided whenever possible, it is not always feasible to do so. Indeed, often such a cooperation might be the only course of action available to us if we are to avoid an even greater harm to the common good.[20]

The Principle of Cooperation (*Cooperatio ad Malum*)[21]

THEOLOGIANS HAVE DEFINED "cooperation" as a physical or moral contribution to someone's morally evil action. It would seem, at least at first sight, that if I associate myself with the evil action performed by someone else, I (the cooperator) should become guilty of the sin committed by the main agent. Nonetheless, theologians asked themselves whether it would be possible, under certain circumstances, to cooperate with somebody else's

---

19. Dom Odon Lottin, a distinguished representative of our Catholic moral tradition in this century, presents his treatment of the principle of *cooperatio ad malum* as one of the examples of an action with a double effect: Odon Lottin, *Morale fondamentale* (Tournai: Desclée, 1954), 286–87, 289–90.

20. John Paul II, *Evangelium Vitae*, 73, offers a good example of a licit cooperation in evil in order to avoid an even greater evil.

21. I will follow basically, although not exclusively, the account of the traditional principle given by James F. Keenan, "Prophylactics, Toleration, and Cooperation: Contemporary and Traditional Principles," *International Philosophical Quarterly* 39 (1989): 205–20. See Bernard Häring, *La legge di Cristo* (Brescia, Queriniana, 1959), 3:112–29; James F. Keenan, "Institutional Cooperation and Religious Directives," *Linacre Quarterly* 64, no. 3 (1997): 53–76; Odon Lottin, *Morale fondamentale*, 289–90.

evil action without sinning oneself. The usual premise, both in this case as well as in the situations considered under the principle of the counsel of the lesser of two evils, is that we are talking about cooperating with the evil or sinful action (at least objectively sinful, to use the classical language) performed by someone who is already determined to sin. It would not be permissible to cooperate with an evil action when I can easily persuade the prospective evildoer to act rightly, that is, in conformity with the demands of the moral law.

The moral manualists argued, for example, that a wife should not cooperate with her husband's desire to engage in so-called onanistic intercourse, whether through withdrawal or through the use of some device such as a condom, when she knows that he could be easily persuaded to sustain a complete sexual act: Therefore, the question is whether A (the cooperator) can assist B (the main agent) to realize an evil action, when B is fully determined to act illicitly.

Theologians developed a series of distinctions that served as analytical tools to discern when it is allowable to carry out such assistance in the realization of an evil action, without involving ourselves in the commission of evil (sin). The first is the distinction between *formal* and *material cooperation*. Formal cooperation implies assistance or cooperation that is a clear participation in the evil *intention* of the main agent. Usually authors say that formal cooperation implies an approval of the main agent's sin. It could happen through an interior approval of the evil action or through a contribution that, by its very nature, represents such an approval.[22] Formal cooperation is always wrong. There is no situation in which it could be morally justified. The distribution of needles and syringes with the purpose of promoting the use of illicit drugs or with an internal approval of such a use would be formal cooperation. It would also be formal cooperation, for example, to sell cocaine to drugs users, even if the individual would, at the same time, claim that he disapproves of its use as an illicit drug. The claim is totally incompatible with his action.

On the other hand, material cooperation can be morally acceptable under certain circumstances. The action performed by the person who cooperates materially must in itself be good or indifferent, although it can be used by the main agent to commit a morally unacceptable action. There are some classical examples of material cooperation in the textbook tradition:

---

22. B. Häring gives an example that can be helpful to clarify this point. A servant who is commanded to take off the door of his master's mistress's room can hardly say that he does not intend to cooperate in his master's sin. Certainly, to break into a room, in general, can be considered an indifferent action, but not in these circumstances. See *La legge di Cristo*, 114–15.

the servant who carries letters between a man and a woman in an illicit relationship, or the orderly or nurse who assists in an illicit operation, among others. The doctor who performs a direct abortion can hardly claim that he is not in favor of abortion, alleging that he is just respecting his patient's constitutional right to exercise control over her body, which includes the right to interrupt her pregnancy. His participation in the operation is of such a nature that it could never be considered mere material cooperation. But the nurse or the orderly who prepares the instruments or hands them to the doctor during the intervention is in a very different situation. He or she prepares the instruments for every single operation, whether it is an abortion or an appendectomy.

Of course, material cooperation cannot be justified in every situation. The manualists developed a set of criteria to determine when material cooperation is morally permissible. But before we enter into the criteria for the moral acceptability of material cooperation, it is necessary to determine whether the distribution of clean needles and syringes to drug addicts in exchange for their used ones, in the context of a risk-reduction program, qualifies as material cooperation.

In my opinion, the answer to this question cannot be but affirmative. Needle exchange programs do not approve the evil of drug addiction. Indeed, needle exchange is usually—and ideally—part of a constellation of services which include referral to drug treatment programs. Needle exchange programs assume, however, that many users of illicit drugs will not get into treatment, either because they do not want to or because they will be unable to (at least some of them on account of the unavailability of drug treatment programs). In this situation, the best that we can do for the welfare of those individuals and for the protection of the common good is to reduce the risk of morbidity and mortality.

Through educational interventions and the exchange of clean needles and syringes for used ones, we can reduce the risk of transmission of HIV and other infectious agents through drug injection. This intervention does not only reduce health harm among drug users, but it also reduces the danger of sexual transmission to their partners and of perinatal transmission to their offspring. Moreover, the distribution of clean needles and syringes is not necessary for the morally objectionable activity (injecting illicit drugs) to happen. These individuals are going to inject anyway. The program does not contribute directly to the evil of drug injection. It simply reduces the physical evils associated with that behavior. Therefore, it seems to me that we are clearly before a case of material cooperation. Let us turn now to the conditions that demonstrate when material cooperation is licit, in order to determine whether our material cooperation with the evil of drug addiction is morally justified.

Proximate or Remote

PROXIMITY IS A matter of degree. The closer a cooperator's act is to the action of the principal agent, the more proximate it is. If the act of the evildoer and the act of the cooperator are one and the same, we talk about immediate cooperation. Therefore, in *immediate cooperation* we have proximity at its fullest. When cooperation is not immediate, it is called *mediate cooperation.*[23] There are several degrees of proximity in the cases of mediate cooperation. Proximity can go from very proximate to very remote. The greater the proximity, the more serious the reason for cooperating must be.

Is the cooperation with the evil of a needle exchange program proximate or remote? This question is not as easy to answer as the first one about material and formal cooperation. However, if the manualist tradition has considered that the servant passing on letters and the orderly preparing instruments for an illicit operation are cooperating remotely, why can we not say that cooperation in the evil of injecting illicit drugs by a needle exchange program is also remote? However, even if it were to be considered proximate cooperation, it does not mean necessarily that it is morally illicit. It only means that a stronger reason is required to justify it. And certainly, as we have seen in our analysis of the empirical claim, the reasons to support needle and syringe exchange programs are of the greatest importance: diminishing morbidity and mortality related to addiction among drug users, their sexual partners and their offspring. In other words: saving human lives, including the lives of innocent children and perhaps unsuspecting partners or partners otherwise unable to protect themselves because they are in a position of submission (such as poor women in certain cultural environments), in addition to avoiding the social and financial costs that such morbidity and mortality entail for society as a whole.

---

23. Cooperation is immediate when the object of the cooperator's action—i.e., the act in itself, independently of the agent's intentions or of its consequences—is one and the same with the object of the main agent. This distinction is not considered in this paper because, generally speaking, immediate cooperation is formal cooperation. The only exception would be when the cooperator has acted under constraint. For example, a woman is captured with her son by a band of robbers, and then she is forced to take part in a robbery, while her son is kept as a hostage. If she does not take part in the robbery, they will kill her and her child. Certainly her cooperation would be immediate, but one can hardly say that her cooperation would be formal.

Necessary or Contingent

WE SAY THAT cooperation is necessary if it is an essential requisite for the realization of the evil act of the main agent. Otherwise, the cooperation is contingent. It is evident that the reasons to justify necessary cooperation must be more serious than the reasons to justify contingent cooperation. It is also evident, in my opinion, that the distribution of clean needles and syringes in a needle exchange program is in no way necessary for injecting drugs. Indeed, the fact is that drug users will inject drugs anyway, using infected needles and syringes, and increasing the risk of the illicit activity itself. The distribution of clean needles and syringes is totally contingent for the realization of the evil action. It is, however, essential in order to reduce the harms that ensue thereof.

In conclusion, I think that it has been shown that needle and syringe exchange programs represent a case of material and justified cooperation. Moreover, material cooperation can be, at times, not only permissible but even obligatory, as B. Häring has pointed out.[24] In my opinion, in the case of needle exchange programs to avoid the transmission of HIV, we are facing a case of material cooperation with an evil action which is not only permissible, it is probably obligatory. Society has a duty to use the most efficacious and cost effective means available to slow down the expansion of the pandemic. Needle and syringe exchange programs seem to be, according to our best scientific knowledge today, both efficacious and cost effective. At the very least, society has the obligation of not hampering private efforts to fight the expansion of the epidemic through the establishment of responsible programs of needle and syringe exchange.[25]

---

24. Häring, *La legge di Cristo*, 116.

25. My colleague Prof. Philip Schmitz, S.J., from the theology faculty of the Gregorian University in Rome, suggested that my interpretation of the principle of cooperation, based on the traditional textbook understanding, could be insufficient at the present time. It could be argued that Pope John Paul II redefined the principle of cooperation in a somewhat stricter fashion both in *Evangelium Vitae* 74 and in his letter to the German bishops on the question of the counseling certificates issued to women seeking abortion by church-sponsored counseling centers ("Eindringliche Bitte," *Herder Korrespondenz* 52, no. 3 [1998]: 122–24). Indeed, the pope seems to insist on the avoidance of scandal or misunderstanding in a way that perhaps could be understood as going beyond the requirements of the traditional textbook doctrine. Nonetheless, in my opinion, it is clear that the pope's intention is to reaffirm, not to redefine, the traditional teaching (see *EV* 74, first paragraph). In *EV* the pope

The Principle of the Counsel of the Lesser of Two Evils

As I SAID before, this principle is closely connected with the principle of cooperation. The starting hypothesis is practically identical. If we have a person determined to commit a sin, is it licit to counsel them to commit a lighter sin? One of the classical examples is to advise fornication to a man who is decided to commit adultery. Catholic authors developed this doctrine beginning in the sixteenth century. Most theologians accepted as morally licit counseling the lesser of two evils to someone who was already determined to commit a sin and could not reasonably be persuaded to act rightly, in agreement with the moral law. E. T. Hannigan studied about a hundred authors from the sixteenth to the beginning of the twentieth century. Before the eighteenth century, thirteen authors accepted the affirmative position without reservations, twenty-three accepted it with reservations, and twelve rejected it entirely.[26]

In the eighteenth century, the affirmative position was accepted by St. Alphonsus Ligouri. Alphonsus teaches that it is licit to counsel the lesser evil to someone who is determined to realize a greater one, because he who counsels the lesser evil does not intend the evil but its reduction.[27] Alphonsus teaches that it is licit to induce someone to drunkenness in order to avoid a greater sin, such as sacrilege or homicide. This is important because some authors had defended that the lesser evil must be virtually included in the greater one (such as fornication in adultery). St. Alphonsus' opinion was more flexible: it is enough to counsel the lesser evil, even if it is not formally included in the greater one.[28] After St. Alphonsus, most

---

refers to direct participation in the taking of innocent human life or to the immoral intention of the person who does it. In the German case, the objection to the certificate given by church-sponsored institutions is that such a document becomes, in fact, the key to gain access to the realization of a legal abortion (*"Es ist nicht zu übersehen, dass der gesetzlich geforderte Beratungsschein, der gewiss zuerst die Pflichtberatung sicherstellen will, faktisch eine Schlüsselfunktion für die Durchführung straffreier Abtreibungen erhalten hat,"* 123). It is clear that the situation is different in the case of risk-reduction. One can hardly argue that the distribution of clean needles in exchange for used ones, in the context of a holistic program of health education, has a *Schlüsselfunktion* in relation to the immoral activity of injecting illicit drugs. In any case, it has such a function in relation to the reduction of risks for drug users themselves and for society as a whole.

26. E. T. Hannigan, "Is It Ever Lawful to Advise the Lesser of Two Evils?," *Gregorianum* 30 (1949): 104-129.

27. St. Alphonsus Ligouri, *Theologia Moralis* (Roma, Typographia Vaticana, 1905–12, edition prepared by L. Di Gaude), 1:353.

28. St. Alphonsus Ligouri, *Theologia Moralis*, 2:762–63.

authors accepted as licit the counsel of the lesser of two evils, although some of them continued to insist that the lesser evil must be formally included in the greater. For our purpose here this point is secondary, since certainly the evil of injecting drugs with sterile needles is virtually included in the greater evil of injecting them with infected needles.[29]

The famed textbook of Noldin and Schmitt argues that it is not only licit to counsel the lesser of two evils, but it is also licit to cooperate in the evil action, if there is no other way to impede its realization. According to this textbook, it would be licit, for example, to help a thief, if it is the only way to avoid a greater evil, such as killing the owner.[30]

It seems rather safe to conclude that a needle and syringe exchange program could also be justified using this principle. To counsel the use of sterile needles for injecting illicit drugs is a clear example of counseling the lesser evil to someone who is determined to act wrongly. The one who counsels the lesser evil is not guilty himself or herself of the evil, since he advises it *sub specie boni*, in order to reduce the harm or evil that the other is about to commit and the counselor does not approve of. If we accept with Noldin-Schmitt, as I do, the possibility of cooperating with the evildoer, if there is no other way to impede the greater evil, then the exchange of the clean syringe for the dirty one is a case of licit cooperation in the lesser evil.

Conclusion

THE APPLICATION OF these traditional principles has shown that needle exchange programs are certainly justified and are possibly morally obligatory. Needle exchange programs do not promote evil. They intend to diminish the evil that drug users are determined to inflict upon themselves and upon society as a whole. Indeed, the lesser evil of using clean needles and syringes is promoted *sub specie boni*. It is no longer a sin but an act of the virtues of fraternal charity and social solidarity.

---

29. It is interesting to remember here the position of Marcelino Zalba, for many years professor of moral theology at Rome's Gregorian University and probably the last of the great pre-Vatican II manualists. In his opinion it is licit to counsel the lesser evil *simpliciter,* even if it is not included in the greater one or if it is directed against a different person. See Zalba, *Theologia moralis compendium* (Madrid: BAC, 1958), 2:112–13.

30. Hieronymus Noldin and Armin Schmitt, *Summa theologiae moralis* (Barcelona: Herder, 1945), 2:114–15.

AN AMERICAN CATHOLIC HOSPITAL SPONSORS A SUPPORT GROUP FOR GAY MEN

John Tuohey

A CATHOLIC HOSPITAL outside Washington, D.C., recently established a support group for couples using natural family planning. The group provides married couples with the opportunity to share the difficulties they experience and to encourage each other to maintain the self-discipline necessary with NFP. The group has been so popular that the staff of the HIV/AIDS clinic operated by this hospital in the district wondered if a similar support group might be of value to some of its clients.

Because of its location and history within the district, the majority of clients who make use of the clinic are gay men. A disturbing trend throughout the United States today is an increase in the incidence of HIV infection among adolescents and teenagers. The clinic has noted that young gay men are not immune from this trend. Although there are any number of reasons for this rise, the experience of the staff is that this younger population often lacks sufficient motivation to exercise either abstinence or sexual practices that reduce the risk of infection. The staff believes that through a support group for young gay men similar to the one formed for couples using NFP, they might motivate each other to exercise greater self-discipline, and in turn lower the HIV infection rate. After further exploration of the idea, it was learned that a local chapter of Courage, a Catholic organization for gay men wishing to live lives of sexual abstinence, offers such a support group. The clinic therefore began referring clients to Courage.

Soon, the staff noted that the majority of those people the clinic would like to reach were not interested in Courage. Some were either not Catholic or religiously minded, or were not comfortable in that setting. Some others were not interested in abstinence, which was the explicit goal of Courage. These clients told the staff they would be interested in a support group if it were open to the idea of motivating them to exercise greater responsibility in their sexual behavior as well as to embrace abstinence. Plans were thus made to explore the idea of setting up a support group at the clinic.

The purpose of this support group was to be nearly identical to that of the NFP group. It would offer clients an environment in which they could discuss, freely and without embarrassment or judgment, their sexual fears, frustrations, and desires. The goal of conversation would be to allow participants to help and encourage each other to exercise greater discipline in their sexual lives than they otherwise might in order to reduce individual risk of HIV exposure. The support group would not be a professionally directed seminar. It would run itself. The clinic would simply facilitate the coming together of the participants and make available appropriate professional resources when needed.

The staff understood that to be effective, the members of the support group must be allowed to explore practical ways of coping with sexual desire, just as do the couples in the NFP support group. If it were to succeed where Courage had not, this would have to include the discussions of exercising discipline within sexual behavior. In light of its Catholic identity as well as the seriousness of the goal of the group, however, the staff also recognized that some ground rules were in order. The pursuit of self-discipline did not mean discussions that promoted, for example, pornography or self-gratification. It was agreed that it would be clear that these meetings were not "safer sex" seminars. The sole aim of the group was to allow participants to motivate each other to exercise greater sexual discipline than they might otherwise show as a way of reducing the risk of HIV infection.

As a support group, the clinic recognized that the dynamics must be primarily between the participants. Still, it was felt appropriate to have professional resources available. It was proposed that an infectious disease staff person should be present at each meeting. This person would answer any questions regarding HIV that might come up, or the medical implications that may be inherent in some behaviors. Also present would be a social worker/psychologist. This person would be able to respond to comments or suggestions that might reflect unhealthy attitudes regarding sexuality or sexual activity. It was deemed important that this person approach sexuality from the perspective of church teaching on the dignity of the human person.

Finally, because this support group was being sponsored by a Catholic clinic, it was felt that someone from pastoral care should be present. It was also proposed that this person would open each meeting with a simple statement that facilitation of this support group by a Catholic facility was not to be interpreted as meaning that the Catholic Church approved of or encouraged homosexual behavior. Rather, it would be explained that it was the church's interest in motivating individuals to act in ways that protected personal and public health within a pluralistic society that allowed such a support group to exist in this setting. The pastoral care person would also be available to respond to any questions that might come up regarding church teaching.

Having done the planning, the only question that remained was whether, as a Catholic clinic, it could with integrity move ahead and implement the support group.

Catholic teaching on human sexuality is not at all ambiguous. As summarized in the Catechism of the Catholic Church, human sexuality is ordered to the procreative, conjugal love of man and woman (CCC 2360). Defined within that context, homosexual acts are described within the Catholic moral tradition as intrinsically disordered (CDF, *Persona humana* 8). In a comment especially relevant to this discussion, the *Catechism* also states that "under no circumstances can they be approved" (CCC 2357).

Like all Christians, homosexual persons are called to live lives of chastity in keeping with their particular state of life (CCC 2348, 2359). For the young gay men who will be participating in the proposed support group, this means a sexual life not unlike that of professed virginity or consecrated celibacy. For the homosexual person, chastity entails a life of total sexual abstinence. The moral concern with this case study, then, arises from the fact that the support group has acceded to the requests of its participants in allowing them to encourage both greater sexual discipline within ongoing sexual behavior and abstinence. The end for which the group is formed by the clinic is the reduction of the risk of HIV infection. It achieves this end by facilitating the mutual support and encouragement that come from sharing the difficulties and frustrations of maintaining self-discipline. This may include the pursuit of chastity on the part of some individuals, but chastity itself is neither the end sought nor the means used to achieve the end. For this reason, it is correct to say that the sponsors of the support group, the Catholic clinic, will be cooperating in the performance of sexual acts considered intrinsically disordered.

The end being sought by this support group is, as stated, the reduction in the incidence of HIV infection among a specific and targeted population. Such an end is in conformity with Catholic social teaching. However, the means to achieve that end is not that chastity to which the Catholic sexual teaching says these young men are called. The focus on sexual discipline is directed instead toward a thoughtful and responsible response to and expression of sexual desires. This may include but is not limited to abstinence. The means to the end is not sexual abstinence, but a self-discipline that is not closed to the possibility of sexual activity. It is this factor which suggests that the group will not simply be tolerating behavior that the church teaches is intrinsically disordered. It will be cooperating in such behavior by virtue of its decision to achieve its end by facilitating a context that will allow participants to encourage and motivate each other to choose those types of behavior in addition to abstinence that will help to reduce the risk of HIV infection.

The question then is whether such cooperation is justified. It will be as long as it is material and mediate, there is sufficient moral distance on the part of the clinic from the wrong, a commensurate relationship exists between the gravity entailed and the good to be achieved, and there is no undue risk of scandal. As the following analysis will show, these conditions are met.

Clearly, the cooperation proposed in this case is not formal cooperation. There is no intention on the part of the clinic to bring about, encourage, or approve of any moral wrongdoing. The group certainly does not exist for the sake of promoting homosexual behavior. Rather, the end of the support group is the prevention of HIV infection among a specific population and within society as a whole. That this is not formal cooperation is further borne out in the clinic's initial attempt to take advantage of a group within Courage.

The organizers of the group do not assume that sexual activity will necessarily continue among its members as much as it recognizes that some of the participants have not made a choice for the chastity to which the church says these young men are called. Similarly, the boundaries for conversation that have been set and the disclaimer at each meeting point to the absence of any intent to promote or approve homosexual behavior. It is true that the support group does not overtly discourage engagement in such sexual activity, and in fact seeks to influence any decisions that might be made regarding such behavior. Hence, there is some level of cooperation. However, the group in no way seeks to encourage or offer approval of such behavior. In contrast, it overtly discourages some types of wrong behavior, although it must be admitted that this has to do with health concerns more than sexual morality.

It should also be fairly clear that the cooperation is neither implicit formal or immediate material cooperation.[1] The act through which cooperation takes place, the facilitation of a support group aimed at fostering greater self-discipline on the part of its members, is at least morally neutral in itself. Note that the clinic is engaged in facilitating the encouragement of sexual self-discipline as a means to an end. The clinic does not actively engage in the process, but merely facilitates it. Also, the means to the end is not the teaching of so-called safer-sex practices. The end is achieved through the members encouraging self-discipline known to take forms other than sexual abstinence. Suppose for a moment that the clinic was conducting seminars for safer-sex practices intended to reduce HIV risk. The support group would still not constitute immediate material cooperation as defined by the *Ethical and Religious Directives*, for the object of the group will always be different from the object of the sexual

---

1. Although I refer to the distinction between implicit formal and immediate material cooperation here, a distinction seen in the *Ethical and Religious Directives for Catholic Health Care Services,* I am not convinced that one truly exists. It appears to me that these are different expressions of the same reality. See also Clarence Deddens, "A Theological Analysis of the Ethical and Religious Directives for Catholic Health Facilities in the United States," dissertation, Rome, Pontifical University of St. Thomas in the City, 1980, 155.

act.[2] If even this much more proximate cooperation is not immediate, though morally more problematic, then what is happening in the proposed group cannot be described as immediate.

A support group that achieves its end by facilitating the achievement of self-discipline is, then, at least morally neutral and in fact probably good. In its most generic form, a support group such as this entails nothing more than the sharing and discussion of the frustrations and difficulties in exercising sexual self-discipline. This is not dissimilar to the nature of the conversation that takes place at the NFP support group after which this group has been modeled. Indeed, it is not that different from the conversation that takes place in any support group aimed at fostering personal self-discipline, be it Over-Eaters Anonymous or Alcoholics Anonymous. In these settings, people simply share among themselves the difficulties of maintaining the ongoing discipline necessary to achieve some good end.

Individuals or groups who seek to exercise greater self-discipline in their lives may be said to be seeking to foster the virtue of temperance. Temperance is that virtue "which seeks to permeate the passions and appetites of the senses with reason" (CCC 2341). Pursuit of this virtue often entails the "long and exacting work" of what the *Catechism* calls "self-mastery." As the *Catechism* goes on to note, this mastery, which "presupposes effort at all stages of life" (CCC 2342), can be greatly enhanced by the kind of mutual support and friendship that a support group exists to provide. As the *Catechism* notes, "whether it develops between persons of the same or opposite sex, friendship represents a great good for all" (CCC 2347). The means to the end in this case, therefore, can be characterized as good even as it is recognized that it entails cooperation in wrongdoing. The cooperation is therefore mediate material cooperation.

Before this mediate material cooperation can be allowed, there must be a commensurate reason for and some element of duress requiring it. The commensurate reason or just cause would appear to be fairly clear: the prevention of and reduction in the rate of HIV infection among a specific population that appears to be at renewed risk. It does not seem necessary to develop this point beyond this simple recognition. This brings us to the question of duress.

The precise description of what constitutes "duress" is a matter of debate among theologians today. Some have assumed that duress requires the lack of *any* other realistic and feasible option to attain some good or prevent some greater harm. Others suggest that duress refers to an episode

---

2. "Material cooperation is immediate when the object of the cooperator is the same as the object of the wrong doer." NCCB, *Ethical and Religious Directives for Catholic Health Care Services,* Washington, D.C., 1995, appendix.

of such exceptional coercion that failure to cooperate would entail a catastrophic loss.[3] In this analysis, I suggest that duress be understood to refer to the existence of circumstances such that a person or persons cannot otherwise reasonably achieve a good end or prevent some greater harm except through mediate material cooperation in some wrong. Support for such a definition is grounded both within the manuals[4] and documents from the NCCB Committee on Doctrine.[5]

Using this understanding of duress, it would seem that sufficient duress exists for this mediate material cooperation. These young gay men, no differently from any other group of young men and women, benefit more from the mutual support available from an intimate and safe setting where desires and frustrations can be faced and explored than from simple "just say no" approaches. Indeed, Cardinal William Keeler has spoken of the value of a group called "True Love Waits" for young men and women striving to live chaste lives before marriage in the archdiocese of Baltimore.[6] Further, it must be noted that the clinic first tried to enlist the resources of an organization fully within the teachings of the church. For various reasons, however, this avenue was not effective. There appears to be no ready way available to the clinic to work to reduce the risk of HIV infection among its client population except by facilitating a support group which of necessity allows its participants to encourage each other to exercise not only abstinence, but also disciplined sexual activity.

Is this mediate material cooperation in homosexual acts proximate or remote? This is not a simple determination of proximity in this case. Although it is clear that not all the participants are embracing a life of chastity, there is little if any temporal and certainly no spatial proximity between the support group and the occurrence of homosexual activity. More importantly, any decision by a participant to engage in sexual activity

---

3. Russell E. Smith, "Duress and Cooperation," *Ethics and Medics* 21 (1996): 1–2.

4. See, for example, the justification of cooperation in the promotion of false doctrine through participation in a lottery for the sake of harmonious relations and goodwill within a community. J. McCarthy, "Moral Notes," *Irish Ecclesiastical Record* 83 (1955): 279–82. John Connery warns that a "too strict approach to such cooperation" can at times undermine such worthwhile ends, "Notes," *Theological Studies* 16 (1955): 558–90.

5. "Material cooperation will be justified only in situations where the hospital because of some kind of duress or pressure cannot reasonably exercise the autonomy it has." See *Commentary on the Reply of the Sacred Congregation for the Doctrine of the Faith on Sterilization in Catholic Hospitals*, Washington, D.C., 1983, 7.

6. See *Time*, 21 December 1998, 17.

will come as a separate decision outside the context of the group. The group is set up in such a way that it does not encourage sexual behavior per se. It is hoped simply that the mutual support resulting from participation in the group will influence the individual's choices as regards to the timing and manner of any possible future sexual behavior.

This seeking to influence a sexual act, should it take place, does introduce the element of cooperation. However, there is no expectation on the part of the group that the individual will or should engage in sexual behavior. Remoteness is also assured in the presence and purpose of support staff: to discuss clinical issues of infection, assure that the dignity of the topic is preserved, and offer the pastoral presence of the church.

On the other hand, it can be argued that the cooperative involvement of the clinic is through its facilitation of a mechanism meant to influence individuals to make decisions whether to engage in homosexual activity. Further, it is also meant to influence the decisions of those who decide for sexual activity regarding with whom, when, and in what manner. For the support group to be effective, it must have a direct influence on the participants' multifaceted decisions regarding sexual behavior. This will include influencing the person's decisions both to abstain from and engage in sexual activity. If the person chooses to engage in sexual activity, the hope of the group is that the decision will be with greater discipline than might otherwise be exercised. From this perspective, it can be argued that the cooperation is morally proximate.

I am not certain that the characterization of the mediate material cooperation as proximate or remote is always helpful, especially in cases like this in which the cooperation can be characterized as being either one or the other. The question is not so much whether the cooperation is proximate or remote, but whether morally permissible cooperation is prudent. That is to say, whatever proximity or remoteness is present, is it—in light of the moral gravity present, the end being sought, and the duress shaping the situation—reasonable to proceed?

Characterizing the cooperation as proximate or remote may be helpful in discerning the prudence of doing so, but the characterization itself is not definitive. Simply because the cooperation is remote will not necessarily mean it is prudent to proceed, and likewise the fact that it is proximate will not necessarily mean it is imprudent to do so. What is more important is that there be a comfortable fit with the cooperation and the identity/mission of the institution. In light of the church's teaching regarding the homosexual person, as distinct from the homosexual activity, its concern for the individual and common good, and the absence of more readily available means, it can be judged prudent to form the support group, however the moral distance is characterized.

Finally, there is the question of scandal. Scandal should not be an issue for those who understand the history and format of the group. The disclaimer at each meeting also makes clear the beliefs and role of the Catholic sponsor of the clinic. In addition, the concern for scandal can be minimized if one keeps in mind that the gay men who participate "must be accepted with respect, compassion, and sensitivity. Every sign of unjust discrimination in their regard should be avoided" (CCC 2358).

It should also be admitted that the risk of scandal does not exist solely when cooperation in wrongdoing takes place. There may also be a risk of scandal in the failure to offer the same resources and opportunities to develop the virtue of temperance in the sexual lives of the homosexual person as offered to others, even if doing so requires some mediate material cooperation in wrongdoing. If one looks at the support group within the larger perspective of the church's mission to lead all people to holiness, it may be that this mediate material cooperation is to be preferred over the alternative of doing nothing in a way not dissimilar from Pius XII's statement that it is sometimes preferable to tolerate rather than oppose wrongdoing.[7] As the *Catechism* states, "by the virtue of self-mastery that teaches inner freedom, at times by the support of disinterested friendship, by prayer, and sacramental grace," the homosexual person "can and should gradually and resolutely approach Christian perfection" (CCC 2359). Through mediate material cooperation in homosexual activity, this support group may do more than reduce the incidence of HIV infection among a targeted audience. It may also facilitate the gradual but resolute pursuit of Christian perfection.

A CATHOLIC HOSPITAL IN INDIA IS ASKED TO COOPERATE WITH AN HIV PREVENTION PROGRAM

Clement Campos, C.Ss.R.

A GROUP OF *religious sisters were approached by a nongovernmental organization (NGO) for the use of an unoccupied section of their hospital. This organization wished to use the premises for their work among people with HIV/AIDS. Initially the sisters appeared open to the idea. It was brought to their attention, however, that the organization followed the advice of the World Health Organization that "a range of options should be offered to*

---

7. Pius XII, *Ci riesce*, AAS XX (1953): 798–811.

young people, including postponing the first sexual activity and, for those already active, nonpenetrative sex and the use of condoms for protected intercourse." One of the stated objectives of the organization was "*controlling and containing the spread of HIV infection among a defined vulnerable target population, through education, awareness, and the promotion of safe sex.*" The sisters then sought the advice of some Catholic experts and eventually decided not to place their property at the service of this group.

This case is illustrative of one of the major dilemmas facing Catholic Church institutions in India in their response to the AIDS pandemic: To what degree may they be involved in ministry among people with AIDS, especially when their involvement necessarily includes cooperation with groups that do not share the same vision as the Catholic Church and, in fact, use means that the traditional teaching of the church considers immoral?

In this study we shall first look at the situation in India and then briefly see the response of the church before addressing the major ethical issues raised by this particular case.

The Indian Context

IT IS VERY hard to establish the extent of the spread of HIV/AIDS in India. The National AIDS Control Organization (NACO) reported that as of 31 March 1999, out of 3,457,080 samples screened, there were 7,012 cases of AIDS and 85,312 were confirmed HIV seropositive. The seropositivity rate is 24.68 per thousand. The epidemiological data indicate that the prevalence of HIV continues to increase and spread mostly through the heterosexual route, from the urban to the rural areas, and from the individuals practicing risk behaviors to the general population. Critics point out that these figures are flawed, because the samples do not cover all the states and the survey has been mainly limited to high risk groups—sexually active women attending prenatal clinics, and men and women attending clinics for sexually transmitted diseases. The figures refer to people tested and not to the entire population. But even making allowances for these drawbacks, the picture is grim. There is a great deal of under-diagnosis involved and the real figures are not showing up in hospital records.[1] Another study states that there are

---

1. For example, an analysis of Mumbai's mortality data for 1994 showed an abnormal increase in deaths due to tuberculosis, diarrhea, and hepatitis (infections common among HIV-positive people), especially among young adults and teenagers. *Express Magazine* (13 September 1998): 4.

four million adult HIV infections, the highest in the world, with one million new infections every year. It further states that nearly 30,000 newborns are infected and 20,000 die every year due to HIV.[2]

"A Strategic Plan for Prevention and Control of AIDS in India" was prepared for country-wide implementation for the period 1992 to 1997, but it is hard to determine the impact and effectiveness of these programs.[3] From time to time the media carry reports of the failure of the authorities to deal with the pandemic and the appalling lack of awareness among the population.

It must also be noted that insurance in the health field for both patients and medical professionals is restricted to a small group. While the poor may have access to the government-run hospitals free of cost, the quality of care and the reliability of tests leaves much to be desired.

There are a number of incidents of violence against AIDS patients.[4] This is the result of fear that arises out of a lack of education. At the same time a serious study analyzing household and community responses to HIV in predominantly lower income households and communities in greater Mumbai (Bombay) indicates a supportive and positive attitude toward people with HIV/AIDS.[5]

The Church's Response

THE CATHOLIC CHURCH in India is comparatively small. Numbering close to 15 million, it makes up just 1.51 percent of a population that is fast approaching a billion. The entire Christian population is about 2.3 percent of the total population. Yet the contribution of the church, especially in the

---

2. UNAIDS, Geneva, 1998.

3. The aims were to establish a program which would prevent HIV transmission, decrease the morbidity and mortality associated with HIV infection, and minimize the socio-economic impact resulting from HIV infection. These goals were to be achieved through meeting a series of medium-term objectives: a)To establish effective surveillance in all states to monitor the epidemic; b) To provide sound technical support; c) To ensure a high level of awareness of HIV/AIDS and its prevention in the population; d) To promote the use of condoms; e) To target interventions at groups identified as high risk; f) To ensure the safety of blood; g) To develop the services required to provide support to HIV-infected persons, AIDS patients, and their associates. See *National AIDS Control Programme, India: Country Scenario, An Update,* published by the Ministry of Health and Family Welfare, Government of India, December 1996.

4. *The Times of India,* 13 June 1998, 12.

5. Shalini Bharat, *Facing the Challenge: Household and Community Response to HIV/AIDS in Mumbai, India* (Mumbai: Tata Institute of Social Sciences, 1996).

field of health care, is quite significant. It is estimated that the church hospitals, dispensaries, and health centers provide about 10 percent of the health care in the country. With the Governmental Health Care system in India proving grossly inadequate, the burden of looking after the needs of the poor often falls on voluntary agencies—those that belong to the church and other religious organizations as well as nongovernmental organizations (NGOs). At present the NGOs seem to be taking the initiative in responding to AIDS. On an institutional level the church has not done much. But with its modest resources, its contribution can only be limited. What is required, apart from ministering to people with AIDS who come to their institutions, is networking with governmental and other secular agencies.[6] The Catholic Hospital Association of India (CHAI) in its policy statement has in fact recommended working with other agencies. But it is precisely here the church faces a conflict. How is it to cooperate with agencies that promote responses not in keeping with the teaching of the church? More specifically, how does the church cooperate with agencies that make the use of prophylactics an essential part of their response to AIDS? These questions do not seem to have been addressed either by CHAI or by the bishops of India. A recent consultation of church bodies held in Delhi in April 1999 dealt with some of these issues with many participants, representing groups involved in ministry to people with AIDS, seeking direction and support from church leadership to respond to this thorny but urgent pastoral problem.

In its response to the AIDS crisis, the church has to combine prophetic witness to the truth with pastoral compassion. The compassionate face of the church in India has traditionally been revealed especially by the charitable hospitals, orphanages, hospices, and developmental activities that are mostly run by religious. The church also has the reputation of normally being the first to respond to major natural calamities. Yet in the face of the HIV/AIDS pandemic there has been a certain reluctance shown by church personnel to get involved.

Two reasons have been suggested by them in private discussions. First, there is a certain amount of discomfort and unease in relating to the HIV-infected persons because one is not comfortable with the subcultures to which many belong—the gay community, "commercial sex workers," drug addicts. Second, there is a conflict between the views of the church and the programs of other agencies, especially with regard to the use of condoms, which makes it difficult to get involved in this ministry.

---

6. Pope John Paul II has also stated that the struggle against AIDS calls for collaboration among all people. *Dolentium Hominum, Church, and Health in the World* 5.1 (1990) 1:6–9.

With regard to the first reason, what is required is that one learn to distinguish between compassion and condoning morally inappropriate behavior. Compassion does not discriminate on the basis of moral behavior as Jesus showed in his ministry. The second reason raises a problem that needs to be addressed. To deal with this issue, we will examine first the ethical problem of "safe sex" and then deal with the response of the church on the individual and institutional levels.

The Issue of Condoms and Safe Sex

SAFE SEX SEEMS to be the major agenda of politicians, scientists, and the media. In India this is part of the official strategy to combat AIDS. The guidelines underlying this proposal are twofold: to avoid sex with people likely to pass on the infection, and to use condoms when there is a risk. The criticism generally leveled against this approach is that while the condom is effective to some extent, it does not guarantee complete protection, and it is wrong to speak of it as safe sex. Moreover, this approach tends to encourage irresponsible sexual behavior. Technical solutions ignore the root causes of such behavior.

It is important that the church take a prophetic stand against the state when it advocates safe sex through public advertising and promotion and distribution of condoms. It must be conceded that the state has the duty to take necessary measures to avoid the spread of the epidemic, always keeping in mind the right of the citizen to privacy and the right to civil tolerance. But for the state to advocate and make available prophylactics is to run the risk of encouraging irresponsible moral behavior, and in fact exposing society to widespread diffusion of the contagion. It is not the state's objective of containing the contagion that is being disputed, but the means which are technically insufficiently reliable and morally questionable.[7]

The church's approach is to suggest sexual abstinence for unmarried people and fidelity by both partners within a monogamous and indissoluble marriage. According to the traditional teaching of the church, the use of a condom as a contraceptive is immoral. Moreover, in the context of the AIDS pandemic the church is also critical of the promotion of condom usage as part of the "safe sex" campaign. But, in a country that is as culturally diverse and religiously pluralistic as India, the Catholic pastor/counselor/physician is confronted with several difficulties in putting across this point of view.

---

7. Carlo Caffarra, "AIDS: General Ethical Aspects," *Dolentium Hominum*, 68–72.

Problems on the Level of Individuals and Institutions

THE GOVERNMENT HAS for many decades strongly advocated family planning. Apart from the objection to the use of coercion, the vast majority of Indians do not have any ethical objections to the use of contraception, sterilization, and even abortion. Hence, on an individual basis, it is not easy to convince people of the rightness of the Catholic position with regard to the use of condoms. In fact, it appears difficult at times to convince Catholics. There have been reports of religious distributing condoms as part of their ministry among commercial sex workers and people with AIDS. They seemed to justify this as a way of limiting the extent of evil when individuals refuse to desist from irresponsible moral behavior.[8]

There is also a problem on the institutional level. In the case cited at the beginning, we saw the difficulty in being associated with groups working for people with AIDS but promoting the distribution and use of condoms.[9] International funding agencies also often make the distribution of condoms one of the requisites for obtaining financial help. To what extent and in what manner can a Catholic or a Catholic institution get involved?

The response of the Catholic Church should be on two levels. It must bear witness to the inclusive nature of its compassion, protesting against discrimination by a broad policy of acceptance of people with AIDS and providing care. It must further be involved in the task of "responsibilization"—educating people to responsibility especially in the areas of prevention, transmission, and healing.[10]

Educating Individuals to Responsibility

IN THE TASK of educating people to responsibility, we must be clear about the content and limits of our teaching. In Catholic institutions one is bound by what the Catholic Church regards as a Catholic vision and a Catholic ethic.

---

8. At the National Consultation of Catholic Church Bodies mention was also made of such incidents as providing clean needles to drug addicts to prevent HIV infection.

9. This also seems to have been the view of Archbishop Roger Mahoney who withdrew permission for the use of church facilities for an AIDS education program which he discovered would promote the use of condoms. *Origins* 16.28 (1986): 506.

10. Marciano Vidal suggests that the two basic criteria of the ethics of AIDS are "responsibilization" and "nondiscrimination." See "The Christian Ethic: Help or Hindrance? The Ethical Aspects of AIDS," José Oscar Beozzo and Virgil Elizondo, eds., *Concilium: The Return of the Plague* (1997/5): 89–98.

What happens when one is confronted with a person or a group of persons who belong to another faith or who do not share the same ethical values as the Catholic? I believe that guidelines must be clearly given so that Catholics know what is expected of them. With regard to the prevention of the spread of AIDS, the U.S. bishops provide a useful indicator of a possible approach. Facing the ground realities, they suggest that educational efforts, if rooted in a proper moral vision, could include accurate information about prophylactic devices or other practices proposed by medical experts. They clearly state that they are not promoting the use of prophylactics, but merely providing information. They do so only after a critique of "safe sex" and an insistence that chaste sexual behavior and avoidance of intravenous drug abuse are the only correct and medically sure ways to prevent the spread of AIDS.[11]

Problems of Cooperation with Others

WITH REGARD TO the problem of collaborating with other agencies that promote and distribute condoms as part of the strategy, the answer to these dilemmas may be found in the traditional principle of moral theology—namely, the principle of cooperation in evil.

In using the principle of cooperation it is important to keep several factors in mind. To state that we must be careful not to cooperate in or promote actions of others when those acts are immoral is, in a sense, to state the obvious. But life is not so simple. We are called to live and carry out our mission in the world and the real world is complex. It is a world of interdependence and ethical pluralism, a world where good and evil coexist. It is not always easy to pursue the good without in some way incurring some degree of evil. One cannot opt to withdraw totally from the world in order not to be contaminated by evil. That would involve an inability to do any good as well. Yet, if we even appear to compromise, we can scandalize people by giving them the impression of involvement in evil.

The traditional doctrine has been clear: it is always unethical to cooperate formally with an immoral act (intend the evil act itself), but it may be permissible to cooperate materially with an immoral act (only indirectly intending its harmful consequences) when only in this way can a greater harm be prevented, provided that (1) the cooperation is not immediate and (2) that the degree of cooperation and the danger of scandal are taken into account.[12]

---

11. USCC Administrative Board, "The Many Faces of AIDS: A Gospel Response," *Origins* 17 (1987): 482–89.

12. James F. Keenan has suggested that we keep in mind some preliminary insights before appealing to the principle. It is a guiding principle and not a

In the light of this doctrine, How would one make a moral decision in the case given above? As James F. Keenan suggests, at least six questions must be answered to determine whether A can legitimately cooperate with B. "First, what is the object of A's activity? Second, is A's cooperation in B's illicit activity formal or merely material? Third, is the cooperation immediate or simply mediate? Fourth, is the cooperation proximate or simply remote? Fifth, does A have sufficient cause for acting? Sixth, is A's cooperation indispensable?"[13]

Applying this principle to the case given, we might draw the following conclusions:

1. In the matter of renting rooms for the NGO, we could say the object of the sisters' act would not in itself be immoral. They merely provide space for the care of people with AIDS.

2. The cooperation is not formal because they do not show approval of the use of prophylactics or intend the act. It is possible for them to detach their concern for people living with HIV/AIDS from the use and promotion of condoms which they do not intend. Such cooperation is only material.

3. Their cooperation is not immediate, since the object of their action is not the same as the object of the illicit activity, nor are they involved in any essential part of the illicit activity.

4. Further, the cooperation is remote from the illicit activity. The act of renting out space is radically different from the acts of the religious who decide to distribute condoms to commercial sex workers and people with AIDS.

5. Yet another question that is traditionally asked is whether there is a sufficiently grave reason for the cooperation. Taking into consideration the nature of the AIDS pandemic and the urgent need to provide care and prevent an epidemic in the interest of the common good, one could claim that there are sufficiently grave reasons.

6. We may also state that the cooperation is not indispensable to the performance of the immoral act.

7. But one final factor needs to be taken into account—namely, the danger of scandal. It is precisely this factor that seems to have prevented

---

permitting principle. It is a principle that we avoid as far as possible because cooperation in evil is regrettable. One of the purposes of the principle is to contain evil. The principle cannot be used mechanically, but has to be applied with human reasoning. James F. Keenan, "Institutional Cooperation and the Ethical and Religious Directives," *Linacre Quarterly* 64 (August 1997): 53–76.

13. James F. Keenan, "Prophylactics, Toleration, and Cooperation: Contemporary Problems and Traditional Principles," *International Philosophical Quarterly* 29 (1989): 209.

the sisters from renting out their premises. It could be interpreted as an endorsement of an approach that was at variance with the official stance of the church insofar as their building was being used for the promotion and distribution of prophylactics for people with AIDS.

Could this problem have been resolved positively? Perhaps an alternative may have been to ensure through a contract that in this instance, the organization would limit its work for people with AIDS in such a way that usage of condoms would not be promoted at this center. In this manner, the sisters would have shown support for the good work done by the organization for people with AIDS while publicly showing disapproval of the promotion of "safe sex."

But it should also be clear from the principle that distribution of condoms by Catholics either as a way of preventing infection or in order to obtain funds for caring for people with AIDS does not meet the criteria for legitimate cooperation and cannot be morally justified. The reason is that the cooperation is so immediate as to almost make them primary agents.

A further question needs to be asked: Would networking with these agencies be construed as unlawful cooperation in evil? Could individual Catholics be involved with these groups in working for people with AIDS? It would in fact appear to be easier to justify these cases than the cases just dealt with. Provided it is clearly indicated that one distances oneself from the promotion and distribution of prophylactics, one could legitimately cooperate with such agencies as an effective way of promoting the good. It would be an effective way of making the Christian presence felt and the Christian voice heard in this area. It would be possible through counseling and education to limit the damage done by these agencies—NGOs or state agencies. There is support for this approach in the traditional teaching and the pastoral practice of the church.[14]

It is important that the church issue directives along these lines so that its members and institutions can more actively respond to the AIDS crisis.

Social Dimension

BECAUSE OF THE attention constantly given to the issue of prophylactics, the impression often created is that AIDS is essentially an issue of sexual

---

14. One example of an attempt to limit evil is provided by *Evangelium Vitae* 73 in the area of the civil law on abortion. Keenan also mentions cooperation implied in the involvement of the Vatican's institutional engagement of other institutions, some of which entail evil—concordats with other states, involvement in agencies like the U.N.—agencies that do not always promote what the Vatican considers morally right. Keenan, "Institutional Cooperation," 62.

morality. It is not. It is more an issue of social justice, involving human rights and the conflict between the rights of the individual and the protection of the common good. The Christian response must be on both the micro and the macro levels.

There is a need for the practice of what Vidal calls "nondiscrimination," stated more positively as the criterion of inclusion or solidarity. The starting point is the criterion of acceptance of the other whom I cannot "shut out" but whom I must "bring in" in a special way to the dynamic of solidarity of human actions.[15] India has had a long history of discrimination that included a practice known as "untouchability." Untouchability was formally abolished in the Indian Constitution, no. 17, but discrimination still continues. There is a danger of people with HIV/AIDS becoming the new untouchables. The reason is that the disease carries a social stigma. In the public perception persons living with HIV/AIDS are seen as having brought it on themselves by immoral behavior. As a result people with AIDS are discriminated against in the area of employment, housing, and access to health care. At times they are denied basic rights such as liberty, autonomy, and freedom of movement. This constitutes an attack on the foundations of justice based on the equal dignity of all human beings, and violates the claim to just and fair treatment irrespective of a person's physical condition or the cause of it.[16]

The Catholic Hospital Association of India (CHAI) has rightly decided that health care institutions have an obligation to establish a policy that guarantees optimum care, resists any form of discrimination, helps in promoting research, and provides educational and counseling support. As Dr. Edmund Pellegrino suggests, there is also a collective responsibility to reaffirm the obligation of all doctors to treat HIV infection, to take action against those who do not, and to support physicians who have become infected. The profession has great influence on society and should be an advocate for nondiscriminatory, compassionate, and competent care of all HIV-infected patients.[17]

Unfortunately, despite the guidelines of CHAI that state that no one must be denied admission or treatment in hospitals because they suffer from

---

15. Vidal, "Christian Ethic," 94.

16. *Gaudium et Spes* clearly states that because of the dignity proper to human persons their rights and duties are universal and inalienable. It further declares that every form of discrimination, whether social or cultural, whether based on sex, race, color, social condition, language, or religion, is to be overcome and eradicated as contrary to God's will (no. 26,29). A similar statement can be found in the *Universal Declaration of Human Rights*.

17. Edmund Pellegrino, "Treatment Decisions and Ethics in HIV Infection," *Dolentium Hominum*, 116–17.

HIV/AIDS, some institutions are reported to have flouted these norms and turned away people with AIDS. This is ethically unacceptable. The reasons usually given are fear of contracting the disease, lack of protective equipment, lack of insurance coverage, or the fear that other patients will keep away due to the fear of contracting AIDS. From the physician's perspective, this goes against all the basic principles of medical ethics (beneficence, nonmaleficence, respect for persons, and justice). Ignorance accounts for much of the attitude of fear. People are afraid of what they do not comprehend. However, this cannot be an excuse for violent or discriminatory behavior against those who are infected. While individuals have the right to reasonable protective cover in terms of procedure, gear, and insurance, as well as protection from infection, this cannot be done in a way that dehumanizes or victimizes those already infected.

As Pellegrino points out, the physician's primary obligation is to treat the sick without discrimination. He grounds this duty in the nature of medical knowledge and the covenant physicians enter into with society when they accept a medical education and take an oath of commitment to the care of the sick.[18] There is a fiduciary relationship that exists between physician and patient that justifies the invasion of the patient's privacy. To refuse treatment violates this relationship. Medical care is not a marketable commodity in the sense of being a matter of price and quality and distribution, and a physician is not free to deny care to a patient in need of it. Medical knowledge is nonproprietary, and doctors also enter into a social covenant with society for a social purpose. It is this that enables them to acquire knowledge gathered from all patients by all physicians.

It is also society that largely supports their education. Society has a rightful claim on the services of physicians in public emergency. The medical professional enters into this covenant to provide a service that at times involves some risk. The covenant cannot be nullified because of a danger now present—very much as a fireman or policeman cannot refuse to help because of danger.[19] Catholic physicians and medical institutions must give the lead in this regard.

The conflict between individual rights and the common good is seen in the development of programs to control, reduce, or eradicate AIDS. One such area is that of mandatory testing of individuals and mass screening. Only if some proportionate health or medical objective is being served, can such an invasion of a person's right to autonomy and right to privacy be

---

18. Pellegrino, "Treatment Decisions," 113.

19. Pellegrino's arguments published elsewhere have been summarized by Richard J. Devine, *Good Care, Painful Choices: Medical Ethics for Ordinary People* (Mahwah, N.J.: Paulist Press, 1996), 163–64.

allowed. But the fact that this often leads to further discrimination and denial of health care, and that at present there is no therapeutic benefit to the patient, indicates that there is no justification for such mandatory screening or testing.

Another area concerning justice is the allocation of resources. The exorbitant cost of providing care to people with AIDS places a strain on society. There is sometimes an objection made that society is not obliged to provide for people who have freely brought the disease on themselves through their behavior. However, this would also constitute unjust discrimination. Access to health care is a right for all persons. There is also a global dimension to be kept in mind. The distribution of resources for the treatment and care of AIDS patients and the prevention of HIV transmission has been extremely unequal. Although more than 80 percent of all HIV infections occur in less-affluent countries, they receive only a small portion of the international resources spent on HIV/AIDS. This raises a serious issue of distributive justice.[20]

As the study document of the WCC indicates, socio-economic and cultural contexts are determining factors in the spread of HIV/AIDS. The WHO currently estimates that nine out of ten people with HIV live in areas where poverty, the subordinate status of women and children, and discrimination are present.[21] Apart from its response to the immediate effects and causes of HIV/AIDS, the church, conscious of the link between poverty and AIDS, must continue to promote just and sustainable development. It also needs to pay attention to situations that increase vulnerability to AIDS—migrant labor, commercial sex activity, and the drug culture. Finally it must also stand up for the human rights of persons living with HIV/AIDS who are often denied their fundamental right to security, freedom of association, movement, and adequate health care.[22]

---

20. *Facing AIDS: The Challenge, the Church's Response*, WCC Study Document (Geneva: WCC Publications, 1997), 66.

21. *Facing AIDS*, 13. According to Dr. Elizabeth Reid, "it is critical to explore the relationship between economic, social, and cultural variables and the spread of HIV—who becomes infected with the virus and with what spatial distribution. Examples which have been identified as having a causal role in the spread of the virus include gender (more specifically the economic, social, and cultural lack of autonomy of women, which places them at risk of infection); poverty and social exclusion (the absence of economic, social, and political rights); and labor mobility (which is more than the physical mobility of persons and includes the effects on values and traditional structures associated with the processes of modernization). At the core of the transmission of HIV are issues of gender and poverty." Quoted in *Facing AIDS*, 14.

22. *Facing AIDS*, 95, 105.

In the context of India, the church cannot do this on its own. It needs to collaborate with governmental and other secular agencies. That is why it is important to clearly establish ethical guidelines for such cooperation.

HIV/AIDS presents the church in India with a challenge to become a genuine healing and reconciling community, boldly bearing witness to the truth, yet unafraid to examine its own theory and practice, and revealing to the people of our day the compassion of God.

6.
COUNSELING

DIFFERENCES IN CONFESSIONAL
ADVICE IN SOUTH AFRICA

Stuart C. Bate, O.M.I.

THEMBINKOSI NGCOBO IS *a truck driver on the N3 highway. This multilane highway is one of the busiest in Africa carrying goods between the port of Durban and the industrial center of Johannesburg, and then on to many countries of south and central Africa. The highway has created its own culture fulfilling the wants of the truck drivers who ply its route. Petrol stations, food centers, stopover points, and tollgates dot the 600 kilometers of concrete and tar. Poor people of the surrounding area are attracted to the highway in search of money. They work in the toll booths. They sell food at the restaurants. Many are "sex workers."[1] HIV transmission is part of the culture of the highway.*

Thembinkosi is married to Nomusa. Their home is in Durban and they have four children. Nomusa is a devout Catholic, while Thembinkosi is one of the reliable men of the parish who helps Father when he is in Durban. He was an altar boy as a youth and likes his Catholic faith. It is part of his "township culture."[2]

Township culture was originally a migrant culture. The apartheid migrant labor laws made it impossible for migrant workers to bring their families to towns, and so it became quite common for men to have a "family" at home in the rural area and another "family" in the township.[3] This

---

1. The government's current politically correct term for those who sell sex for money or food. For the role of commercial sex workers in HIV spread, see Lorenzo Togni, *AIDS in South Africa and on the African Continent* (Pretoria: Kagiso, 1997), 20–24.

2. Township was the name given to urban areas for black South Africans in the apartheid era. A "township culture" emerged as an amalgam of traditional African culture, secular Western culture, and Christianity as people from different backgrounds became urbanized.

3. See Philip Mayer, *Townsmen or Tribesmen* (Capetown: Oxford University, 1971), 263ff.

too has come to form part of the "township" culture. Thembinkosi's work means that he spends time at the two ends of his journey: Johannesburg and Durban. It comes as no surprise to find that he also has a "family" in Johannesburg where he supports a younger woman who is the mother of two of his children. He has no formal marriage relationship with this woman. She is his "girlfriend." He pays for the upkeep of these children and stays with her when he is in Johannesburg. His wife suspects something but doesn't ask.

In a routine medical checkup required by the medical insurance program of the company he works for, Thembinkosi was found to be HIV positive. Initially he was afraid to tell anyone, but after some months he told his wife and upon testing it was found that she too was positive. Their HIV counselor explained to them that it was essential to avoid retransmission of the disease and that if they were to continue sexual relations, they should both wear condoms to prevent reinfection and thus to prolong their lives. As Catholics they were aware that condoms were not something usually acceptable to the church. At Nomusa's insistence they went to discuss the issue with their parish priest.

The priest was very disturbed about the case. He was very compassionate to the couple, but insisted that the teaching of the church did not allow them to use condoms. He counseled them to abstain from sexual relations for the rest of their lives. He also suggested that they speak to one of the Catholic HIV counselors employed by the diocese. This they did and during the session it became very clear that Thembinkosi and Nomusa wished to continue their sexual relationship. Nomusa was deeply unhappy with the advice of the priest as she wanted to continue following the teaching of the church and to live her faith, but thought that the burden of sexual abstinence on top of the tragedy of Thembinkosi's disease would drive him away from her to his "family" in Johannesburg. She was also afraid of what the other members of the church women's society would think if she did not go to communion.

Margaret, the counselor, went to speak to the priest and suggested that he leave the counseling of this couple to her as she was more experienced. The priest was delighted to do so as he too was unhappy with the advice he had given, saying that he felt constrained to follow the teaching of the church but unhappy about how it applied in this case.

During the counseling session, several issues arose. First, it was clear that every means possible should be taken to prevent retransmission of the disease, since every reinfection increased the viral load and weakened the already struggling immune system. However, abstinence was not a viable solution, since this would add another burden to their lives besides the ones they already had. The sexual expression of their love was a value to each of them, helping to bring them close to one another and cementing their marriage relationship. They wished to remain faithful to one another and look for ways to build their bond until death. But they did not want to go to hell when they died for disobeying the teaching of the church.

As a result of this counseling, the couple decided to use both male and female condoms when having sexual relationships. Nomusa said she would go to confession every week but Thembinkosi didn't feel this was necessary. The confession was always a nightmare for Nomusa since their parish priest continued to tell her in the confessional that what they were doing was wrong and a sin, and so they should abstain from sex. Each week she promised to try but always failed.

Their sexual relationship was now becoming a source of anxiety for Nomusa and Thembinkosi and they went back to the AIDS counselor who suggested that they go to confession to another priest who was more experienced in this field. The discussion with this priest seemed much more helpful. He pointed out to them that the primary moral value was the sanctity of their marriage and the maintenance of their bond. Factors supporting the growth of the bond were their support for one another in the face of this crisis, the love they had for one another of which their sexual relationship was an important expression, and their openness to one another in the wish to remain together. Factors militating against the bond were things like the anxiety and stress brought on by their knowledge of the disease, their standing in the church as "sinners" not going to communion or continually having to confess the use of condoms, and the fact of being unable to live a celibate lifestyle as a married couple. The priest suggested that while in normal cases the use of condoms would not be acceptable, there were some mitigating reasons in this case. Clearly unprotected sex would make both open to reinfection and so the sex act, rather than being open to life, would be detrimental to it. The possibility of bringing more children into the world when their parents might soon die was another issue they needed to consider. Abstinence might drive Thembinkosi to look for other outlets thus endangering other people. The priest asked the couple to take all these factors into account and to use their own consciences in deciding what was in fact sinful. For Thembinkosi it was clear. He did not consider any sin in the condoms and he would go to communion without confessing. Nomusa was less sure but she said she would prefer to come to confession to this priest who seemed "so understanding" and helpful. He showed her that she was not just being a sinner when she had to disobey this law of the church.

Symptom of a Deeper Social Ill

IN EASTERN, CENTRAL, and southern Africa the reality of HIV and AIDS is somewhat different from that in the rest of the world. Here it is not something which infects a small minority of people. It affects most people. With infection rates either having passed or approaching 20 percent of the population, the majority of families either have someone who has died of AIDS or is HIV positive.[4] The rapid rate of HIV infection here can be put down to social and cultural factors.[5] In this part of the world HIV transmission has to be linked with social breakdown and disorganization leading to fluidity in social mores, cultural values, and worldview.

In southern Africa, we see an increasing acculturation of local belief and ethical systems into some of the western ones. This often results in people having two or more moral systems to articulate their lifestyle choices: an African traditional one, a modern western materialist one, and a Christian one. People often dip into these, choosing the most convenient to justify and maintain their lifestyle choices.

Economic forces have led to a struggle for money in a continent of poverty. Economic necessity and attraction leads to people today being far less rooted and much more mobile than in the past. Money has become a basic and fundamental need particularly for those who have very little. Most are forced by this need to accept whatever means they can to get access to money and the life it can buy. This too has become a major cultural value today.

The migratory labor system has had a major impact on the value system of black Africans throughout sub-Saharan Africa, but particularly in South Africa where it was codified by the apartheid regime into a rigorous system of laws. As men were unable to bring their families to their place of work, the migratory labor system forced migrant workers into a variety of heterodox sexual practices which would be termed immoral in terms of both African traditional culture and Christianity. Among many other things, this has led to a relatively common South African phenomenon of a man with two families: one at home and one in the city of work. Often the former is a more formal "marriage" whereas the latter is a less formal arrangement and the woman is a "girlfriend." Migrants are commuters and consequently major highways have become conduits of culture in a

---

4. Around one in four adults is HIV positive in countries like Zimbabwe and Botswana. See Marian Westley and Erika Check, "Is AIDS Forever," *Newsweek US Edition* (6 July 1998): 60–61. In the KwaZulu-Natal province of South Africa, the incidence of HIV positive pregnant mothers rose from 1.6 percent to 25 percent between 1990 and 1996; See Diakonia, *An AIDS Kairos for Durban Churches*, June 1997, 5.

5. For the influence of social and cultural factors on HIV infection rates, see Willem Saayman and Jacques Kriel, "Toward a Christian response to AIDS," *Missionalia* 19, no. 2 (1991): 154–67, and Willem Saayman, "AIDS" in *Doing Ethics in Context,* ed. Charles Villa Vicencio and John De Gruchy (Cape Town: David Philip, 1994), 174–75.

continent with very few material resources. As goods and people travel up and down the highways, new cultural forms and symbols are continually created and inserted into existing worldviews to create new ways of life with their own "value" systems.

Women are often the principal victims of this situation. Through no fault of Nomusa, the continuation of a genital relationship with her husband now becomes a roll of the dice with the disease. And what of Thembinkosi's "girlfriend" and family in Johannesburg? She is dependent on him for money to support herself and her children, but there is no formal relationship and so she will probably be abandoned if Thembinkosi deteriorates and is forced by his illness to leave his job. This is a tragedy played out daily in the lives of many women left to look after their children and forced to use whatever means they can to support them.

The Church's Response

MINISTRY IN A world of HIV/AIDS must contain a social and cultural response. Similarly, the theological response to HIV/AIDS must at the same time be a theological response to the underlying social and cultural phenomenon, or it will provide pastoral praxis which does not touch the life of people. The church's moral theology is sometimes unhelpful in this context since it is often based on western anthropological categories stressing the individual as the fundamental moral agent. Often, as in this case, the moral issues affecting individuals have social and cultural components which must form part of the moral response. At the same time the teaching of the church cannot be abandoned on the altar of social expediency, and for these reasons a pastoral moral theology should imply the interpenetration of authentic teaching and an effective pastoral response.

An Authentic Teaching

The parish priest in our case was correctly concerned about maintaining an authentic teaching. However, on the pastoral level, authentic teaching implies the effective catechesis of morality. This requires values which are incarnated in an inculturated faith responding to human life in a context. The human sciences and social and cultural analysis have to be part of such a pastoral moral theology. There have been some efforts to do this on the psychological level in recent years, but fewer attempts to relate socioeconomic and cultural factors to issues of moral theology.

People often ignore the church's teaching because it seems so far from the reality of their lives and the inhuman system of disvalues in which we become entrapped. Our society is in need of moral reconstruction, but this has to occur in a way that is socially possible. How can the church develop a moral position regarding human sexuality which will not just be ignored and disregarded by the vast majority of Catholics as inapplicable? Social studies here show, for example, that as people become more affluent, they have fewer children and practice birth control. Poorer people tend to have more partners and are often less committed to the stable bonds of marriage. Social facts like these affect behavior even when people are trying to live a Christian moral life.

At the same time our cathechesis is called to be countercultural. Clearly Thembinkosi's cultural value of two families needs to be challenged. His township culture is in need of evangelization here. But what is the worldview that we offer as Christians? It needs to be realistic or it will not be taken seriously. Promiscuity, and relationships without formal commitment such as the one Thembinkosi has with his "girlfriend," may be short-term expediencies but they often lead to human suffering and single-parent disadvantaged poor families. Such families are somewhat of a cultural norm here, but this does not mean that the church should assimilate such cultural disvalues into its own vision. Strong promotion of a Christian sexual morality, together with strategies of how to live it, are an essential part of youth formation today in our context.

An Effective Pastoral Response: The Mission to Heal

People in moral crisis often turn to their priests. But as in our case study, clergy are often unequipped to deal with the complexity of the social issues around moral crises. The parish priest's advice in terms of the church's teaching was unhelpful to the couple; while it affirmed ideal principles, it proposed unworkable solutions. Ultimately his advice was largely ignored by the couple and only served to add to their worries. He too was aware of its inadequacy and was happy to give up his responsibility to the counselor.

An effective pastoral response to people in need cannot be just the articulation and application of clear principles and norms. There is a time and place for strong and effective catechesis, but when people experience sickness, suffering, and crisis, the focus must change. Jesus took account of people in their need and was accused of breaking the law when responding to people in their concrete experience of suffering. He mandated his followers to continue his mission to heal.

The second priest was more helpful in raising some of the important issues around their situation. He was able to provide a better link between the ideals of the church's moral teaching and the context of their human life. The ability to make this link would seem to be essential for ministers in our modern world but often it is lacking. What kind of theological approach can help ministers to make these links and thus respond to people in their human context as Jesus did?

I would suggest that the mission to heal offers a better framework within which such moral issues can be approached whether in the sacrament of penance, counseling, or even ordinary prayer. This fundamental missionary mandate is often overlooked, yet when we look at the ministry of Jesus we see that his principal concerns were to preach good news, to heal the sick, and to form a group of disciples to continue his work. Each of these is subsumed and transformed by his death and resurrection into salvation for all people. In transmitting his mission to his followers it is clear that he wanted them to follow what he did. So in the mission mandate of Matthew 10 we read how the disciples are given authority over unclean spirits to cast them out and to heal every disease. The words used for healing in the Greek always refer to the whole person and not to individual members of the body,[6] and "always in such a way that the reference is not to medical treatment which might fail but to real healing."[7]

When we try to understand what our mission to heal is today, we should not be confused by modern western culture where the "medical model" of sickness and health is the primary cultural framework for healing. Medically, HIV/AIDS is currently incurable. But does this mean that it cannot be healed?

In contemporary medical anthropology, *disease* is used to refer to organic malfunction, whereas *illness* "refers to the psychosocial experience and meaning of perceived disease."[8] The construction of illness out of disease is always a cultural process following cultural categories of sickness and health. Consequently the healing process is also always a cultural process.

It is worth noting that healing refers to two related but distinguishable clinical tasks: the establishment of effective control of disordered biological and psychological processes, which I shall refer to as the "curing of disease," and the provision of personal and social meaning for life problems created by sickness which I shall refer to as the "healing of illness."[9]

HIV/AIDS exhibits aspects of being an illness and a disease. Because of the way society has stigmatized this sickness and because it is a sickness unto death, people who contract HIV go through a process of cultural and

6. See Gerhard Kittel and Gerhard Friedrich, eds., Theological Dictionary of the New Testament, 10 vols. (Grand Rapids, Mich.: Eerdmans, 1964–1976), 7:990.

7. Ibid., 8:129.

8. Arthur Kleinman, *Patients and Healers in the Context of Culture* (Berkeley: University of California, 1980), 72.

9. Ibid., 82.

social isolation which is in many ways much more "sickening" than the clinical symptoms themselves. Often testing is avoided since this will construct the illness out of the disease and move people into the socially ostracized group of "HIV/AIDS victims."

Now the mission to heal may concern itself with the curing of disease, but it should not focus on that for a number of reasons:

- *AIDS is an illness and needs healing as much as, if not more than, curing.*
- *Healing is concerned with the human person, whereas curing is concerned with scientific processes which require scientific expertise.*
- *Curing is often "out of our hands" as missionaries and Christians, whereas healing is our vocation.*
- *Care, affirmation, hope, and acceptance are not provided by the curing model which is concerned with organic processes, not human processes.*

Clearly those involved in any form of work with persons affected by HIV/AIDS need to see themselves as healers doing the church's healing ministry and following the theological categories appropriate to that ministry.

Healing is an essential ministry today, especially in a world beset by cultural, social, and psychological sickness. We need to search actively for the means of human healing in our ministry. In our case the second priest was more of a healer whereas the first, even while trying to do good, actually contributed to the illness by increasing the stress of Thembinkosi and especially Nomusa. Cultural and religious healing is fundamentally a question of care and prayer in an accepting human environment. So we need to look for ways to set up "caring structures" which help people to cope and live human and Christian lives. Counseling, group therapy for HIV positive people, and family-based care of people with AIDS would be examples of effective healing. We can contribute to healing an illness even when the disease may be incurable by removing the sickness which is exacerbated by the culture of silence and fear around the disease. Here healing demands a move to a healthier worldview from the sicker one of the past. This is evangelization, since healing occurs through living a moral and coherent human life.

Let us come finally to the issue of condoms and the marriage of Thembinkosi and Nomusa. Here we see a marriage which has been compromised by several social, cultural, medical, and religious factors which impinge upon the humanity and Christianity of this married couple. At the same time we see a couple who are trying to save their marriage and who are living with a lot of stress. The confession and their parish priest's response have contributed to the stress and are not healing. At the same time, a sexual act separated by two plastic condoms, male and female, must be deeply ambiguous to the human relationship. How to resolve this? Is the saving of the marriage a deeper, more fundamental issue than the integrity of the sexual act? We would have to answer yes. This couple needs one another right now more than ever, and they need whatever expression of their love they can find.

At the same time we should be careful not to generalize here. Condom-focused pastoral responses to the AIDS issue are bound to fail because they tackle only part of the issue. They do not resolve the healing of illness even though they may provide a temporary preventive measure to the spread of the disease in a cultural context which is allowing a large measure of sexual promiscuity. As one of the diocesan AIDS workers noted: "throwing condoms at the AIDS problem will not solve it. We have learned this from fifteen years work in ATIC and now in the diocesan AIDS program."[10] Condoms can never be a morally acceptable part of the genital act since in a certain sense they destroy its humanity by changing the nature of what is happening. They promote precisely the sort of promiscuity and irresponsibility in human relationships which has led to where we are now.

However we do not find ourselves in a normal social situation, but in one of a pandemic coupled with cultural and social disorganization. If people refuse to live according to the gospel in society and spread disease, then what to do? A more holistic response to the spread of HIV/AIDS has emerged recently. It is currently being promoted in several parts of Africa and is called the ABC program. ABC stands for: Abstain, Be faithful, or use a Condom. This puts the use of the condom in a better context as a response which goes together with the active decision to be promiscuous: a decision which some people in our society do make but which can never be a Christian one. However, the human and Christian values of abstinence and faithfulness are seen as a more *effective* human and Christian response as well as being more *moral* ones.

The ABC program is part of the National Campaign against AIDS in Uganda[11] and has won some support there from church authorities. The Diakonia Council of Churches in Durban largely supports this approach, although the Catholic archdiocese of Durban does not accept the condom part of this strategy. It is abstinence and faithfulness which will promote moral reconstruction and clearly the issue of moral reconstruction is a vital one in Africa today. This is where evangelization and catechesis to a

---

10. Interview with Liz Towell and Sabbath Mlambo, full-time workers in the archdiocese of Durban AIDS homecare project, 3 March 1998. The "AIDS Training and Information Centres" (ATIC) is a nongovernmental organization offering training, counseling, and support services for people with AIDS in KwaZulu-Natal province.

11. Diakonia, *AIDS—A Problem Shared: Report on a Study Visit to East Africa*, May 1997, 22.

better way of life are essential. The church needs to play the role of society's "conscience," showing that lifestyle changes are required if people are to avoid the kind of chaos in our societies of which HIV/AIDS is but one symptom. Functionalist solutions to these problems such as condoms, pills, and injections together with structural solutions such as national campaigns and legislation are important, but the underlying problem is a cultural one and so the long-term effective remedy needs to operate on this level. Cultural reconstruction is vital at this period of African history, and cultural reconstruction implies moral reconstruction. In helping the moral reconstruction of our society, the church plays a vital pastoral role in the healing of our communities.

WHEN FIDELITY AND JUSTICE CLASH: TESTING THE LIMITS OF CONFIDENTIALITY IN AUSTRALIA

Gerald Gleeson and David Leary

"ANDREW," A YOUNG *man of aboriginal descent, was told he was HIV positive as a result of an infected blood transfusion in the same week his adoptive father died from a brain tumor. These events marked the beginning of his withdrawal from his family and the breakdown of his peer support. His subsequent acting out behavior included criminal offences and multiple drug use, and in 1985, at sixteen years of age, he was incarcerated in a juvenile detention center. Andrew was the first adolescent detainee in Australia known to be HIV positive, and he was subjected to significant racial and HIV-related discrimination. He was referred to the Come In Youth resource center prior to release, in the hope that he could begin to establish a network of support within the community. On release, he attended the center, received counseling, and was helped to find secure, long-term housing. The center became his advocate with outstanding legal issues, including matters of discrimination.*

As his illness progressed, Andrew became more desperate and more difficult to assist. Although no longer engaging in criminal activity, he placated his fear of illness and death with increased drug use, financed by occasional prostitution. Staff of the center assisted with counseling and material aid, and because of the potential harm to others, he was on occasion supplied with condoms, needles, and syringes. Soon Andrew began a relationship with "Jane," who was fifteen years of age. She had recently run away from home and was living in a refuge. Though not "street wise," and much in need of protection, Jane was highly resistant to intervention.

Once the center became aware of the relationship between Andrew and Jane, complex legal, psychosocial, and ethical dilemmas arose. Both adolescents were clients of the center, both were withdrawn and uncommunicative. The team was perplexed by issues of knowledge and responsibility. Did Jane know of Andrew's medical status? How could this be established when both were unwilling or unable to discuss the issue? Did the duty of care to Jane override confidentiality with Andrew? As they pondered these questions, the staff knew that to break confidence with Andrew would be to risk his withdrawal from his only professional support. There was a further potential conflict of interest because the director of the center was both clinical supervisor to other counselors (including Jane's), and counselor to Andrew.

In addition, the center's association with the local Catholic parish prompted concerns about the distribution of condoms, needles, and syringes. Andrew and Jane were counseled about responsible sexual and drug-related behavior, but were known to be using drugs, and presumably were sexually active. The staff tried to persuade Andrew to tell Jane that he was HIV positive and warned Jane of the dangers of unsafe sexual and drug-related activity, but she was never directly informed of Andrew's medical status. In time, she too became HIV positive. Given the potential for multimodal transmission, it is not known how the infection occurred. Andrew died from an AIDS-related condition in June 1991.

"Andrew" and "Jane" are representative of many young people living on the streets of affluent cities in the developed world.[1] Among the ethical questions their story raises, few are more difficult to resolve than those about when confidentiality should be breached in order to protect another from harm. We will argue that this question is best understood in terms of a clash between the claims made on counselors, ministers, or health workers in the name of *fidelity* to their clients, and the claims made on them in the name of *justice* to others. The resolution of this conflict demands *prudence* or practical moral wisdom.

---

1. See Richard Eckersley, "Failing a Generation—The Impact of Culture on the Health and Well-Being of Youth," *Journal of Paediatrics and Child Health* 29/1 (1993): 16–69.

Ministry to the Marginalized

FOR OVER TWENTY years the Come In Youth resource center has provided counseling, advocacy, and practical assistance to disadvantaged and marginalized young people, who either reside in or move through the innercity of Sydney (Australia). The center, which operates in association with the Catholic parish of St. Francis, at Paddington, comprises a central base, a small residential unit, and outreach activities. It deals with homelessness, juvenile offending, adolescent health problems, HIV and AIDS, drug and alcohol concerns, poverty, and the sundry emotional difficulties associated with family dysfunction and breakdown. The center also assists with education, employment, and training. The principal aim is to provide long-term support to highly disaffected youth.

Despite the grave plight of our homeless youth, some will question whether a Catholic parish should support a refuge for those caught up in immoral behavior. Will not such a center bring its staff uncomfortably close to wrongdoing, and to the moral dilemmas it generates? These are not abstract questions for, in the case of this particular center, some Catholics complained that it was "purveying the *culture of death*" and "openly promoting, supporting, and co-operating in intrinsically evil acts . . . and giving grave scandal to young people." Happily, these charges were refuted to the satisfaction of church authorities. Nonetheless, since attacks on the center and others like it continue, it is important to rebut the charge that one should not try to assist young people like Andrew and Jane.

Motivation and Intention

CRITICS OF THE center's work remind us that continuing ethical reflection is incumbent on anyone seeking to assist vulnerable people caught up in the seedy world of illegal drugs and promiscuous sex. In the Catholic tradition, this reflection should examine both *motivation* and *intention*. Motivation looks back to the conscious and unconscious desires, feelings, and dispositions out of which one acts. Intention, by contrast, looks forward to one's goals and the means one rationally chooses to realize them. (The English word "motive" is ambiguous between these two notions.) Motivation describes the source of the one's willing; intention describes the order in one's reasoning. Ideally, motivation and intention are in harmony: out of love for others, one intends and does what is morally right.

In practice, motivation and intention may come apart: a loving motivation does not guarantee that one will intend and act rightly. Good people often intend and act unwisely, and those who appear to be acting rightly may well be hypocrites.[2] Moreover, the goodness of one's motivation is ultimately known only to God, for the heart is devious, and motivation is always flawed and partially unconscious. Nonetheless, the "normal" expressions of a loving motivation—that is, of God's love "poured into our hearts" (Rom. 5:5)—are easily recognized, since compassion for the wounded in our midst is love shown for Christ himself (Mt. 25:31–46).

The staff of the center, and others like it, aspire to give practical expression to God's own compassion for some of the most wounded people in our society—marginalized, homeless youth. However, for this compassion to be *wisely exercised*, it must be shaped by sound reasoning about the appropriate ways in which to promote the good of the human person. Accordingly, the focus of our discussion will be, not motivation, but rather practical wisdom as to *what* one should do when faced with dilemmas about confidentiality.

Sound Moral Reasoning: The Case of Cooperation

MORAL REASONING LEADING to intentional action embraces the complex ordering of chosen means to desired ends: *what* I am doing and *why* I am doing it. Of course, one's intended goals are normally "good" under some description. The real challenge for moral reasoning concerns the rightness of the "means" chosen to attain one's goals. For example: a health worker's goal may be to minimize the danger of HIV infection, but are the chosen means—providing someone with condoms or clean needles—"rightly ordered" and appropriate in the circumstances, or do they rather facilitate life-threatening and immoral conduct, and implicitly endorse it?

The Catholic Church's approach to moral reasoning about cooperation with others steers a middle course between *consequentialism*, on the one hand, and *moral neutrality*, on the other hand. Consequentialism adopts the viewpoint of an external observer who tries to calculate whether cooperation or noncooperation would produce greater good overall. This approach bypasses the prior question of the meaning and moral status of one's cooperative action in itself, and of its significance for the person cooperating. The moral neutrality approach focuses narrowly on what *I* do, in isolation from what is done by those others with whom I am cooperating. This approach inflates individual autonomy and ignores the complex ways in which our actions, and our responsibilities, are interwoven.

---

2. See James F. Keenan, *Goodness and Rightness in Thomas Aquinas's* Summa Theologiae (Washington, D.C.: Georgetown University Press, 1992), and Gerald Gleeson, "When a Good Conscience Errs," *Pacifica* 8 (1995): 53–73.

Catholic moral reasoning, by contrast, takes up the viewpoint of the "acting subject," and so the first-person perspective of the agent in relation to other agents.[3] From this viewpoint, "formal" cooperation in which an agent shares in the wrong intentions of another can be distinguished from "material" cooperation in which, even though an agent gives some assistance to another who is acting wrongly, the agent's own action remains morally upright. Material, but not formal, cooperation may only be justified when the right effects of cooperating outweigh the wrong effects of not cooperating with another. It was on the basis of this long-standing Catholic teaching on material cooperation that the work of the help center was vindicated against its critics.

Confidentiality and the Virtues

IN CONSIDERING QUESTIONS about the limits of confidentiality, we likewise aim to move beyond both "consequentialist" thinking and "moral autonomy" thinking. Consequentialism, perhaps endemic to the social welfare culture, looks only to the external consequences of actions; deciding whether to maintain or to breach confidentiality is a matter of "counting heads," of calculating what course of action would do more good in the circumstances, irrespective of one's relationships to the people involved. Moral autonomy thinking, on the other hand, refuses to look beyond the confines of a fiduciary relationship, supposing my duty to my client to be entirely self-contained.

A Catholic "virtues" approach to moral reasoning seeks to acknowledge the significance of one's chosen actions both for the agent and for those to whom the agent is related. In James Keenan's restatement of the "cardinal" virtues, *justice* is the virtue governing one's relationships with other human beings in general, and *fidelity* is the new cardinal virtue he proposes as governing one's relationships with those to whom one is specially related (family, friends, clients).[4] Keenan subsumes the traditionally "instrumental" virtues of courage and moderation under the virtue of *self-care*, by which we esteem ourselves and our own integrity, and give due regard to our legitimate needs. Justice, fidelity, and self-care can thus be redefined in terms of relationships to self and others. *Prudence* is the virtue of practical wisdom to integrate and resolve the competing claims of the virtues. The moral

---

3. See Pope John Paul II, *Veritatis Splendor* (Vatican City: Libreria Editrice Vaticana, 1993), 78.

4. See James F. Keenan, "Proposing Cardinal Virtues," *Theological Studies* 56 (1995): 709–29.

conflict in the case of Andrew and Jane well exemplifies this relational account of the virtues.

Fidelity

The pressing ethical issue for staff of the center was whether to breach confidentiality with Andrew in the hope of protecting Jane. Fidelity is partly constitutive of every counseling relationship, and so, in normal circumstances, not even a client may release a professional from the duty to maintain confidentiality. Confidentiality belongs to the relationship itself, rather than to the individuals who enter into the relationship. Because the director was related to Andrew in a way in which he was not related to Jane, he was not free to stand back as an external observer of these two young people, nor free simply to "calculate" what action would do the most good overall.

In addition, at sixteen years of age, Andrew was becoming a responsible adult. In the experience of the center's staff, sixteen is a crucial turning point at which young people (especially those "living on the streets") really do take charge of their lives. The director sought to foster Andrew's movement to adulthood by trusting his promise to tell Jane of his HIV status. Not to have allowed time for this, would have been to undermine the trust vital to Andrew's growth. But how long could the director afford to wait?

Justice

In addition to his fidelity to Andrew, the director had other responsibilities as a professional and as a human being: to his peers, to counselors under his supervision, and to the wider community. Every professional is also a member of society, and as such his relationships with other people fall under the virtue of justice—what is owed to others because they are our fellow human beings. A potential conflict between fidelity and justice arises when *as privy to confidential information* one learns of threats to the well-being of others.

Once the director realized that Andrew's behavior could endanger Jane's life, he was conscious of the need to protect Jane as a matter of justice, and indirectly, as a matter of fidelity, since Jane was a client of the center. He also knew that women can be more vulnerable to HIV transmission because often they are less able to demand the protection to which they are entitled. The Catholic tradition holds that in principle (apart from the sacrament of reconciliation) confidentiality may be breached, as a last resort, when there is a grave threat to others or to the common good. The gravity of the situation in this case, given Jane's age and vulnerability, would in principle entitle a counselor to tell Jane what Andrew was withholding from her.

And yet, as much as a claim in fidelity should—*for sufficiently grave reasons*—give way to the claim of justice, this conclusion did not seem open to the director. His overriding concern was to stay in relationship with Andrew, for if this relationship broke down, he would be in no position to assist either Andrew or Jane. If the director had simply told Jane of Andrew's medical status, he risked her breaking with Andrew, and Andrew reacting in ways destructive to himself, to Jane, and to others. Indeed, the director believed there was a danger that Andrew might become more reckless in his sexual behavior, or return to prostitution and endanger the lives of many others. Finally, the director felt trapped by Andrew's refusal to say whether or not he had told Jane. What if he breached confidence only to learn that Jane already knew?

Prudence as Practical Wisdom

In retrospect, of course, it is tempting to conclude that Jane should have been told earlier. There was room for such a judgment in the Catholic moral tradition, even if Jane's exposure to HIV was likely to persist whether she was informed or not. But how does one make a prudential judgment in circumstances like these?[5] "Prudence" in contemporary English often means little more than self-interest. For Aristotle and Thomas Aquinas, however, prudence is the mark of the morally mature and wise person, and a prudent or practically wise judgment is a judgment in accord with "right desiring." It is the judgment which "feels right" to the person whose attitudes and feelings for the situation are right.[6] What makes one's "feelings" for a situation right?

Right feelings and attitudes are shaped, first, by right reasoning about the requirements of justice and fidelity. Justice identifies the minimum requirements for civil society, the peace and good order within which personal relationships may flourish. From this viewpoint, the claims of justice are prior to those of fidelity because if justice for all is not safeguarded, the context for fidelity to a few will be undermined. However, there is good reason to think that unless a person can relate to a few, special people, it

---

5. For a general discussion of cases and issues, see James F. Keenan, "Notes on Moral Theology: Confidentiality, Disclosure, and Fiduciary Responsibility" in *Theological Studies* 54 (1993): 142–59.

6. See Yves R. Simon, *Practical Knowledge* (New York: Fordham University Press, 1991), 1–26.

will be very difficult for him or her to relate to many, let alone to society as a whole. From this viewpoint, the experience of specific relationships (chiefly within the family and with peers) is prior to the experience of one-self as a member of the wider society. Without the experience of mutual fidelity, the claims of justice will remain abstract and remote.

Justice and fidelity are thus mutually supportive. It would have been from within his experience of faithful relationships (with counselor and peers) that Andrew might have become trusting enough to accept his responsibilities to others. To break confidence with Andrew on the grounds of others' right to know his medical status would have been not only to undermine his trust, but also to diminish the chances of his ever coming to recognize the claims of justice. This is not to deny that at some point, it might have been prudent to tell Jane of Andrew's HIV status.

Self-Care in Decision Making

Right feelings and attitudes for decision-making are shaped, secondly, by care of oneself, and by growth in those virtues like courage and modera-tion which govern the emotional dispositions without which one's judg-ments are likely to be flawed. The director needed both courage to face the consequences of his decision in the face of Andrew's likely reactions and moderation to ensure he neither settled for easy procrastination, nor was caught up in the excitement of crisis management. He needed to recognize his limited power to resolve a terrible situation in which his best efforts were likely to be frustrated. Drawing on his inner resources of moral char-acter, the director had to make a prudential judgment, which would inte-grate the claims of each of these virtues in a final, practical judgment, a "reasoning of the heart," based on his instinctive feeling for when it would be right to intervene directly with Jane.

A virtuous approach to moral reasoning is often criticized for not telling us exactly what to do. In truth it does something more important: it tells me what kind of person I should become, if I am to have any hope of knowing what to do. To be sure, a virtues approach does rule out some kinds of action—namely, those which *contradict* justice and fidelity (theft, murder, and adultery). But in most cases that matter, no code, law, or principle could possibly resolve our moral dilemmas. A virtues approach challenges our temptation to look for a definitive moral answer outside of ourselves and our own grasp of a situation. In the end, a person can and must trust their instinctive judgment for what is right. But whether one's decision really is right will depend on the extent to which one has become a morally wise per-son—that is, a person of sound character whose reasoning, feelings, and dis-positions are rightly ordered in relation to self and to others.

New Insight into Confidentiality

THIS CASE SHEDS new light on the claims of fidelity and justice in relation to vulnerable young people and HIV prevention. In many western societies today, the claims of justice and the common good are in the ascendant: political parties compete to be seen as proponents of "law and order," policing and sentencing policies are resulting in overcrowded jails, and it is commonly presumed that disclosure of someone's HIV status must be in the public interest. Yet, contrary to those forces which would erode confidentiality it is our conviction that the greater public interest often lies in ensuring that people with HIV/AIDS are not deterred from seeking help.

Marginalized youth have little sense of, or respect for, the common good and the social fabric. What they most desperately seek is trusting support within a safe environment where their confidences will not be betrayed. They need to experience fidelity in relationship—both with their peers and with significant adults—a fidelity which connects them to others, and which enables them to move beyond the overwhelming sense of betrayal which typically marks their approach to society at large. This is not to suggest that fidelity is an isolated absolute. It is equally crucial that those entering into special, confidential relationships are led to recognize the just claims others may make. Every relationship of fidelity is located within the wider, moral context of society, which is defined by networks of relationships also governed by fidelity and justice. Social workers and other professionals must constantly assess the claims of justice and fidelity with a view to the needs of the person before them, and in the light of the convictions that guide their thoughtful and responsible interventions.

The case of Andrew and Jane led staff of the help center to refine their policies on confidentiality. Clients are now told that what they say will be held in confidence by the team, rather than by the individual counselor, so that fidelity is not reduced to a privatized relationship between client and counselor. This approach allows for (nonidentified) external consultation when expert advice is needed. In this way, the mutually supportive relationship between fidelity and justice is modeled for those whose own experience of relationship is so fragmented. Clients are also informed of the limits to confidentiality, and told that a serious threat of self-harm or of harm to others constitutes grounds for re-evaluating the confidentiality agreement struck between client and counselor.

A judgment of prudence must always be made *before* the actual consequences are known. A judgment may still have been prudent even if things turn out badly. We cannot say the director waited too long, simply because Jane became HIV positive. In the words of Cardinal Newman, our duty is to strengthen our capacity for prudential judgment, "and in every case as it comes to do our best."[7]

This discussion has sought to identify the basis for "doing our best," when faced with moral dilemmas as an education in the moral virtues. One's capacity for sound moral reasoning depends on a grasp of the relevant facts and their importance, on the right ordering of one's emotions and attitudes, and on an ability to recognize and to integrate the various moral claims at stake. We have highlighted the different kinds of relationships we have with other people, and the significance of these relationships for our self-understanding as moral agents.[8] The "Andrews" and "Janes" of our world need us to be both faithful to them and just to others, and prudent when fidelity and justice seem to clash.

AUSTRALIAN PARENTS OF YOUNG GAYS AND LESBIANS: SUPPORT AND PROTECTION

Peter Black, C.Ss.R.

THE CONFLICT BETWEEN *support on the one hand, and the condoning of what one believes to be a harmful or even immoral lifestyle on the other, is a common experience for many parents today. Recently a very concrete expression of such a conflict was brought to my attention. A seventeen-year-old boy asked his parents for permission to join a support group for young gay men because he was experiencing a lack of support and understanding at the local Catholic school and from his peer group.*

The teenager came out to his parents and explained that he could not be himself most of the time, especially in the school environment where he felt constrained in what he said, what he did and how he appeared, and that he lived with the constant fear of some form of harassment by fellow students. This type of experience by young gay and lesbian students has been identified recently in a popular gay magazine in Australia:

7. John Henry Cardinal Newman, *An Essay in Aid of A Grammar of Assent* (Westminster, Md.: Christian Classics, 1973), 359.

8. See Charles Taylor, "The Dialogical Self," D. R. Hiley, J. F. Bohman, and R. Shusterman, eds., *The Interpretive Turn* (Ithaca: Cornel University Press, 1991).

Lesbian and gay students are encouraged to live a school life of constraint; constrained in what they can say, in what they can do, and in how they appear. They often endure harassment, the fear of harassment, in silence, because they are scared of speaking out. They are fearful of the consequences of speaking themselves, not only to peers, but to teachers and family. But when it comes to expressing heterosexuality, students are far less constrained. They are encouraged to be loudly straight, in the way they act, appear, and speak.[1]

The teenager had discovered two groups that met on a regular basis in the city, one was called Breakaway and the second Other Voices. He read about these support groups in a small booklet entitled "You Are Not Alone," a joint project of the Gay and Lesbian Counseling Service and the local AIDS council. His parents remained open and took the time to examine the contents of the booklet and the description of the two groups. Breakaway was described as a friendly social group for young guys who are attracted to other young guys. They get together once a fortnight and go to movies, horse riding, coffee, and the screening of videos. Other Voices is run by young gay and bisexual guys to offer support and social contact for young men between the ages of fifteen and twenty-five. With the assistance of the western Australian AIDS council, the group runs the highly successful Escape Explore youth retreat which helps in the creation of HIV prevention campaigns for young gay men and also organizes social and fund-raising events to fund its programs.

In reading the entire booklet "You Are Not Alone," the parents come across statements such as: "It's OK to be attracted to someone of the same sex. Being attracted to people of the same sex is a natural and healthy way to be," and "being gay, lesbian, or bisexual is as natural, normal, and healthy as being heterosexual. The vast majority of psychologists and psychiatrists consider it unethical to try to change a person's sexual orientation" (USA Psychiatric Association; USA Psychological Association; British Psychiatric Association). There is also a section on sexually transmissible diseases, which reads: "If you choose to have sex with someone, regardless of their sex, you should think about STDs, including HIV/AIDS. Remember always use protection, such as a condom, dam (square piece of latex), or latex gloves with water-based lubricant to keep both you and your partner safe."[2]

---

1. Greg Curran, Michael Crowhurst, and Louise Halliday, "Being Lesbian and Gay in a Catholic School," *Campaign* (March 1998): 31-32.

2. Graham Brown, Pia Coates, and Melissa Gillet, *You're Not Alone* (a joint project of the Gay and Lesbian Counseling Service WA and the WA AIDS Council, 1997), 1, 8.

Naturally, conflicting thoughts and emotions run through the minds and hearts of these parents. The first thought might be, "How do I continue to love and support my son in the light of what he understands as his coming out?" The initial feelings of the parents may be grief, shock, denial, anger, guilt, a sense of loss, or even relief and acceptance. The second thoughts might be: "Can I presume that at seventeen years of age my son knows that he is gay, or is this experimenting with some homosexual attractions and attitudes merely part of the process of discovering his sexual identity?"

They are not alone in their conflict. One may remember that the first version of *Always Our Children* (pastoral letter to parents of gay/lesbian youth by the U.S. Catholic bishops) suggested that during the early stages of sexual confusion "sometimes the best approach may be a wait-and-see attitude, while you try to maintain a trusting relationship and provide various kinds of support, information, and encouragement."[3] The revised version of the same document on the other hand suggested:

> What is called for on the part of the parents is an approach that does not presume that your child has developed a homosexual orientation and which will help you maintain a loving relationship, while you provide support, information, encouragement, and moral guidance. Parents must always be vigilant about their children's behavior and exercise responsible intervention when necessary.[4]

The conflict of approaches is even evident in the two versions of this document: wait and see, or intervention?

The fears of the parents may be legion. Remembering church claims that the orientation is objectively disordered[5] and homosexual acts are intrinsically disordered and contrary to natural law,[6] they could wonder: "If we encourage him or at least give him permission to join these support groups, will he be in contact with views on homosexuality and homosexual activity that are in conflict with the teaching of the church?" Perhaps the most worrying thought would be: "Would we in some way be placing him at risk in relation to HIV/AIDS if we gave him permission to be a part of

---

3. National Conference of Catholic Bishop's Committee on Marriage and Family (NCCB), "Always Our Children: To the Parents of Homosexual Children," *Origins* 27/17 (1997): 287–91.

4. NCCB, "Always Our Children: To the Parents of Homosexual Children," (revised) *Origins* 28/7 (1998): 97–102.

5. *The Catechism of the Catholic Church* (London: Geoffrey Chapman, 1994), no. 2358.

6. The Pontifical Council for the Family, *The Truth and Meaning of Human Sexuality* (Homebush, NSW: St. Paul Publication, 1996), no. 104.

the support groups?" In subsequent discussion with their son they may realize that he is not seeking to join the groups to make sexual contacts. Yet the fear persists: Will the older and more experienced young men take advantage of him?

What are some of the central issues with which the parents have to come to terms? In affirming their son's emerging sexual identity and giving him permission to be part of a support group, are they giving him an indirect message that sexual relationships, in particular homosexual relationships, are acceptable? In so doing are they exposing him to the risk of contracting HIV/AIDS?

On the other hand, they have read in a second booklet, also brought home by their son, that research has shown that gay and lesbian youth who are shut out by their parents and family have a comparatively high incidence of suicide and drug and alcohol abuse.[7] If they refuse to talk about the issue or perhaps refuse to give the young man permission, will he go underground with his sexuality, resort eventually to drug and alcohol abuse, and therefore be at greater risk regarding HIV/AIDS?

Certainly one cannot limit the possible damage done to the young man due to the lack of parental support or to drug and alcohol abuse, which in turn could place the teenager at a greater risk of contracting HIV/AIDS. More crippling still, the nonsupport of the parents could also undermine the young man's self-confidence, decrease his sense of self-esteem, and engender a confused sense that the homosexual must always lurk in the shadows of deception and play the double life. Such attitudes can be a major factor in causing gay individuals to engage in high-risk activities and desperate expressions of their homosexuality.

From the start, one would have to maintain that affirming someone's sexuality does not necessarily imply that one affirms their sexual activity. Affirming the sexuality of a seventeen-year-old heterosexual young man does not suggest that the parents are therefore encouraging him to engage in premarital sex, which in turn could put him at risk regarding HIV/AIDS. The distinction between sexual identity and sexual activity would need to be clearly drawn by the parents in talking to their son. Granted that this distinction is made by the parents and understood by the young man, does the granting of permission to join the support group become the central issue for the parents?

Before examining the question of such a permission, we need to reflect on the concept of support. Is it possible that besides the parents themselves,

---

7. Graham Brown, Pia Coates, and Melissa Gillet, *Someone You Love: Information for Parents, Friends and Family of Young Gay, Lesbian, or Bisexual People* (a joint project of the Gay and Lesbian Counseling Service WA and the WA AIDS Council, 1997), 1.

others could offer a satisfactory level of support and encouragement for healthy maturation? This may prove difficult. As we have seen, a young gay man's peers do not seem to offer an essential atmosphere for support and self-expression inasmuch as the majority of those peers are straight. Moreover, some homosexual teachers who would be naturally concerned and most understanding, may keep a distance from the student for fear that their peers may raise questions about their own sexual orientation and lifestyle. Perhaps there are, as a recent church document suggests, "agencies that operate in a manner consistent with Catholic teaching."[8] Such agencies do not seem to exist in most dioceses. Fearful and suspicious attitudes by local churches toward homosexual persons tend to prevent the establishment of any such agencies or support groups. They leave young people with no other option except to join groups that perhaps do not operate in a manner consistent with Catholic teaching on human sexuality.

How then does support affect the parents' decision to give or refuse permission? The parents would need to consider whether their son would go to the meetings anyway without their permission and knowledge. Or, perhaps he would unhappily obey their decision, but that could lead either to isolation from his parents or to some form of open rebellion to prove to them that he is gay. Or, perhaps he would obey their advice not to attend the group and understand their reasons, such as: he is too young to be categorizing himself as homosexual at this stage; the attitude and practice of many of the other young adults at the meetings would be in conflict with the teaching of the church on human sexuality, particularly homosexuality; and he would be placing himself in a vulnerable and dangerous situation.

For the sake of argument let us consider some of the many difficult scenarios. First, the young man wants to be a member of the group and disagrees with the reasons suggested by the parents for staying away. He assures them that he is only seeking friendship and support, that he accepts all they have taught him about sexuality, and that sooner or later he is going to have to contend with other gay people who do not accept that the only option open to gay men and women is a life of celibacy.

Or, suppose he is a rather precocious child and he quotes the figures from the Faculty of Health Sciences at La Trobe University in the state of Victoria in Australia, which conducted a study entitled *Secondary Students, HIV/AIDS, and Sexual Health.*[9] The 1997 study provides nationally representative data on the knowledge, attitudes, and practices of

---

8. NCCB, *Always Our Children*, 104.

9. Jo Lindsay, Anthony Smith, and Doreen Rosenthal, *Secondary Students, HIV/AIDS, and Sexual Health, 1997.* (Carlton, Australia: La Trobe University, 1997).

secondary school students in years ten (15–16 years of age) and twelve (17–18 years of age). He came across the study in the local library. He quotes the figure that 48 percent of males his age have had sexual intercourse already, so his parents "need to get real" and face the fact that young people, including homosexual people, are sexually active. He does not intend to be celibate for the rest of his life; and wouldn't he be better meeting people in a more wholesome environment where he can discuss problems and ask questions, rather than eventually going to more seedy bars when he can legally drink at the age of eighteen?

In the light of so many variables, one may argue that the safer and more clear-cut option is for the parents to simply say no to his request. In this way they are clearly not cooperating in any way with what could be seen as an introduction of their son to an immoral and dangerous lifestyle. They do their best to cope with his disappointment or anger, and attempt to give him all the support they can.

However, I believe this case highlights the role of prudence in moral theology. It is not just a matter of parents not cooperating with possible harmful consequences. It is also a question of parents' positive cooperation for the overall good of their son. One cannot restrict the process of socialization as in the past. Do we tell young men and women not to associate with atheists, agnostics, and people of other faiths because it could cause them to doubt their own Catholic belief? One can be so diligent in saving people from so many "occasions of sin" that a new sin is introduced into their lives—namely, they have no occasions to develop, mature, relate, and live. More to the point, all seventeen-year-old sons are not the same, the relationships between parents and such a son are all different, and cultural and social environment can differ vastly. A high percentage of youth suicides in rural Australia are young gay men. Depending on the temperament of the young man, his support or lack of support, the harassment or lack of harassment, the care or lack of care by parents and teachers, wouldn't such a young man have a better chance of survival in the city, attending such a support group despite the inherent dangers?

Thus, let us take the case a step further in our imagination. In the light of these variables, prudence requires foresight. The parents in giving or refusing support need to anticipate the eventual possibility that their son will engage in sexual activity. Quite apart from whatever decision they make, the young man joins the support group and after six months it becomes obvious that he is sexually active. Or, perhaps the teenager does not join the support group but still becomes sexually active. What are the parents to do? Their fears are heightened because they have now read for themselves the 1997 study, cited above, which reveals that 26 percent of seventeen- and eighteen-year-old males have sex without a condom. The parents firmly believe that abstinence outside marriage and fidelity within marriage are the true expressions of sexual responsibility and maturity. In the case of their son, if he is definitely homosexual, then a life of celibacy is the ideal option for him.

They are also aware of the teaching of the church. "In this situation parents must also reject the promotion of so-called safe-sex or safer-sex, a dangerous and immoral policy based on the deluded theory that the condom can provide adequate protection against AIDS. Parents must insist on continence outside marriage and fidelity in marriage as the only true and secure education for the prevention of this contagious disease."[10]

The concerned parents find an opportunity to have a prolonged talk with their son. They stress again what he has already been taught at the Catholic school—namely, that sex outside of marriage is harmful to the person—and that sexual relationships are to be expressed in a genital way only in the monogamous, heterosexual bond of a loving and faithful commitment in marriage. Perhaps, though, these words have little influence. Not wanting to go down the destructive road of "if you do not change your ways, you are out of this house and no longer a member of this family," they direct the discussion to HIV/AIDS. Their son seems reluctant to discuss this matter,[11] yet they insist that it is irresponsible to believe that condoms are 100 percent safe. At the conclusion of the conversation both parents realize that the sexual behavior of their son is not going to change. Can they urge him to at least lessen the harm he might do?

A teacher in a Catholic school faced a similar dilemma with a particular student and posed the questions as follows: "What if I give him to the best of my ability the teaching of the church on human sexuality, what if I stress that condoms are no guarantee against HIV, can I say to him in desperation, 'if you choose to ignore the wisdom of the church, the advice of your parents and teachers, and engage in immoral sexual activity, at least know the facts about safer-sex so that you limit the harm you are doing to yourself and others'?"

---

10. Pontifical Council for the Family, *The Truth and Meaning*, no. 139. One of the most important studies on this question was published by De Vincenzi in the *New England Journal of Medicine* (1994): 341–46. This study evaluated HIV-discordant couples who were counseled to use condoms consistently during intercourse. At the end of two years, 121 couples who reported inconsistent condom use documented 12 new HIV infections in the previously uninfected member of the couple, while among the 124 couples who used condoms consistently there were no new HIV infections despite an estimated 15,000 acts of intercourse.

11. Thirty percent of seventeen- and eighteen-year-old boys have little or no confidence in talking to parents about HIV; see *Secondary Students, HIV/AIDS, and Sexual Health*.

The question concerning the private counseling of one who is determined to continue immoral sexual activity, to at least engage in "safer-sex," has had a great deal of literature devoted to it.[12] Any teacher or parent faced with the above situation does find it difficult to wade through the arguments and finds it disconcerting when theologians disagree and church statements are so subtle in what they say or what they do not say that one wonders if they contradict each other.[13] If the person concerned is your own child, do you not recommend "safer-sex" because in advising "safer-sex" you run the risk of giving scandal if your private advice was to be made public? Do you conclude that such an approach of recommending "safer-sex" is actually promoting behavior that is unacceptable, and do you reason that, strictly speaking, the principle of lesser evil does not apply in this case because there is always the option over time for the young person to opt for chastity? Or do you conclude, if this young man is determined to act in this way, at least he should lessen the chances of being infected or infecting others with HIV?

At the heart of this dilemma is the question of whether the traditional moral principles of lesser evil on the part of the wrongdoer and the justified material cooperation on the part of the one giving the advice apply. If a parent or parents know that their son has no intention of changing or stopping his sexual activity, despite all their protests, then I believe they can validly use the principles of lesser evil and justified material cooperation. Is it not common sense to advise the young and determined man to at least lessen the risk for himself and others? Would it not be asking heroic virtue of parents to adopt the following attitude: "I am certain as a parent can be that my son is not going to change his behavior, but there always is the slight chance that he may for some reason, therefore my advice of "safer-sex" could jeopardize this chance, my advice could be made public and give scandal, therefore I will keep insisting on abstinence and pray that he does not contract

---

12. James Keenan, "Prophylactics, Toleration, and Cooperation: Contemporary Problems and Traditional Principles," *International Philosophical Quarterly* 29 (1989): 205–20; Brian Lucas, "The Condoms Question," *The Catholic Weekly* (NSW) (2 April 1995); Gerald Gleeson, "The Harm Strategy," *The Catholic Weekly* (NSW) (23 April 1995); Germain Grisez, "Dear Fr. Gleeson," *The Catholic Weekly* (NSW) (14 May 1995); Gerald Gleeson, "Fr. Gleeson Replies," *The Catholic Weekly* (NSW) (21 May 1995).

13. The French bishops' social commission, *Sida: la société en question* (Paris: Bayard/Editions le Centurion, 1996); United States Conference of Catholic Bishops (USCC) Administrative Board, *The Many Faces of AIDS: A Gospel Response*, in *Origins* 17 (1987): 482–89; NCCB, *Called to Compassion and Responsibility: A Response to the HIV/AIDS Crisis*, in *Origins* 19 (1989): 422–34; Pontifical Council for the Family, *The Truth and Meaning*.

HIV." In fact such an approach may not be heroic virtue on the part of the parents but rather a refusal to face the reality before them. If they adopted the above approach, they would be casting their wish upon a star so as to avoid engaging the reality of this young man's life and the real dangers to his continued healthy existence.[14] For example, if parents know that their teenager is going to drink too much at a party and that the only two options before them in the situation are that the son drives himself home or they agree to drive him, I think they would drive him home. For even though the offer of driving may in fact encourage him to drink more, since he knows he does not have to get behind the wheel, the cooperation of the parents in this difficult situation will avoid greater harm.

More cynical parents have often said that by the time young men or women reach the age of seventeen, what you teach them about a Catholic approach to sexuality will have little or no influence on their real lives. Even if you were to teach them "safer sex," this too would have little impact. While I do not completely share their cynicism, their sense of reality highlights an insight into the meaning of moral education, be it concerned with sexuality, social justice, or some other area. Moral education is primarily concerned about who I am and who I hope to become. There is always the temptation to reduce education in human sexuality to dilemma ethics and to give less attention to the shaping of attitudes, dispositions, and vision that young people have of themselves and to the project or dream they are attempting to construct or hold on to for the future. Parents can be in an unenviable situation at times, for instant problem-solving may seem more practical and exciting to a young mind and a young life than the slow task of character formation. Naturally, parents themselves want answers to urgent and practical problems, and struggle to apply the old maxim, that in areas that are certain there needs to be firmness, in areas of doubt liberty, and in all things charity. Enabling young people to have a healthy pride in themselves, including their sexuality, and alerting them to the destruction that distorted attitudes of prejudice, discrimination, and oppression bring may be more preventative of HIV/AIDS in the long run.

---

14. The following advice given to healthcare professionals seems applicable also to parents. "On the more personal level of the healthcare professional, the first course of action should be to invite a patient at risk, or one who already has been exposed to the disease, to live a chaste life. If it is obvious that the person will not act without bringing harm to others, then the traditional Catholic wisdom with regard to one's responsibility to avoid inflicting greater harm may be appropriately applied." USCC, *The Many Faces of AIDS: A Gospel Response*, no. 4. from the appendix.

A Spaniard Resists Disclosing His HIV Status to His Girlfriend

José Carlos Bermejo Higuera, M.I.
Translated by Mario Alberto Torres, S.J.

Constantino is a forty-year-old male admitted to the hospital for respiratory problems and overall debilitation of an uncertain origin. After several diagnostic tests, and with the patient's informed consent, it is determined that the ailments are related to HIV infection, which up to that time had been an unknown ailment. After being informed by the doctor of his condition, the patient receives the visit of a pastoral agent, who having been advised by the doctor of the patient's diagnosis, attempts to engage in conversation about the illness and its implications in order to bring him some spiritual support.

Constantino lives alone in a city-owned apartment which he rents. His girlfriend lives in another city, 600 kilometers away, and she comes to visit him almost every weekend. He has two brothers in another city with whom he does not have a good relationship. He does not want to tell them of his hospitalization so as not to revive old conflicts between them, conflicts that led to his distancing himself from them fourteen years ago. He does not have any friends and his only significant relationship is with a co-worker who brings him some personal hygiene items.

The pastoral agent engages in daily conversation with Constantino and gets to know his girlfriend. As a result of his conversations with the couple, the pastoral agent comes to know things that they voluntarily disclose to him, including the fact that they sporadically engage in sexual relations.

Constantino does not mention his HIV-positive status either to his girlfriend or to the pastoral agent. They both talk of "an infection" but never disclose the fact that he suffers from an HIV infection. The pastoral agent attempts to encourage open dialogue about his illness, but is not successful.

Faced with the fact of Constantino's upcoming discharge from the hospital, and aware of the plans that he and his girlfriend have made to spend Christmas together in a rented apartment, the pastoral agent makes more incisive attempts to engage in open dialogue with the patient. Constantino acknowledges in very vague terms his HIV-positive condition. Then the pastoral agent, after attentively listening to the patient's concerns, presents the problem to the patient and confronts him with the ethical duty of informing his partner, but Constantino expresses his unwillingness to do so.

I present this as a reflection centered on prevention, with a particular pastoral concern. Pastoral reflection has to consider the specificity of the case, as well as the individual, personal, and emotional factors that color the experience of the people involved, while ethical reflection occurs within a more rational framework (in the sense of being less susceptible to emotional biases).

The first issue that emerges following this brief description of the case is the question of whether the confidentiality of the patient has been violated by the fact that the pastoral agent has been informed by the doctor of the patient's HIV-positive status. To make both medicine and the integral care of the patient more humane entails that the patient be treated comprehensively:

> . . . as a complex and total personality well beyond any reduction of the patient to his/her ailment or symptomatology. An important consequence of this comprehensive approach would be a deep respect for the privacy of the patient, privacy that can be compromised by a comprehensive approach to treatment. Undoubtedly, knowing the intimate secrets of the patient is a form of potential power that can, within the framework of socialized medicine, be shared with others, thus violating the most intimate self of the patient.[1]

For the case at hand, keeping the pastoral agent abreast about the patient's diagnosis seems to be justified by the interdisciplinary nature of the work—if this is well used. This would facilitate a comprehensive intervention in which the pastoral agent occupies a relevant role in the prevention of infection of third parties. It is not always the case in interdisciplinary work that the proper role of each health agent is recognized, the result being that their skills are not fully utilized. Unfortunately, too often in Spain pastoral agents work on the margin of the rest of the health treatment team with little specific information.

The fundamental problem in this situation appears to be the conflict between the respect of the liberty and the autonomy of the patient[2] and the professional duty to defend the health of third parties (the partner) and of the community. The autonomy and the liberty of the patient entail a right

---

1. Javier Gafo, *10 palabras clave en bioética* (Estella: Verbo Divino, 1994), 35–36.

2. In terms of morality, autonomy refers to the capacity of the individual to govern oneself—that is, to provide oneself with norms and principles of conduct and to guide one's life in conformity with one's own personal values. See J. Barbero, *El acompañamiento a personas con VIH/SIDA: Claves ideológicas, contextuales y relacionales* (Madrid: CREFAT, 1997), 34.

to privacy, and at the same time reveal other underlying issues about the relationship with the partner, with whom it will be necessary to encourage the exercise of responsibility and sincere communication.

As far as we know, in Spain, the failure to communicate the HIV diagnosis to the partner results from the fact that such a communication would imply a double disclosure, illness and an involvement in unfaithful sexual relations. On rare occasions it is a matter of drug use.

We face an ethical conflict whose implications must be analyzed using the reflection unique to the field of bioethics, but also involving the ethics of daily life and the attitudes and social skills which the pastoral agent will use to seek, together with the patient and his partner, the best possible good. It would seem of crucial importance for health professionals to acquire such attitudes and social skills. The field of bioethics, which does not always pay enough attention to these, should include them in their reflections so as to provide a more complete spectrum of itself.

Certainly, the best possible good would be an education in values with those for whom sexual relations is the most authentic mode of communication, keeping in mind the fact that, according to Catholic doctrine, this mode of communication is found within the conditions created within a monogamous relationship and implies a public, religious, and definitive commitment.

However, we also face the freedom of individuals who, though wanting to be faithful to the gospel values, do not always share all the moral teachings of the magisterium or who in any case follow the most immediate instance of morality—that is, the individual conscience.[3] Still, as Elizari notes: "the Catholic Church presents a proposal that tries to bring together two values, one of hygiene (effective prevention of the HIV) and the other of a moral nature, in accordance with a sexuality that is lived within the human and Christian stipulations. Faithful to a particular notion of sexuality, the Christian proposal is defined by the following two standards: sexual abstinence for the unmarried and mutual fidelity within monogamous and indissoluble marriage."[4] Over and beyond the critical stance that could be taken about this position, it is true, as Gafo comments, that a shallow way of understanding sexuality, in which the human dimension, so rich in meaning, is taken as one more object for consumption and makes a taboo of anything that represents a restraint in the sexual realm.[5]

From the perspective of the pastoral agent, in the case at hand it seems clear that what is most important are the attitudes and skills that the pastoral agent uses to establish an effective *helping relationship* for both

---

3. *Lumen Gentium* 16.
4. F. Javier Elizari, *Bioética* (Madrid: San Pablo, 1991), 311.
5. Gafo, *10 palabras clave en bioetica*, 302.

Constantino and his partner. For this to be achieved, the good will of the pastoral agent is not enough, nor is a correct appraisal of the ethical issues involved in the case. What is required is a particular *interpersonal*[6] and *emotional*[7] *competence* so that the encounter with the persons involved becomes an authentic and effective encounter in which the Lord accomplishes through the Spirit[8] the salvific work, of which the pastoral agent is nothing more than a sheer intermediary.

One of the fundamental aspects of the helping relationship is the capacity to confront without moralizing. In this case, it is a matter of helping Constantino appraise his situation and be aware of the implications of his attitude with his partner. Most particularly, the agent should assist Constantino in reckoning with the fact that he has not faced the truth of his infection and its implications for himself (which could be explained as denial), his partner, and the community.

The high point of the art of confrontation lies in the capacity to persuade the patient of the necessity to carefully examine the situation in which he finds himself, to become aware of the meaning that sexual relations have for both him and his partner, and to decide freely and responsibly, with fidelity to the gospel values. Nevertheless, the couple continues to have sexual relations. Thus the pastoral agent must persuasively face the necessity of preventing possible infections, both of his partner as well as possible future partners. In this sense, it seems opportune to verify the patient's knowledge of the hygienic practices associated with the prevention of HIV. It is also necessary to consider the possibility that the couple is already infected. In this case, the responsible course of action would be to explore what would be needed for each person as well as to encourage responsible action with future third parties.

Certainly, good confrontation and good persuasion are not possible if these are not preceded in the dialogue by the unconditional acceptance of the person and by the capacity to understand him and to make him feel that he has been understood. A display of empathy in listening and in responding are prerequisites for any type of confrontation.[9]

The situation becomes complicated when, even after taking this course of action, the patient expresses his unwillingness to communicate his HIV-positive status to his partner. This is an issue that has been closely studied

---

6. José Carlos Bermejo, *Apuntes de relación de ayuda* (Santander: Sal Terrae, 1998), 104.

7. José Carlos Bermejo and Rosa Carabias, *Relación de ayuda y enfermería* (Santander: Sal Terrae, 1998), 104.

8. Bermejo, *Relación pastoral de ayuda al enfermo*, 26.

9. Bermejo, *Comprender y ayudar al enfermo de Sida* (Chile: Caritas, 1995), 88.

by several bioethicists. It has even been proposed that confidentiality not be respected and that the patient's HIV diagnosis be revealed to the partner. This proposal is founded on the premise that confidentiality[10] is not an absolute which imposes a law without exceptions, but instead that it imposes limits that stem from the fact that there is a social dimension to health which is no less important than the personal dimension.[11]

The opinions of bioethicists do not achieve complete agreement. Some have even affirmed that confidentiality is a cornerstone of medical practice in HIV cases and that its violation would reduce the number of people who present themselves for HIV testing. The consequence of this would mean that fewer people would receive crucial guidance about reducing the risk of transmission. This would result, in turn, in the suffering and death of a larger number of people than would result from maintaining confidentiality, even while acknowledging the complete innocence of those who may be infected by persons who refuse to disclose their HIV diagnosis.[12] Without the assurance of confidentiality, patients, it is argued, would be resistant to communicate the necessary information and would be less willing to undergo diagnostic tests.

This reflection is pertinent and, above all else, brings our attention to the exceptional nature of a violation of confidentiality. Nonetheless, we share the opinion of "most ethicists who in this case would assert that a violation of confidentiality would be justified as the lesser of two evils and could even be mandated by law."[13] In this regard, Spanish law indicates that in extreme cases confidentiality may be sacrificed in the interests of other rights, but not so much from the perspective of a juridical duty as from the existence of a situation of need that justifies it, since it would limit the right to privacy of the patient, which is a lesser evil than the one that is being avoided.[14]

---

10. We do not consider the issues associated with confidentiality within the sacrament of reconciliation, since these go beyond the case at hand. A reflection on these issues would include several new elements.

11. Manuel Cuyas, *Diritto all'intimitá e diritto alla veritá in AIDS: Segretezza professionale* (Padova: Liviana Editrice, 1989), 7.

12. See, for instance, G. Gillet, "AIDS and confidentiality," *Journal of Applied Psychology* 4 (1987): 16, quoted by Jorge J. Ferrer, *Sida y bioética: de la autonomía a la justicia* (Madrid: Comillas, 1997), 155.

13. Harry Edmund Emson, "Segretezza: un valore modificato," in *AIDS: Segretezza professionale*, 26.

14. Javier Sánchez Caro and José Ramón Giménez Cabezón, *Derecho y Sida* (Madrid: Mafre, 1995), 39. The "Ley General de Sanidad" in Spain (1986) seems ambiguous. Legally, these situations are defined as a conflict of juridical goods.

Given the exceptional nature of a violation of confidentiality and its serious implications for the physician-patient relationship, it seems appropriate to specify the conditions which would justify such a violation. Elizari has proposed four conditions which would make a disclosure to the partner legal and perhaps ethically obligatory: the unwillingness of the infected party to inform the partner, in spite of attempts to make him/her assume such responsibility; the ignorance by the spouse or partner of the danger involved; a real danger of new infections; a familiarity with the person who is the likely recipient of the information.[15]

The underlying problem lies in the notion of the relationship between person and society. Catholic tradition would not consider it licit to sacrifice the confidentiality of a person just for a potential social benefit, since this would amount to making the human being a pure means at the service of society, thus opening the door to a utilitarian ethical perspective. Nevertheless, I am of the opinion that revealing the diagnosis is licit and obligatory since "the carrier of HIV who refuses to warn his/her partner . . . places him/herself outside the moral community inasmuch as his refusal goes against the community's most fundamental basis: the respect to the individual and nonmaleficence. The pretension of using the moral norm of confidentiality as an indirect instrument in order to continue hurting other people seems to me to be contradictory. Moral norms cannot be invoked to undermine the bases upon which the moral community is founded; it is the moral community which constitutes the framework upon which any moral claim makes sense."[16]

As a pastoral agent, I experience more intensely the obligation to inform the partner than simply recognizing the legality of doing so. In Spain, the opinions of the experts vary. Barbero, who has ample practical experience in direct contact with AIDS patients, positions himself against a break in confidentiality, acquiescing to such a violation only in exceptional cases, yet he criticizes at the same time the Spanish nongovernmental organizations that call for an absolute observance of confidentiality.[17] Barbero, too, affirms that practical experience indicates that when a patient has been well informed and properly advised, it is very difficult for him/her to refuse to disclose the fact of an HIV infection to his/her partner .

As I see it, the pastoral minister would have the obligation of informing the patient of both the moral dilemma in which the patient has placed the minister and the minister's intention of notifying the partner. The patient is

---

15. F. Javier Elizari, *Bioética*, 306.

16. Jorge J. Ferrer, *Sida y bioética: de la autonomia a la justicia*, 160.

17. J. Barbero, *El acompañamiento a personas con VIH/SIDA: Claves ideológicas, contextuales y relacionales*, 34.

to be informed that such a notification will only be done after a careful evaluation has revealed that all the possible consequences of notification are not worse than the consequences of maintaining the confidentiality.

And, in any case, the duty of the health professional would not end with revealing the seropositive status to the partner. Such a notification would also require a commitment to provide emotional and spiritual support to both the patient and the partner, to facilitate all the means that would help them cope with the impact of such a revelation, and to do whatever is possible to prevent future infection. In effect, one of the fundamental roles of the pastoral agent is that of an intermediary.[18]

Once again we see that attitudes and skills are necessary to relate to the patient. It is not only a matter of figuring out the ethical problem in order to make a judgment on the legality or ethical duty to reveal the diagnosis. The efficacy and the ethical nature of whatever health professionals do will also be determined by the quality of the relationships and by the interpersonal skills of the health professional.

It could be asked if all that is said about confidentiality among physicians is also applicable to pastoral agents, and if the pastoral agent is the most appropriate person to accomplish the task of revealing the diagnosis to the partner. Regarding the first issue, the answer appears to be obvious: it is the professional team—not only the physician—that is bound by the duties of confidentiality and of protection of communal health. As a member of the interdisciplinary team that struggles against the causes and consequences of the illness, the pastoral agent is also bound to this team and its duties. With regards to the second question, it is my opinion that the communication of diagnosis is a medical act, and that in order for this to be done by another member of the health team, there should be reasons that are both valid and favorable to the patient. In any case, it would not make sense for any of the professionals to act without the accord of the other members in the team. Thus, HIV-positive diagnosis would be understood as a process reflecting the attitudes of all the professionals, rather than as a decision that is brought up and resolved in an instant.

One more aspect remains outstanding. In the case that we have discussed, we have considered the relationship between the patient and the partner as one with the solidity of stable relationships, in spite of the distance that separates them and the nature of their relationship (they are lovers, not spouses). Some authors would be more restrictive when considering possible violations of confidentiality. Sgreccia states: "information that is external to the care group should be given only to those who

---

18. José Carlos Bermejo, *Sida: vida en el camino* (Madrid: San Pablo, 1990), 169.

have rights and responsibilities in relationship to the patient, the relatives, and above all the spouse, and only after having advised, in the proper manner, the interested party of the necessity to give out such information."[19] It is my understanding that the couple in this case meets the conditions specified when Sgreccia refers to the spouse (though I admit that this is a debatable question) because the risks and the nature of the relationship, of which I have firsthand knowledge, are equivalent in a certain sense.

In any case, the professional should have exhausted all the persuasive possibilities which I understand should be exercised by a competent person not only from the technical point of view but also from the ethical, interpersonal, and emotional perspectives in order to help the patient and his/her partner to make responsible and meaningful decisions about the values that are in conflict.

And, in any case, the pastoral agent, as an expert in humanity, should also count on the experts in bioethics in order to be able to handle complex situations such as the one referred to in this essay. For example, entities such as the "bioethics committee" should be consulted, since through them pastoral agents can enhance their knowledge of the implications of the problems, and then focus on the person of the patient whom agents encounter and serve.

AN HIV-INFECTED ITALIAN WOMAN SEEKING TO HAVE CHILDREN

Maurizio P. Faggioni, O.F.M.
Translated by Andrea Vicini, S.J.

LAURA AND MARCO *are in front of me, visibly tense. They have been sent to me by their pastor who told them: "I have a friend who is a professor of moral theology in Rome. Surely, he will be able to help you in finding an answer to your dilemma." I hope I will not disappoint them and their expectations but, unfortunately, life is always a little more complex than the theorems of the moral theology that I teach.*

---

19. Elio Sgreccia, *Bioética* (Milan: Vita e Pensiera, 1986), 17.

Laura is twenty-four years-old, Marco is twenty-five. They are two former substance abusers and both are HIV positive. They met in a therapeutic community and there, while they found again their dignity and their desire to live, their relationship began and led them to marry. Now, after their first year of marriage, Marco has been able to find a job and both desire to have a child.

They had addressed themselves to a gynecologist of the Italian National Health Service (SSN) with their request: "Could we have children?" The gynecologist, says Laura, was speaking in a calm and distant way. Theoretically, he was saying, it would be possible to have sexual intercourse without the protection of the condom during the woman's fertile period to increase her probability of becoming pregnant but, even without considering the risk that nonprotected contacts could accelerate the evolution of the disease, the possibility of transmitting the infection to the future child advises against the pregnancy. Because Laura and Marco did not seem to be impressed by that information, the gynecologist, continuing with his inexpressive tone, presented the difficulties that an HIV positive child would face from a medical, social, and economic point of view. He also insinuated that the baby, whether infected or not, could soon become an orphan and ended by saying: "Reflect well on what you want to do. You are only thinking of your own well-being and not of that of the child. You have already had so many problems in life. Why would you like to create for yourselves a problem that can be avoided?"

How is it possible to speak about a child as a problem to be avoided? How is it possible that so limited a risk would be stronger than the desire? Why should abortion of a baby with a low probability of being infected be considered a good for the baby while to desire having the same baby is an evil? Laura and Marco left that consultation extremely confused. Now they are sitting in front of me and, together, we will try to understand.

Since AIDS has reached the proportions of an epidemic, HIV transmission from a mother to her infant has represented one of the crucial aspects of the infection for its medical, epidemiological, social, and ethical implications. The World Health Organization (WHO) estimates that in the year 2000 there will be 40 million people HIV positive, and among them more than 3 million will be children; 80 percent of those children are destined to die without treatment before they will be five years old.[1] It is shocking that almost 1.8 million of those HIV positive children will be in Central Africa;

---

1. The world data comes from *UNAIDS/WHO Working Group on Global HIV/AIDS and STD Surveillance, Report on the Global HIV/AIDS Epidemic.* December 1998, at http://www.unaids.org/ highband/ document / epidemic.

they will be the children of the 8 million HIV positive women who live in that region. *Before the year 2000, the epidemic will have left orphaned more than 9 million children, that is, boys and girls below the age of fifteen who are HIV negative but who have lost one or both their parents because of AIDS.* The story of our couple who long to have a child is placed in this dramatic background. Although 90 percent of the anticipated new cases of HIV infection will be in the Third World, the drama of pediatric AIDS affects all geographic areas of the world, even if specific medical, social, and cultural aspects qualify each particular context.

According to the data of the *Italian Registry for HIV Infection Among Pediatric Patients* for the period 1982 to 1998, in Italy almost 95 percent of HIV positive children have been infected by the mother; only in a very limited percentage the infection results from a blood transfusion as in the case of hemophiliac and thalassemic children or because of other causes.[2] Forty percent of HIV positive mothers have a history of drug addiction and an extra 27 percent of them, besides using drugs, have had repeated sexual contact with people HIV positive, often in the context of prostitution. Another 26 percent of HIV positive mothers do not have a history of drug addiction and they have been infected through sexual intercourse, mostly with people drug dependent.

Vertical transmission from a mother to her baby represents one of the main sources of HIV infection and can occur during pregnancy, delivery, or breast-feeding. At birth all the newborns of HIV positive mothers are HIV positive on antibody testing. This does not indicate that the newborns have contracted AIDS, but it merely reveals the *passive passage* of antibodies through the placenta; in the majority of the cases those antibodies disappear during the second year. Only a limited percentage of babies are infected and will continue to be HIV positive: the transmission rate goes from 40 percent reported in some African studies to the 15–20 percent of many North American and European studies, with an 18 percent rate in Italy.[3] Recent studies have confirmed the possibility of drastically reducing the transmission rate to 1–2 percent by treating pregnant women with antiviral drugs from the second trimester of pregnancy (to avoid possible damage to the fetus it is not possible to begin this treatment earlier), by treating

---

2. Centro Operativo AIDS, "Aggiornamento dei casi di AIDS notificati in Italia al 30 settembre 1998," *Notiziario dell'Istituto Superiore di Sanità* 11, n. 11, suppl. 1 (1998): 1–8.

3. C. Giaquinto, and E. Ruga "Epidemiologia della trasmissione verticale," *AIDS 1998: Il contributo italiano all'AIDS*, ed. F. Dianzani et al. (Padova: Piccin, 1998), 17–21.

newborns, and by using a cesarean delivery.[4] Where mothers breast feed their infants, another 14 percent risk is added because babies can be infected by their mothers who are HIV positive. In Italy this occurrence is not epidemiologically relevant.[5]

In an infected, untreated baby, AIDS progresses more rapidly than in an adult: in world statistics it appears that almost 80 percent of HIV positive children will die before the first five years of life from AIDS related pathologies. In developed countries, two patterns of disease progression in HIV positive children have been recognized: a first group, short-term survival, will develop AIDS within the first two years of life and a second group, with long-term survival, which is the majority, will develop AIDS during the school years. In Italy, because of the presence of specific therapies and highly specialized health care, 60 percent of HIV positive children are still alive when they are ten years-old.[6]

By considering these medical and epidemiological data, and by examining the policies that have been established by governments and their agencies to prevent AIDS, a question spontaneously rises—that is, whether, for an HIV positive couple, it is right or not to procreate. The question becomes even more unavoidable in a Christian context where the meaning of procreation as a fruit of the incarnated love of the spouses and a privileged expression of their service to life is a value generally understood and accepted.[7]

In this area of reflection, a principle often reaffirmed is the respect due to the reproductive choices of every HIV positive woman. However, if it is true that nobody has the right to interfere with the choices of a woman or a couple, it is equally true that human life cannot be transmitted without showing an attitude of responsibility that values the many ethically relevant factors which are at stake and, particularly, those concerned with the well-being of

---

4. E. G. Hermione Lyall, C. Stainby et al., "Review of Uptake of Interventions to Reduce Mother to Child Transmission of HIV by Women Aware of their HIV Status," *British Medical Journal* 316, n. 7127 (1998): 268–69; L. Mandelbrot, J. Le Chenadec et al., "Perinatal HIV-1 Transmission: Interaction Between Zidovudine Prophylaxis and Mode of Delivery in the French Perinatal Cohort," *JAMA* 280, n. 280 (1998): 55–60.

5. M. De Martino, P. A. Tovo, L. Galli et al., "Human Immunodeficiency Virus-type 1 Infection and Breast Milk," *Acta Paediatrica* 83, suppl. 400 (1994): 51–58; J. Kreiss, "Breast Feeding and Vertical Transmission of HIV," *Acta Paediatrica* 86, suppl. 421 (1997): 113–17.

6. M. De Martino, P. A. Tovo, L. Galli et al., "Features of Children Perinatally Infected with HIV-1 Surviving Longer than 5 Years," *Lancet* 343, n. 8891 (1994): 191–95.

7. For the multiple ways of service to life to which the married couples are called, see John Paul II, *Familiaris Consortio*, 22 November 1981, no. 28–41.

the weak and defenseless—that is, the child at risk. In the dialectic of autonomy and responsibility, some mostly focus on the autonomy of the individual, others emphasize the responsibility toward the future child. For the first group, the more important elements are the relevance of the couple's desire of procreating and the psychological benefits that a pregnancy could have for a couple affected by such a terrible infection. Their choice of having a child becomes almost a counteraction of life against the disease and death. For the second group, the consideration of what is the best interest for the child prevails. Therefore, the risk of transmitting AIDS, with its poor prognosis sooner or later, and with a future of difficulties and marginalization that this child will face, is relevant for making a decision.

For this purpose, it appears strange to us that Saint Thomas and the tradition suggested that it is right for a man affected by leprosy to father an infected baby because "it is better being this way than not being."[8] It could be meaningful to apply this principle in the case of eugenic abortion when it is asked whether it is better to leave the infant the life that it already has, although it is a life marked by some anomaly or to suppress the life. However, in the case of a life that is merely anticipated this comparison does not have any meaning: it is obviously better not to be conceived than to live only to suffer. According to our understanding, to affirm the contrary would be an untenable *vitalism*, a celebration of biological life that is not concerned for its quality.

It is not possible to underestimate the strength of one's desire for parenthood, even in relation to the psychological benefits that could come to the couple, but a child cannot be considered the equivalent of a therapy, nor reduced to an instrument to achieve another goal than being himself or herself. Women have the right to autonomous reproductive choices, but this does not mean that a woman has a *right to a child*: there is not a right to have a child because rights only concern objects and a child cannot simply be the projection of one's desire or the instrument to achieve one's self-realization. On the contrary, there is a child's right not to have to suffer a wrongful life because of the lack of responsibility or egotism of the parents, at least when this birth can be avoided.

My reasoning becomes even more careful when it concerns the frequent case of HIV positive women in Italy.[9] Even if it is necessary to consider each case separately, it is largely presumed that it is not possible to

---

8. Thomas Aquinas, *Scriptum super libros Sententiarum*, 4, dist. 32, disp. 1, 7. See Alphonsus Liquori, *Theologia Moralis* (Rome: Polyglotta Vaticana 1912) vol. 4, n. 951.

9. European Centre for the Epidemiological Monitoring of AIDS, "HIV/AIDS Surveillance in Europe," *Quarterly Report* n. 59 (September 1998): 20.

responsibly give life and welcome it. The substance abuser has not shown an ability to welcome, lead, and organize her life and, therefore, it is not clear how she will be able to take adequate care of her child's life. Probably drug dependent people have a sincere desire of motherhood and fatherhood but, in all likelihood, they will not be able to transform into concrete actions this desire. For this reason, too, besides the risk of transmitting the disease, it appears to be wiser to advise against procreation.

Very different is the case of those who, after an experience of drug dependence, have been able to get out of this tunnel, rebuild their existence, and earn anew their autonomy and dignity. However, even in these cases, it will be wiser to refer to the suggestions of the therapeutic community and, generally, of all those who have helped them to be cured of drug addiction.

By considering all the multiple factors which intervene, and by moving away from any irresponsible affirmation of autonomy as well as all defense of the right to procreate without the boundaries set by principles and criteria, it seems more reasonable that the HIV positive couple expresses its reproductive freedom by responsibly choosing not to procreate. This choice is determined neither by depreciation of the fecundity of marriage nor by fear of it, but should be taken to avoid a certain and extremely serious damage to a percentage, even if limited, of newborns and to avoid calling into life a creature whom, probably, the parents would not be able to take care of in the due way because of the progression of their own disease. "In taking the decision of generating or not generating, the spouses should let themselves be inspired neither by egotism nor frivolousness, but by a prudent and responsible generosity that values the possibilities and circumstances and, particularly, that places at its center the well-being of the future born. When, therefore, there is a reason for not procreating, this choice is allowed, and it could be even due."[10]

Finally, it is not possible to underestimate the spouses' risk which depends on nonprotected sexual intercourse. Generally speaking, the high risk of contagion justifies, from a biomedical point of view, the advice of abstaining from sexual intercourse as well as other erotic manifestations that could increase the risk of transmitting the HIV virus. This also applies in the case of spouses who are both HIV positive because the repeated exposure to the HIV virus accelerates the passage from being HIV positive to full-blown AIDS. It is known, in fact, that the defense which is offered by the condom is only partially effective and, by frequent sexual intercourse, the probability of being affected by the disease becomes extremely high. For this reason, in every case, repeated sexual

---

10. John Paul II, "Discorso all'Angelus," *L'Osservatore Romano* (18–19 July 1994): 5.

intercourse with a spouse HIV positive puts in serious danger the health of the other spouse.[11]

Surely, neither of the two partners can impose having sexual intercourse on the other, particularly when it is not protected, because putting in danger the life of the partner radically contradicts the meaning of the sexual union that should manifest love and care for the other partner. According to some moral theologians, the danger of being infected or of worsening the disease, even when regularly using the condom, would be a sufficient reason for considering illicit any sexual intercourse because it would put at risk one's health. But it is not possible to exclude that, at least in some circumstances, the spouses could be ready to consciously run a risk to show with their own concrete acts their mutual love, their closeness, and their reciprocal support. During any sickness, the tangible manifestation of affection by the other spouse can assume a symbolic value that goes beyond the natural and rightful need for sexual intimacy of the spouses. In this way the ancient moral theologians were used to solving the issue of conjugal sexual intercourse in the case of infectious diseases that were menacing and untreatable, like leprosy and syphilis, just as AIDS is today. For the same reason, two spouses who, in conscience, feel called to express the human and Christian value of married fecundity by having a child, for such a noble motive can reasonably expose themselves to the danger of contagion or the possibility of worsening their health condition.

In the context of counseling, in the case of HIV infection, the same rules of behavior that are ordinarily accepted in genetic counseling and, particularly, in nondirective counseling (also called value neutrality) are usually suggested. The physician who, consulted by an HIV positive couple, led their decision in one way or another would go beyond the physician's role of offering them precise and correct information. By answering the question of an HIV positive woman, "Could we have children?" as the gynecologist did in our opening story, shows, in spite of its appearance, a paternalism which does not respect the autonomy of the person, limits one's liberty of choice, and, probably, prompts the couple to more strongly seek the contrary of what the untimely advisor tried to prohibit.

On the other hand, the nondirective counseling often appears to be not entirely adequate to address the problems of an HIV positive couple who deal with the issue of procreation. Educational counseling appears to be more helpful. It requires a more active role from the advisors. They try to help the couple to accurately focus on the motives and decisional steps that lead to decisions about the pregnancy and to identify the existential meaning

---

11. J. Suaudeau, "Le sexe sûr et le préservatif face au défi du SIDA," *Medicina e Morale* 47.4 (1997): 689–726.

of the various types of choice. Compared with the simple neutral information given in the context of nondirective counseling, educational counseling helps to clarify the values that are lived by the people involved. The couple can realize whether they undermine or deny the gravity of the infection, whether the responsibilities and duties that depend on procreation have been accurately considered, whether objectively it is possible to take adequate care of a child. It is also possible to suggest a visit to hospital departments where HIV positive children are treated in order to personally experience what it means to have a child HIV positive.

The task of counseling is not to lead to one or another choice, but to help the woman and the couple to appropriately consider the fact of their being HIV positive as a reality that, in some ways, is opposed to pregnancy.

In any case, nobody has the right to substitute oneself for the couple's conscience or to put any pressure on the making of such a personal decision, even if we often assist inappropriate interventions into people's freedom by health practitioners who consider those couples egotistic and irresponsible, and who give very pressing advice, to the point of psychological terrorism, to avoid pregnancy absolutely. In Italy, both a strong medical paternalism that seems will never die and a very common eugenic pressure lead many health practitioners to invade with self-styled medical suggestions what should be the field of the couple's free and informed choice. In the context of counseling, the issue of social responsibility to prevent the diffusion of AIDS can be more easily in conflict with the couple's pondered motivations in favor of procreation. The authentic neutrality, which is practiced in the case of genetic diseases as cystic fibrosis or thalassemia, is replaced by a more directive approach (often unconscious) in the case of a feared disease like AIDS.

IN CONCLUSION, WHAT seems to be more appropriate to a Christian vision is the attitude that advises against transmitting life when the status of being HIV positive endangers the integrity of the future child, without even considering the harm caused by a premature death of one or both the parents. However, this approach, with its negative propensity, does not equal a prohibition: for every couple the right to decide remains intact, whether to procreate by assuming consciously their responsibilities and by being, at the same time, committed to use any means which are available to avoid unnecessary risks and harm to the baby. The couple's choice for procreation needs to be concretely respected by making available to them all the care and assistance that are offered to other pregnant women and families.

In its substance, this was the teaching that Pope Pius XII expressed on the responsibility of advisors and parents when they foresee that they can transmit, with a high probability, serious genetic diseases to their future children:

Certainly, there exists the motive for and, in the majority of cases, the duty to advise those who are certainly carriers of serious hereditary diseases about the burden that they are on the brink of imposing on themselves, their partner, and the descendants. This burden would probably become unbearable. But to advise against is not to prohibit. There could be motives, especially moral and personal, of such a great importance that they authorize those affected by these diseases to exercise the marriage even in those circumstances.[12]

By meeting Laura and Marco there emerges with clarity the profile of a couple who are healing from the injuries of drug addiction and who have discovered in themselves a great capacity for love. I remind them that, if the well-being of the future child can sometimes advise against procreation, this is not enough to stop the fecundity of their conjugal love that can express itself in multiple ways in serving and welcoming life, particularly in those who are weaker and marginalized. I understand how much pain and love are present in their lives. I realize the genuineness of the motivations that lead them to desire a baby. I imagine how important for them is the possibility of giving life to a creature. It is a victory of life over against that death which, by crawling slowly, seems to corrupt the roots of human existence. Probably, it is when someone lives with death within oneself that more than ever one realizes the need of feeling that, from within, from one's being and love, new life can pour out. I know that within myself I will not disapprove of them if they decide, hoping against hope and, by consciously facing the challenge of uncertainty, they will welcome with responsibility and love the life that God will place in their arms.

---

12. Pius XII, "Al I Simposio Internazionale di Genetica Medica" (7 September 1953) in *Discorsi e Radiomessaggi*, vol. 15 (Vatican City: Polyglotta 1954), 265.

Part 2: Fundamental Moral Issues for HIV Prevention

7.
PROGRESS IN THE MORAL TRADITION

Marciano Vidal, C.Ss.R.
Translated by José Carlos Coupeau, S.J.

IN THE FOLLOWING pages, I attempt to analyze the meaning of tradition in the field of moral theology. More precisely, I am concerned with developing the criteria that govern progress within the Christian moral tradition. This question bears great epistemological import, since together with Scripture and the magisterium, tradition constitutes one of the proper theological "loci."[1]

Human reason needs to be added to these three strictly theological "places." According to what John Paul II has recently reminded us once again in his encyclical *Fides et Ratio*,[2] human reason is the necessary mediation to live and express the meaning of faith. This articulation between the specifically theological places and human reason was happily formulated by Vatican II when it said that the moral problems of our times need to be analyzed "in the light of the gospel and human experience."[3] In this way, human mediation is not reduced to "reason," but rather assumes the full meaning of "human experience." Moreover, the theological places obtain unity when they are understood as the "gospel." Even more, the copula "and" stresses the relation between the gospel and human experience. This expression leads us to see the connection as neither an incoherent juxtaposition, nor as a confusion, nor as a sterile copulative.

I have recalled this basic structure of moral-theological epistemology in order to place tradition within this framework and to emphasize the importance that tradition has in constituting a coherent ethical-theological discourse. One needs to say, however, that this question, generally acknowledged by everyone as of great importance, has been hardly studied.[4]

---

1. *Dei Verbum*, 10.
2. *Fides et Ratio*, 36–48.
3. *Gaudium et Spes*, 46.
4. For two studies on the subject, see Brian Johnstone who analyzes the subject in general terms in "Faithful Action: The Catholic Moral Tradition and

I have two goals. First, I mean to offer a description of the state of the question, confirmed in magisterial statements. Second, I give a number of systematic perspectives over two aspects of progress in moral tradition: the forms of development in the Christian moral tradition and some advances achieved during the last few decades in the field of Catholic ethics.

Lacking enough specific theological reflection on the development of tradition in the field of Christian ethics, we need to turn to the texts of the magisterium if we want to know the state of the question, naturally, still in an embryonic or basic stage. I limit my references to three documents of church teachings: the Constitution *Dei Verbum* from Vatican Council II (1965), and John Paul II's encyclicals *Veritatis Splendor* (1993) and *Centesimus Annus* (1991).

Dei Verbum (DV)

TO MY KNOWLEDGE, there is no study analyzing the references that *DV* made to the question of progress in tradition and Christian ethics. I consider, however, that turning to this document is of great interest and importance if we want to put the question about the possibility and form of moral development within the tradition of the church correctly. I point to those perspectives that I consider most decisive and pertinent.

The Meaning of Tradition

Undoubtedly, the most decisive orientation of *DV* consisted in referring to divine revelation in personalist[5] categories of communication.[6] These categories do not originate from the "truth" of God but from God's "wisdom and goodness."[7] These categories seem to invite humans into the trinitarian

---

Veritatis Splendor," *Studia Moralia* 31 (1993): 283–305. A more concrete study of the changes in usury, marriage, slavery, and religious freedom morals, is in John T. Noonan Jr.'s "Development in Moral Doctrine," *Theological Studies* 54 (1993): 662–77.

5. René Latourelle, "La Révelation et sa transmission selon la Constitution *Dei Verbum,"* *Gregorianum* 47 (1966): 5–40.

6. *Dei Verbum* 2: "By this revelation, then, the invisible God . . . , from the fullness of his love, *addresses* men as his friends, and *moves among* them, in order to invite and receive them into his own *company*" (stress added).

7. Ibid.: "It pleased God, in his *goodness and wisdom*, to reveal himself" (stress added).

8. Ibid.: "His will was that men should have access to the *Father*, through *Christ* . . . in the *Holy Spirit*, and thus become sharers in the divine nature" (stress added).

dynamism and so "to become sharers in the divine nature."[8] Making use of the same expression adopted by the Council of Trent, Vatican II calls divine revelation "gospel."[9] Such a category denotes a rich scriptural flavor and allows for ecumenical convergence.

Broadly understood here as "divine revelation," the gospel is "source of all saving truth and moral discipline." Vatican II borrowed this formulation from Trent.[10] Thus, Christian ethics is implicated by faith in general terms. This implication with different nuances often appears underlined in recent documents of the magisterium.[11]

Vatican II's concern with tradition was, before anything else, to deepen and express its relationship with Scripture anew.[12] It also offered valuable perspectives to understand its nature and its functionality.[13]

The council text does not use the word *tradition* consistently.[14] One can distinguish between "apostolic" or constitutive tradition (the sacred tradition) and postapostolic or "church" tradition (continuing tradition). The apostolic tradition, which includes the sacred Scriptures, "comprises everything that serves to make the people of God live their lives in *holiness and to increase their faith*."[15] I emphasize these words to highlight the moral content of the apostolic tradition.[16] As opposed to the Scriptures,

---

9. Ibid., 7.

10. Trent, *Tamquan fontem omnis et salutaris veritatis et morum disciplinae* (Denzinger, 1501); Vatican II: *Dei Verbum*, 7.

11. *Gaudium et Spes*, 33; *Veritatis Splendor*, 4, 27, 28, 29, 30.

12. Ibid., 9. On the postconciliar reception of this doctrine, see the study by Achim Buckenmaier, *"Schrift und Tradition" seit dem Vatikan II. Vorgeschichte und Rezeption* (Paderborn: Bonifatius, 1996).

13. Two recent works interpret the teaching of Vatican II on tradition and place it in an historical context: Angel Maria Navarro Lecanda, *"Evangelii traditio." Tradición como Evangelización a la luz de Dei Verbum I-II* (Vitoria-Gasteiz: Eset, 1997), 2 vol.; Jean Georges Boeglin, *La question de la Tradition dans la théologie catholique contemporaine* (Paris: Editions du Cerf, 1998).

14. See César Izquierdo, "La Tradición en Teología Fundamental," *Scripta Theologica* 29 (1997): 397, note 16.

15. *Dei Verbum*, 8.

16. Josef Rupert Geiselmann's opinion is well known. For him everything pertaining to faith is contained at the same time in the Scriptures and tradition, whereas the latter contains its own elements pertaining to disciplinary and moral orders, and is not contained in the Scriptures [*Sagrada Escritura y Tradición, Historia y alcance de una controversia* (Barcelona: Herder, 1968), 381–82; also "Tradición," *Conceptos Fundamentales de Teología* (Madrid: San Pablo, 1979) second ed., vol. II, 818.] As is well known, the council did not want to solve this theological question.

this moral content of the tradition lacks a particular "organ" of verification.[17] It is the entire life of the church that manifests the "moral content of the apostolic tradition." "In this way the church, in her doctrine, life and worship, perpetuates and transmits to every generation all that she herself is, all that she believes."[18]

The riches of the apostolic tradition "are poured out in the practice and life of the church, in her belief and her prayer." That tradition becomes a "living presence" through the "conversation" of the church, spouse of the Trinity. The text attributes to the Holy Spirit the fact that "the living voice of the gospel rings out in the church."[19] Constituted as such, the tradition appears to convey a richer theological meaning (trinitarian, ecclesiastical, and eschatological) than the cold and miserly one given by the neoscholastic epistemology: "place of probation."[20] Although the council did not teach in detail and with precision what is the subject of the tradition,[21] it clearly stated that the entire church, infallibly and in communion, lives and fleshes out the "living voice of the gospel."[22] The "great tradition" is constituted, then, through the life of the entire church; the smaller "traditions" obtain their meaning by referring themselves to this greater tradition.[23]

The Dynamic Character of Tradition

In this theological context, Vatican II introduces the dynamic character of tradition. Vatican II explicitly refers to Vatican I at this point and labors within the framework provided by the previous council. Vatican II makes

---

17. The apostolic tradition "lacks its own organ of transmission and, therefore, it is transmitted via church tradition that includes the magisterium of the bishops, the teaching of the Fathers and theologians and, to some extent, the sense of the faithful" (Bartomeu Maria Xiberta, *La tradición y su problemática actual* [Barcelona: Herder, 1964], 32).

18. *Dei Verbum*, 8.

19. Ibid.: "Thus, God who spoke in the past, continues *to converse* with the spouse of his beloved Son."

20. On the theology of tradition, see M. Semeraro, *"Temi eclesiologici nel capitolo secondo della 'Dei Verbum'"*; Nicola Ciola, ed., *La "Dei Verbum" trent'anni dopo* (Rome: Libreria editrice della Pontificia Università Lateranense, 1995), 123–45.

21. Angel Maria Navarro, *"Evangeli traditio,"* vol. II, 913–17, mentions this silence among the lacunae of *Dei Verbum*.

22. *Dei Verbum*, 10.

23. *Catechism of the Catholic Church*, no. 83. Yves Congar's study in *La Tradition et les traditions*, 2 vol. (Paris: Fayard, 1960) echoes in this distinction between "great tradition" and "traditions."

the next general statement: "The tradition that comes from the apostles makes progress in the church, with the help of the Holy Spirit." We would want to know the concrete meanings of this important statement. The council seems to limit "growth" to the "insight into the realities and words that are being passed on." Such comprehensive growth takes place through the next passages: "through the contemplation (of the words and the institutions transmitted) and the study by believers who ponder these things in their hearts (see Lk. 2:1–51). It comes from the intimate sense of spiritual realities which they experience. And it comes from the preaching of those who have received, along with their right to succession in the episcopate, the sure charism of truth."[24]

Although Vatican II did not dwell on it, there is no doubt that the council stressed the dynamic character of the forms and passages of progress within the church tradition: "The church is always advancing toward the plenitude of divine truth, until eventually the words of God are fulfilled in her"; "the Holy Spirit . . . leads believers to the full truth."[25] Such a dynamic understanding of the church tradition cannot be underestimated.[26] On the contrary, the role of "creativity" in tradition needs to be continuously studied, along the lines chosen by Avery Dulles or in some similar way.[27] The spirit and the letter of the Constitution *Dei Verbum* direct us toward a dynamic understanding of tradition—that is, to a living tradition.

Veritatis Splendor (VS)

JOHN PAUL II'S encyclical *VS* (1993) is the recent document of the church that most powerfully shows both the normative character that tradition has in the field of ethics and its dynamic and, therefore, progressive structure. The document, however, does not provide an elaborate development of its statements.[28]

---

24. *Dei Verbum*, 8.

25. Ibid.

26. See the open interpretation of this statement by Vicente Gómez Mier, "Sobre tradición y tradiciones de investigación," *La Ciudad de Dios* 209 (1996): 231–70, as opposed to Latourelle's minimalist stand in his article cited above.

27. Avery Dulles, "Tradition and Creativity in Theology," *First Things* 27 (November 1992): 20–27.

28. See Brian V. Johnstone, "Faithful Action," "The theme of Tradition or 'living tradition' has a central place in the encyclical" (283). "However, it does not provide an analysis of what tradition is, or how tradition functions" (284).

Normative Character of Tradition in Ethics

VS, 27 shows in an explicit way the normative character that tradition bears in the field of ethics. This paragraph presupposes the teaching of Vatican II on the ecclesiastical sphere within which divine revelation is transmitted: "In this way the church, in her doctrine, life and worship, perpetuates and transmits to every generation all that she herself is, all that she believes."[29] Apart from this general statement, it underlines two aspects.

First, 27 emphasizes the continuity of the "ecclesiastical tradition" in relation to the "apostolic tradition." "Promoting and preserving the faith and the moral life is the task entrusted by Jesus to the apostles (see Mt. 28:19–20), a task which continues in the ministry of their successors." Secondly, it insists on the signs of the ecclesiastical tradition as witnessed by the teaching of the fathers, the lives of the saints, the church's liturgy, and the teaching of the magisterium.

Adopting an expression already used by the *Catechism of the Catholic Church* (no. 83), it locates this doctrine as belonging to the "great tradition." *VS*, 27 applies this very doctrine to the field of ethics: "By this same tradition Christians receive 'the living voice of the gospel,' as the faithful expression of God's wisdom and will. Within tradition, the authentic interpretation of the Lord's law develops with the help of the Holy Spirit. The same Holy Spirit present at the origin of the revelation of Jesus' commandments and teachings guarantees that they will be reverently preserved, faithfully expounded and correctly applied in different times and places."

Therefore, the encyclical *VS* comes to underline a statement usually assumed in the ethical-theological etymology: the normative character of tradition. Church ethics is "a moral teaching based upon Sacred Scripture and the living tradition of the church."[30]

"Dynamic" Interpretation of Tradition

VS does not understand tradition as a static number of truths handed down from one generation into the next. On the contrary, it means tradition as a dynamic or "living" reality. The latter adjective usually accompanies the substantive tradition. The expression "living tradition" arose in the context of nineteenth-century Catholic romanticism, more precisely in the theology of Johann Adam Möhler, and then passed into the Roman school of

---

29. *Dei Verbum*, 8.
30. *Veritatis Splendor*, 5; it cites *Dei Verbum*, 10.

theology, influencing Yves Congar's reflection on tradition and traditions in particular.[31] Currently, it is a formulation that is regularly repeated in magisterial documents.[32]

Apart from the expression "living tradition," VS uses other verbal phrases denoting dynamism and emphasizing the "dynamic" character of the tradition. In no. 27 the following details appear: "This tradition, which comes from the apostles, progresses in the church"; "Within tradition, the authentic interpretation of the Lord's law develops, with the help of the Holy Spirit."

At the same time, we need not forget that the "living" or dynamic character of the ecclesiastical tradition does not point to an increase of divine revelation, since revelation was closed at the end of the apostolic age.[33]

"Doctrinal Development" within the Tradition

VS goes one step further. It not only receives and develops the teaching of DV on the dynamic character of tradition, but from such a general comprehension, it deduces an important concrete application for epistemology and for the discourse of moral theology. For the first time in a church document, the principle of "doctrinal development" applied to the truths of faith is carried up to the field of ethics. Such a clear formulation of this application will not be found even in previous academic expositions of moral theology.

VS, 28 formulates the principle, places it in its context, and explains how it operates. The formulation of the principle is clear: The church "has achieved a *doctrinal development* analogous to that which has taken place in the realm of the truths of faith." This principle retrieves its meaning from the context of faithfulness to the received word of God: "The church has faithfully preserved what the word of God teaches, not only about truths which should be believed but also about moral action." Here the principle is applied to three references: 1) The subject of doctrinal development is the "church assisted by the Holy Spirit." 2) The search for "all the truth (see Jn. 16:13)," which becomes the final goal, rules over this dynamism. 3) According to the guideline given by *Gaudium et Spes*, 22,

---

31. See M. Semeraro, *"Temi eclesiologoci,"* 123–45.

32. *Veritatis Splendor,* n. 5 ("Living Tradition of the Church"), n. 27 ("Living Tradition"), *Familiaris consortio,* n. 29 ("living tradition of the ecclesiastical community"); *Centesimus annus,* n. 3 ("the church's tradition . . . being ever living and vital"); *Donum veritatis,* n. 6 ("Living Tradition of the Church").

33. *Dei Verbum,* 4.

and so often quoted by John Paul II, the way to realize the evolving process is "to illuminate the mystery of the human" by scrutinizing "the mystery of the Word made flesh."

As will be noted, VS's exposition on the principle of doctrinal development in the field of Christian ethics is remarkably original and doctrinally rich. Nevertheless, some decisive questions remain open to further analysis. I refer to two of them. The first one concerns the explanation of doctrinal development in a general sense, "within the limits of the truths of faith." The second one deals with the meaning of the adjective "analogous" (*similis* in the Latin original) when applied to development within the moral field: What is the distinctive characteristic of moral development when compared with development in the field of the truths of faith? VS does not answer these questions, leaving them open for theological reflection.

In this regard, the special contribution of VS is its reference in paragraph 4 to the doctrinal development of the papal magisterium: "At all times, but particularly in the last two centuries, the popes, whether individually or together with the college of bishops, have developed and proposed a moral teaching regarding the many different spheres of human life." It notes the positive function of doctrinal development for different areas of human life: "With the guarantee of assistance from the Spirit of truth, they [the popes] have contributed to a better understanding of moral demands in the areas of human sexuality, the family, and social, economic and political life." It formulates a general principle, referring to previous pronouncements by Pius XII and John XXIII: "In the tradition of the church and in the history of humanity, their teaching represents a constant deepening of knowledge with regard to morality."

The last sentence clearly shows the newness of VS's contribution to the "development of doctrine" in the moral field: "In the tradition of the church" and in relation to "the history of humanity," "a constant deepening" takes place with regard to all that implies "moral knowledge." It is up to the theological reflection to explain, harmonize, and to make more concrete this doctrine.

Centesimus Annus (CA)

ONE MAY DETECT some creative air in the arrangement of CA. In no. 3, I spot the most explicit references, that I know of, by the magisterium to "look to the future" and to read the tradition of the church with a prospective and creative hermeneutics. The pope writes: "I invite you to look to the future," when we glimpse the third millennium of the Christian era, so filled with uncertainties, but also with promises that together appeal to our imagination and creativity, and reawaken our responsibility.

It is in this context of invitation to the creative and responsible imagination that the pope asks for the unveiling of the "treasure of the church's tradition" which he says is "always living and always vital." He exposes the sense of tradition by turning to the gospel image of the "scribe who has been trained for the Kingdom of Heaven," whom the Lord compares to "a householder who brings out of his treasure what is new and what is old" (Mt. 13:52). The pope does not hesitate to apply this image to the tradition of the church: this "treasure is the great outpouring of the church's tradition, which contains 'what is old'—received and passed on from the very beginning—and which enables us to interpret the 'new things' in the midst of which the life of the church and the world unfolds." The discovered "new things" are "incorporated into tradition" and, thus, "they become old," "enriching both tradition and the life of faith."

I want to finish my description of the·state of things with this excerpt because, in my opinion, it provides us with the spirit in which we should analyze the unsettled questions on moral progress in tradition. In the life of the church, particularly in periods like ours, "so filled with (serious) uncertainties but also (hopeful) with promises," we need to understand the tradition from a creative fidelity approach, like the scribe "who knows to communicate the new and the old."

Systematic Perspectives: Planning

IN LIGHT OF the magisterium, I will try to offer two sets of systematic perspectives about moral progress in the Christian tradition. I mean, more specifically, the ways or forms through which this progress may happen and the spheres in which, as a matter of fact, moral advance has taken place.

John T. Noonan has analyzed development in Catholic moral doctrine focusing on four topics: usury, marriage (dissolution of the bond), slavery, and religious freedom. Only the last one, and to some extent the second, refer to recent situations. In order to explain evolution in moral doctrine, Noonan basically makes use of the criteria proposed by John Newman for the development of dogmatic questions.[34] He summarizes these criteria: the deeper knowledge of Christ and the meaning of human experience.[35]

---

34. See Noonan, "Development," 670–72. Noonan (677) assumes Owen Chadwick's opinion in Newman (Oxford: Oxford University Press, 1983), 47, for whom "the idea of development was the most important single idea Newman contributed to the thought of the Christian Church."

35. Noonan, "Development," 672–75.

For my part, I take into account Noonan's reflections, but I direct my own thoughts along complementary ways. I address recent changes, not failing to acknowledge, however, the importance of analyzing other changes that happened in the history of moral theology. Moreover, I consider those changes insofar as they bear positive progress in moral theology. Finally, I attempt to systematize those factors (or ways or forms) conditioning the advance of Catholic moral tradition.

Advances in Catholic Moral Theology

I DO NOT intend to show all the changes and advances achieved in moral theology, which are impossible to state in this essay. I will limit my considerations to some topological examples, framed most recently by the church. Yet I present the formulation of these changes from the documents of the ecclesiastical magisterium. Thus, we will be assured that we are dealing with moral "progress" in the Christian "tradition."

Advances in Social Ethics

It is obvious that in this field of moral theology, many "advances" have been achieved. I point to the most outstanding ones in the last decades:

- Agreeing with Noonan, I note first the awareness and strengthening of the *rights to religious freedom and freedom of conscience*, a "revolutionary" advance of Vatican II.[36]
- The *moral reappraisal of war*: We have shifted from the "just war" theory to "undertake a completely fresh reappraisal of war,"[37] to finally the point of saying no to war.[38]
- The formulation of *solidarity* as a "new virtue"[39] and a "new principle"[40] of social life.[41]
- The acceptance of the ethical-juridical category *human rights*: After the reticence specific to the eighteenth, nineteenth, and the first half of the

---

36. *Dignitatis Humanae*, 2.
37. *Gaudium et Spes*, 80.
38. *Centesimus Annus*, 52.
39. *Sollicitudo Rei Socialis*, 39.
40. *Centesimus Annus*, 10.
41. See its development in Marciano Vidal, *Para comprender la Solidaridad: virtud y principio ético* (Estella: Verb Divino, 1996).

twentieth centuries, the encyclical *Pacem in Terris* marked the change by stating that "the explicit acknowledgment of human rights" constitutes "the fundamental principle of work for man's welfare"[42] and "an authentic and solid foundation" of democracy.[43]

- The magisterium has introduced such nuances into the right to *private property* that one can talk about a "substantive variation" in its understanding today.[44]
- The *preferential option for the poor*[45] has been affirmed as a moral principle that "far from being a sign of particularism or sectarianism, manifests the universality of the church's being and mission,"[46] bearing noteworthy repercussions for understanding and formulating the "social responsibilities" of the Christian.[47]

Advances in Personal Ethics

Those advances that have taken place in the understanding of the person, the value of human life, and of corporal and sexual dimensions pertain to this section. These changes bear considerable influence when focusing on moral problems pertaining to bioethics and sexual ethics. I note some of them:

- In many commentators' opinion there is a progress in the *comprehension of the person* in *Gaudium et Spes,* and particularly in its reference to the "nature of the human person" (no. 51), where a "wholistic" comprehension of each human being is offered to us.
- The *value of human life* has gained depth, above all in John Paul II's magisterium,[48] so that one can talk about an authentic "progress" in Catholic moral theory on this value; especially in the morality of abortion, euthanasia, capital punishment, and so forth.[49]

---

42. *Redemptor Hominis,* 17.

43. *Centesimus Annus,* 47.

44. *Populorum Progressio,* 23; *Laborem Exercens,* 14; *Sollicitudo Rei Socialis,* 42; *Centesimus Annus,* 30.

45. See Marciano Vidal, "La preferencia por el pobre, criterio de moral," *Studia Moralia* 20 (1982): 277–304.

46. Congregation for the Doctrine of Faith, *Christian Freedom and Liberation* (1986), no. 68.

47. *Centesimus Annus,* 42.

48. Particularly by means of *Evangelium Vitae* (1995).

49. See Marciano Vidal, *El evangelio de la vida humana* (Madrid: San Pablo, 1996).

- The understanding of the *corporal dimension* of the human condition has moved beyond the staggering "biologist" (or physicalist) consideration to a distinctive "personalist" comprehension.[50]
- *Human sexuality* is placed today within the framework of an integral vision of the person.[51]

Advances in Fundamental Ethics

Catholic moral theory has also achieved many advances in this field. I note only three:

- Chapter 5 of *Lumen Gentium* states that the *universal call to holiness* implies an extensive development in our understanding of Christian ethics.[52] This is no longer a "morality of sins" but the pursuit of the "exalted vocation of the faithful in Christ."[53]
- The limits of the morality "of acts" have been overcome by accepting the complementary category of *fundamental choice,* which "ultimately defines the moral condition of a person,"[54] although it should not be separated from the "concrete choices."[55]
- The *sin of structures*[56] or structural sin is an advance in the formulations of objective and subjective culpabilities.[57]

If we realize that these thirteen topics belong to the Vatican II era, it can be stated that in the short period of the last thirty to forty years a spectacular progress has happened in Catholic moral theory, whose implications and consequences have not been fully developed.

---

50. *Veritatis splendor,* 50; *Donum vitae,* introduction, 3.

51. Congregation for the Doctrine of Faith, *Human Person* (1975), no. 1; Congregation for Catholic Education, *Educational Orientations on Human Love* (1983) nn. 4–6; Pontifical Counsel for the Family, *Human sexuality: Truth and Meaning* (1995) nn. 8–15.

52. See Marciano Vidal, *Moral y Espiritualidad* (Madrid: PS, 1997).

53. *Optatam Totius,* 16.

54. *Persona Humana,* 10.

55. *Veritatis Splendor,* 65–70

56. *Sollicitudo Rei Socialis,* 36.

57. See M. Vidal, "Structural Sin: A New Category in Moral Theology"; Raphael Gallagher and Brendan McCovery, *History and Conscience: Studies in Honor of Sean O'Riordan, C.Ss.R.* (Dublin: Gill and MacMillan, 1989), 181–98.

Factors of Moral Progress

In a schematic fashion, I point now to the factors working toward moral progress in Christian tradition. These factors are, at the same time, the ways through which the developing dynamism happens; they may be considered also as the forms adopted by moral development.

Noonan's advice is valuable: progress in moral theory does not depend on a singular factor but rather comes from a "complex constellation of elements."[58] Thus, the following factors should not be understood separately, but as building a meaningful whole:

- The most profound understanding of the *mystery of Christ* and its meaning to explain and orient the mystery of the human person is, without doubt, the principal and omnipresent factor in all moral advances in the Christian tradition.[59] Vatican II formulated the principle governing progress in the understanding and orientation of the human condition: "It is only in the mystery of the Word made flesh that the mystery of humanity truly becomes clear."[60] Christian ethics is nothing but a "patterned" anthropology whose original reference is Christ; this is the reason why all progress in Christian moral theory implies a more profound knowledge of the incarnate Word.
- The urgency to answer the questions posed by *historical reality* in a Christian manner constitutes the other major factor that, indissolubly bound to the ever-deeper knowledge of the mystery of Christ, prompts moral progress in the Christian tradition. Vatican II proposed a new hermeneutical category: "the signs of the times," that the church has to "read" and "interpret" in the light of the gospel.[61] All "historical newness" carries as well a "challenge" to the Christian conscience. The answer to that challenge has to be born from a "re-creation" of the data of the tradition to combine "the old things" and "the new things," according to the suggestive interpretation that John Paul II made of Mt. 13:52.[62]
- The rich and diverse *human experience,* the gift of God the "creator," opens up new ways to the truth that are fully revealed in Christ and inherited (*depositum*) by the church. "The church is not unaware of how much it has profited from the history and development of mankind. It profits from the experience of past ages, from the progress of the sciences, and from the riches hidden in various cultures, through

---

58. Noonan, "Development," 676.
59. *Veritatis Splendor,* 28. Cf. Noonan, "Development," 672–73.
60. *Gaudium et Spes,* 22.
61. Ibid., 4.
62. *Centesimus Annus,* 3.

which greater light is thrown on the nature of man and new avenues to truth are opened up."[63] This "vital exchange between the church and different cultures"[64] has an especially meaningful function in the field of ethics.

- The *scientific-technical advances* discover new possibilities in human realities. They present new ethical questions postulating answers that are also new within the Christian tradition. Christians have "to incorporate the findings of new sciences and teachings and the understanding of the most recent discoveries with Christian morality and thought."[65] This "integration" requires putting into practice a "creative fidelity," for which tradition is not an obstacle but a sphere of security and guarantee.

Moral theory, letting itself be questioned by all the factors that we have just seen, needs to advance. This is what John Paul II has noted in the Catholic ethical reflection carried out in accordance with the spirit of Vatican II. "The work of many theologians who found support in the council's encouragement" has allowed that Christian truths be today "offered in a form better suited to the sensitivities and questions of our contemporaries."[66] This new presentation does not go against tradition, since "there is a difference between the deposit of the truths of faith and the manner in which they are expressed, keeping the same meaning and the same judgment."[67]

The goal of those advances in moral theory that happen in the Christian tradition is that "thus the knowledge of God will be made better known (*penitus percipi*); the preaching of the gospel will be rendered more intelligible to man's mind (*mellius intelligi*), and will appear more relevant (*aptius proponi*) to his situation."[68] Therefore, while "listening to and distinguishing the many voices of our times and to interpret them in the light of the divine word,"[69] theologians know that they remain creatively faithful to Christian tradition.

---

63. *Gaudium et Spes*, 44.
64. Ibid., 44.
65. Ibid., 62.
66. *Veritatis Splendor*, 29.
67. *Gaudium et Spes*, 62. Quoted in *Veritatis Splendor*, 29.
68. Ibid., 62.
69. Ibid., 44.

8.
CATHOLIC MEDICAL ETHICS: A TRADITION WHICH PROGRESSES

Raphael Gallagher, C.Ss.R.

CARDINAL NEWMAN ADVANCED a hypothesis to account for the difficulty which the evident development of doctrine posed. Ethical issues pose a different though analogous quandary for the theologian. On the one hand there is the myriad of new questions, strikingly so in the biomedical area; on the other hand there is the unmistakable evidence that moral theology has changed its use and formulation of some principles and rules in response to new questions. If moral theological rules are not permanent, but change, how can they help us respond to new problems? Understanding how the tradition of moral theology has developed could be useful toward an adequate response to a crisis such as AIDS.

Instead of talking about the relationship between existing moral theological rules and AIDS, I will look at another issue: How was the principle of totality used in justifying organ transplants? Of course, to the contemporary reader, the need to justify organ transplants may seem unnecessary. However, at one point in history we needed that justification because it seemed wrong to take the organ that God gave one person and give it to another.

When moral theologians invoked the principle of totality to justify these donations, they were interpreting the principle in a wholly different way. Still, their predecessors had over the centuries also applied the principle of totality in a variety of ways. The principle developed, then, through the moral tradition.[1] But we cannot simply assert that development occurs: the why and how of this development are worth examining to discern what lessons we may learn in the application of other principles to other cases.

---

1. A wider historical perspective can be found in: Thomas R. Kopfensteiner, *Paradigms and Hermeneutics: The Essential Tension between Person and Nature in the Principle of Totality*, dissertatio ad doctoratum (Rome: Gregorian University, 1988).

Why a Moral Tradition Develops

THE MANUALS TAUGHT that self-mutilation was wrong according to the principle of nonmaleficence. Furthermore, this view was considered to be immutable, since the manuals held that the action was intrinsically evil.[2] The individual's body was defined as a self-contained physical totality of which God alone was sovereign. Initial efforts to widen the application of totality to include the needs of society were rejected precisely on these grounds: one cannot redefine the physical nature of an action.

Theoretical discussion and practical medical advances were to question this presumption. On the level of theory, it was pointed out that there is a difference between charity as an internal end of the agent (*finis operantis*) and the bond of charity as the good of virtue (*bonum virtutis*) that became a legitimate qualifying circumstance. On the practical level, the breakthrough in the possibility of kidney transplants made it possible to envisage that a good done for another was not necessarily the direct result of an evil done to oneself: medicine made it safe to live a full life on one kidney.

What we see here is the transformative development of a principle (totality) through the recovery of a virtue (charity) into a reformulation of the principle which we can now, perhaps, call totality-as-solidarity. That this is a case of development, and not abandonment, is evidenced by the retaining of the term *totality*, though obviously with a new meaning. The hesitancy about the possibility of transplants was overcome by the recovery of a more genuinely Christian view of the person-in-society: an individual is never an end in oneself, and we have an obligation to return something to society in lieu of all we have received from it.

It was the moral prophets of a previous generation who unfroze the presumed immutable principle of bodily totality through a recovery of a more comprehensive vision of charity and social solidarity. The basic insight that enabled the development to occur was an anthropological one: we looked at the person as a more integrated social-spiritual-moral reality. The body was no longer seen as a private physical entity: it was seen to have a social significance, something that scientific advances helped to make clear.

Acquiring a fuller anthropological vision of the meaning of the body facilitated another development. A questioning of the appropriateness of the particular principles and their application began to occur. The older formulation of the principle of totality is given a presumptive priority: there is a prima facie duty not to harm oneself or to use a person as a means

---

2. A standard presentation is available in Henry Davis, *Moral and Pastoral Theology* (London: Sheed and Ward, 1949), 2:141–99.

in any situation. But once we enter into what Aristotle called the particulars of a case, we begin to see that we cannot properly understand an action without a consideration of the various contingencies and variabilities.

A moment of interpretive uncertainty occurs: is the case we are studying really covered by the principle of totality? This interpretive uncertainty forces us to hesitate: this can be the result of either ambiguity (is this really an act of self-mutilation?) or conflict (the duty of self-preservation versus the duty of helping another person in greater need). What happens is that a more correct specification of the action in question enables us to ask whether the prima facie presumption in favor of a particular principle holds up in view of the doubts raised by new cases and new evidence. In the issue of transplants it clearly did not: development occurs in that an older formulation of a principle is found to be not applicable in a particular case. This change in the application of the principle of totality is an aspect of the underlying anthropological shift which I noted. Once totality is understood in terms of the spiritual-moral person, rather than in those of the merely physical body, it is obvious that the application of the principle will change.

These reasons for development are all aspects of the fact that moral theology includes the art of practical deliberation. There is, consequently, an ongoing need to interpret and decipher what is occurring in changing circumstances.[3] It is rarely immediately obvious what virtue requires: integrity and character. Centrally important as they are for the moral life, they do not yield automatic solutions to specific problems. The moral theologian must incorporate the skill of practical hesitancy into a theological method: hesitancy implies doubt, doubt implies uncertainty, and uncertainty implies the possibility of development. This possibility of development is, for some, bewildering because it seems to imply that right and wrong changes depending on the decade we live in. The theoretic explanation of the reason for moral development offered here is more nuanced: what develops is the insight into the anthropological value which is presumed in the principle. Quite simply, when the theory of a particular principle is tested in practice, it can become clear that the formal application of the principle would, in fact, undercut the presumed anthropological value.

In the development of the principle of totality what happened was that the anthropological meaning of the principle was expanded. The principle was not abandoned, tempting as that option must have seemed to some. With the expanded anthropological horizon something new became clear: the principle of totality could be seen to be of benefit to the donor as well

---

3. The issues are well presented by Richard Miller, *Casuistry and Modern Ethics* (Chicago: University of Chicago Press, 1996), 17–27, 168–72.

as to the recipient. The benefit to the recipient was always clear, but it is only when we work with a wider anthropology that we can see that the donor is also a beneficiary. Totality is, thus, not abandoned; it develops a new meaning on the basis of an anthropological insight.

A useful analogy is St. Thomas' discussion of theft: the principle "do not steal" is not applicable in certain circumstances where the protections that normally surround property no longer apply because certain normally presumed conditions are lacking. Once we accept the need for practical deliberation as an aspect of moral theology, it seems logically imperative to posit the possibility of development, particularly when we consider that what we are deliberating about is the anthropological meaning of the human.

I believe the above reasons for moral development can be seen as operative in the period between the end of World War II and the opening of Vatican II. Organ transplants were generally forbidden at the beginning of this period, given that they were judged to be a direct mutilation of one's physical body. A first move in the direction of development happened when it was suggested that mutilation was not covered by the principle of double effect (thus removing the problem of "direct" mutilation) but, rather, by the principle of totality. This is not a view held by all, but I suggest it is a tenable position on the basis that the principle of totality is an aspect of anthropology while the principle of double effect is an aspect of the practical application of a principle. Largely due to a pioneering thesis by B. Cunningham, it was increasingly accepted that the totality referred to was not simply one's own physical body but the mystical body of Christ.[4] As the possible justification for transplants was thus established, medical progress began to convince moralists that the appropriate principle to invoke was, indeed, totality, but no longer understood in a restrictive physical sense. It was not that something was "wrong" in 1945 and "right" in 1962, *tout court*.

In the light of the arguments advanced above, the reasons for development are coherent rather than random in that there is a gradual discovery of an anthropological insight. A principle develops in the light of and in response to the questions which are put to it by new cases. The principle of totality is an excellent example: the new cases raised the basic anthropological question of what it means to be human. Development occurs, therefore, through a process of differentiation and distinction, and this of a fundamental kind. The insight that the body is a social organism rather than a self-referring physical entity was the catalyst for developing the principle of totality. A new anthropological horizon of meaning became possible.

---

4. B. Cunningham, *The Morality of Organic Transplantation* (Washington, D.C.: Catholic University of America Press, 1944).

How a Moral Tradition Develops

UNDERSTANDING WHY A tradition develops leads to a second question for the theologian: How is this development expressed and articulated?

The use of distinctions with a view to greater clarity suggests itself as the first step in how moral theology has developed its principles and rules.[5] Take the older and, for the manuals, standard definition of mutilation: the destruction of some part or the suppression of some function of the body. The ambiguity of this definition was exposed once theologians saw that the definition did not distinguish between sterilizing and nonsterilizing mutilations, a critical distinction for the manual tradition. Further, the view that mutilation was intrinsically evil was undermined by the observation that in some cases mutilation was both justifiable and licit.

It is possible for a tradition to find a coherent way of development by using distinctions in order to understand the total picture. True, moral theology has too often used distinctions to obfuscate and confuse. This need not necessarily be so. A carefully made distinction helps to maintain a dialectic between what we understand a principle to be and what our experience of reality is telling us. From this dialectic emerges a greater clarity, precisely because of the proper distinction, and from the emergent clarity it is possible to develop one's theory.

Using distinctions in a discerning way not only develops the tradition in terms of accurate formulation. There is the further benefit of indicating which principle one should use in which case. Mutilation, once covered by moral theologians under the rubric of the double effect theory, was later treated under the principle of totality, in its various formulations. Transplants opened up the possibility of competing principles: the good of one's own body versus the good of humanity in a more general sense. Unless one accepted the positive value of distinguishing, precisely in order to clarify and unify, moral theology would have remained frozen, unable to distinguish between a physicalist understanding of totality and one that was more anthropologically inclusive of the spiritual and social dimensions of the human.

Given the importance of magisterial statements in the tradition of moral theology, it is not surprising that the interpretation of such texts gives a further clue as to how tradition develops. Earlier in this century, most moralists seemed to agree that the principle of (physical) totality was the only principle applicable in instances of bodily mutilation. In defense of this position it became standard to quote a classic text of Pius XI in *Casti*

---

5. This paragraph owes much to the insightful article of John Mahoney, "The Challenge of Moral Distinctions," *Theological Studies* 53 (1992): 663–82.

Conubii which upheld that the good of a part was always subordinate to the good of the whole.[6] Once theologians began to examine the historical context of the philosophical attitudes which the pope was attacking, it became clearer that such a restrictive interpretation of the magisterial text was not necessarily consonant with the papal intention. This indicated that, in using magisterial statements, a theologian should not merely repeat the verbal text but, crucially, should seek the intention of the text within the context in which it was written. Textual criticism, in this sense, was a determining factor in a development to which we have already alluded: the move away from a physicalist understanding of totality to seeing it as totality interpreted through charity-solidarity.[7] It was this development of the principle that allowed for the resolution of the problem of transplants.

How a tradition develops has, in the above three modes, been illustrated in what might seem like marginal details: distinctions, clarifications, and textual criticism. Underlying these is one central issue: once the basic anthropological reference-schema is changed, there is an inevitability in how principles and rules develop.[8] I will use a series of assertions, followed by a qualification, to illustrate this. The body is a value, but not the highest value; God is sovereign of life, but humans have a responsibility of stewardship; totality is an important principle, but wholeness is a better indicator of the human vocation. These three positions indicate important anthropological shifts that have occurred within moral theology. The first part of the anthropological assertion is never denied; however, the qualifying clause in each case has implications for moral principles. Mutilation, to take a precise example, would be judged in a different way depending on whether one followed the first part of the above assertions or whether one accepted the qualifying clause. The acceptance of the qualifications is of profound anthropological consequence. It is my belief that it is at this point we can best see how the tradition has developed in recent decades.

In an anthropological horizon of physical bodily integrity, obligations to the self, and a biocentric view of life, transplants are defined in a restrictive way, as in the moral manuals. In an anthropological horizon of social harmony, responsibilities toward the good of society and a transcendental view of the human destiny, transplants are judged quite differently. The

---

6. Encyclical Letter *Casti Conubii*, AAS 22 (1930), at 565.

7. A notable early contribution on this point was that of Gerald Kelly, "The Morality of Mutilation: Toward a Revision of the Treatise," *Theological Studies,* 17 (1956): 322–44.

8. These arguments are treated at greater length by Antonio Autiero, "Quale obbligo c'è di donare un organo?," in *La Questione dei Trapianti: tra Etica, Diritto, Economia,* ed. S. Fagiuoli (Milan, 1997), 139–49.

anthropological horizon changes: a transplant can be a gift that transforms our self-understanding and transforms a role-construction of society into a mutually supportive community. Transplants can become, in this changed definition of anthropological responsibility, a meritorious Christian gesture.

Looking over the developments within moral theology and its use of principles with regard to mutilation and transplants, I think a four-stage pattern is discernible. At first the moral tradition is presumed to be immutable, and there is nothing to do but apply the unchangeable principle and rule. In a second moment, more obvious in the early part of this century, it is the physicalist interpretation of natural law that is the stabilizing reference point. By mid-century, these first two stages are subsumed into a voluntarist (and, at times, literalist) interpretation of magisterial texts. In a fourth moment, the central reference point becomes the spiritual-social consideration of the human person in relation to others and with God.

No doubt, this general schema may appear too neat and simple. I use it not to defend the schema in detail, but to indicate how a change within the dominant horizon of anthropological reference is a decisive catalyst in moral development. It is important to note how the change in anthropological emphasis refers back to the earlier arguments. Moral theology, using practical discernment, often has to move into new or strange territory. This is relatively straightforward where there is a simple development of case studies within a stable paradigm. It becomes more problematic when the major reference points are changed, as in the anthropological shift just noted. Development then becomes more a questioning of presumed positions than a positive addition of new formulations; these come later.[9]

Within the issues under consideration here, one can note a questioning of underlying ideas (the definition of the body, the meaning of human nature, and the like) that tries to ensure that any moral principles used correspond to the best possible formulation of the relevant facts and eschew any false use of ideologies. How development occurs is, thus, not just through positive additions and clarifications; the negative elimination of outdated ideas has also been a crucial factor, even if the full fruits of this stage of development are yet to be reaped. The fact, for instance, that there may not be consensus on a definition of "the person adequately considered" does not mean that we have to revert to older biological formulas. An anthropological benchmark has been struck, and it too will be filled out in time by the use of distinctions and clarifications.

---

9. Though not sharing all his conclusions, I am indebted to the contribution of John T. Noonan, "Development in Moral Doctrine," *The Context of Casuistry,* ed. James Keenan and Thomas Shannon (Washington, D.C.: Georgetown University Press, 1995), 188–204.

I have noted a number of ways how a moral tradition develops: greater clarity though more precise distinctions; a more accurate choice of the appropriate principle; the use of proper norms for textual interpretation; changes within the horizon of interpretive reference; and a *via negativa* elimination of ideas that obfuscate proper moral classification.[10] In each of these ways, one can note a slighter or greater development of the tradition. We now turn to the more important consideration: Can the why and how of development indicate any signposts or parameters for further development?

Signposts for the Future

A BASIC PREMISE of this chapter is that moral theology is formed within a tradition. The arguments presented above suggest that it is a tradition that can develop in a coherent way. By coherence I do not wish to imply that every step is at once logically clear; this need not necessarily be so. The coherence is connected with the direction of moral development. This always seeks a more accurate understanding of the anthropological basis of any principle. Given this sense of coherence, I believe we can establish three processes that may apply to future development, and from these we can formulate three further likely inferences as to how that development is likely to take shape.

It is evident, firstly, that development has occurred in overlapping stages: the point where one formulation of a principle ends and another begins is never exactly definable. The principle of totality was, for instance, variously defined in terms of physicalist, ecclesiastically positivist and personalist categories. I am referring here to the statement of the principle as a normative theory rather than entering the separate question of metaethical verification. Though the stages overlap, there is no doubt that, by the end of the process, the first stage of the formulation of the principle had been superseded. Future development is likely to follow this same stage-by-stage pattern of redimensioning the formulation of principles.

Secondly, the evidence shows that the development of a principle includes residual elements of the previous definition (or formulation) of the

---

10. As background material to these arguments I suggest a rereading of some articles that have become standard reference points: G. Kelly, "Pope Pius XII and the Principle of Totality," *Theological Studies* 16 (1955): 373–96; M. Nolan, "The Positive Doctrine of Pius XII on the Principle of Totality," *Augustinianum* 3 (1963): 28–44, and 4 (1964): 537–59; Augustine Regan, "The Basic Morality of Organic Transplants between Living Humans," *Studia Moralia* 3 (1965): 320–61 and "Man's Administration of his Bodily Life and Members: The Principle of Totality and Organic Transplants between Living Donors," *Studia Moralia* 5 (1967): 179–200.

principle. With regard to transplants the principle of nonmaleficence ("do no harm") was, with time, seen to be less important than the principle of beneficence ("do good to others"). But the consensus around the principle of beneficence did not cancel out crucial residual elements of the principle of nonmaleficence: for instance, mentally incompetent persons would be ruled out as donor-candidates because of an inability to give free consent. This process will apply to future development: the present formulation of a principle can be said to have a *prima facie* claim to acceptance, but this is not an absolute claim if compelling reasons or conflicting cases force us to reconsider the formulation.

In this reconsideration, the evidence shows that moral theology attempts to preserve, at least in a shadow form, values that are considered enduring. The benefit to the donor, which is one of the gains of the developed principle of totality-as-solidarity, does not cancel out the enduring benefit to the recipient which, clearly, remains a constant factor.

The third process that seems incontrovertible in the light of the evidence studied is that the development of moral principles involves a process of theological reception. Development is slow, and occasionally contorted. One could argue that the justification of transplants is "self-evident." Why was moral theology so tardy in responding? My analysis would suggest that the careful distinctions and clarification of cases were not refusals to be realistic. The issues at stake are most serious, involving the definition of life, relationships in society, and the future direction of humanity. The way moral theology tends to develop does not block progress but allows time and space for the reception of new insights to be tested in a variety of appropriate ways. This infuriates many people, of course, but I judge that this painstaking process of reception is the more normal route of theological development.[11]

From the above I believe we can draw three likely inferences for future developments. First, it is more likely that moral principles will function as a hermeneutic of interpretation rather than as a probabilist theory of reflex principles. This will happen not just because of the (happy) demise of the casuistry of the manuals but, more importantly, because of interpretive uncertainties with regard to new evidence and the necessity of deciphering the practical meaning of obligation in unforeseen circumstances. Principles will remain, but their interpretive function will be different.

Linked to this is a second inference. Moral theology is concerned with all that really matters in life, and what matters most is the need for personal

---

11. That patient and closely argued debate leads to a good quality of development is implicit in the study of David Kelly, *The Emergence of Roman Catholic Medical Ethics in North America* (New York: Mellen Press, 1979).

survival in a crisis of suffering. Principles will function, therefore, as a mode of deciphering what is ultimately important for the person in this dilemma of pain and distress. It was more usual for principles to function, in the broadest sense, as a method of meaning-making in the face of life's inevitable moral dilemmas. I am impressed by the evidence, particularly from studies in medical anthropology, that the urgent current quest is not the search for meaning (some forms of suffering seem utterly meaningless) but the need for personal survival.[12] If this is true, it would imply that principles serve this latter need rather than the former search.

The third inference is a placing of the first two in the context of faith, and more specifically of theodicy. The heart of moral theology is neither the principle nor its function, new or old. Moral theology's first question is how, in this experience, God is revealed to us. Too often the theodicy question was absent from moral theology.[13] This happened because of presumptions about the centrality of sin and a certainty that principles clearly reflected God's will. If our primary sensitivity is to the suffering person(s) we encounter then, I believe, the experience of God will be formulated differently. That this would have consequences for the formulation and application of principles and rules seems obvious.

I have focused on the questions of how and why a moral principle develops. I believe a certain pattern has emerged. Principles seem to function as a way of pausing before perplexity and diversity; they are a sort of plateau where the moral theologian works out residual hesitations about the implications of any development for the anthropological meaning of the human. The tradition develops because principles, however important, are seen to be at the service of the fuller truth that always lies ahead. Precisely because it is a tradition, and not an abstract theory, moral theology can develop to meet new challenges along the lines indicated above.[14]

If my central analysis is correct—namely, that the principle of totality developed because of an insight into anthropology—the application to the crisis of AIDS seems almost too banal to mention. It is humanity that has AIDS, and not simply an isolated person. Any moral principle that tries to

---

12. For an introduction to the issues, a useful article is A. Kleinman, "Everything that really matters: Social Suffering, Subjectivity, and the Re-Making of Human Experience in a Disordering World," *Harvard Theological Review* 90 (1997): 315–25.

13. Strong arguments for its inclusion can be found in J. B. Metz, "God and the Evil of the World," *Concilium* 5 (1997): 3–8.

14. Allen Verhey and Stephen E. Lammers, ed., *Theological Voices in Medical Ethics* (Grand Rapids, Mich.: William B. Eerdmans, 1993) is a useful overview of how traditions develop in medical ethics.

deal with whatever aspect of AIDS simply by referring to the past applications of the principle will fail the test for development which my analysis indicates. It was the anthropological question of what life means (a physical entity or a social organism) that was determinative in the development of the principle of totality. AIDS is forcing us to ask the question: How can human life survive now? That it can and will, I have no doubt. But those of us who use moral principles in dealing with AIDS must pause and hesitate, precisely because of the human dimension of AIDS. The epidemic raises the question of the *humanum* on every level: the behavioral choices that people make, the political options implicit in medical programs, the religious inferences in attributing blame. If it was a new anthropological insight that enabled the principle of totality to develop into its current understanding, we may be surprised at how placing the AIDS crisis in its wider anthropological context may enable a development of some principles that, at first sight, seem immutable. What is at stake is the quality of human survival. That should make any theologian pause for thought in the use of principles and in the discernment of their possible development.

9.
AIDS, JUSTICE, AND
THE COMMON GOOD

Lisa Sowle Cahill

T HE THESIS OF this essay on the global AIDS pandemic and Catholic
social teaching is that the primary cause of the spread of this horren-
dous disease is poverty. Related barriers to AIDS prevention are racism; the
low status of women; and an exploitive global economic system, which
influences marketing of medical resources. After considering structural
agents of AIDS transmission, I will explore the resources Catholic social
thought can provide for an ethical analysis.

AIDS: Social Causes and Remedies

AIDS IS A justice issue, not primarily a sex issue. AIDS as a justice issue
concerns the social relationships that help spread HIV and fail to alleviate
AIDS, relationships of power and vulnerability that are in violation of
Catholic norms of justice and the common good.

Clearly, HIV infection depends on individual behaviors, especially sexual contact and IV drug use. These should be addressed in their own right.
However, an exclusive focus on sexual promiscuity or drug abuse, condoms
or needle exchange programs, obscures the fact that the behaviors that transmit HIV are strongly influenced by social conditions. Likewise, a choice to
engage in different behavior patterns—like sexual fidelity in marriage to an
uninfected spouse and a healthy lifestyle—is only possible when one's social
circumstances offer those different patterns as real possibilities for oneself.

Ninety percent of people infected with HIV live in developing countries, where eight hundred million people lack access to clean water, and
are grievously wanting for basic health care and perinatal care, primary
education, nutrition, and sanitation. The fact that poverty and poor health
are linked hardly needs argument; when people lack access to the basic
means of subsistence, their physical well-being obviously declines. Poverty
also denies people social access to the means of preventing or avoiding specific health threats. This includes their ability to avoid contracting or
spreading HIV/AIDS.

Even though only 10 percent of persons with AIDS live in industrialized nations, it is affluent societies that enjoy availability of preventive education, treatments, and care for the disease. The $15,000 annual cost of treatment is far beyond the reach of most of the thirty-four million people now infected. The World Health Organization has estimated that HIV prevention programs could be implemented successfully in developing nations for between $1.5 billion and 2.9 billion a year, which represents only 5 percent of the amount spent on Operation Desert Storm. Although the U.S. spent $7 billion on AIDS education, care, and research in 1993, for instance, 95 percent of that budget went to efforts in the First World. According to a recent estimate, to make the standard AIDS treatment globally available would cost $36.5 billion. But the United Nations has calculated that for roughly the same amount ($35 billion to $40 billion), basic health care, nutrition, and social services could be provided to the world's poorest people. Providing for these basic needs would be the most effective way to prevent AIDS by eradicating the dire poverty that provides its seedbed. Yet political and ecclesial controversies over AIDS sidetrack identification of the *unjust ultimate social causes* of the spread of HIV by focusing myopically on more volatile proximate causes and deterrents—sex outside marriage and condoms.[1]

People living in poverty not only suffer a general loss of physical well-being, they often are forced to adopt "survival strategies" that expose them to health risks. Married couples may be split apart when men leave traditional agricultural work to find higher paid employment in the cities. There they may meet women who, themselves under economic duress, have either turned to prostitution, or are willing to enter a more long-term arrangement, in which they trade regular sexual access and emotional or domestic support to a man in exchange for financial support for themselves and possibly their children. Meanwhile, the rural wives of the city-employed men remain financially dependent on their wages, and socially dependent on the marriage relationship for recognition and respect in the local community. Their men may bring home disease along with their pay. Upon the deaths of such men, their wives may in some cases be by custom passed on to male relatives, through whom HIV is transmitted ever-more widely in the extended family. Granting the centrality in some cultures of an ethic of promoting

1. The above statistics were taken from Robert J. Vitillo, "Theological Challenges Posed by the Global Pandemic of AIDS," reflection paper presented to the Theological Study Group on HIV/AIDS, Boston College, 23 March 1994; Lawrence K. Altman, "AIDS Meeting Ends with Little Hope of Breakthrough: Emphasis on Prevention," *New York Times*, 5 July 1998, A1, A11; Blaise Salmon, "Poverty is Scourge Behind Global AIDS Epidemic," "Letters to the Editor," *New York Times*, 11 July 1998, A14.

life through childbearing, and the value of levirate marriage in providing for widows, the unequal position of women in defining these traditional priorities certainly plays a role in exposing women and children to HIV/AIDS.

Perhaps an even more basic issue than economic and gender relations in the countries most affected by AIDS is the justice of the interlocking local and global economic systems that disrupt traditional societies, displace economic and educational infrastructures, and cut off access to kinds of prevention and treatment of disease whose efficacy in Europe and North America is well established.

Some seemingly self-evident points still bear repeating in the context of social vulnerability to AIDS:

> Power, the ability of individuals and groups to gain their ends . . . is unequally distributed in human societies. . . . [A]ccess systems implicitly or explicitly evaluate the relative claims of individuals or groups by using criteria which commonly include ethnicity, class, gender, and sexual predisposition. A common result of differential entitlement is that the more powerful or privileged groups frequently scapegoat those less powerful or otherwise marginalized, for dangers or risks from which the latter may actually suffer the major casualties.

Ethnic and gender relations are named among the most important causes of marginalization, leading both to vulnerability to HIV infection and to adverse social consequences of infection.[2]

Those prominent in the worldwide fight against AIDS are well aware of these factors. Richard G. Parker, secretary general of the Brazilian Interdisciplinary AIDS Association, in a speech to the 11th International Conference on AIDS in Vancouver in 1996, asserts that AIDS has never been a democratic disease, and that its causes are as much structural as individual. By focusing on social vulnerability, it is possible "to more fully comprehend the consequences, with regard to HIV infection and AIDS, of the sexual stigma and discrimination so often faced by gay men or sex workers, of the gender power relations and gender oppression so often faced by women, or of the social and economic marginalization faced by the poor."[3]

---

2. Tony Barnett and Rachel Grellier, "Cultural Influence on Society Vulnerability," in Jonathan M. Mann and Daniel Tarantola, eds., *AIDS in the World II: Global Dimensions, Social Roots, and Responses* (New York: Oxford UP, 1996) 445, 446.

3. Richard G. Parker, "Empowerment, Community Mobilization, and Social Change in the Face of HIV/AIDS," paper presented at the XI International Conference on AIDS, Vancouver, July 1996, 6–7.

At the 1998 12th World AIDS Conference, one participant pointed out that gaps in care existed in the United States and other affluent countries, as well as in less privileged areas. "When we talk about the North-South gap, we must remember that the South includes Mississippi, and it includes the South Bronx," said Mark Harrington, a representative of an AIDS action group in New York City.

Another speaker, Dr. Hoosen Coovadia, of Durban, South Africa, who is chairman of the next World AIDS Conference in 2000 in Durban, said he had never used any anti-HIV drugs. His hospital, a large facility serving the city's black population, has a forty percent infection rate among the children it treats; however, it cannot afford drug treatments for AIDS. Moreover, giving pregnant women the anti-viral drug AZT and delivering their children by Caesarean section could reduce the risk of the infection of the infants to about one percent. But many obstetricians in developing countries do not perform Caesarean sections because of the risk of surgery and the lack of adequate infection-control measures on their hospitals.[4]

I want particularly to highlight the unequal position of women globally in claiming access to human goods and in making choices about their own destiny. Among the poor, women are the most poor, both materially and socially. Without transformation of the unequal power relations that exist between the sexes in virtually every culture of the world, "women will continue to be preferential targets of HIV infection and will be unable to guarantee their own safety."[5] In many cases, women lack sexual self-determination both before and after marriage. This means that they have little choice of sexual partners, no say in the sexual practices of husbands, and no freedom to refuse sex even to a spouse who is infected. In some cases, women and girls are forced into prostitution. In many cases, women who develop AIDS are abandoned or cast out, whether they are prostitutes, concubines, or wives. Needless to say, children of these women often meet a similar fate.

Catholic Social Teaching, Justice, and AIDS

REGARDING GLOBAL RESPONSIBILITY for the plight of nations disproportionately affected by AIDS, Parker in 1996 asserted that "we have begun to

---

4. Altman, "AIDS Meeting Ends."

5. Ibid., A11; See Maura O'Donohue, MMM, *Women and Children and the HIV/AIDS Pandemic*, unpublished document, *Catholic Fund for Overseas Development (CAFOD)*, England, April 1995; and, Robert Vitillo, "Ethical Challenges Posed by HIV/AIDS: Can Christians Confront Them in the Light?," paper presented at the *Eighth National HIV/AIDS Ministry Conference*, Chicago, July 1995.

understand the perverse consequences caused by specific models of economic development (most often imposed from above) that have in fact functioned to produce and reproduce structures of economic dependence and processes of social disintegration."[6] Yet another expert has cautioned that while the AIDS pandemic has a "simple" solution in the reduction of the gap between rich and poor, the methods to accomplish this goal are, to say the least, "unclear." What can be done concretely? With whom should one collaborate? And what can motivate fundamental societal changes in the economic and social disparities that cause AIDS?[7]

While no simple answer to these questions is available, it is just at this point that Catholic social teaching bears fruit. Catholic social teaching offers a framework of analysis that clarifies the mutual rights and responsibilities of members of local and global communities. It urges the right and duty of all to participate in the common good, and to support such participation for others. Catholic social teaching motivates persons and communities to achieve the common good by using religious symbolism and by evoking a sense of our common humanity.

Key elements in the Catholic vision of social justice and the common good are the dignity of the person; the comprehensive common good of society; the need for affirmative action toward those currently most excluded from participation in the common good (preferential option for the poor); the reality of structural sin; and the principle of subsidiarity, designating the reciprocal functions of local, national, and international structures of justice.[8] Each of these terms shall be discussed in turn, with brief applications to the AIDS crisis.

Dignity of the Person

TRADITIONAL SOCIETIES, CHRISTIAN and otherwise, usually understand individual identity and worth primarily in terms of social roles. Modern liberal individualism, on the other hand, tends to so stress individual rights and liberty that social responsibilities can be severely neglected. The encyclical

---

6. Parker, "Empowerment," 4, 11.

7. Jeffrey O'Malley, " Societal Context and Response," in Mann and Tarantola, eds., *AIDS in the World*, 459.

8. Although Catholic social teaching is rooted in ancient authors, especially Augustine and Aquinas, it has been developed in modern times by means of a series of papal social encyclicals beginning in 1891. A resource is John A. Coleman, ed., *One Hundred Years of Catholic Social Thought: Celebration and Challenge* (Maryknoll, N.Y.: Orbis, 1991).

tradition has tried to strike a balance by making the individual an inviolable value in himself or herself, while strongly affirming the inherently social nature of the person. Particularly in light of the AIDS crisis, it must be stressed that, in Catholic social teaching, the dignity and equality of each and every person, no matter what his or her condition, is the cornerstone of social justice.

According to John XXIII's encyclical, *Peace on Earth* (1963), every well ordered and just society is founded on the principle that all human persons, by definition, share rights which are "universal, inviolable, and inalienable," including food, clothing, shelter, medical care, "the necessary social services" (nos. 9, 11), and marriage "with equal rights for man and woman" (nos. 15, 16). These rights are the necessary preconditions of the person's contribution to society. "Since men [and women] are social by nature they are meant to live with others and to work for one another's welfare" (no. 31).

Although the recognition of gender equality is a relatively recent development, it has received increasingly greater emphasis in the writings of John Paul II. In *On the Family* (1981), he affirms "the equal dignity and responsibility of men and women" (nos. 22, 23). The Christian message about human dignity is violated when any person is treated simply as "an object of trade" or of the selfish interests of others. "The first victims of this mentality are women." The pope condemns all forms of discrimination against women, and specifically targets organized prostitution, and oppression of childless wives, widows, and unmarried mothers (no. 24).[9]

The basic equality of persons of different classes and races has a long history in Catholic social ethics. The first of the modern social encyclicals, *On the Condition of Labor* (1891), was written to address exploitation of workers that had occurred as a result of capitalism and industrialization. In 1968, Paul VI called all those who are "blessed with abundance" *(On the Development of Peoples,* no. 3) to exercise greater solidarity with all those "who are striving to escape from hunger, misery, endemic diseases, and ignorance," and who seek "a wider share in the benefits of civilization" (no. 1).

This brings us to the central concept of this teaching, the common good. In Catholic tradition *justice* means precisely the association of persons in community according to relationships and structures that serve the

---

9. See also John Paul II, "Letter to Women," written in preparation for the 1995 United Nations World Conference in Beijing on the Status of Women. Therein the pope apologizes for the complicity of representatives of the church in creating discrimination against women, and condemns sexual violence and prostitution as offenses against women.

good of all. Insofar as poverty and gender bias assist the spread of HIV, the recognition of the dignity of every woman and man is an essential precondition of diminishing infection.

The Common Good

EVERY HUMAN PERSON is social by nature, and all persons interdependently exist in communities providing structures that either facilitate or impede their just cooperation. John XXIII's definition of the common good, albeit expressed in male-oriented terminology that has become less pervasive in more recent teaching, well expresses the tradition:

> [T]he common good touches the whole man, the needs both of his body and of his soul . . . the common good of all embraces the sum total of those conditions of social living whereby men are enabled to achieve their own integral perfection more fully and more easily (*Peace on Earth*, nos. 57, 58).

The message is that every member of society has a right of participation in the common good, claiming rights and fulfilling responsibilities; the ultimate purpose of the common good is to enhance the well-being of every single member of society, as well as of society as a whole. The common good includes both the material and the social aspects of human flourishing.

The most notable development of this concept in the decades since the Second Vatican Council is its increasingly global scope. All the members of the world's various communities, large or small, live in solidarity with their fellow human beings, and are called to mutual responsibility. John XXIII and Paul VI frequently use the term "universal common good." John Paul II stresses global interdependence and the need to close the gap between rich and poor in his 1988 encyclical *On the Social Order*. He also has exhorted all cultures to reaffirm the value of all lives, and exhorts every culture to "respect, protect, love and serve life, every human life! Only in this direction will you find justice, development, true freedom, peace, and happiness!" (*Gospel of Life*, no. 5). Writing in celebration of the one hundredth anniversary of the first social encyclical by Leo XIII in 1891, John Paul notes that the "grave imbalances" in wealth among different geographical regions of the world make the task of social ethics fully international (*One Hundredth Year*, 1991, no. 21).[10] Calling for cooperation and solidarity, as

---

10. This is a recurrent theme in the encyclicals. See for example John XXIII, *Mother and Teacher* (1961), no. 157: "[T]he nations that enjoy a sufficiency and abundance of everything may not overlook the plight of other nations whose citizens

well as the restraint of market forces by juridical structures (no. 42), the pope denounces "with absolute clarity" the economic and social exploitation that permits western prosperity while elsewhere reinforcing poverty so abject that it amounts to little more than slavery (no. 61).

The framework of the common good applies to the AIDS crisis on many levels. Obviously, it is incompatible both with the rejection of HIV infected persons in their local communities and with the economic greed that creates the conditions in which AIDS thrives. If prevention is our main concern, then the common good demands that dollars spent for education, testing, and perinatal treatment of infants be much more equally distributed than they are at present. Preventive measures consistent with the common good also mean that equal access to education, health care, and sexual responsible self-determination be guaranteed for all social groups, and to women within every group. Researchers in scientifically advanced cultures have no absolute right to monopolize the benefits of their discoveries, reaping economic rewards while HIV/AIDS runs rampant elsewhere. Trials for AIDS tests and vaccines are conducted in countries like Uganda, Zambia, and Thailand, where many sufferers may be too poor to buy the products developed. While profits are not in themselves immoral, the principle of distributive justice within the common good sets limits of proportion on self-enrichment. To deny the moral necessity of broad, redistributive measures of preventing AIDS is to violate clear and urgent Catholic Church teaching.

Preferential Option for the Poor

THOSE WHO HAVE in the past most greatly suffered from exclusion have a right to preferential compensation in access to social goods. Affirmative action toward those most grievously affected by the AIDS crisis is a duty both of human justice and of Christian love.

John Paul II adopts a "preferential option for the poor" as a biblical value *(One Hundredth Year*, no. 11). He has repeatedly urged a duty of solidarity toward those who are most vulnerable to social ills and direct abuse. "It is above all the 'poor' to whom Jesus speaks in his preaching and actions" (*Gospel of Life*, no. 32), especially those who are sick, suffering, or outcast by society. The pope calls for "solidarity" in "the common good of the entire human family" to end the AIDS crisis, and specifically places persons living with AIDS and their families in a category of preferential concern.

---

experience such domestic problems that they are all but overcome by poverty and hunger, and are not able to enjoy basic human rights. This is all the more so inasmuch as countries each day seem to become more dependent on each other."

The AIDS epidemic calls for a supreme effort of international cooperation on the part of governments, the world medical and scientific community, and all those who exercise influence in developing a sense of moral responsibility in society. The threat is so great that indifference on the part of public authorities, condemnatory, or discriminatory practices toward those affected by the Acquired Immunodeficiency Virus, or self-interested rivalries in the search for a medical answer to this syndrome, should be considered forms of collaboration on this terrible evil which has come upon humanity. . . . Those members of the church will continue to play their part in caring for those who are suffering with AIDS, as Jesus taught his followers to do (Mt. 25:36). . . . Our individual and collective concern for them is a definite measure of our humanity, taken in the loftiest sense of the word.[11]

Most troublesome in this regard are anecdotal accounts of church representatives who discriminate against AIDS sufferers, and who discourage preventive measures because of lack of compassion or outright denigration and hatred of at-risk populations. An international HIV/AIDS educator from an international church-based agency has recounted personal experiences with a bishop who insisted repeatedly at a conference that AIDS was God's punishment on the unrighteous; of another who asked how his clergy could "spot" AIDS patients and so avoid contact with them; and of church workers who argue, against demonstrated facts, that sex education increases illicit sexual activity, and that condoms do not really prevent AIDS infection. In order to preserve the *bella figura*, or "good image" of the church's structures and of its adherents, some Catholics, even those highly placed in the ranks of pastoral responsibility, are willing to distort the truth and to compromise the church's mission of compassion for all.[12] What a disappointment of the pope's promise that "members of the church will continue to play their part in caring for those who are suffering, as Jesus taught his followers to do."[13]

In reality, there are good arguments, well-grounded in Catholic teaching itself, that could justify the use of condoms specifically as means of disease prevention (not contraception), and that could accept needle exchange as a way of reducing the disastrous effects of drug addiction (in programs like those already implemented by Catholic agencies in Australia).[14] Failure

---

11. John Paul II, "The AIDS Epidemic," Address to the Diplomatic Corps in Tanzania, 1 September 1990, *Origins* 20.15 (20 September 1990): 241–43, nos. 3 and 4.

12. Vitillo, "Theological Challenges," and "Ethical Challenges."

13. John Paul II, "The AIDS Epidemic," no. 4.

to be open to these arguments in the face of the increasing toll of the AIDS virus on millions of people who ultimately have little or no responsibility for their infection, raises serious questions about motivation and about sinful social structures in which even the church participates.

Structural Sin

PERSONAL SIN IS not the only cause of the spread of HIV/AIDS. In fact, its role pales in comparison to the aforementioned structures of poverty and gender discrimination that placed most HIV-infected persons at risk. Some of those structures have been described above. Here I will only note that recent Catholic teaching has become ever more sensitive to the social dimension of sin, a reality which makes it morally impossible to "scapegoat" victims without taking a hard look at the pressures that constrain their individual behavior. John Paul II's *On the Social Order* insists that "structures of sin" is a category that should be applied to contemporary social relations more frequently. Moreover, structural sin does not refer to impersonal forces beyond human control, but to "the concrete acts of individuals who introduce these structures, consolidate them, and make them difficult to remove," allowing them to grow stronger "and so influence people's behavior" (no. 36). Local and global institutions of employment, marketing, health care, medical research, marriage, family, gender roles, and sexuality (including a global sex trade in women and children) are all contributing factors in the AIDS crisis.

The development and distribution of vaccines to prevent HIV/AIDS can serve as an example. Results of vaccine trials can be obtained more quickly and with fewer participants when they are conducted in areas, like Botswana and Zimbabwe, where the rate of infection is extremely high. Thus there is a market incentive for First World drug companies to test in these nations. In 1992, at the Amsterdam International Conference on AIDS, Uganda's minister of health made a plea for more equitable access to the fruits of research: "The people of Uganda are offering themselves as subjects in the vaccine trials for the good of all humanity; do not forget us when the vaccines arrive at the marketplace!"[15]

An ethics panel convened by the United Nations has recently recommended easing guidelines requiring that HIV vaccines be tested in the

---

14. See Jon Fuller, "AIDS Prevention: A Challenge to the Catholic Moral Tradition," *America* 175 (28 December 1996): 13–20; and "Needle Exchange: Saving Lives," *America* 179 (18–25 July 1998): 8–11.

15. Vitillo, "Theological Challenges," 5.

manufacturer's country before trials in developing countries.[16] The reason for this is that these trials are still the only realistic means of access to vaccines for *the majority* of people infected with HIV. Those infected by the disease in the most heavily hit countries are still not able to afford the drugs when they are ready for sale. Representatives like Sophia Mukasa Monico, director of an AIDS support organization in Uganda, have been reduced to asking for "more flexibility in the [testing] guidelines right now."[17] The ironic fact that the people of Uganda and similarly devastated countries are in a position of pleading for the privilege of being research subjects for the ultimate well-being of the wealthy nations, whose economic practices have contributed to the spread of HIV/AIDS in the first place, illustrates well the health effects of structural sin in a global economy in which profit overrides personal dignity and human rights as the reigning standard of the social order.

Subsidiarity

SOCIAL STRUCTURES, OF course, are complex and multilayered. A continuing theme of the encyclicals is the interdependence of local, national or federal, multinational and global levels of organization and authority. While the principle of subsidiarity was originally proposed to protect the autonomy of local associations from heavy-handed control by the state (Pius XI, *Fortieth Year*, 1931, no. 79), the converse meaning of the principle is that governmental authority should intervene to correct imbalances among groups and institutions in society (for example, John XXIII, *Mother and Teacher*, nos. 53, 54).

Both kinds of efforts are necessary to combat AIDS. Many examples of international and regional efforts can be found in the literature of Caritas Internationalis, as well as instances of local outreach, aid, and education programs.[18] Representatives at international conferences increasingly highlight the importance of grassroots efforts at AIDS education and prevention. One reason for the relatively great effectiveness of community-based programs is that they alone can be fully sensitive to the cultural conditions that transmit or discourage HIV infection. Only at the local level can the relationships of trust be established that are so necessary to motivate

---

16. Lawrence K. Altman, "Ethics Panel Urges Easing of Curbs on AIDS Vaccine Tests," *New York Times*, 28 June 1998, A6.

17. Ibid.

18. See the educational packet, *Caritas Internationalis and the Global AIDS Pandemic*, Rome, Caritas International.

change in long-standing, culturally sanctioned practices. Caritas has stimulated local response to AIDS by providing HIV testing kits; medical supplies; home based care; training personnel to raise awareness of AIDS; training in pastoral care, counseling, and family support; provision of educational materials, and programs for AIDS orphans. To the degree that all these efforts raise consciousness about HIV/AIDS and encourage empathy with and respect for at-risk populations, driving AIDS out from under the cover of shame and secrecy that allows it to breed, all are part of the preventive effort. Such initiatives are most effective when they nurture networks of collaboration and accountability in a spirit of solidarity, building partnerships that "empower people to improve their own situation."[19]

---

19. Maura O'Donohue, M.M.M., "A General Overview of the HIV/AIDS Pandemic," in *Caritas Internationalis and the Global AIDS Pandemic,* 22.

10.
CASUISTRY AND AIDS: A REFLECTION ON THE CATHOLIC TRADITION

Paulinus Ikechukwu Odozor, C.S.Sp.

THE HIV/AIDS SITUATION in Nigeria, as in many other parts of Africa, is becoming serious. Some researchers suspect that about four percent of the one hundred ten million Nigerians might be HIV positive. This would represent a significant increase from 1992 when about two percent of the population was thought to be carrying the AIDS virus.

This essay is about the strengths and weaknesses of casuistry when faced with the personal and social complexities of a phenomenon like AIDS and HIV prevention. Already the HIV/AIDS epidemic is forcing us to rethink some of our moral principles and presuppositions. To illustrate this point, I shall begin the discussion by examining two real life cases from a hospital in Nigeria. Anyone who is familiar with AIDS and HIV infection anywhere in the world will recognize the familiar challenges which stories like these pose to casuistry in the Catholic tradition.

Case 1

OKAFOR AND AMAKA have been married for twenty-five years. During a recent trip to the doctor, Okafor tests positive with HIV. He forbids the doctor from letting anyone know of his condition, including his wife Amaka, who was at this time HIV negative. Amaka is uneducated and knows very little about symptoms associated with HIV/AIDS infection. Sometime later, Okafor comes down with AIDS. It is only at this point that he decides to tell his wife of his condition himself. The wife returns to hospital for tests and discovers she is HIV positive. The case for casuistry here is whether the doctor should have maintained confidentiality or not?

It is generally recognized that the doctor has a duty as a physician to uphold confidentiality. This duty is grounded in the patient's right to control sensitive information about himself or herself. As John Arras and Bonnie Steinbock note, "confidentiality provides vital protection both to the interests of patients and to the very existence of the physician-patient relationship. It functions to maintain the very possibility of a productive relationship between physician and patients." If prospective patients doubt the physician's willingness to keep secrets, they may not seek help in the first place.[1] The question here is whether there are limits to confidentiality. Should the doctor have insisted on letting Amaka know of Okafor's condition? How would traditional casuistry handle such a case?

Traditional moral theology would maintain the duty of the professional such as a doctor in regard to his/her patient, the lawyer in regard to his/her client, the priest in regard to the penitent to absolute secrecy concerning matters they have come to know about in their professional capacities. However, while the tradition is uncompromising regarding the obligation of the priest to maintain confidentiality in matters pertaining to the confessional, it makes room for possible exceptions in other cases.

Edwin Healy, who authored one of the handbooks of moral theology which was used in Catholic seminaries and universities before Vatican II, maintains, for example, that doctor/patient confidentiality is binding at all times except in the following situations: the one who entrusts the secret consents to its divulgement; the secret has become public knowledge; such a disclosure would avert grave harm to society in general; the revelation is necessary in order "to avert grave harm from the one communicating or from the one receiving the secret;" or in a situation where guarding the secret may cause harm to an innocent third party. Healy illustrates this last point this way:

> If a man who is about to marry a healthy girl is found to be infected with a venereal disease in its active state, the doctor should urge him to inform the girl of this disease or else postpone the marriage until a complete cure can be effected. If the patient refuses and insists on going ahead with the marriage, the physician may warn the girl of the impending danger to health. He need not warn her if to do so would entail grave inconvenience for him, since the obligation is one of charity only.[2]

---

1. John D. Arras and Bonnie Steinbock, "Foundations of the Health Professional–Patient Relationship," in *Ethical Issues in Modern Medicine*, fourth edition (London: Mayfield Publishing Company, 1997), 47.

2. Edwin F. Healy, *Moral Guidance: A Textbook in Principles of Conduct for Colleges and Universities* (Chicago, Ill: Loyola University Press, 1942), 307. See also Leroy Walters, "Ethical Aspects of Medical Confidentiality," in Tom L. Beauchamp and Leroy Walters, eds., *Contemporary Issues in Bioethics*, second edition (Belmont, Calif.: Wadsworth Publishing Company, 1982), 198–203.

There are two related sets of issues in the Okafor/Amaka story. The first is the question of the conflict of goods: Okafor's reputation versus Amaka's life. The casuistic resolution of this aspect of the case would be similar to that of the hypothetical case reported here by Healy and based on proportionate reasoning. The solution was arrived at on the basis of a hierarchy of values. In Healy's example above, the reasoning seems to be that the health of the girl ranks higher than the harm to the man's reputation. Ultimately, however, the convenience of the physician seems paramount to any other consideration, including, even the health of the girl. Healy considered the obligation to protect the life of the woman in this case a duty of charity only. However, there is also in this case, as in the Okafor/Amaka case, a conflict of duties of justice to two different parties. Here as well the notion of a hierarchy of values should help us determine which is the higher and therefore more important value to pursue in the case.

An important question to ask is whether HIV/AIDS cases like Amaka and Okafor's introduce any new feature which could alter the casuistic approach of traditional theology in matters relating to confidentiality in patient/physician relationships? The physician involved in the case told me that Okafor gave him two reasons for insisting on the doctor's silence. He feared the social ostracism that might result from a third party (even his wife) knowing of his condition. More importantly he feared Amaka might leave him if she knew he had HIV. In other words, he feared for his reputation and for his marriage, especially as he was a man of some standing in the society. These features are not necessarily new, however.

The "new" feature which would play a prominent part in our consideration is the morally obliging consciousness concerning the equality of women. Such consciousness brings out more clearly the right of the wife both in Healy's example and in the Amaka/Okafor story to be told the truth even if that meant going against the husband's preference to risk her life to save his reputation and keep his marriage. It shows up the injustice to the woman in the situation where confidentiality, reputation, and professional convenience can be preferred to the health and life of the woman.

Case 2

JANE AND JOSEPH are devout married Catholics with three children, ages eighteen, fourteen, and twelve. Jane, a hospital worker, contracted HIV at work, through exposure to infected blood. Her HIV infection has not yet led to AIDS. Jane and Joseph have both been to their pastor for advice on whether to use condoms or not. The pastor is genuinely sympathetic to the plight of the couple but states that the teaching of the church absolutely prohibits the use of condoms. Joseph loves his wife, who on all accounts appears very healthy still. They have no intention of living as brother and sister. The question for casuistry here is how to preserve the value of openness to fecundity through noncontraceptive intercourse, maintain this marriage, and even keep an innocent third party (Joseph) from being infected.

Analysis

IN ROMAN CATHOLIC theology, casuistry signifies that aspect of moral theology which deals with the application of moral principles to singular facts.[3] Casuistry presupposes rules. And to talk of casuistry is to wrestle with the force and function of moral norms, especially in situations of moral conflict. In the first case above, the rule of confidentiality is in conflict with the need to spare an innocent third party from contracting HIV with possibly fatal results. In the second case, the important values inherent in noncontraceptive intercourse are in conflict with values of Christian marriage and again with life.

The role of casuistry in these cases is to find practical solutions which would safeguard all the values intrinsic to the situations thus described. As Werner Stark points out, beside being a claim that rules have limits, casuistry is also an admission that rules are not self-interpreting and can neither resolve ambiguities nor settle the claims of conflicting moral principles. In its best sense, Stark says, "casuistry is opposed to inflexible or legalistic interpretation of moral rules; indeed casuistry rejects any attitude which absolutizes a general and abstract norm, and insists on its all-round unyielding and quasi mechanical application, while at the same time denying any abatement or adjustment to contingencies."[4]

Moral norms are an important way that communities capture and preserve in a rather terse manner some of the values they consider important for human flourishing. From experience built up over the years and from many authoritative sources, communities come to some appreciation of these values. Because norms are a human articulation of value, they may sometimes be incomplete in their expression of the values in question. Thus, the need for constant revision of some of the norms that govern human conduct. Casuistry is an important way of effecting these revisions, which may lead to the abrogation of particular norms, the enlargement of some others, or the refinement of yet others. Casuistry is thus an important

---

3. Edouard Hamel, "Casuistry," in *The New Catholic Encyclopedia* (San Francisco: Catholic University Press, 1967), 3:195.

4. Werner Stark, "Casuistry," in *The Dictionary of the History of Ideas* (New York: Charles Scribner's Sons), 1:257.

way that individuals and communities negotiate their ethical beliefs when faced with moral issues.[5]

In the cases above, the community's ethical belief comes in contact with new realities which raise questions about the principles. The question of confidentiality, whether in the priest/penitent or the doctor/patient setting, is understood by the Catholic tradition as important on the ground that everyone has a right to his/her good name and must not be deprived of it without proportionate reason. There is, at least in the confessor/penitent setting, also a strongly consequentialist fear of the violation of such a principle. Some philosophers would add that there is also a human right involved here—the right of privacy.

Concerning this particular right, Samuel Warren and Louis Brandeis wrote that the common law secured "to each individual the right of determining, ordinarily, to what extent his thoughts, sentiments, and emotions shall be communicated to others."[6] The kind of people we are as a Christian community thus forbids the spreading of information about anyone which would expose them in ways that could be detrimental to their well-being. This is an indication of a particular construal of the world. It is this mode of construal of the world which is the source of the moral quandary in this case. For, assuming that confidentiality were not considered as important as it is here, there would be no moral quandary. The same is true also of the second case. The Catholic tradition has constantly condemned in rather strong terms the disvalue in contraceptive intercourse. When faced with AIDS and its consequences, the question of contraception assumes new dimensions. The question here is whether the use of condoms to prevent AIDS in a marriage where one of the partners is already a carrier of the AIDS virus is contraceptive. Some people argue that contraception in this case is only an unintended side effect of the effort to prevent the transmission of disease, and therefore does not amount to a violation of the law forbidding contraceptive intercourse even within marriage. Thus the use of condoms in this instance, the argument continues, is one more example of the hierarchy of values at work in the casuistic tradition. Life and marriage are here seen as higher values to be preserved when faced with this rather regrettable choice. Thus, when faced with AIDS and its consequences, the community is forced to rethink its moral principles and presuppositions. The goal is not to abandon the result of many years of communal wisdom taught authoritatively by the

---

5. See James Keenan, "Making a Case for Casuistry: AIDS and its Ethical Challenges," *Hva er Kasuistikk? Om moralsk laering og refleksjon tilknytning til forbilder og eksempler*, Jon Wetlesen, ed. (Oslo: Universitet, 1998), 163–86.

6. Walters, "Ethical Aspects of Medical Confidentiality," 199–200.

magisterium of the church. Rather, it is to find imaginatively creative ways of understanding or coming to terms with the community's ethical commitment in the face of this entirely new and devastating phenomenon. As Stanley Hauerwas has shown, this role belongs to casuistry. Says Hauerwas, "casuistry is the mode of reflection a community employs to test imaginatively the often unnoticed and unacknowledged implications of its narrative commitments."[7]

Catholic moral casuistic tradition has always paid attention to circumstances, principles, and the individual conscience in the search for solutions to the problems which new phenomena raise for the individual and society.[8] In the words of Thomas Aquinas, circumstances can be defined as "whatever conditions are outside the substance of an act, and yet in some way touch the human act."[9] Aquinas believed that the commensurability of an act to an end, the goodness or evil of an act, as well as the voluntariness of an act can sometimes depend very much on the circumstances.[10] Thus, circumstances "highlight the uniqueness of one situation from all others" and can make an enormous difference in the way we see a case and arrive at an appropriate moral judgment.[11] Even so, the casuist tries to establish the connection between differing yet similar cases and, through the use of analogy, tries to find a solution to new cases.[12] Principles are also important as one tries to negotiate one's ethical beliefs in the face of new moral problems. These serve as guides to illumine agents' ways as they wade through the maze of often confusing data.

There are two possible pitfalls in regard to principles. One is to overgeneralize their effectiveness and relevance, and to seek to force all moral problems to yield to their demand. However, as Jonsen and Toulmin have

---

7. Stanley Hauerwas, "Casuistry as a Narrative Art," *Interpretation* 37 (1983): 381.

8. See Albert R. Jonsen and Stephen Toulmin, *The Abuse of Casuistry: A History of Moral Reasoning* (Berkeley: University of California Press, 1988), 123–36. See also James F. Keenan and Thomas Shannon, "Contexts of Casuistry: Historical and Contemporary," in *The Context of Casuistry*, James F. Keenan and Thomas A. Shannon, eds. (Washington, D.C.: Georgetown University Press, 1995), 221–31.

9. Thomas Aquinas, *Summa Theologiae* (translated by the Fathers of the English Dominican Province), I–IIae, q. 7, art. 1.

10. Ibid. See also ST, 1–IIae, q. 18, art. 10.

11. ST, 1a–IIae, q. 100, art. 1. See also Paulinus I. Odozor, "Proportionalists and the Principle of Double Effect: A Review Discussion," *Christian Bioethics* 3.2 (1997): 124.

12. James Keenan and Thomas Shannon, "Contexts of Casuistry: Historical and Contemporary," 223.

pointed out, every moral maxim, rule, or other form of generalization "applies to certain actual situations centrally and unambiguously, but to others only marginally or ambiguously."[13] The other pitfall to avoid is the antinomianism which can result from the urgent need to help people who are struggling with weighty matters in situations of moral conflict. Sound casuistry is therefore not restricted just to definition, interpretation, and application of principles of conduct to past or future action. Its purpose extends, as Kenneth Kirk says, "to the discovery of methods along which those principles can truly be interpreted and applied as need arises, or along which conflict of principles can be solved; and in virtue of which the solutions proposed can be vindicated."[14]

Casuistry and AIDS: Strengths and Weaknesses

THE ISSUES OF confidentiality and contraception apropos of HIV/AIDS, though among the earliest and most persistent questions posed by the epidemic to moral reasoning, are by no means the only ones. The HIV/AIDS phenomenon is raising extraordinary moral questions in other ways as well. James Keenan has noted the problem posed by the drug thalidomide which was pulled out of the market initially because of its side effects. Many babies were born with phocomelia by mothers who used the drug. It has been discovered recently that thalidomide is effective in the cure of some AIDS-related conditions. The problem is whether the drug should be used knowing that even men can pass the drug through their sperm to women. Thus there is no zero risk situation for unborn children. Other problems concern the allocation of scarce medical and financial resources; the question of experimentation either on humans or on primates in the effort to find a cure for HIV/AIDS; and the rights of individual patients, especially pregnant women, to refuse treatment on the grounds of intrusion into their privacy, even though such refusal would almost certainly jeopardize the health of the unborn child.[15]

One of the strengths of casuistic discourse is its pliability. Many authors have shown how casuistry has expanded to include new developments in the areas of usury, slavery, marriage, and religious freedom, for example.[16] In this sense casuistry is an open-ended affirmation of the different

---

13. Albert R. Jonsen and Stephen Toulmin, *The Abuse of Casuistry*, 8.

14. Kenneth E. Kirk, *Conscience and its Problems: An Introduction to Casuistry* (London: Longmans, Green, 1927), 111.

15. James Keenan, "Making a Case for Casuistry," 9.

16. See John T. Noonan Jr., "Development in Moral Doctrine," in *The Context of Casuistry*, 188–220.

ramifications of truth. In spite of the newness and complexity of HIV/AIDS, there are powerful instruments which are available in the casuistic tradition that provide a context and guidelines for appropriate moral responses to the HIV/AIDS epidemic. One instrument is the notion of an *ordo bonorum*.

The casuistic tradition's belief in an *ordo bonorum*—that is, a hierarchy of values—goes back to Cicero's time. In the third book of his *De Officiis*, which has been described as "the cradle of casuistry,"[17] Cicero discusses the way "a decision ought to be reached, in case that which has the appearance of being morally right clashes with that which seems to be expedient."[18] In cases of doubt and ambiguity, there is need to examine the available options closely for it could happen, "owing to exceptional circumstances, that what is accustomed under ordinary circumstances to be considered morally wrong is found to not be morally wrong."[19] Such examination is made easier if we recognize that within particular situations, some things are more important and therefore take precedence over others. And the idea of a hierarchy of values implies that "all things being equal, the higher value has to be given priority."[20] For example, the casuistic tradition has given special place to human life as the basis for the actualization of all other values. Thus solutions that are in favor of life are more in keeping with the best insights of our moral tradition. The two cases above can certainly benefit from this bias toward life.

Although life is a very high priority, it is not, however, an absolute value. The casuistic tradition is conscious of the fact that life cannot be maintained at all costs. In the issue of the allocation of scarce resources for the cure of AIDS, for example, it could imply that in each circumstance, people should be given whatever is possible at that particular time in their locality, without overtaxing available resources. Sometimes the AIDS lobby can become too powerful and therefore force public authority to allocate a disproportionate percentage of public resources to the search for cures of AIDS, while other medical needs are left unanswered. The casuistic tradition can help us in the search for ways of prudently allocating scarce resources to all medical needs by conscientizing us to the urgency of some problems over others.

It is one of the strengths of the casuistic tradition that it recognizes that certain urgent situations can call for extraordinary actions—the parent

---

17. Albert Jonsen and Stephen Toulmin, *The Abuse of Casuistry*, 83.

18. Marcus Tullus Cicero, *De Officiis*, trans. W. Miller (Cambridge Mass.: Harvard University Press, 1961), Bk. III. 2 (8).

19. *De Officiis*, III 4 (18).

20. Louis Janssens, "Norms and Priorities in a Love Ethics," *Louvain Studies* 6 (1977), 229.

who steals a loaf of bread to save a child dying of hunger, or the person who equivocates when he knows that telling the truth would cause mortal harm to a third party. These insights are present in the casuistic tradition and can be used *mutatis mutandis* to treat HIV/AIDS related cases.

HIV/AIDS infection is extraordinary in many ways. The most important is that it is a total assault on the human person. Other diseases attack some aspects of the human body. By attacking the immune system, HIV/AIDS affects the total person in every ramification: physical, social, spiritual, and psychological. The very personhood of the human being is the basis for all other goods—even the good of eternal life. Any casuistic attempt to find a solution to the moral problems raised by HIV/AIDS must take this fact into account. Even if it cannot find a solution to all other moral issues involved in the HIV/AIDS question, it must help the patient toward the rediscovery of her/his personhood. Okafor, in our first case above, was very much aware of the total loss entailed in HIV/AIDS.

Casuistry at its worst can lead to the loss of moral idealism. This happens when the method is used as a means to escape what Edward Leroy Long describes as the "high demands of God," thereby forcing conscience to settle for "less than perfect expressions of the standard to which it gives full devotion."[21] As Jonsen and Toulmin demonstrate, this has happened at various times in the past. The result is that even today, some people still consider casuistry to be synonymous with sophistry, for example.

There are two ways casuistry apropos of HIV/AIDS can escape the twin temptations of both the loss of moral idealism and a reactive rigorism. One is to make sure that it has as its goal the search for the good of the human person integrally and adequately considered. This means that the person's social, psychological, physical, spiritual, religious, and other needs have to be considered in the *ordo bonorum*. Another way is to ensure that the search for casuistic solutions to moral problems posed by HIV/AIDS is directed by persons with common sense who are able "to recognize what is at issue in new and hitherto untried situations" and are capable of coming to terms with the demands of varieties of persons and situations by drawing from past experiences and considering future possibilities.[22] Only prudent people like this can be of help in the search for ways to find solutions to the ethical problems which the HIV/AIDS phenomenon is constantly raising for individuals and communities all over the world.

---

21. Edward Leroy Long Jr., *Conscience and Compromise: An Approach to Protestant Casuistry* (Philadelphia: Westminster Press, 1954), 18.

22. Jonsen and Toulmin, *The Abuse of Casuistry*, are actually summarizing the views of St. Thomas Aquinas on the notion of a prudent person, at 130.

11.
FROM RESPONSIBLE TO MEANINGFUL SEXUALITY: AN ETHICS OF GROWTH AS AN ETHICS OF MERCY FOR YOUNG PEOPLE IN THIS ERA OF AIDS

Roger Burggraeve

I AIM TO develop an ethical model of thought concerning relational upbringing which is educational. Concretely, I intend to do justice to both the contribution of Christian-human ideals of life as well as the contribution of experience and the social sciences. In addition, we should not lose sight of the factual modes of experience in their concrete societal situation as in our western European society affected by, among others, the current AIDS problem.[1] Otherwise, we will neither educationally guide young people "from where they stand," nor concretely help them grow toward a meaningfully human and Christian sexual life.

Responsible Sexuality

As A STARTING point, we take the concrete reality of the sexual behavior among young people. This does not mean, however, that I pose this reality as an ethical or educational norm.

Generally speaking, I can state that in Western society, there are more and more young people who first have sexual contacts—and this happens even more early and frequently—before they start "going steady," which is

---

1. Roman Bleistein, "Zwischen Antipädagogik und postmoderner Pädagogik. Neuere Theorieen in der Erziehungswissenschaft," *Stimmen der Zeit* (1992), 147–62.

to say, before they have a stable relationship with a more or less pronounced prospect for the future.

What is of great importance for our discussion is the distinction between the different types of coital behavior among adolescents, even if in reality these cannot be easily separated from each other.

Regarding a first type, we can speak of casual sex where the momentary genital experience takes center stage, detached from or performed only within a minimal relational context. We can also call these "detached" or "occasional" sexual contacts, insofar as they are characterized by momentary interactions. What is notable is that young people who turn to such sexual "experiences" often make a clear distinction between occasional or transient sex partners and real friends with whom they do not have sex. The latter are there for friendship—to exchange feelings, experiences, and mutual understanding.

Another type of intimate sexual behavior is embedded in a more and more pronounced form of relationship, one that is not without quality but continues to bear, nonetheless, a temporary character. The perspective toward the future is not *a priori* excluded, but neither is it included; it is rather left in the middle. Insofar as this form of relationship represents a kind of in-between form between "detached" and "stable," we speak of a "semidetached" relationship where the emphasis falls on the "detached" rather than on the "stable."

Then again, intimate sexual behavior within semidetached forms of relationships must be distinguished from—and this not only factually-sociologically but also ethically and educationally—the sexual intimacy within a stable relationship with a clear future prospect or a steady relationship in the strict sense of the term.

The Ethical Bottom Line: The No-Harm Principle

On the ethical level, the possible consequences of HIV infection and the ever fatal AIDS as well as undesired pregnancies require first of all the application of the "ethical minimum." This can be formulated both positively as "just sexuality" and negatively as the "no-harm principle." Whatever view one may have on "meaningful sexuality," in each type of sexual behavior, justice must be respected. The negative rule of action, "you shall do no harm," guarantees a minimum of human dignity in situations where the meaningful is only minimally or partially realized.[2]

---

2. Rita Süssmuth, *AIDS: Wege aus der Angst* (Hamburg: Hoffmann und Campe, 1987), 92–100.

The absolute minimal responsibility for young people who move into intimate sexual contact with their occasional, varying, or semidetached partners, concretely consists in taking the necessary efficient measures so that pregnancy, HIV and other sexually transmitted diseases (STDs), and infections are prevented. This is a form of respect for life, the bottom line of which is expressed by the commandment "you shall not kill." Not only does it require respect toward one's own life and health, but also toward that of the partner and of the possible third person who can be conceived (or infected by oneself or the partner). It is also a form of honesty toward society which is often saddled with the "consequences" when one does not take up one's responsibility. This prevention is an urgent moral duty and not a noncommittal advice or recommendation. To maintain the contrary —which is to say, to not recognize this minimal duty of responsible sexuality—would manifest either a hopeless naivety and a lack of common sense, or a far-reaching cynicism.

Responsible sexuality implies also the task of obtaining information. Individuals should correctly inform themselves about risky behavior—that is, about the actual scope of their actions and about adequate prevention of unacceptable results of their behavior. Ignorance is a terrible adviser. Due to the seriousness of undesired pregnancy and all sorts of infectious diseases, the person involved surely cannot disregard this aspect.[3] However, it is not as simple to determine which information is the most reliable and which information best serves human dignity. That is why society, which is responsible for the general welfare and public health, has a duty toward prevention and information. This can be achieved, among others means, via adequate and responsible campaigns and support programs, with respect for privacy, human rights, and different ethical convictions and principles.

An Educational Perspective: The Formation of Motivation

Responsible sexuality, however, not only presupposes that one aptly informs oneself, but also that one is prepared to act accordingly to prevent more serious consequences. This requires necessary motivation. When obtaining correct information is not coupled with sufficient motivation, adequate preventive action will easily fall through.

Not only is a "knowledge of affairs" necessary; there is also a need for "conviction" and decisiveness in the sexual dealing with others to live up

---

3. August Wilhelm von Eiff, AIDS. Gefährdung und Vorsorge. Strategien einer Aufklärung (Freiburg: Herder, 1988), 33–35; Patrick Verspieren, "SIDA: la nécessaire vigilance," Études 366 (1987): 481–83.

to safe-sex behavior and to refuse nonsafe-sex behavior. At the same time, a constant initiative and perseverance is needed not only to maintain responsible sexual behavior toward possible partners, but also to maintain and carry this through when large or small obstacles appear. By the fact that the condom was known as an "anti-AIDS-measure" it can easily take on a negative connotation. Sexologists point out that this could lead to people making more use of the condom only in the first time of acute AIDS-fear, but afterwards in intimate relationships resist it as a demeaning medium. There are indications that young people consider the pill as a contraceptive measure that establishes love and trust, while the condom is associated with loose sexual behavior or "dirty sex," and furthermore becomes a symbol of distrust toward the partner.[4]

The need for motivation also presupposes the necessary training in assertiveness, namely in the "art of saying no" when one does not want to have sex, or in the ability to say no to risky behavior when one does engage in sexual contacts or relations. Young people must therefore be prepared for the implications of sexual behavior so that they actually learn to take responsibility for their own actions. In this way, surprises from the first can be avoided. In this regard, some sexologists point to how girls especially should develop a stronger feeling of self-worth and become more assertive toward boys. Naturally, it is just as important that boys commence a similar process of consciousness-raising so that they become cognizant of the actual imbalances and possible male dominance structures of the "negotiation process." They should especially learn to take the girls themselves—their experiences, feelings, concerns, and their choices—into consideration.

The No-Violence Principle

We reach a second ethical principle that is of utmost importance not only in a minimal sexual ethics, but in every sexual and relational upbringing—namely, the "principle of equality," formulated in the negative as the "no-violence principle." From our fundamental orientation toward the other, we are essentially relational beings. For the experience of sexuality, it follows that we are not only to approach ourselves with respect, but that we also need to be aware of the dignity of the other person—that is, the equality of every other, of the partner in particular. Equality on a relational and sexual level then implies that one accords the other just as much value as oneself. Minimally, this means that in no way whatsoever—whether by

---

4. Xavier Thévenot, "Le parti de l'existence," in Emmanuel Hirsch, ed., *Le sida. Rumeurs et faits* (Paris: Éditions du Cerf, 1987), 185–87.

physical violence, or by emotional, moral or social blackmail (for example, by making use of the group or societal-ethos as a means of exerting pressure)—should a person be forced, directly or indirectly, to have sexual contact. In no way should a person force another to have sex or to violate the exclusive committed relationship of others.

The norm of equality likewise rejects all double standard sexual morals which discriminate against certain persons or groups to the advantage of others on the basis of an alleged "difference of values," whether or not it is legitimized metaphysically, social-scientifically, or socially. Thus, there can be no separate sexual ethics for men and another for women by means of which men would have easier and more access to sexual fulfilment than women, and this on the basis of one or another claim of the so-called female inferiority.

From a minimal interpretation of our human-Christian view on humane sexuality, justice and equality become the foundation for a meaningful experience of sexuality. These minimum values should not be lacking in any sexual experience if it is to be worthy of human dignity.

From Responsible to Meaningful Sexuality

HOWEVER NECESSARY THE appeal to responsible sexuality may be, it is surely inadequate for a sexual and relational upbringing which intends to be qualitative and Christian at the same time. That is why I wish to make it clear that prevention, even if it is based on the ethical minimum of responsibility and a principle of "do-no-harm," cannot even be our starting point for a Christian ethics.

An Ethics of Fear

A number of (converging) risks are involved in an ethics that primarily concentrates on the consequences of a behavior. If in the weighing of consequences we stop especially at the negative results, then there is a chance that we may end up in an "ethics of fear." Undoubtedly it can be a sign of common sense and a sense of reality that one takes into account the consequences of certain actions in an honest way. But by means of an exaggerated focusing on the sometimes pernicious consequences of certain behaviors, the ethical accompaniment can evolve into an "ethics of fear" that tries to induce people, especially young people, toward obedience or a return to the norm (posed by the church, for instance).[5]

---

5. Helmut Piechowiak, *Eingriffe in menschliches Lebens. Sinn und Grenzen ärztlichen Handelns* (Frankfurt am Main: J. Knecht, 1987), 238–45.

That such an "ethics of fear" is not entirely illusory today can be proved, among other means, by the negative-moralizing way in which the AIDS problematic at times was and is manipulated ethically and educationally, from a religious perspective or otherwise. Some see AIDS as a good opportunity to return to the former repressive and negative morals of control. From the frightening consequences of interchanging sexual contacts, they try to make young people especially, and adults as well, return to premarital and extramarital sexual abstinence and monogamy. These norms intending to protect the quality of sexual relational life deserve better arguments, however.[6]

Instrumentalization of Sexuality

The "ethics of fear" sketched above has an ally in the purely medical-hygienic contention that is present especially on the functional level of "instrumental values" and pays little or no attention at all to the level of "final or goal values." Concretely, such a contention provides information ("advice") about the function of the sexual organs and on the negative consequences that this function can have, among others, on life and health. At the same time, it discusses how these negative results, deadly or otherwise, can be avoided or remedied, for instance, how HIV infection can be prevented by means of "safe sex" and an efficient use of condoms. This discourse ("how does it work and how do you prevent it from happening"), however, is not framed within a view of the qualitative formation of relationships.[7]

A technical-instrumental approach to the prevention of AIDS (and other negative consequences) easily evolves into a clinical and objectifying view on the formation of relationships and sexuality. By putting emphasis on "safe" sex, for instance, one runs the risk of reducing sexual experience to a dangerous activity when one has unprotected sex. A technical prevention discourse, usually framed medically, often sees "no further than the tip of a condom" so that one loses track of the psycho-sexual and emotional components which make the use of condoms a not always so smooth—and therefore risky—learning process. By a merely technical and informative approach, moreover, attention both to the integral-human meaning of

---

6. Ernst Fuchs, "Le sida, réflexions éthiques," in Jean Martin, ed., *Faire face au SIDA* (Lausanne: Favre, 1988), 62–65.

7. R. and A. Gaedt, "Die Last mit der Lust: Im Religionsunterricht über Liebe und AIDS sprechen," in Friedrich Koch, ed., *Sexualerziehung und AIDS* (Hamburg: Bergmann and Helbig, 1992), 21–28.

sexual experience and to the quality of human relationships is in danger of being lost. This form of "psycho-sexual and educational negligence" has nonetheless been frequently present in sex education projects in school, in youth-training, and in public life.

We should not start, then, with the AIDS-problematic and its medical and instrumental aspects, nor from the fears of an unwanted pregnancy, nor from contraception aimed at preventing that pregnancy, if we want to help young people toward competency in relationships and a meaningful experience of sexuality. Preventive realism cannot be the decisive foundation for an actual humane sexual ethics which approaches human sexuality as a potential for contact, relationship, solidarity, and fertility.[8] As "good" news, the gospel endorses no negative ethics of fear or anxiety, but rather a positive ethics of love that "as the qualitative ethics of human excellence" appeals to "that which is humanly beautiful." From this foundation, a sensitivity to relationships and the love-competence of every person give shape to sexual faculties. Even the "calamity" that ensues from possible immoral or ethically less edifying sexual activity becomes, for a Christian inspired ethics, a summons and a challenge to investigate how such behavior implies a denial of love.[9]

Tenderness and Authenticity

All these considerations on the relationship between prevention and sexual ethics illustrates how urgent it is to pose the question of "what is humanly desirable." On the sexual level, this is the question of "meaningful sexuality" and of the way in which this "meaningful sexual life" has its best chances and possibilities.[10]

Out of Christian inspiration, a relational and sexual education guides young people in their growth toward a "meaningful sexual life" by facing the task of providing an "ethical optimum" as a "goal to strive for" (Zielgebot). This literally "pro-vocative" or "forward-summoning" contribution must therefore happen through an inviting, youth-friendly, and communicative language which provides color and beauty to its argumentation. This "aesthetics of ethics" brings reflection and taste into an educational unity in the awareness that the way toward a meaningful experience

8. J. Gründel, "AIDS-ethische Herausforderung an die ganze Menschheit," in Jurgen Mickisch and Raul Niemann, eds., Positiv oder Negativ? AIDS als Schicksal und Chance (Güterslöher: Haus Mohn Verlag, 1988), 119–20.

9. Johannes Reiter, AIDS. Wege aus der Krankheit (Cologne: Heilen, 1988), 19–22.

10. Guy Durand, L'éducation sexuelle (Montreal: Fides, 1985), 15–18.

of sexuality sometimes runs over twisting paths. Some young people do not or only partially reach this goal, marked as they are by a number of psychosocial conditions.[11]

Responsibility and equality must therefore become tenderness, understood in a rather broadened sense as a quality of presence not only to oneself but likewise and especially to the other. I opt for the word tenderness because it evokes a bodily connotation which renders a merely "spiritual" interpretation of quality of presence impossible. In this way, the bodily as sensitivity and longing is not only a means but also a source of the so-called spiritual. We understand tenderness in a relationship as a mutual acceptance of each other as one actually is, with one's specific sexual qualities, vulnerabilities, imperfections, wealth, and opportunities. Tenderness, however, is more than accepting and concurring with oneself and one's partner; it also promotes each other to become what one can most profoundly become both as a person and as a man and woman, without destroying each other's differences in a blended unity. That is why it is not coincidental that the Christian tradition connects exclusivity and fidelity as foundational conditions for sexual activity.

This quality of presence, being not only spiritual but integral and thus bodily, requires in its turn an authenticity, the minimal condition of which is given by the commandment "you shall not bear false witness." Sincerity means living as much as possible in harmony of thought, feeling, and action. The authenticity of partners toward each other consists in their manner of approaching each other, keeping pace as much as possible with the intimacy of the whole relationship. This implies that bodily gestures express signs of and incentives toward a deeper involvement, that the body represents what lives within the whole person and adds an extra dimension to it out of its very own dynamism.

It is common experience that one cannot give a univocal meaning to any particular gesture. Gestures, expressions, and signs have their own inner force of meaning and expressive depth. They expound a particular level of feeling and intimacy. To the extent that the body is more deeply involved in the relationship with the other, all the more is the entire person expressed therein. And, conversely, to the extent the relationship goes deeper, all the more intimately is the body involved therein. This growing force of expression of bodily gestures and signs, however, does not happen automatically. Body languages can be poor or rich, sincere or hypocritical, superficial or profound, formal or warm. The more intimate the gesture, all the more does it engage the whole person in all her or his dimensions, feelings, thoughts, and deeds.

---

11. Dietmar Mieth, "Christliche Sexualethik," Wilhelm Ernst, ed., *Grundlagen und Probleme der heutigen Moraltheologie* (Würzburg: Echter, 1989), 256–64.

This is seen in the Christian experience discovered in coitus, the symbol of the "coire," literally "going together."[12] The sexual deed through which man and woman give themselves to each other is, as John Paul II writes in *Familiaris Consortio* (no. 11), much more than a mere biological given. It touches the inner being of the person. The complete bodily surrender is a lie if it is not a sign and a fruit of the full personal surrender wherein the entire person, even in one's temporal dimension, is present.[13]

An Ethics of Mercy for Young People on the Way

FROM AN OPTION for an ethically qualitative and at the same time realistic education for a meaningful experience of relationship and sexuality, I want to sketch a few elements of a growth-ethics for the actual sexual relational behavior among young people. I do not undertake this out of a kind of fear of being ethically radical, but because the gospel reveals Jesus as redeemer who exhorts the healing and redemption of people in their concrete lives, according to their own possibilities and limits. Jesus' exhortation is, then, that they be shown mercy. I dare to speak in this regard of an "ethics of mercy," which is an ethics of liberation at the same time. I can concretely mark this ethics of liberation as a "transition ethics" that approaches the period of youth as a growth phase, with all that this implies in terms of temporariness and a not yet developed freedom. In line with the "law of gradualness" employed by John Paul II in *Familiaris Consortio* (no. 34), we can also speak of a "graduality ethics" without lapsing into the "graduality of the law." What is involved, therefore, is not a separate or closed "youth ethics" which would pose its own values and norms as valid definitively and of themselves, without any prospect for an ethical maturity that yields the meaningfully human.

A Realistic Growth-Ethics

An "ethics of being on the way" or a "growth-ethics" attunes its evaluation and guidance to the real situation of young people—that is, to that which they are effectively capable of in their psycho-genetic phase and

---

12. Jack Dominian, *Sexual Integrity: The Answer to AIDS* (London: Darton, Longman and Todd, 1988), second ed., 92–97; ibid., *Passionate and Compassionate Love: A Vision for Christian Marriage* (London, Darton, Longman, and Todd, 1991), 94–95.

13. Denise Lardner Carmody, *Caring for Marriage: Feminist and Biblical Reflections* (New York: Paulist, 1985), 17–30.

social situation. At times such an ethics is an "ethics of the unpermitted," however paradoxical this may sound. There are situations or behaviors that, objectively speaking, have to be labeled "unpermitted"—that is, they are in no way meaningful in the context of the Christian-human vision. This does not mean, however, that in such situations the ethical is no longer under discussion. Ethical meaning must be brought into even the unpermitted.

Naturally, an exploration of the many subjective and social reasons, factors, and occasions that lead to loose sexual contacts or semidetached forms of sexual relationships among young people can (and should) lead to a certain "understanding." In some circumstances they can lead even to a certain subjective exoneration of their actual sexual behaviour, even if it is clearly not meaningful nor qualitatively edifying. But if we leave it at this, we end up in a generalized exculpation which at the same time would mean a "de-ethicization." If sexual behavior among young people is pardoned—simply speaking, by returning it to its psycho-social context—then, ethically speaking, it is also "explained away." The ethical moment—namely, the appeal to responsibility for one's own growth in being human—would disappear then and ethical education would lead only to the prevention of accidents and nasty consequences.

That is why we should look beyond the subjective and social conditioning of actual sexual behavior among young people and search for elements that can address and stimulate their partial but indeed real responsibility. The ethical challenge remains valid in order to strive for as much human dignity as possible, and this in a progressive sense—namely, toward the direction of the humanly meaningful. This is precisely what we call a realistic "growth-ethics." That we take the factual situation as a starting point for this growth-ethics does not mean that we allow ourselves to be enticed into an "interim ethics" that considers the youth period in isolation. On the contrary, we want to provide elements for a relational and sexual "continuing growth-ethics" that challenges and guides young people toward the direction of a meaningful experience of sexuality in the context of a love project. The growth-ethics we advocate, therefore, must literally be a "continuing growth-ethics" that is exceptionally vigilant against choices, global orientations, and behaviors that mortgage or even impede growth toward the meaningfully human.[14]

---

14. Roman Bleistein, *Jugendmoral. Tatsachen, Deutungen, Hilfen* (Würzburg: Echter 1979), second ed., 137–47.

Minimal Conditions for Starting a Sexual Relationship

A growth-ethics promotes the educational task of stimulating young peo-ple—who have de facto turned to sexual relational behavior—toward the direction of a qualitative deepening and broadening of their relational and sexual experience. Starting from an ethical minimum, I now sketch a few important elements of this "continuing growth-ethics."[15]

A first series of orientations on a relational level is concerned with the entrance itself into a sexual relationship. The minimal requirement direct-ly ensues from the already mentioned rule of equality of which the no-violence principle represents the "bottom line." This means that entering into a sexual relationship must take place in freedom. From an ethical per-spective, it is utterly impermissible that a sexual relationship would be imposed in one way or the other—that is, by any form of individual or social pressure, blackmail, or violence.

Moreover, the step toward sexual relationship should not only be based on necessary external freedom but also on sufficient internal freedom of the partners themselves. If entrance into a sexual relationship flows too much from a strong sexual-emotional impulse, there is a very real chance that the necessary distance and reflection for a real personal decision would be lacking.

The rule of equality also requires that the decision for sexual contact would be a dialogical decision. This implies that there should always be a cer-tain time between the upcoming and growing longing for sexual contact and the decision, not only from the separate individuals but also from both of them together, after they have taken the time for thoughtful consideration.

Finally, it is desirable that the step toward sexual contact would be pre-ceded at least by a certain relational quality. By this I mean mutual affec-tion, most preferably with a prospect for the future. Mere emotional attraction and romantic love is not enough; a personal involvement is required that has already withstood some test of time and reality.

Relational and Sexual Growth-Imperatives

Once the decision has been taken toward intimate sexual behavior, we can formulate a number of growth orientations on a relational and sexual level. First, the rule of freedom applies not only for the beginning, but also for the continuation and even the possible termination of the sexual

---

15. William Spohn, "The Moral Dimensions of AIDS," *Theological Studies* 49 (1988): 89–109.

relationship. Freedom of assent should never be hindered either in the start or in the continuation of a sexual relationship.

Next, a growth-ethics approach to actual sexual relational behavior among young people requires that they also work on the quality of their relationship itself. Here, I introduce the "goal to strive for" or the "end norm" of tenderness as a quality of presence. This means that mere emotional intimacy should be transcended by a certain commitment and awareness of mutual responsibility. This implies the conscious will to work on the broadening and the deepening of the relationship: to grow in knowledge of each other, to learn to give of each other, to be worth each other's trust, to show respect toward each other's feelings and sensitivities, to overcome possessive jealousy so that each one has enough space to be oneself, to not attack the partner "below the belt" nor ridicule in the presence of others, to become free to be able to express feelings and opinions in all honesty, to show interest for each other's fields of interest, to learn "to negotiate" concessions as two independent persons, to learn to dialogue about the way in which tensions and conflicts are dealt with, and so on.

The growth imperative to work on the quality of the relationship also implies the appeal to work on the sexual dimension of the relationship. Along with this, the criterion of authenticity stands central, with its summons to strive for as much expressive quality as possible, taking into account the opportunities and mishaps of the situation and the nature of the relationship. This can be expressed in a number of questions which serve as guidelines. Is the erotic and sexual behavior integrated in the relationship? Or is the relationship as such so dominated and consumed by the sexual that the relationship stands in function of the sexual? Are the two so obsessed with each other because of the sex that they lose necessary distance, privacy, and freedom toward each other? In other words, how is the sexual experience related to the relationship? Is the sexual experienced as part of a growing quality of relationships and of tenderness? Other questions involve the quality of the sexual experience itself. Is "sex" considered a right that one has over the other from the moment that the sexual relationship began? Who "asks" ("demands") sexual contact and who "gives in"? Is it always the same one who asks and the same one who gives in? Or does a mutuality of longings grow slowly, listening to each other and taking each other into account on an erotic and sexual level? Does one concentrate on the coital in the sexual experience or does the "in-between-area" of non-coital erotic expressions also receive sufficient time and opportunity? By means of these questions, we suggest that the erotic and sexual experience itself should become a "quality of presence."

A Growing Humanization of Preventive Behavior

The ethical option for a qualitative development and deepening of sexual relational behavior between young people implies that attention is thereby paid to the humanization of the prevention-imperative, as far as prevention of both HIV as well as unwanted pregnancy are concerned.

This concretely means that both ethically as well as educationally sexual upbringing must go farther than the mere formal positing of the minimal duty in order to prevent the negative consequences of premarital intimate sexual behavior. However necessary, the no-harm principle is insufficient as an orientation for the humanization of this behavior. Ethics cannot confine itself to the affirmation that preventive action is an ineluctable task wherein human rights play a role in their respect for the life and the health of oneself and of others. It must also question how this preventive action itself can be performed as humanely as possible, where the relational character of this preventive action immediately comes to the fore.

A first element in this growing humanization is the desirability that the application of necessary prevention evolves into a commonly shared, commensurate responsibility of both partners (just as this in fact also applies to condom use for HIV prevention and other infections). Here, we simply apply the equality rule. To pass the responsibility of prevention to the other, in the case of contraception for the girl, shows that the equality of the partner is not really taken seriously. This means that young people are faced with the task of compensating as much as possible for the asymmetry or imbalance that can be introduced by the prevention method.

A second important element in the growing humanization is examination of the preventive behavior itself. Concretely, does one only apply prevention in order to be sexually free and safe, and to avoid "accidents," or is the preventive behavior also positively motivated by respect for human life? From an educational perspective, it is important to confront young people—especially boys—with the insight that careless, faulty, or simply nonexistent contraceptive behavior in cases of loose or semidetached sexual behavior goes against respect for life and human rights.

Furthermore, we cannot pass over the fact that preventive behavior can steer young people in the direction of a negative attitude toward life and fertility. Since in loose and semidetached sexual relationships, preventive behavior does not take place in the framework of a life project and of responsible parenthood, young people are time and again confronted in a negative way with having to avoid disease or pregnancy, and not at all with the positive choice for life or with the fulfilling realization of one's own faculty of fertility in a loving future-oriented project with a partner. The emphasis is placed mainly on the preventive and the contraceptive, which in a midrange or longrange term can undermine a positive and noble "yes" toward life and children, so much so that an ambivalence toward life and children can begin to grow and even an "antilife" mentality can arise.

Conclusion: In the Perspective of an Ethics of Redemption

TIME AND AGAIN, a Christian-inspired ethics is challenged to lay open the perspective of the meaningful for a particular domain of life and to make this argumentatively and esthetically communicable. Hence we pursue both meaningful sexuality as a "goal commandment" as well as qualitative relational and sexual education. Only against this background is it possible to develop a growth-ethics that not only understands and approaches in a nuanced way the intimate sexual behavior of adolescents, but also situates it critically and evocatively in the "continuing growth-ethics" of a meaningful sexual life as horizon and task.

Christian-inspired ethicists and educators, moreover, do not resign themselves to the facts, but let themselves be led by the confidence that "everything is possible for those who believe." From an indestructible hope, sometimes "against all hope," they believe that opportunities for "continuing growth" are present in every intimate sexual behavior of young people. The Christian-inspired ethics is also constantly an "ethics of liberation"—that is, an ethics of grace, liberation, and redemption from powerlessness and evil whereby people can become new again and, notwithstanding everything, can find the path toward meaningful life and action, even if they now follow the wrong path or go astray. This perspective of redemption and healing thus liberates not only from pessimism, but also from any anxiety about approaching young people. Only a future-directed education that never becomes cynical, but constantly keeps its sense of joy and mild humor is capable of "touching" young people whereby this "touching" heals them and "sets them on their way" toward a "meaningful" relational and sexual life.

12.
THE REIGN OF GOD: SIGNPOSTS FOR CATHOLIC MORAL THEOLOGY

Enda McDonagh

FAITH IN A creator-redeemer God, a God of love and power, may be more readily threatened in the face of human or natural disaster. The Lisbon earthquake in the seventeenth century became a classic occasion for a renewal of the old-Job debate about evil and the existence of a Christian-style God. The twentieth century has provided more than its share of such catastrophes, natural and human, raising the same basic questions. Doing theology after Auschwitz proved too much for certain Jewish and Christian thinkers. Recurring genocide and ethnic cleansing combined with devastating famines, floods, earthquakes, and nuclear disasters continue to trouble believers to the point where they may feel like a Samuel Beckett character that God's only justification in the face of such evil is that "the bastard doesn't exist." In that tradition the theological impact of the pandemic of HIV-AIDS is first of all to reopen or, better, to reenforce the questioning of the very existence and certainly the nature of the God of the Christian faith. It is a questioning that is always valuable to the health of theology and of faith. Even if it does not elicit any new light on the issue, it keeps theologians and believers from complacent security, alert to the risk and vulnerability of believing.

One of the early reactions within the Christian community was to regard HIV-AIDS as divine punishment for human sinfulness, particularly sexual sinfulness and more particularly homosexual sinfulness. The widespread dismissal of this response by pastors, theologians, and other Christians did not entirely remove either the suspicion of guilt attached to many living with the virus or the social stigma incurred, sometimes with violent consequences. Deeper understanding of God's ways and more effective love of neighbor are required to overcome the prejudice and neglect which too many people with the virus still have to endure.

Apart from its precedents in the Hebrew scriptures such as the story of Sodom and Gomorrah with their New Testament echoes, the interpretation of AIDS and other human disasters as divine punishment has at least the merit of taking God's involvement in the world seriously. And this is a God who takes the world seriously. Attempts to distance God from the evil in the world to protect God's goodness and omnipotence can easily result in distancing God from the world entirely. The whirlwind God of Job insisted on God's involvement in the most intricate aspects of world-making. If the divine response did not explain in human terms the mystery of human suffering, it both rejected the conventional view that it was a matter of divine punishment and refused to distance God from the reality of the world and its suffering. With Jesus' ministry and teaching, suffering and death begins a new phase of divine involvement and of human understanding.

The disciples' question about the blind man in chapter 9 of John's Gospel, "Who sinned, this man or his parents?" is rendered superfluous in the new manifestation of God's glory, the healing mission of Jesus and his solidarity in suffering with the least ones. Only when Jesus is lifted up on the cross will he be finally glorified, will the glory of God be fully manifest. The paradox of Job is transcended in deeper paradox as the power and commitment to heal of the creator-savior (healing) God is realized in undergoing human suffering and death. God's involvement with the evil in this world, God's promise and power to overcome it are revealed by solidarity with humanity in suffering that evil. So shall the kingdom or reign of God be achieved which Jesus announced at the beginning of his mission and ministry.

The Reign of God: Christian Symbol and Moral Imperative

IN THE HISTORY of Christian thought and practice, the kingdom, or as it is now more usually termed the reign, of God has followed an erratic course. Even in the New Testament, the frequent usage of this term by Jesus in the synoptics contrasts sharply with its sparing use in John and Paul. The debates still continue both about how far in its synoptic usage it refers to the present (already, among you) or to the future, a future that is imminently and mistakenly expected or simply unknown, and about its invisible, internal, and eternal character (not of this world) as opposed to its visible and historical realization. These debates and others such as the one about how far it is uniquely the work of God and how far it involves human cooperation are clearly relevant to any discussion of Christian morality or moral theology. The description of the reign of God as Christian symbol is not intended to short-circuit the debates, still less to remove the reality of Jesus' announcement from the contested terrain of contemporary history. To do so would be to make it irrelevant to the crisis provoked by HIV-AIDS and to the whole enterprise of moral theology.

In its origin, symbol (*symballein*) signals a drawing together of diverse, even conflicting ideas or realities. In the Christian tradition it declares and realizes some compound of the divine and the human. The sacraments are primary instances. Creeds like the Nicene or individual doctrines like the incarnation could in this traditional usage also be described as symbols. The reign of God as Christian symbol calls attention to the complex nature of the presence, power, and activity of creator in creation, of God in human and cosmic history. The presence, power, and activity of God in creating and sustaining, healing, transforming, and fulfilling humanity and creation combines much of the elusive material suggested by references to the reign of God in both Old and New Testaments, while leaving the manner and timing of the divine presence and activity open to more precise determination. The more precise determination manifest in Jesus by divine solidarity with the suffering and excluded reinforces the description of divine reign as symbol, indicating and realizing the drawing together of such apparently distant realities, the all-powerful creator and the most powerless of creatures, not in some simple alliance or even mercy mission but in genuine solidarity, in com-passion, in suffering with.

The key, then, to interpreting the saving and moral significance of the reign of God is the climactic presence of God with the poor and deprived in Jesus Christ. The call of the poor and oppressed is the call which God hears and responds to in such radical personal terms.

It is the call to which those who follow Jesus must also listen and respond. For disciples the moral imperative of God's reign focuses first of all on the least ones, on those oppressed or ignored by the mighty in their seats of power and privilege, even episcopal or clerical. In this vision the moral thrust is toward recognizing and seeking to overcome unjust structures and relationships in solidarity with those suffering such injustices. In this analysis, justice would seem to be the primary Christian virtue and not charity.

The justice-seeking of Jesus Christ, exemplary and efficacious as it is, was a supreme instance of the primacy of the charity he preached. "Greater love has no one than that somebody lays down his life for his friends." "Out of love in search of justice" might be a useful summary of many saints and heroes inspired by the teaching and example of Jesus. Political heroes of our own time, from Gandhi and Bonhoeffer to Martin Luther King and Nelson Mandela, plus thousands of the unknown and unsung, have followed this Christian pattern, out of love in search of justice for the oppressed even to the laying down of one's life. The anger and indignation of Jesus' prophetic predecessors in Israel at the injustices of the powerful and wealthy against the powerless and poor had its roots in love also and was frequently voiced at serious risk to the prophet's own life or well-being. Attacking and even slaying the prophet would be the Hebrew equivalent of blaming and even killing the messenger.

The Reign of God and the Shape of Catholic Moral Theology

THE MORAL IMPERATIVE of the reign of God requires some systematic expression. This might be developed in a variety of ways. In the manualist tradition of moral theology, the reign of God did not figure. The law of God as formulated in the Ten Commandments or as interpreted in natural law was the dominant model. The return of moral theologians to Scripture in the fifties and sixties offered some theological modifications, although most revisions retained the underlying law model, particularly some version of natural law. Only one serious attempt was made to use the reign of God as starting point and leitmotif by a moral theologian, Johannes Stelzenberger.[1]

This essay proposes one possible framework for moral theology based on analysis of some aspects of the reign of God as announced and inaugurated by Jesus and attempts to incorporate some of the excellent insights of natural law and biblical morality. For Christians the God who reigns, would reign, and will reign is first of all the creator God of Genesis, Isaiah, the psalms, Job, the synoptics and Paul, to take some quick biblical soundings. A moral theology which takes creation seriously is capable of integrating "natural law" insights derived from an investigation of (created) human nature (in person and community) by (created) human reason (personal and communal). The historical and dynamic dimensions of human existence and natural law find a place in the reign of God's moral structure along with its personal, social, and ecological dimensions. Creation includes cosmos and (human) community. The creator God is also the (Mosaic) covenant God of the dialogue. Creation itself is the original covenant. Later covenants from Noah, Abraham, and Moses through the promised New Covenant of the prophets to be realized for Christians in Jesus offer critical biblical data on the continuities and discontinuities in the reign of God and in the human responses to it. Recurrent crises in divine-human relations, frequently manifested in the breakdown of human-human relations, prompted fresh initiatives from God and fresh covenants. God's growing involvement in human and cosmic history was directed to the sustaining, healing, and transforming of humanity and cosmos, to the development of the divine reign.

What is of immediate significance for understanding the moral imperative of the reign of God is the divine strategy pursued in the progress from creation (covenant) through crisis (in human response) to *kairos* as

---

1. See his *Lehrbuch der Moraltheologie, Die Sittlichkeitslehre der Koenigsherrschaft Gottes* (Paderborn: F. Schoningh, 1953).

the opportune time perceived by God for a new loving initiative. This strategy is far removed from the imperialism often attributed to God and more often appropriated by God's called or "chosen" people. The antiimperial character of God's reign only becomes fully clear in Jesus, the culmination of humanity's crisis and of God's involvement. "Last of all he sent his son, saying they will reverence my son." The recurring human crises and the continuing divine responses in loving surrender to human need have reached their climax as the divine Son emptied himself, taking the form of a servant and entering the human condition even to the point of suffering and death (Phil. 2).

This self-emptying (*kenosis*) of which Paul speaks so eloquently was no masochistic search for suffering, but the fateful consequence of unconditional loving. Through this mortal surrender of God in love of humankind, death itself was overcome as if creation, history, and the tomb could no longer contain the "dead" God. The bonds of history were broken and a new covenant and a new community were established. In that other piercing phrase of Paul in 2 Corinthians 5, a new creation emerged. The journey from creation (*ktisis*) through crisis (*krisis*) becoming *kairos* and involving a radical divine self-emptying (*kenosis*) reached its destination in the new covenant and new community *(kaine koinonia)*, and more comprehensivley in the new creation *(kaine ktisis)*. In the great K words of (biblical) Greek, the God of *ktisis* confronted *krisis* as *kairos* and in the engagement of *kenosis* achieved *kaine koinonia* and *kaine ktisis*. These are the real signposts of the reign of God which human beings are called to follow in their imitation of God and in their discipleship of Jesus, the framework for a moral theology of compassion and inclusion, of seeking justice and peace out of love.

The more systematic structure of moral theology can and should take seriously this saving strategy of the divine reign. The more detailed analysis of particular moral cases and the direction of particular decisions will observe the same pattern. Whether story or virtues or law provide the subsidiary structures, the great K-pattern will provide the crucial shape.

Catholic Moral Theology and the HIV/AIDS Pandemic

HIV/AIDS HAS PRECIPITATED a serious crisis for humanity with devastating cosmic and community dimensions. The rapid spread of the virus with its devastating biological consequences as it develops into AIDS has presented one of the most serious public health hazards of the century. Creation as cosmos and as good, the human body as God-given and as good are radically threatened. Creation in its human and loving personal and community dimensions faces a major crisis. The reign of God faces total eclipse by these breakdowns in the illness and death of the many infected by HIV and AIDS, and by the immoral exclusion and neglect which they encounter from the healthy, wealthy and powerful. Compassion or "suffering-with" remains the divine strategy's first imperative. It ought to be followed by the allocation of all the resources available in a movement of justice and inclusion on the model of Jesus' own promotion of the reign of God.

Such a moral response, where the crisis becomes *kairos,* will involve sacrifice by the powerful. It will have to follow the kenotic line of God and of God's Son, the surrender in compassion and loving service of the reign of God. In terms of personal caring this may be very difficult for many family members, partners, friends, and neighbors as well as for the professional physicians and paramedics. But it is at least understandable in the love-of-neighbor kenotic terms of the gospel. The structural demands of justice in allocation of resources and of inclusion in community are not always so evident. Yet they are the deeper and more far-reaching demands which members of the Christian community must strive to promote themselves and strive to persuade, more by example than word, the broader community to emulate. Crisis as *kairos* demanding *kenosis* at this socio-economic level is more difficult to make manifest and to implement.

In the world of HIV-AIDS the poor, the weak and the excluded are the most vulnerable to infection and the least likely to be attended. In the steps of Jesus, attention to these people above all enables *kairos* to issue in *kaine ktisis* (new creation) and *kaine koinonia* (new community). It is the way to ensuring that the reign of God is emerging among us, however partially. Catholic moral theology must be structured to give precedence to this work of compassion, justice, and inclusion, characteristics of the Reign of God.

The Risk of God and the Reign of God

THE REIGN OF God as adumbrated in scripture and particularly in Jesus Christ might be rewritten as an account of the risk of God. Creation itself could be seen in this way, including the creation of potential partners for God, created in the divine image, risks that proved failures in many ways, drawing God into further *kenosis*—that is, into greater involvement and heavier risk. Crisis and *kairos* leading to *kenosis* in the incarnation, suffering, and death of Jesus showed the growing risks God was prepared to take. The final return in resurrection, new creation, and new community is still far from complete.

The disciples of Jesus are called to follow the risk-laden example of Jesus in seeking the sick and the poor, the stigmatized and excluded. They have to be prepared to be stigmatized and excluded themselves in challenging some of the orthodoxies of their time in serving the deprived.

Healing or plucking ears of corn on the Sabbath may be near blasphemy to certain "orthodox" leaders, but they illustrate the priorities of the reign of God: people before rules, the needs of the sick and the hungry before the concerns of the comfortable and powerful. In the face of HIV/AIDS Christians and Catholics, the Catholic community and Catholic moral theology, must be prepared to take risks with their own rules. The divinely inspired risks of Jesus and of the reign of God might shed a new light on such disputable but secondary issues as the use of condoms and the exchange of needles in attempting to prevent or reduce the spread of HIV/AIDS. Such practices are indeed secondary to the practices of compassion, justice, and inclusion needed to turn the crisis into *kairos*. They are secondary, too, to the *kenosis* required of all Christians for the new creation and new community of the reign of the God of Jesus Christ.

CONCLUSION: A MORAL THEOLOGIAN FACES THE NEW MILLENNIUM IN A TIME OF AIDS

Kevin Kelly

OUTSIDE MANY CHURCHES in the north of England there is a notice which reads: "The Millennium is Christ's 2000th birthday. Worship him—here—now." In this time of AIDS a more challenging message might be: "The body of Christ has AIDS. Worship him—here—now."

"The body of Christ has AIDS" was the message on a banner held aloft at an international AIDS conference in the Vatican a few years ago. It was a message repeated a few week ago in Zimbabwe at two Winter Schools I helped to facilitate. Both had the same theme: "The pastoral care of people living with HIV/AIDS: opportunities and challenges for the church." One of my abiding memories of that experience is sitting among a group of about sixty Zimbabweans while John, my fellow facilitator, reminded us that 25 percent of adults in Zimbabwe are HIV positive. That meant that, statistically at least, about fifteen of our group had the virus. In that setting, statistics were no longer figures on a page; they suddenly became living—and dying—people. This was even truer a little later on in the course, when two of the participants actually living with AIDS shared their personal experience with us. We were all deeply moved by their honesty and openness; but also shocked and chastened by their accounts of being rejected by many of their fellow Christians, even to the extent of people in church moving away from them when they sat down. The truth of the statement, "The church has AIDS," suddenly struck home to us all. AIDS was not something "out there" that only touched other people. It touched us all.

After their sharing we began to speak in much more inclusive terms. "We" and "us" replaced "they" and "them." We were all in this together, whether we were infected or affected. In that particular group, virtually everyone could name someone, a family member, friend, fellow priest or religious, who had died of AIDS. We experienced tangibly the truth of the statement, "The body of Christ has AIDS." This came home to us very powerfully in our liturgy, most poignantly when we followed Sister Kay Lawlor's stations of the cross in which each station tells of the sufferings of named individuals known to Kay who had died of AIDS in Uganda. In using the expression "The body of Christ has AIDS," we wanted to express our solidarity with all those living with HIV/AIDS. Together we form the one body of Christ. As St. Paul reminds us, if one member suffers, the whole body suffers. To respond as Christians to the AIDS pandemic we need to take time out from our often overactive lives and simply contemplate Christ suffering with (com-passioning) all those infected. In their bodies they bear the wounds of Christ. Enda McDonagh has emphasized this point.

An African theologian, Teresa Okure, in a paper delivered to a theological symposium on HIV/AIDS held in Pretoria, South Africa, in 1998, startled her hearers by saying that there are at least two other viruses which are even more dangerous than HIV and which are the carriers enabling this virus to spread so rapidly among the most vulnerable in society.

One is a virus which affects people's minds and their cultures—almost a form of human madness. It is the virus which makes people look on women as inferior to men—and it affects women as well as men. Each year this virus causes ten million cases of female genital mutilation in Africa alone—a practice that leaves girls and young women at greater risk of HIV infection. It is also the virus which fuels the sex industry—in which young girls (in reality, victims of sexual and child abuse) become HIV-infected and then pass on the virus to others—tragically in many cases, even to their own babies. This virus is responsible for the shocking fact that in many countries of the developing world the condition which carries the highest risk of HIV infection is that of being a married woman! Lisa Cahill has already highlighted many other ways in which this virus of looking on women as inferior to men facilitates the rapid spread of HIV/AIDS. It is one of the major reasons why HIV/AIDS is now the number one cause of death for African women.

The other virus enabling the devastating spread of HIV is a virus which is found mainly, though not exclusively, in the developed world. It is the virus of global injustice which is causing such terrible poverty in many parts of the developing world. What James Keenan and Stuart Bate write about AIDS ("a social problem" and a cultural illness) is similar to the point made by Teresa Okure.

This makes us face the possibility that the expression, "The body of Christ has AIDS," can have a second meaning radically different from the one already considered. It still has to do with solidarity, but this time it refers to the solidarity of the church, the body of Christ, in the sinful structures which constitute the underlying causes of the rapid spread of AIDS.

One of the problems unearthed in both Winter Schools in Zimbabwe was that of silence and denial. AIDS was the great unmentionable. It was not talked about in polite society. No one ever died of an AIDS-related sickness. Sometimes a similar veil of silence and denial can exist with regard to admitting that the church, the body of Christ, has AIDS, in the sense of sharing some responsibility for the sinful structures which contribute to the rapid spread of HIV/AIDS. At an institutional level, this possibility needs to be faced, without in any way denying that, at the level of preventative HIV/AIDS education and pastoral care, there has been a magnificent response, especially on the part of a number of religious congregations and many local Christian community groups throughout the world.

As we face the new millennium, therefore, the question before all of us as church is: if the church, the body of Christ, has AIDS, what aspects of its life and teaching need to change if it is to become a more effective sign and instrument of healing for our whole AIDS-infected human family? In this time of AIDS, what would be the marks of a church which is living *positively* with AIDS? Do we find any clues for future renewal in the case histories and fundamental analyses presented in this book?

However, before looking at the institutional church, it is only fair that I and my fellow moral theologians should first examine our own consciences. It seems that information-based HIV prevention programs in developing countries are unable to motivate people to change their sexual behavior which is the primary channel of HIV infection. Perhaps that should make us moral theologians look again at the kind of sexual ethics we are promoting. Is it the kind of sexual ethics which is likely to give people the positive motivation needed if they are to think seriously about the quality of their relationships? Does it come over as being in tune with what people today consider to be the important values in life? Does it see our human sexuality as a wonderful gift of God, given to us so that we may find joy and happiness in the kind of loving relationships which we find most fulfilling as human beings? People will only be motivated into behavior change if they find it attractive and in tune with their deepest needs.

Perhaps we moral theologians too often criticize official church teaching on sexual ethics for being too negative without offering any more positive formulations. I do not believe that is because we have nothing to offer. When pressed, I suspect most of us would agree substantially on a positive sexual ethics which goes beyond the current official teaching, and yet which we believe to be fully in line with the central core of our Christian tradition at this stage of our developing understanding of ourselves as human persons, and in the light of reflecting on contemporary experience through the lens of the gospel. Are moral theologians colluding in a fear-induced silence, not unlike the silence and denial hindering HIV prevention in Zimbabwe? A "time of AIDS" is not a time for keeping quiet.

May I offer the following tentative proposal to my fellow moral theologians.

To help the church, the body of Christ, live positively with AIDS, moral theologians need to have the courage and confidence to formulate and teach a positive and attractive person-centered sexual ethics which is both truly human and truly Christian.

Such a sexual ethics would need to be heard by all people of good will as "good news." It should tap into our deepest desires. It should primarily be about our feeling at ease with ourselves and each other as sexual persons, deeply grateful to God for the gift of our sexuality, and able to enjoy and appreciate each other in this way. Its aim should be to help us grow as loving and loved persons, whose loving is truly life-giving in the fullest sense—loving new persons into life, if and when appropriate, but always striving to love each other into fuller life, through mutual healing and positive encouragement. It would be about enabling us to find security in relationships of personal intimacy, mutual trust, and faithful commitment. It would repudiate the appalling caricature of a Christian sexual ethics captured so strikingly in Hugh Lavery's phrase, "In the beginning was the word, and the word was 'no.'" The only "no" that would have any place in such a person-centered sexual ethics would be to whatever violates the dignity of a human person, whether ourselves or others. Hence, such a sexual ethics would be prepared to say no even to the institution of marriage if, in some cultures, it takes the form of such an unequal power relationship that the dignity of the woman as a human person is seriously compromised. Such a no would certainly strike a chord with all people of good will. They too would refuse to approve of anything which destroys or corrupts love between persons or erodes our capacity for loving. That is precisely why child abuse is held in such abhorrence by all right-thinking people. Such a positive, person-centered sexual ethics would be light years away from a sexual ethics which gives the impression that the main concern of Christians should be to oppose all use of condoms, for whatever reason!

A positive, person-centered sexual ethics must remain true to its emphasis on life-giving love (in the fuller sense explained above) even, or perhaps especially, in the context of HIV prevention. Hence, it would acknowledge not just the irony, but also the tragedy, of an act of supposedly life-giving love actually involving the transmission of a life-threatening virus. Failure to do one's best to ensure that this did not happen would be a failure in responsible loving. In such a context, granted the scientifically established capacity of good quality condoms, properly used, to diminish considerably the risk of HIV infection, would not condom use be more accurately described, from a moral perspective, as life-preserving rather than life-preventing, prolife rather than antilife? And would not such a conclusion be more in keeping with the positive, person-centered approach of Vatican II? Of course, other personal and social factors might also need to be taken into consideration in a couple's decision-making process in such a situation.

Such a person-centered sexual ethics should also be "good news" equally to gay and lesbian persons as to heterosexual persons. The earlier description of such a sexual ethics should hold both for heterosexual and homosexual persons:

> It should tap into our deepest desires. It should primarily be about our feeling at ease with ourselves and each other as sexual persons, deeply grateful to God for the gift of our sexuality, and able to enjoy and appreciate each other in this way. Its aim should be to help us grow as loving and loved persons, whose loving is truly life-giving in the fullest sense, loving new persons into life, if and when appropriate, but always striving to love each other into fuller life, through mutual healing and positive encouragement. It would be about enabling us to find security in relationships of personal intimacy, mutual trust and faithful commitment.

I have tentatively tried to explore further such a positive, person-centered Christian sexual ethics in chapter 6 of my *New Directions in Sexual Ethics* (London: Geoffrey Chapman, 1998). I have also tried to show that such a sexual ethics constitutes progress, rather than deviation, within the tradition, in keeping with the rich meaning of tradition outlined earlier by Marciano Vidal and Raphael Gallagher.

Information about the dangers of certain so-called high-risk activities does not seem to have produced the desired pattern of behavior change needed to achieve effective HIV prevention. The predominant motivation arising from danger-focused information campaigns is one of fear. However, fear too easily consolidates feelings of poor self-worth on the part of those pushed to the margins of society and for whom the future offers little hope—and these tend to be the people most at risk of HIV infection. Fear-inducement is also linked to heavyhanded law enforcement. If religiously induced, such fear can seriously harm any positive image of a loving God.

The reason why crowds flocked to listen to Jesus was not because he induced fear in them. They were attracted by the "good news" he offered. He enabled them to appreciate their own God-given dignity, a message they did not hear from their own religious leaders. If we are made in the image of a loving, relational God, for moral theologians to allow themselves to be trapped into colluding with a negative sexual ethics is a form of blasphemy.

If the church is to be an effective participant in the field of HIV/AIDS prevention, we moral theologians must face up to our responsibility to provide the church with a sexual ethics which is positive and attractive to people today and one which appeals to the best in them. We would be failing the church if we settled for anything less than that. And we must not let ourselves be discouraged or diverted from our task in the face of discouragement or even disapproval on the part of church authorities.

What, then, about the two viruses identified by Teresa Okure, the sexual and economic subordination of women, and the terrible poverty resulting from social injustice and their key role in facilitating the rapid spread of HIV/AIDS, especially in developing countries? Is the church, the body of Christ, completely immune from these two viruses, or is it, too, challenged by Okure's diagnosis? Again, I would offer a tentative suggestion.

If the church, the body of Christ, is to live *positively* with AIDS, I would suggest that two "marks" of the true church in a "time of AIDS" should be:

(1) It should be a church which in its life and teaching offers a credible witness to its belief in the full and equal dignity of women, and which repudiates as contrary to the gospel any way of thinking or acting which implies that women are in any way of inferior status to men.

The church must have the humility to examine whether it needs to put its own house in order before championing the full and equal dignity of women in the world at large. In the Catholic Church certainly, and to a large extent in most other Christian churches, the power of decision-making rests firmly in the hands of men, even though the vast majority of people actively involved in church life are women. Moreover, the male preserve of decision-making is not restricted merely to matters of practical action. It also includes decisions about what is authentic Christian teaching. For the church to be true to its belief in the infallibility of the whole people of God, it must make sure that the voice of women is not only heard and listened to in any debate on authentic teaching, but that the minds and hearts of women are actively involved in the whole process of discerning what is true teaching.

This might seem far removed from those cultural practices which, through sexual or economic subordination, leave many women virtually defenseless in the face of HIV exposure from infected males, be they husbands, partners, clients, or other men in positions of domination through a whole variety of unequal power relationships. However, it is all part of one and the same mindset. Most women with whom I have spoken on my visits of Africa and Asia have told me that, for the most part, they find the institutional church and its representatives to be part of the problem rather than part of the solution. In extreme cases, and sadly such cases are not that rare, this can even take the form of explicit sexual exploitation of women, including women religious, by priests—and even, on occasion, by bishops. It is the existence of the unequal power relationship (partly cleric/lay but primarily man/woman) within the church which makes such abusive behavior possible. There are even grounds for saying that the Vatican seems to take a stronger line against minor (and sometimes very debatable) deviations from doctrinal orthodoxy than it does against the serious and blatant violation of gospel values involved in such abusive behavior. The implications of the words of Jesus, "the Sabbath is made for persons, not persons for the Sabbath," are far-reaching and need to be a permanent feature on the church's agenda for critical self-examination. They also have their application within the cultural field. Cultures are made for persons, not persons for cultures. Hence, the comment of Stuart Bate: "Cultural reconstruction is vital at this period of African history and cultural reconstruction implies moral reconstruction."

In listening to the "signs of the times" we need to remember that the new millennium is not just a "time of AIDS." It is also a "time of women." Recent popes, including Paul VI and John Paul II, have acknowledged this. If the church fails to respond positively to the Spirit's invitation to open the church up to equal "ownership" on the part of women, it will hardly be able to eradicate from its own system the first of Teresa Okure's two fatal viruses. As long as this virus continues to live in the church's bloodstream, anything church leaders say about the full and equal dignity of women will lack any real credibility. That would be a tragedy not simply for the church, but also for the cause of HIV prevention in our world living with AIDS.

(2) *It should be a church which uses the full power of its authority and influence to change and eradicate the basic causes of poverty in our world today, especially the many factors which owe their continued existence to human agency and which constitute global structural injustice on a worldwide scale. Likewise, it needs to be a church which is prepared to name and shame corruption wherever it is found, but especially when it exists among those who are the guardians and promoters of the common good in society and whose corrupt practices result in serious damage to the lives of the poorest in the community, often even contributing to their death.*

It is a long time since I saw such extremes of poverty as I did when I accompanied the home-care teams round the outskirts of Livingstone in Zambia. Sadly, I am aware that these conditions are the norm rather than the exception in many developing countries, especially in sub-Saharan Africa. In our day and age such poverty is completely unacceptable. It is a violation of the divine image in these people. For us to allow it to continue in an age of such affluence is a form of blasphemy. That must be the church's bottom line, before we embark on any kind of social analysis aimed at unraveling the complex web of interconnected causal factors which have created and continue to sustain such poverty. We are simply failing to proclaim the gospel if we do not name this violation of the gospel message loud and clear. In a statement which, by repeated ratification by episcopal conferences throughout the world, has almost achieved canonical status as an inspired text, the 1971

Synod of Bishops left us in no doubt that the elimination of such inhuman poverty is intrinsic to the very proclamation of the gospel:

> Action on behalf of justice and participation in the transformation of the world fully appear to us as a constitutive dimension of the preaching of the Gospel, or, in other words, of the church's mission for the redemption of the human race and its liberation from every oppressive situation.

Viewed from any angle, the eradication of such extreme poverty is a moral imperative of the highest order. In this "time of AIDS," however, it has acquired even greater urgency, since failure to eradicate this level of poverty is, at the same time, failure to tackle one of the major underlying causes of the rapid spread of HIV/AIDS in our world today.

There has been a growing consensus that one essential ingredient in this process of eliminating poverty lies in tackling the scandal of the way developing countries are bleeding to death through their interest repayments on debts owed to Western countries and financial institutions. As always, it is the poor in these countries who bear the brunt, usually in the form of massive cut-backs in their health care, social services, and education. Many Christian churches and local congregations in the West have shown great commitment in espousing this cause. The Jubilee 2000 campaign has been particularly important in this regard and has been given a lot of church support. Many bishops' conferences have issued powerful statements on this theme and have made strong representations to their governments. Nevertheless, there is still some way to go. Commitment to eradicating such blasphemous poverty, while seen by many as a serious moral imperative, has still not achieved what, in the Protestant tradition, would be described as a *status confessionis*. In other words, such commitment is not yet accepted as intrinsic to our Christian profession of faith.

However, it is not just in the West that Teresa Okure's virus of social injustice is to be found. It is also rampant in developing countries. My recent visit to Zimbabwe and Zambia left me in no doubt about that. The virus of economic injustice infects many people in positions of power in the developing world. This shows itself in the widespread corruption, reaching even (or perhaps, especially) into the highest echelons of government. There can be no really effective HIV-prevention policies until these countries are healed from this virus of corruption. It is a virus which is crippling the health service in many developing countries, with the result that often government hospitals can do little more than offer a diagnosis without any subsequent treatment. They are often bereft of even the most basic drugs.

Without properly supervised conditions ensuring that the poor will benefit directly as a result of debt remission, debt relief on its own could amount to continuing collusion in structural sin. It would simply be financing still further high-level corruption without bringing any benefit to the poorest, who are the very ones at highest risk of HIV infection. Local church leaders have a particular responsibility to name and shame such corruption, and many have done this at great personal risk to themselves. Sadly, a few have joined the corruption bandwagon themselves.

IN HIS INTRODUCTION to this book James Keenan has reminded us that recent scholarly writing has clearly demonstrated that the tradition of moral theology is sufficiently robust to be able to respond positively to the demands of HIV prevention with regard to the issues of (1) condom use as a direct means to safeguard health and prevent fatal infection; and (2) needle exchange for the same purpose. The case studies in this book provide us with positive examples of how to deal with the cultural variables which are inevitably part of the scenario of a worldwide pandemic such as HIV/AIDS. The concluding essays on closely related foundational issues provide a rich and varied backdrop to this whole exercise. Thus we enter the new millennium with a moral theology which is fundamentally healthy.

In this final chapter I have gone on to suggest that this rich inheritance of moral theology has the potential to show up the in-built weaknesses inherent in some aspects of human culture, particularly with regard to the position of women within society and the church. It can also reveal the person-destroying malfunctioning in our global politico-economic system. It can even help us so refine our self-understanding as sexual persons that we are able to see that we may have been identifying moral ambiguity where perhaps none exists.

As the new millennium approaches, many people fear that the so-called millennium bug will affect the functioning of some of our major institutional systems. Perhaps our hope should be that the church will play a major part in dislocating the functioning of some of the major systems of our human community—not with a view to creating chaos but to ensure that they function for the benefit of all, not least those whose human dignity takes a back seat at present. If the church is able to act as a kind of millennium bug in such a positive fashion, it will enable our human family to build up its immunity to Teresa Okure's two fatal viruses, and hence will be making a major and indispensable contribution to HIV prevention in the new millennium.

At the ninth International Conference on AIDS in July 1996, Professor Richard Parker suggested that the way we respond to the challenge of HIV/AIDS today "will write the history of the epidemic for years to come." I would even dare to suggest that what is in the balance is not just the future of the epidemic, but the future of a large section of our human family. In the words of Enda McDonagh, that is the "risk" God is prepared to take—here—now—in this "*kairos* time of AIDS."

About the Authors

Stuart Bate, O.M.I., is a lecturer at St. Joseph's Theological Institute, Cedara, South Africa. He is the author of *Inculturation and Healing* (New York: Edwin Mellen, 1999) and has edited *Serving Humanity* (Pietermaritzburg: Cluster Publications, 1996).

José Carlos Bermejo Higueroa, M.I., is director of the Centro de Humanización de la Salud in Madrid. His recent books include *Humanizar el sufrimiento* (Bilbao: Desclée de Brouwer, 1999) and *Salir de la noche: Por una enfermería humanizada* (Santander: Sal Terrae, 1999).

Peter Black, C.Ss.R., teaches moral theology at Notre Dame University in western Australia. He has written "Do Circumstances Ever Justify Capital Punishment?" *Theological Studies* 60 (1999), and "Talking Points for Moral Theology," *New Theology Review* (Summer 1999).

Roger Burggraeve is professor of moral theology at the Catholic University of Leuven. He has written several articles including "Prohibition and Taste: Bipolarity in Christian Ethics," *Ethical Perspectives* 1 (September 1994), and "Une éthique de miséricorde," *Lumen Vitae: Revue internationale de catéchèse et de pastorale* 49 (September 1994).

Lisa Sowle Cahill is J. Donald Monan, S.J., Professor of Theology at Boston College. She is the author of *Sex, Gender, and Christian Ethics* (Cambridge: Cambridge University Press, 1996) and has written "Goods for Whom? Defining Goods and Expanding Solidarity in Catholic Approaches to Violence," *Journal of Religious Ethics* 25 (1998).

Rev. Clement Campos, C.Ss.R., is a professor at St. Alphonsus College in Bangalore, India. He wrote "Homosexuality: Psychological, Ethical, and Pastoral Perspectives," *Kristu Jyoti* 10 (March 1994), and "Accompanying the Dying: The Role of a Pastoral Minister," *Word and Worship* 30 (September–October 1997).

Maurizio Pietro Faggioni, O.F.M., an associate professor of bioethics at the Accademia Alfonsiana in Rome, was recently appointed as a consultor at the Congregation for the Doctrine of the Faith. He is the author of "Aspetti Bioetici dell'AIDS Pediatrico," in L. Bruscuglia, ed., *AIDS Pediatrico. Problematiche Guridiche e Medico Sociali* (Milan: Giuffrè, 1997), and "Veritá al Malato" in G. Cine et al., eds., *Dizionario di Pastorale Sanitaria* (Turin: Camilliane, 1997).

Paul Farmer, an infectious-disease physician and anthropologist, is associate professor at the Harvard Medical School and medical director of the Clinique Bon Sauveur in rural Haiti. He is the author of *AIDS and Accusation: Haiti and the Geography of Blame* (Berkeley: University of California Press, 1992) and *Infections and Inequality: The Modern Plagues* (Berkeley: University of California Press, 1999). He is also the editor of *Women, Poverty and AIDS* (Monroe, Maine: Common Courage, 1996).

Jorge J. Ferrer, S.J., is professor of moral theology at Seminario Regional in San Juan, Puerto Rico, and is adjunct professor at the Gregorian University in Rome. He is also an instructor and consultant in bioethics at the Universidad Central de Caribe in Bayamon. His works include two books on AIDS, *SIDA ¿Condena o Solidaridad?* (Madrid: PPC, 1992) and *SIDA y Bioética. De la Autonomia a la Justicia* (Madrid: Universidad Pontificia Comillas, 1997).

Eileen P. Flynn is a professor of theology at St. Peter's College in Jersey City, New Jersey. She is the author of *Issues in Health Care Ethics* (Upper Saddle River, N.J.: Prentice Hall, 1999) and *Catholicism: Agenda for Renewal* (Lanham, Md.: University Press of America, 1994).

Jon D. Fuller, S.J., M.D., is assistant director of the adult Clinical AIDS Program at Boston Medical Center, associate professor of medicine, Boston University School of Medicine, and adjunct faculty member to both Weston Jesuit School of Theology and Harvard Divinity School. Among his writings are: with D. E. Craven, K. A. Steger et al., "Influenza Vaccination of Human Immunodeficiency Virus (HIV)-Infected Adults: Impact on Plasma Levels of HIV Type 1 RNA and Determinants of Antibody Response," *Clinical Infectious Diseases* 28 (1999), and "Needle Exchange: Saving Lives," *America* 179 (1998).

Raphael Gallagher, C.Ss.R., visiting professor at Accademia Alfonsiana in Rome, is co-editor with S. Cannon of *Sean O'Riordan: A Theologian of Development* (Rome: Accademia Alphonsiana, 1998). He has also written "The Moral Method of St. Alphonsus in the Light of the Vindiciae Controversy," *Spicilegium Historicum* 45 (1997).

Gerald Gleeson is senior lecturer of philosophy and Christian ethics at the Catholic Institute of Sydney. His writings include "When a Good Conscience Errs," *Pacifica* 8 (1995), and "Seeking Understanding," in Richard Lennan, ed., *An Introduction to Catholic Theology*, (New York: Paulist Press, 1998).

James Good left the academy in 1975, after twenty-one years of teaching philosophy, theology, and medical ethics at University College in Cork, to become a missionary in the Turkana desert of Kenya, where he served as the diocesan secretary in the diocese of Lodwar. He recently received a D. Litt. (*honoris causa*) from the National University of Ireland and retired to his home diocese of Cork and Ross, Ireland.

Nicholas Peter Harvey was formerly a professor of moral theology at Downside Abbey and a lecturer of Christian ethics at Queen's College, Birmingham. His works include *The Morals of Jesus* (London: Darton, Longman, and Todd, 1991) and an extended article, "Christian Morality?," in James Woodward and Stephen Pattison, eds., *The Blackwell Reader in Practical and Pastoral Theology* (Oxford: Blackwell, 1999).

Diana L. Hayes is associate professor of systematic theology at Georgetown University. She recently edited *Taking Down Our Harps: Black Catholics in the United States* (Maryknoll, N.Y.: Orbis, 1998) and wrote "My Hope is in the Lord: Transformation and Salvation in the African American Community," in Emilie Townes, ed., *Embracing the Spirit: Womanist Perspectives on Hope, Salvation, and Transformation* (Maryknoll, N.Y.: Orbis, 1997).

Linda Hogan is a lecturer of theology at the University of Leeds in the United Kingdom. She has written *Christian Perspectives on Development Issues: Human Rights* (Dublin: Trocaire Veritas Cafod, 1998) and "Boundaries and Knowledge: Feminist Ethics in Search of Sure Foundations," in Kathleen O'Grady, Ann L. Gilroy, and Janette Gray, eds., *Bodies, Lives, Voices: Gender in Theology* (Sheffield: Sheffield Academic Press, 1998).

James F. Keenan, S.J., is professor of moral theology at Weston Jesuit School of Theology in Cambridge, Massachusetts, and chairperson of the Catholic Theological Coalition on HIV/AIDS Prevention. He recently wrote "Applying the Seventeenth-Century Casuistry of Accommodation to HIV Prevention," *Theological Studies* 60 (1999), and edited with Joseph Kotva, *Practice What You Preach: Virtues, Ethics, and Power in the Lives of Pastoral Ministers and Their Congregations* (Franklin, Wis.: Sheed and Ward, 1999).

Kevin Kelly, a visiting senior research fellow in moral theology at Liverpool Hope University, is a member of the AIDS Committee of the (British) Catholic Fund for Overseas Development (CAFOD), and has written extensively in the field of moral theology, including articles on the church and AIDS. His most recent book is *New Directions in Sexual Ethics: Moral Theology and the Challenge of AIDS* (London: Geoffrey Chapman, 1998).

David Andrew Leary works as the director and senior counselor in the Come In Youth Resource Center in Paddington, Australia. Aside from

"The Fear of (Not) Being: 'Psychic Retreats' in Marginalized Adolescents," *Child Psychoanalytic Gazette* (1999), he has also written "Fast Cars Don't Kill Me: Marginalized Young People, HIV, and Suicide," in S. McKillop, ed., *Preventing Youth Suicide* (Canberra: Australian Institute of Criminology, 1992).

Laurenti Magesa is the pastor at Bukama parish in Tarime, Tanzania. He edited *The Church in African Christianity* (Nairobi: Initiatives, 1990) and wrote *African Religion: The Moral Traditions of Abundant Life* (Maryknoll, N.Y.: Orbis, 1997).

Leonard Martin, C.Ss.R., professor of moral theology and director of the Instituto Teológico-Pastoral de Ceará in Brazil, has written "O Código Brasiliero de Ética e os Direitos do Doente na fase Final da AIDS," in Leocir Pessini and Christian de Paul de Barchifontaine, eds., *Fundamentos da Bioética* (São Paulo: Paulus, 1996), and "A Homosexualidade numa Perspectiva Cristã: Subsídios para Avaliação do Projeto de Lei n° 1.151, de 1995," *Espaços—Revista Semestral de Teologia* 5 (1997).

Enda McDonagh is professor emeritus of moral theology at the Pontifical University of Maynooth in Ireland. His writings include "Theology in a Time of AIDS," in his collection of writings, *Faith in Fragments* (Dublin: Columbia Press, 1997), and "Thirty Years After Humanae Vitae," *Ceide* 2 (1998).

Nader Michel, S.J., is a cardiologist at Caritas-Egypt and professor of moral theology and medical ethics at the Faculty of Religious Sciences in Sakanini, Cairo. His recent works include *Mad'wuun ila al-horeya, Dirasa fi osos al-akhlaq al-maseheya* (Beyrouth: Dar al-Machreq, 1998), and *Le débat moral en Egypte, défis pour la foi et enjeus pour la société* (Paris: Centre Sevres, 1992).

Mark Miller, C.Ss.R., serves as director of the Redemptorist bioethics consultancy in Edmonton, Canada. He has authored *Making Moral Choices* (Mystic, Conn.: Twenty-Third Publications, 1995), and *Living Ethically in Christ: Is Christian Ethics Unique?* (New York: Peter Lang Publishing, 1998).

Orlando Navarro Rojas is director of CECODERS (Centro Coordinador de Evangelización y Realidad Social) in San José, Costa Rica. He has written *Nueva Era: El oportunismo anticristiano* (San José: Edic. Texto Comunicación, 1997) and "Jubileo, celebración y desafio: una perspectiva teológica," *Cristianismo y Sociedad* 36 (1998).

Paulinus Ikechukwu Odozor, C.S.Sp., is both academic dean and a senior lecturer at the Spiritan International School of Theology in Attakwu, Nigeria. He has authored *Richard A. McCormick and the Renewal of*

Moral Theology (Notre Dame: University of Notre Dame Press, 1995) and also written "Proportionalists and the Principle of Double Effect: A Review Discussion," *Christian Bioethics* 3 (1997).

Kenneth J. Owens is a parish priest at St. John Vianney's in Edinburgh.

Jorge Peláez, S.J., serves as both academic vice president and professor of moral theology at the Pontificia Universidad Javeriana in Bogotá, Colombia. His recent articles include "Humanae Vitae: anuncio profético y debate teológico" and "Los divorciados vueltos casar," both in *Theologica Xavieriana* 44 (1994).

Gervas Rozario is the vice-rector of Holy Spirit National Major Seminary in Bangladesh, where he is also the editor of their quarterly review, *Prodipon*. He has contributed articles including "Women in the Teaching of the Church" and "The Call of the Great Jubilee: The New World in the Holy Spirit," both in *Prodipon* 21 (1998).

Maura A. Ryan, assistant professor of Christian ethics at the University of Notre Dame, is co-editor with Todd Whitmore of *The Challenge of Global Stewardship: Roman Catholic Responses* (Notre Dame: Notre Dame University Press, 1997). She has also written "Feminist Theologies and the New Genetics," *Concilium* (1998).

José Antônio Trasferetti is professor of theological anthropology and social ethics at the Pontificia Universidade Católica de Campinas in Brazil. His two most recent books are *Entre a Poética e a Política—Teologia Moral e Espiritualidade* (Petrópolis: Vozes, 1998) and *Pastoral com homossexuais —Retratos de uma experiência* (Petrópolis: Vozes, 1999).

John Tuohey is chair of Applied Health Care Ethics in the Providence Health System in Portland, Oregon. Among his publications are "Moving from Autonomy to Responsibility in HIV-Related Healthcare," *Cambridge Quarterly of Healthcare Ethics* 4 (1995), and "Methodology and Ideology: The Condom and a Consistent Sexual Ethic," *Louvain Studies* 15 (1991).

Marciano Vidal is professor of moral theology at the Universidad Pontificia Comillas in Madrid. His current works include *Moral de Actitudes*, 4 vols. (Madrid: PS, 1990), and *Moral y Espiritualidad* (Madrid: PS, 1999).

John Mary Waliggo teaches at the Uganda Martyrs University and is commissioner of the Uganda Human Rights Commission. He has authored *A Man of Vision: Life and Legacy of Archbishop Joseph Kiwanuka* (Kinubi: Marianum Press, 1993) and "Tourism as Blessing or Curse: The Host's View," *The Way* 39 (January 1999).

David Walton is a research fellow in Harvard Medical School's program in infectious disease and social change. His scholarly work has been on the management of tuberculosis, and he has served as the coordinator of clinical services of the Thomas J. White Center for Infectious Diseases, based in Haiti's Central Plateau. Walton currently coordinates the center's new project, "An Option for the Poor and Faith-based Responses to HIV."

Regina Wentzel Wolfe is assistant professor of theology at the College of St. Benedict and the School of Theology and Seminary at St. John's University in Minnesota. She has co-edited *Ethics and World Religions: Cross Cultural Case Studies* (Maryknoll, N.Y.: Orbis, 1999) with Christine Gudorf, and has written "The Ethical Imperative of the Eucharist: Responding in the Workplace," in Mary E. Stamps, ed., *To Do Justice and Right Upon the Earth* (Minnesota: The Liturgical Press, 1993).

Index

CPSIA information can be obtained
at www.ICGtesting.com
Printed in the USA
LVHW010410250722
724321LV00001B/34